Political Science Internships

Towards Best Practices

Renée B. Van Vechten
Bobbi Gentry
John C. Berg

AMERICAN POLITICAL SCIENCE ASSOCIATION

Designed by Henry E. Chen

Photo Credits
Cover photographs (clockwise from top left): Darren Harold-Golden sits next to District 7 State Senator James Manning during Senate floor discussion, 2019 (Credit: Logan Gilles); Capitol tour guide: Elisa Perkins Cuellar, Perla Aguirre, Michelle Chin (Credit: Andrea Torres); Archer fellows in committee: Evan Mitchell, Isra Abdoolwadood, Kenwoo Kim (Credit: Andrea Torres); Erin Fitzpatrick (Credit: Matthew Cosner); Trip Davis, Nikolas Fotinos, Madison Lockett, Christian Soenen (Credit: Andrea Torres); background cherry blossoms (Credit: Getty/BeeCoolPhoto).

ISBN (Soft Cover): 978-1-878147-66-0
ISBN (Fixed Layout ePUB): 978-1-878147-67-7

For our intrepid University of Redlands Political Science and Public Policy alumni, who inspire and lead by example — RVV

To my students and husband who always challenge me to be better — BG

Dedicated to the thousand-plus Suffolk University interns and their supervisors who taught me so much about both experiential education and politics — JCB

Table of Contents

Preface

The idea for this book was sparked many years ago at an APSA Teaching and Learning Conference (TLC), where our themed track discussions about program assessment touched off numerous side conversations about internships. To take stock of contemporary practices in political science internships, editors Renée Van Vechten and Bobbi Gentry, along with colleague Shamira Gelbman, launched their inquiry in 2015 by surveying internship coordinators located at four-year institutions, followed by a second survey in 2017 examining internship practices at community colleges exclusively. The research took shape in conference papers, roundtables, and workshops, and eventually, this volume. What's clear is that internship practices across the profession vary widely, and in some cases, "anything goes." It's no wonder that so many in the profession dismiss internships as volunteer work. Yet we also learned that many in the discipline are experts on experiential learning with a wealth of insight to share.

Situated within a larger, ongoing dialogue about teaching and learning and the undergraduate curriculum, this book is intended to fill a general need for theory-driven and evidence-based knowledge about internships. Although scholarship examining internships in political science has been around for well over 70 years, pedagogical materials remain scattered across journals, centers for teaching and learning, libraries, and faculty offices. By pooling resources and centralizing knowledge in a book such as this, we offer an overview of internship practices that we hope will assist faculty members and others who want to create, improve, or expand their programs. In essence, these chapters justify further investments in academic internship programs by faculty, their institutions, and internship providers—commitments of time, personnel, and finances to secure the sustainability of programs.

Moving towards best practices, the contributors to this book address different settings and modes for internships, legal aspects, resources, and various approaches to improving interns' learning. The opinions of the authors are their own, as are the examples and experiences at different institutions that they describe. Their studied recommendations are meant to be broad and encompassing so that they can be applied to different institutional contexts. Supplemental materials, combined with practical recommendations, help give this book the feel of a manual for undergraduate internships in the discipline.

This book also endeavors to address issues of equity in access to internships, diversity of stakeholders, and inclusion of all students, regardless of background. In order to promote inclusive writing, the singular pronoun "they" is used to recognize the multidimensionality of students, faculty, and people generally.

The editors would like to thank the American Political Science Association for recognizing the value of such a resource for members of the profession and helping to bring our proposal to fruition. Their sponsorship of the Teaching and Learning Conference (since the first conference in 2004) made this book possible by creating a space for research and collaboration to improve political science education. In addition, we would like to acknowledge the work of former APSA director Michael Brintnall, who, by establishing the TLC, contributed invaluably to the building of a community of teacher-scholars within the profession, and his successor, Steven Rathgeb Smith, for carrying on the commitment of the Association. We also thank former APSA staff member Sheila Mann for her dedication to making the APSA more relevant to the political science faculty whose main duty is teaching, along with Henry Chen, an extraordinarily efficient and capable managing editor, and skillful publications director Jon Gurstelle, for shepherding this project into existence. Lastly, we are grateful for the Political Science

Education section, which lobbied for the Teaching and Learning Conference, created the *Journal of Political Science Education*, and continues to be a kind and welcoming academic community that remains committed to advancing rigorous scholarship of teaching and learning. This member section of APSA remains open to all scholars who support the scholarship of teaching and learning (SoTL) within the discipline.

Because this project is ongoing and further contributions to our knowledge and understanding will continue to inform our collective practices, practical materials and additional research about internships will be available on APSA Educate (https://educate.apsanet.org), an open-source library created for the purpose of sharing information about political science teaching methods. These resources will be updated and expanded periodically. Finally, we would like to thank Charlie Van Vechten, David DuBose, Martha E. Richmond, family, friends, and pets Remo, Winnie, and the late Allegra for their support and patience as we worked to complete this project.

CHAPTER 1

An Introduction to Political Science Internships

THE ORIGINS OF CONTEMPORARY POLITICAL SCIENCE INTERNSHIPS

In 1965, seven distinguished political scientists led an APSA-sponsored conference in Las Croabas, Puerto Rico, an event devoted exclusively to political internships. The title of Harold D. Lasswell's paper, "The Professional and Public Service Potential of Internship Programs," hinted at the discipline's communion with practical politics, while fellow panelist Donald G. Herzberg struck a wry tone with his contribution, "The Care and Feeding of Interns." Considering the earlier results of a 1949 survey by Reed and Reed (1950) that identified only one political science internship in existence and their prediction that internships were "not likely to play any considerable part in the preparation of students for participation in politics" (50), the conference signaled a turning point in the profession and helped galvanize the development of pedagogical resources around political science internships.[1]

Drawing on these elemental works and data from five internship programs, Bernard Hennessy followed with a foundational framework for designing, delivering, and assessing undergraduate and graduate-level internships in his monograph, *Political Internships: Theory, Practice, and Evaluation* (1970). Lauding APSA's Congressional Fellowship Program as one of several examples of how research and job experience could be merged successfully and with purpose,[2] he laid out the case for experiential education in terms that have remained remarkably stable over time. For instance, his advice for providing regular, expert supervision is echoed in the pages of this volume, as is his assertion that political internships must include "the opportunity for the systematic and continuous examination of the experience in relation to generalizations of political science" (9).

What Hennessy helped clarify was that laboring outside a theoretical frame and without critical reflection is simply work or volunteering, regardless of whether it is carried out on Capitol Hill, in state houses, or any other setting. Presence in a political office is not a sufficient condition for earning political science credit, argued Hennessy: "It goes without saying, it is not enough merely to call an experience an internship to make it so" (1970, 9). These arguments have provided generations of political scientists justification for healthy skepticism about the purposes, deployment, and outcomes of for-credit internships, which is often expressed as a fear of creeping vocationalism in academia (Alexander 1982, 128; DiMaggio 2018). Their suspicions are often validated by woeful stories of interns who spent months doing mundane chores in exchange for a line on their résumés, and these reports contribute to a sense that internships are lively and engaging but lack intellectual rigor (Arum and Roska 2011). In the extreme, internships across the board are regarded as an improper substitute for classroom learning.

On the other hand, Hennessy's arguments have supplied a rationale for structuring robust, educational internship programs, and as research on internships has broadened, so too have views about the purposes, nature, and desirable outcomes of experiential learning.[3] Rooted in the practice of apprenticeship through which masters convey knowledge, enable trainees to develop specialized skills, and socialize them into the norms and customs of their trade (Garnett and Donovan 2002, 3), internships have become affixed to the educational landscape not only because they help facilitate the transition from school to workplace, but also because they ground abstract learning in the realities of organizational life (Gabris and Mitchell 1989).[4]

Scholarship about internships has grown steadily over the past few decades, much of it focused on the efficacy of specific practices and experiential learning outcomes. Studies across all major academic disciplines have examined direct and indirect consequences of internships, probing individual-level impacts on academic performance and macro-level outcomes such as liberal education's ability to prepare students for civic life and leadership. In the 1970s, public administration scholars organized internship-themed symposia that sparked new waves of research in that field (Benavides, Dicke, and Holt 2013).[5] In political science, the APSA-sponsored Wahlke Task Force in 1991 recommended that all students be afforded the opportunity to engage in one or more kinds of "real-life" political situations off campus, with internships leading the list of suggested practices (Wahlke 1991). Professional organizations such as the National Association of Colleges and Employers (NACE), the Council for the Advancement of Standards in Higher Education (CAS), Campus Compact, and the National Society for Experiential Education (NSEE) have amplified and extended similar evidence-based conclusions. Experiential learning has been of interest to the Association for American Colleges and Universities (AAC&U), whose data-driven observations and focus on deep learning have helped postsecondary educators reorient liberal education curricula to prepare students for the highly fluid and demanding social, economic, personal, and civic challenges they will confront post-graduation.

Among AAC&U's recent advancements are well-supported conclusions about the benefits of "high-impact educational practices," a category that includes internships (Kuh 2008).[6] In this perspective, undergraduate students must build broad knowledge and strong intellectual skills and develop a grounded sense of civic responsibility; but to achieve the objectives of a liberal education today, they must also acquire global and intercultural competencies, build technological sophistication, hone collaborative problem-solving and transferable skills, and practice and integrate their learning through application (Schneider 2008, 3). Analyzing long-term data from the National Survey on Student Engagement (NSSE), Kuh and his colleagues (2008; 2013) demonstrate that co-curricular activities such as internships can foster the achievement of these essential learning goals, stronger student engagement, improved retention rates, and higher persistence to graduation rates (a point particularly appealing to higher education administrators).[7] High-impact practices (HIPs) can promote deep learning for *all* types of students, but crucially, historically underserved students tend to benefit *more* from engaging in intentionally-designed, purposeful educational activities than their peers in the majority (Kuh 2008, 17).

That last point is worth reiterating: high-impact practices have been shown to have a disproportionately *positive* effect on students who have historically been underserved in education, even as gains have been demonstrated for all types of students. While HIPs such as internships are not a panacea (cf. Kuh and Kinzie 2018; Seifert et al. 2016), research generally demonstrates that when well-formed, these active, collaborative, educational practices can facilitate measurable student academic gains and contribute to graduates' success in the workforce (Brownell and Swaner 2010; Hesser 2014; Kilgo, Ezell Sheet, and Pascarella 2014; Kuh 2013; McClellan, Kopko, and Gruber 2021).

WHAT DO WE MEAN BY POLITICAL SCIENCE "INTERNSHIPS"?

Nearly 50 years after Hedlund (1973) wrote about the "growing interest among students and faculty in using practical political involvement as an adjunct to formal classroom teaching" (19), the literature has matured into a thick body of research scrutinizing the scope, strategy, structure, and curriculum of internships. Even so, while internships have nearly become standard experiences for undergraduate political science majors, in practice they are far from standardized across programs and institutions.

According to one national survey, 90% of four-year political science programs assign academic credit for intern experiences compared to fewer than half of community colleges that do so. Among four-year institutions, more than two-thirds do not require concurrent enrollment in a departmental internship course, more than half of all political science departments (56%) do not require a learning contract that spells out expectations for students, and a few programs assign no academic components at all (Gentry and Van Vechten 2018).[8] Variation stems from an array of factors, chiefly among them: what is treated as a "political science" internship; the goals being pursued; what standards of excellence have been established for all stakeholders; how much intention and forethought are put into coupling academic and worksite experiences; the amount of institutional, administrative, and site resources dedicated to supporting internship programs; and interns' attitudes and attributes (Collins, Gibbs, and Schiff 2012; Eyler 2009; Gryski, Johnson, and O'Toole 1987; Hedlund 1973; Hirschfield and Adler 1973; Hindmoor 2010; McClellan, Kopko, and Gruber 2021).

Basic components are common to internships, although an "exact" definition eludes capture. Internships have been loosely defined as supervised discipline- and career-related work experiences that involve active learning, critical reflection, and professional development (Simons et al. 2012). They tend to be defined operationally, as "experiences through which students can apply their academic knowledge in work settings" (NACE 2021), in contexts that are usually related to their career interests (Kuh 2008). NACE emphasizes that they "give students the opportunity to gain valuable applied experience and make connections in professional fields they are considering for career paths, and give employers the opportunity to guide and evaluate talent" (2021, n.p.). The Council for the Advancement of Standards in Higher Education (CAS) similarly defines them as "planned, practical, educationally purposeful experiences in professional, work-related settings that relate to or complement students' academic and career goals" (2019, 6). True (2002) suggests that we should define internships as "carefully monitored work or service experience in which a student has intentional learning goals and reflects actively on what she or he is learning throughout the experience" (True 2002, 2).

All of these definitions highlight the importance of constructing knowledge through practice and professional supervision, placing internships at the nexus of classroom and potential career. US courts and the federal government through the Fair Labor Standards Act and Department of Labor have clarified certain legal criteria for a job to be considered an internship rather than employment; generally, interns are not considered employees if they work under close supervision of staff, are provided training as an extension of their education, are not in training for a promised job, and do not displace other paid employees. Furthermore, the employer must not depend on the intern's activities and the experience must benefit the interns primarily (Wage and Hour Division 2018; see Supplemental Internship Resources and also Chapter 3 by Yamada).

NACE (2021) also lists seven criteria for determining whether an internship is "legitimate," the first of which emphasizes the experience as an *extension of the classroom* and as a *learning experience* in which students apply classroom knowledge—not merely as an opportunity to advance the operations of the employer.[9] Furthermore, the intern must gain transferable skills or knowledge, and the experience must be structured around specified learning goals that are supported with resources, supervision, and feedback by the host employer.

Education and research tend to be the primary *goals* of all internships. For students of political science, training in public service or simply competent citizenship may be secondary objectives (Hennessy 1970; Hirschfield and Adler 1973), meaning that interns can develop civic awareness, self-efficacy, and political identity through their participation in community-based settings—all of which may be important to a political science intern.[10] Whenever academic credit is awarded, students' learning *is* the central purpose, and Hennessy noted a half-century ago that this fact should be regarded as "the without which nothing" (1970, 22): the *sine qua non* of internships.

The extended classroom enables students to pursue other secondary educational objectives, particularly those related to developing personal and professional capacities, including (but not limited to): cognitive complexity; a sense of civic responsibility and ethics; teamwork; networks and interpersonal skills; workplace competencies; self-understanding; academic portfolios informed by experience; and improved chances for long-term career success (Alexander 1982; CAS 2019). For some undergraduates and certainly graduate students in policy subfields or public administration, making a temporary position permanent may be the primary aim—one that has been encouraged by the Federal Internship Improvement Act of 2011, a law directing federal agencies that have internship programs to hire internship coordinators and facilitate the noncompetitive transition of interns into federal employment, an effort formalized through the federal Pathways Program (Benavides, Dicke, and Holt 2013).[11]

How well internships fulfill their educational purposes tends to be a function of their design, institutional support, and structure, manifest in the standards established at the beginning to the assessments delivered at the end (Sweitzer and King 2019), Furthermore, if "quality" refers to how well students learn through their internship placements, then overall quality is also highly contingent on the values, resources, and performance of major stakeholders: institutions, faculty mentors or internship directors, students, and internship site partners. Variations among these actors guarantee that not all internships can or will yield the same outcomes, but as the Council for the Advancement of Standards in Higher Education (CAS) notes, "Setting standards for internship programs establishes benchmarks for administrators, faculty, and staff members that identify a quality internship and an effective learning experience" (3, 2019). To enable learning by doing, internship program standards need to address the degree of faculty or staff guidance, on-site supervision, types of feedback mechanisms, and also set expectations for student self-study and reflection (CAS 2019). In short, stakeholders should agree on what a quality internship entails.

These imperatives provide stable footings for internship programs. But what kinds of placements merit academic credit in political science? In practice, the power to decide whether a particular field experience is folded into the definition of a political science internship may ultimately lie with faculty internship coordinators who have the authority to approve students' plans. Conceptually, however, there is implicit agreement in the literature that *experiential learning concerned primarily with public affairs and public goods,* rather than private gain and private goods, *lies at the heart of political science internships.* Political science internships deal primarily with *matters related to governance that have an impact on the common welfare*, not profit-making.[12] In them, students regularly *confront concepts that are core to political science*: power, equality, representation, democracy, fairness, liberty, collective action, and agency, among others.

Placements directly associated with politics, policy, and government certainly satisfy these general criteria, but organizations and firms of all types potentially could qualify. Working in the marketing department of a business would not normally justify political science credit at even a basic level, but a position in its government advocacy unit logically would. On the other hand, it's entirely possible that a student could do research or "fieldwork" to test political science-related hypotheses while being embedded in a marketing department of a for-profit business.[13] The distinction resides in the substantive nature of the work: even when placed in a private law firm, for instance, interns directly engage politically- or civically-oriented institutions such as laws and courts whose industry is fundamentally concerned with governance (and self-governance).[14] By this measure, students of politics—and not just political science majors—can capitalize on the transformative effects of internships in which they grapple with the theoretical tensions, dilemmas, and thorny problems that confront political communities in local, regional, state, national, international, or supranational contexts.

TOWARDS BEST PRACTICES IN POLITICAL SCIENCE INTERNSHIPS

In an age of declining college enrollment and persistent achievement gaps, educational practices that could neutralize—if not help reverse—trends such as these demand sustained attention. As this discussion and the chapters in this volume indicate, internships are not a cure-all for what ails higher education, but experiential learning promises significant returns on investments made with intentionality and purpose.

Situated within a discipline-specific frame, this book responds to a peremptory, perennial question: "How do we create educational contexts and practices that help students *of politics, government, and public affairs* improve?" Moreover, "How do we effectively raise the levels of accomplishment for all, with special attention to those whose life circumstances—first generation, low income—may put them at particular educational risk?" (Schneider 2008, 7). Across the discipline, how might we do these things more systematically to achieve preferred outcomes?

One reply—the one Kuh and his associates offered—is that "if the essential learning outcomes are goals, then our curricular, cocurricular, and pedagogical practices need to be recognized as the means to achieving these larger educational ends" (Schneider 2008, 7). Collegiate interns, therefore, are obligated to critically explore the relationships among factual knowledge, concepts, theory, models, and real-world applications, and they need guidance to do so methodically (CAS 2019). Stated differently, for-credit internships should fit into a well-defined program of study with explicit standards and which enables the articulation of relevant and realistic learning goals, all of which are periodically reviewed.

This book leverages that approach by bringing together experts and evidence to illuminate how students, faculty, and internship providers can get the most out of an internship, even when their motives or goals differ. Not surprisingly, many students—and their parents—consider internships an essential step in career preparation that will enable them to rise above their peers in a competitive labor market (Grant-Smith and McDonald 2016). Internship providers or employers, on the other hand, often want interns in order to supplement their staff or eventually fill entry-level positions; some desire to "give back" or "pay it forward" by orienting newcomers to the workplace and equipping them for careers. When fortified with the right resources, faculty can help these stakeholders align their objectives within an educational framework and advance their objectives cooperatively.

This edited volume is designed to address different types of needs. Although theory frames our inquiry, practicality is our guide. Some readers may be trying to establish an internship program in their department from scratch. Others may be looking to shore up existing programs with more resources or justify their expansion. Still others may want to transform an existing internship curriculum into a more meaningful experience for all types of students. In this book, chapter authors describe and evaluate different pedagogical strategies and practical techniques for designing, administering, delivering, and assessing undergraduate political science internship programs, basing their recommendations on different kinds of evidence: qualitative and quantitative data, tried and tested methods, and an extensive literature that spans academic disciplines.

Because all of our authors have direct experience with internship programs, some for many decades, their reflections and observations necessarily shape their views about what works in different contexts. In all cases, to minimize errors arising from human judgment and bias,[15] contributors have braced their expert conclusions with results from course evaluations, surveys, interviews, and secondary data analysis.[16] Even so, "the old-fashioned but still essential metric of faculty members' considered judgment" (Schneider 2008, 7) which is reinforced by assessments that remain in the background, adds to our shared understanding about how to "do internships" best.

Most of the chapters fall into what Gryski, Johnson and O'Toole (1987) called "evaluation research": they focus mainly on process—the "design, administration, and operation of internship programs and how to structure and manage them" (Benavides, Dicke, and Holt 2013, 330)—rather than on the empirical analysis of outcomes. We recognize the continuing need for studies that can improve upon existing knowledge through further explorations of the empirical relationships among intern characteristics and academic success, learning outcomes, intern achievement levels, institutional practices, persistence, graduation rates, career fulfillment, and so on, a point we revisit in the conclusion.

In our collective effort to identify best practices in internships, a search that is never complete, we also hope the messages in this book empower faculty to contribute to the creation of sustainable internship programs that also advance and protect faculty's own wellbeing. Faculty often shoulder the uncompensated work of internships that is administratively cumbersome and which institutions support with miserly restraint. Virtually all our contributors either explicitly or implicitly advocate for institutional investments that will put internship programs on solid academic footings, not only for the sake of students, but also faculty. They delineate roles for their colleges and universities, APSA, and others to play in this endeavor, and identify the tools to deliver better outcomes. The resources in the supplemental materials section ("Supplemental Internship Resources") are intended to ease the burden of reinventing the wheel with respect to creating materials, articulating goals, and assessing outcomes, among other tasks. Some of these materials can and should be directed to students who choose to do internships without the close guidance of a faculty mentor or who undertake them apart from an internship course.

This book makes at least one thing clear: despite the pessimistic prediction in 1950 that the demise of internships was imminent, they are here to stay. Societal norms and competitive labor markets almost certainly guarantee it, while the promise of thrilling, hands-on, co-curricular experiences also ensures their continued appeal for undergraduates. Internship opportunities continue to expand, taking form in new virtual spaces and for more specialized purposes, yet the discipline continues to grapple with how best to deliver academic credit-worthy experiential learning for all students. This book responds to those dilemmas with strategies that are firmly embedded in quantitative and qualitative evidence and a wealth of experience, supplying a robust set of practical, pedagogical tools that will help faculty, site supervisors, and students at every stage and in various aspects of an internship program—moving us closer to collectively achieving best practices in political science internships.[17]

REFERENCES

Alexander, James R. 1982. "Institutional Design of Public Service Internships: Conceptual, Academic, and Structural Problems." *Teaching Political Science* 9 (3): 127–133.

American Political Science Association. 2021. "About APSA: Vision." APSA, Accessed July 1, 2021, https://www.apsanet.org/ABOUT/About-APSA.

Arum, Richard, and Josipa Roksa. 2011. *Academically Adrift: Limited Learning on College Campuses.* Chicago: University of Chicago Press.

Benavides, Abraham, Lisa A. Dicke and Amy C. Holt. 2013. "Internships Adrift? Anchoring Internship Programs in Collaboration." *Journal of Public Affairs Education* 19 (2): 325–353.

Bretschneider, Stuart, Frederick J. Marc-Aurele, Jr., and Jiannan Wu. 2005. "'Best Practices' Research: A Methodological Guide for the Perplexed." *Journal of Public Administration Research and Theory: J-PART* 15 (2): 307–323.

Brownell, Jayne E., and Lynne Swaner. 2010. "Five High-Impact Practices: Research on Learning Outcomes, Completion, and Quality." Washington, DC: Association of American Colleges and Universities.

Collins, Todd, H. Gibbs Knotts, Jen Schiff. 2012. "Career Preparation and the Political Science Major: Evidence from Departments." *PS: Political Science & Politics* 45 (1): 87–92.

Council for the Advancement of Standards in Higher Education (CAS). 2019. "Internship Programs (Revised Standards)." In *Professional Standards for Higher Education*, CAS. Fort Collins, CO: CAS.

DiMaggio, Anthony. 2018. "Is Political Science Relevant? The Decline of Critical Scholarly Engagement in the Neoliberal Era." *Poverty and Public Policy* 10 (2): 222–252.

Eyler, Janet. 2009. "The Power of Experiential Education." *Liberal Education* 95 (4): 24–31.

Gabris, Gerald T., and Kenneth Mitchell. 1989. "Exploring the Relationship between Intern Job Performance, Quality of Education Experience, and Career Placement." *Public Administration Quarterly* 12 (4): 484–505.

Garnett, James L., and Craig R. Donovan. 2002. "The New Old Way to Launch a Career in Public Service." American Society for Public Administration, *PA Times* (Educational Supplement): 3–4.

Gentry, Bobbi, and Renée Van Vechten. 2018. "The What and How of Political Science Internships: Best Practices in the Discipline." Paper presented at the Annual Meeting of the American Political Science Association, Boston, MA.

Grant-Smith, Deanna, and Paula McDonald. 2014. "The Trend Toward Pre-Graduation Professional Work Experience for Australian Young Planners: Essential Experience or Essentially Exploitation." *Australian Planner* 53 (2): 65–72.

Gryski, Gerald S., Gerald W. Johnson, and Laurence O'Toole, Jr. 1987. "Undergraduate Internships: An Empirical Review." *Public Administration Quarterly* 11 (2): 150–170.

Hedlund, Ronald. 1973. "Reflections on Political Internships." *PS: Political Science & Politics* 6 (1): 19–25.

Hennessy, Bernard C. 1970. *Political Internships: Theory, Practice, Evaluation.* University Park, PA: Penn State Studies.

Hesser, Garry. 2014. *Strengthening Experiential Education: A New Era.* Mount Royal, NJ: National Society for Experiential Education.

Hindmoor, Andrew. 2010. "Internships within Political Science." *Australian Journal of Political Science* 45 (3): 483–490.

Hirschfield, Robert, and Norman M. Adler. 1973. "Internships in Politics: The CUNY Experience." *PS: Political Science & Politics* 6 (1): 13–18.

Johnson, Sarah Randall, and Frances King Stage. 2018. "Academic Engagement and Student Success: Do High-Impact Practices Mean Higher Graduation Rates?" *The Journal of Higher Education* 89 (5): 753–781. doi: 10.1080/00221546.2018.1441107.

Kahneman, Daniel, Paul Slovic, and Amos Tversky. 1982. *Judgment Under Uncertainty: Heuristic and Biases.* Cambridge, UK: Cambridge University Press.

Kilgo, Cindy A., Jessica K. Ezell Sheets, and Ernest T. Pascarella. 2015. "The Link between High-Impact Practices and Student Learning: Some Longitudinal Evidence." *Higher Education* (69) 4: 509–525.

Kuh, George D. 2008. *High-Impact Educational Practices: What They Are, Who Has Access to Them, and Why They Matter.* Washington, DC: Association of American Colleges and Universities (AAC&U).

Kuh, George D. 2013. "Taking HIP's to the Next Level." In George D. Kuh & Ken O'Donnell, Eds. *Ensuring Quality and Taking High-Impact Practices to Scale.* Washington, DC: AAC&U.

Kuh George D., and Jillian Kinzie. 2018. "What Really Makes a 'High-Impact' Practice High Impact?" *Inside Higher Ed*, May 1. https://www.insidehighered.com/views/2018/05/01/kuh-and-kinzie-respond-essay-questioning-high-impact-practices-opinion.

Kuh, George D., Ty Cruce, Rick Shoup, Jillian Kinzie, and Robert M. Gonyea. 2008. "Unmasking the Effects of Student Engagement on College Grades and Persistence." *Journal of Higher Education* 79: 540–563.

McClellan, Fletcher, Kyle Casimir Kopko, and Kayla L. Gruber. 2021. "High-Impact Practices and Their Effects: Implications for the Undergraduate Political Science Curriculum." *Journal of Political Science Education* (online): 1–19.

NACE. 2021. "Position Statement: US Internships." National Association of Colleges and Employers. Accessed June 5, 2021. https://www.naceweb.org/about-us/advocacy/position-statements/position-statement-us-internships/.

Office of Personnel Management. 2011. "Hiring Authorities: Students and Recent Graduates." OPM. Retrieved from http://www.opm. gov/hiringreform/pathways/.

Reed, Thomas H., and Doris Reed. 1950. *Evaluation of Citizenship Training and Incentive in American Colleges and Universities.* New York: Citizenship Clearing House.

Schneider, Carol Geary. 2008. "Liberal Education and High-Impact Practices: Making Excellence—Once and For All—Inclusive." In *High-Impact Educational Practices: What They Are, Who Has Access to Them, and Why They Matter*, ed. George Kuh, 1–8. Washington, DC: AAC&U.

Seifert, Tricia A., Benjamin Gillig, Jana M. Hanson, Ernest T. Pascarella, and Charles F. Blaich. 2014. "The Conditional Nature of High Impact/Good Practices on Student Learning Outcomes." *The Journal of Higher Education* 85 (4): 531–564. doi: 10.1080/00221546.2014.11777339.

Simons, Lori, Lawrence Fehr, Nancy Blank, Heather Connell, Denise Georganas, David Fernandez, Verda Peterson. 2012. "Lessons Learned from Experiential Learning: What Do Students Learn from a Practicum/ Internship?" *International Journal of Teaching and Learning in Higher Education* 24 (3): 325–334.

Smith, Michael B., Rebecca S. Nowacek, and Jeffrey L. Bernstein. 2017. "Don't Retreat. Teach Citizenship." *Chronicle of Higher Education* 63: 21. https://www.chronicle.com/article/dont-retreat-teach-citizenship/.

Sweitzer, H. Frederick, and King, Mary A. 2019. *The Successful Internship: Transformation and Empowerment in Experiential Learning, 5th Edition.* Boston, MA: Cengage Learning.

True, Michael. 2011. *Starting and Maintaining A Quality Internship Program, 7th Edition.* Grantham, PA: Messiah College Internship Center. http://www.internqube.com/uploads/4/8/0/7/4807298/starting_an_internship_program_-_7th_edition.pdf.

Wage and Hour Division. 2018. "Fact Sheet #71: Internship Programs Under the Fair Labor Standards Act." US Department of Labor. http://www.dol.gov/whd/regs/compliance/whdfs71.pdf.

Wahlke, John C. 1991. "Liberal Learning and the Political Science Major: A Report to the Profession." *PS: Political Science & Politics* 24 (1): 48–60.

ENDNOTES

1. Hirschfield and Adler (1973) write that of 83 works listed in a "Bibliography of Major Publications on Intern Programs and Participant Observation" published in 1970 [by R. Hedlund], "only 10 relate directly either to the organization or theory of internships," and that seven of those were papers presented at the Las Croabas conference, which was co-sponsored by APSA and the Ford Foundation (13). In addition to those named in the text above, the other five were: Everett Cataldo, "An Appraisal of the Congressional Fellowship Program"; Bernard C. Hennessy, "The Nature and Scope of College Political Internship Programs: Survey and Commentary"; James A. Robinson, "Participant Observation, Political Internships and Research"; John G. Stewart, "The Intern Crisis: Some Thoughts on the Overextension of a Good Thing," and Sidney Wise, "The Administration of an Internship Program" (see footnote 5).

2. APSA's Congressional Fellowship Program (CFP) was established in 1953 and is designed for political scientists (not undergraduates). See: https://www.apsanet.org/cfp.

3. In this volume, the terms *internship*, *experiential learning*, and *experiential education* are used interchangeably. Experiential education, we note for the record, can include other types of activities such as student teaching, simulations, or study abroad, but we use it to refer to internships exclusively.

4. The term "internship" became popular in the legal and medical fields, as young lawyers and doctors received practical training under expert supervision. In the 1930s, professional schools and departments of public administration had adapted the model to imbue public servants with expertise in bureaucratic processes (Hennessy 1973, 6-7). Prior to this, Hennessy writes (in Chapter 1, Footnote 1) that "Jane Dahlberg reports that the internship for training in public administration began in the The New York Bureau of Municipal Research in 1911, and public administration internships began in universities as early as 1914. Letter to the author, March 14, 1968" (ibid., 124).

5. Benavides, Dicke, and Holt (2013) write that scholars of public administration began to look for "tangible evidence" to support the effectiveness of internships, and two symposia were published in 1979: one by the *Public Administration Review* titled, "Internships in Public Administration," and the other by the *Southern Review of Public Administration*—currently *Public Administration Quarterly*—called "Public Service Internships: The Continuing Evolution." Benavides, Dicke and Holt concluded: "Collectively, both symposiums showed the educational value of internships. They are of historical significance because it was the first time that the public administration profession looked at internships as a pedagogical teaching technique meriting symposium status. Few if any other teaching pedagogies have reached such a level" (2013, 328).

6. The widely-tested teaching and learning practices that have been shown to increase student success (variously operationalized, as in "persistence to graduation," for example) are: first-year seminars and experiences; common intellectual experiences (such as common courses); learning communities; writing-intensive courses; collaborative assignments and projects; undergraduate research; study abroad; service learning or community-based learning; internships; and capstone courses and integrative projects (Kuh 2008). Recently, ePortfolios have been added to this list (see: "High Impact Practices," AAC&U, Accessed July 20. 2021. https://www.aacu.org/resources/high-impact-practices).

7. Kuh et al. (2008) make a strong case for persistence as a demonstrable outcome of HIPs, but Johnson and Stage (2018) question the overall effects of high-impact practices on graduation rates. Using primary and secondary data from 101 institutions, they investigated whether offering high-impact practices as required for all students, required for some students, or as optional was related to an institution's four or six-year graduation rate, and they found "limited" relationships between HIPs and graduation rates.

8. A two-wave national survey about internships was conducted in 2015-16; response rates were 20.5% for the 2015 survey of four-year institutions, and 6.7% for the 2016 community colleges iteration (172 respondents, combined). Among 102 four-year institutions, 67.6% reportedly did not offer an internship class (n=73) although five institutions required a campus-wide course, one required an "independent study," and one required students to take a course for which the responsibility was shared by six campuses. Among all universities, 90.3% gave political science credit for internships; among 51 community colleges, only 43.5% did (n=20). PhD-granting institutions were most likely to require an academic component such as a term paper (95.5%, n=21); 90.7% of MA-granting institutions required assignments (n=39); and 84.3% of liberal arts institutions did so (n=43); and only 40.8% of community colleges did (n=20). Overall, less than 2% of four-year institutions required no academic components (n=2), compared to 20.4% of community colleges (n=10). Whether internship class was required did not vary much by institutional type (Gentry and Van Vechten 2018). In a 2018 APSA Community College Faculty Survey, 39.7% (n=112) reported that their institution offered internships for credit. That survey was administered to 2,634 faculty in the US; 298 responded to the online survey between March 26 and May 2, 2018, for a response rate of 11.2%.

9. Spelled out on its website (https://www.naceweb.org/about-us/advocacy/position-statements/position-statement-us-internships/), the NACE criteria are:

    1. The experience must be an extension of the classroom: a learning experience that provides for applying the knowledge gained in the classroom. It must not be simply to advance the operations of the employer or be the work that a regular employee would routinely perform.
    2. The skills or knowledge learned must be transferable to other employment settings.
    3. The experience has a defined beginning and end, and a job description with desired qualifications.
    4. There are clearly defined learning objectives/goals related to the professional goals of the student's academic coursework.
    5. There is supervision by a professional with expertise and educational and/or professional back-

ground in the field of the experience.
6. There is routine feedback by the experienced supervisor.
7. There are resources, equipment, and facilities provided by the host employer that support learning objectives/goals.

10. Although some scholars consider internships a form of civic engagement, they are conceptually and practically distinct. Internships are not necessarily connected to civic learning (Smith, Nowacek, and Bernstein 2017), although they can be structured to foster civic engagement and learning.

11. In 2010 President Obama signed Executive Order 13562, "Recruiting and Hiring Students and Recent Graduates," as a means to establish procedures that would help the federal government more easily recruit college graduates into the federal workforce. He then signed the Federal Internship Improvement Act on December 31, 2011; it "requires government agencies that have internship programs to create an internship coordinator position and publish information about available internships on their websites." The act also facilitates the noncompetitive transition of an individual with an internship into a career with the federal government. According to a study in 2007 by the Partnership for Public Service, the federal government hired only about 6.6% of its interns, *and* the private sector hired half of its interns" (Benavides, Dicke, and Holt 2013, 325-26). More about the Pathways program can be found on the Office of Personnel Management's website for students and recent graduates: https://www.opm.gov/policy-data-oversight/hiring-information/students-recent-graduates/#url=Overview.

12. One could also say that they have implications for the common welfare, not private conditions. As this discussion shows, there is no "perfect" or singular definition of a political science internship, partly because there is no perfect, singular definition of political science (although one could argue that there is agreement at a general level). For example, on its website, APSA (2021) alludes to a definition of the profession where it states that political science "promotes scholarly understanding of political ideas, norms, behaviors, and institutions to inform public choices about government, governance, and public policy." In this text, we consider most *public affairs* internships to be political science internships and use the terms interchangeably, although arguably they are distinct yet overlapping. Again, the nature of the work is key for defining what qualifies as a political science internship: for example, a placement with a public health agency could fall into the public affairs category, but would be considered "political science" only if the intern were engaging the core concepts of the discipline regularly (and at least implicitly) through their work.

13. Highly specified research (such as using marketing department data to test political science concepts) tends not to occupy undergraduates, but students located in rural areas (or who otherwise have limited internship options) might find pathways to an internship by conducting research that is interdisciplinary.

14. Hennessy (1973) dwells on this point at length, explaining that post-World War II, political scientists who generally were focused on policy "urged the collection and codification of data" that could be gathered in the field, such as through federal agencies, and there was general acknowledgement that the "'science' of politics had to be an empirical, replicable, and largely quantitative science" (7). Pure behavioralists, however, tended to view policy analysis (and activism) as value-laden and therefore liable to compromise the objectivity of the scientific enterprise. Some scholars with a "flair for politics who were also scholars" recognized internships as a device through which these concerns could be reconciled. Thus, E. E. Schattschneider and Victoria Schuck, among others, began to experiment with placing students with politicians and supervising their activities (8).

15. For an extended discussion of the pitfalls associated with an overreliance on observation, see Kahneman, Slovic, and Tversky (1982).

16. This is to say that most of our contributors have access to years' worth of supervisor evaluations, student surveys, reports, and other institution-specific data which inform their conclusions, but only protected information that has been approved by an institutional review board is included in this publication.

17. With modest recognition of the continuing need for comparative, longitudinal data to establish causal relationships, we stop short of asserting that the recommendations described in this text constitute a definitive set of "best" practices for delivering internships (for a straightforward discussion of the necessary and sufficient conditions for justifying the term "best practices," see Bretschneider, Marc-Aurele, Jr., and Wu 2005).

CHAPTER 2

A Review of the Literature: Internships and Best Practices

Renée B. Van Vechten, University of Redlands

INTRODUCTION

Are internships worth doing? What can they add to students' education and to a political science degree? What does research teach us about effective practices? To answer these essential questions and others, this review of the research literature takes a panoramic look at published work on academic internships and delves into political science scholarship specifically. While this chapter does not center exclusively on studies specific to the discipline, it provides a larger context for understanding the pedagogical value of internships and explores the evidence-based instructional practices that can help students achieve various experiential learning outcomes.

Following the Introduction that defines the contours of political science internships, this chapter spells out how they have been studied. After a brief look at how researchers have approached the study of internships and a leading theory explaining why experiential learning[1] is generally valued, the discussion turns to an exploration of student learning goals and how these are treated as benchmarks for measuring a mix of educational and career-related learning outcomes from internships. We then review the kinds of benefits and challenges for internship stakeholders that researchers have identified.

Obtaining advantageous outcomes is a concern of internship practitioners in all academic disciplines, and broad consensus about how to facilitate effective learning through specific methods has emerged from a sizable body of scholarship. These prescriptively-labeled "best practices" for faculty, students, and internship providers are reviewed next, followed by a closer look at the evidence-based practices that can reinforce political science internship programs. Significant findings from the literature are condensed into tables for easy reference.

Despite its wide scope, this review is not meant to provide a comprehensive blueprint for conducting internships in all settings. Rather, it is intended to establish an empirical foundation for the chapters that follow, presenting evidence that underpins arguments and recommendations that are woven into this volume. It prepares a stage for contributor insights and thus should prompt the reader to dive into subsequent chapters to learn more. The conclusions from studies reviewed here suggest a basic set of practices that, when implemented systematically and purposefully, can render internships valuable elements of political science programs.

THE LITERATURE EXPANDS

Although internships have existed for over a century, in the 1960s, experiential education became the focus of a movement to connect theory with practice (Dworkis, Thomas, and Weintraub 1962; Hennessy 1970; Hirschfield and Adler 1973; Murphy 1973). Since that time scholars have developed and honed an array of practices to render internships worthwhile learning experiences that merit the awarding of academic credit, their research amounting to a sizable literature that spans academia. Through essays reflecting on firsthand experience and empirical approaches that largely rely on survey responses, internship evaluations, interviews, and student-level data,[2] this scholarship tends to affirm that high-quality experiential learning provides direct and residual benefits for students, departments, institutions, and internship site providers. Despite the continuing need for longitudinal studies, those that contain control groups, and more rigorous statistical controls generally, practitioners and scholars have endorsed the idea that internships are vital, if not *essential,* undergraduate experiences that help bridge education and career (Ahmad 2020; Busteed and Auter 2017; Clark and Martin 2016; Johnson 2016; Kuh 2008).

Much of the very early research on internships tended to lack theoretical grounding, relying mainly on descriptive anecdotes, correlation, and small-n studies whose conclusions were not generalizable (Narayanan, Olk, and Fukami 2010). However, spurred by the recognition of internships as a "high-impact practice" generating multiple benefits for students—especially those who have historically been marginalized or underserved by institutions of higher education[3]—rigorous empirical studies exploring the design of internship programs and their measurable outcomes have multiplied (Finley and McNair 2013; McClellan, Kopko, and Gruber 2021). Despite copious information about how to design internship programs and courses—after all, most recommendations are generalizable across academic disciplines—lack of uniformity in course content, requirements for academic credit, and learning outcomes prevails in political science (Gentry and Van Vechten 2018; Moon and Schokman 2000; Van Vechten and Gentry 2017).

LEARNING THROUGH DOING

Meaningful academic internships place student learning at the center of all internship activities (Whitaker 1989), whether that learning occurs passively, such as through reading or observation and listening, or (preferably) actively, through grappling with concepts and ideas in real time and then reconstructing and reorganizing that knowledge (Dewey 1938; Eyler 2009; Jarvis, Holford, and Griffin 2003). Research generally demonstrates the power of applying knowledge and practicing skills in "authentic, real-world situations, with all the contextual idiosyncrasies and unpredictability that entails"; these activities engender "deep and flexible learning" (Ambrose and Poklop 2015, 55) in environments and in ways that neither simulations nor case studies can fully achieve. Experiential learning extends the classroom, giving students the chance to create and transform knowledge through feeling, observing, conceptualizing, and experimenting (Kolb 1984), and to integrate theoretical or factual knowledge through practice (Ambrose et al. 2010; Ambrose and Poklop 2015; D'Aloisio 2006).[4] This kind of learning is reflected in Whitaker's five criteria for the awarding of academic credit for experiential learning such as internships:

1. Credit should be awarded only for learning, and not for experience;
2. College credit should be awarded only for college-level learning;
3. Credit should be awarded only for learning that has a balance, appropriate to the subject, between theory and practical application;
4. The determination of competence levels and credit awards must be made by appropriate subject matter and academic experts; and
5. Credit should be appropriate to the academic context in which it is accepted. (Whitaker 1989, xvii)[5]

These principles form the bedrock for building and delivering academic internship programs. They imply that learning must occur not only through meaningful work in the internship, but also through supporting assignments, discussions, and reflective activities that are guided by mentors or instructors. Internships, therefore, enable learning in more than one setting and through active integration of theory and practice (Lowenthal and Sosland 2007).

POLITICAL SCIENCE INTERNSHIPS: LEARNING GOALS, LEARNING OUTCOMES, AND BENEFITS

In political science internships, students witness how issues relating to the common welfare are dealt with in the public sphere, often through governmental or legal means (see the Introduction for a fuller definition). What tends to distinguish political science internships from those in other liberal arts disciplines is the centrality of public policy-oriented issues, and key learning goals—either implicitly or explicitly—should be related to the exploration of core political science concepts such as power, equality, fairness, and liberty, among others, and their expression in real-world contexts (Pecorella 2007).

Logically, students also pursue internships in order to develop the attitudes, skills, and aptitudes that will help them transition from college to a career, often perceiving these (and only these) practical outcomes as worthwhile. Although some academics who insist on pure scholarship and rigorous training will object to the "creeping vocationalism" that practical objectives imply (DiMaggio 2018), others argue equally forcefully that transferable skills are absolutely fundamental to the acquisition of 21st century education, recognizing that interns' scholarly capacities should translate into work abilities (Clark and Martin 2016). It is up to instructors and faculty mentors to bridge these two worlds by helping the student articulate a range of goals that integrate academic and practical work as seamlessly as possible.

Whereas individual learning goals should be tailored to the internship placement, another way to measure individual progress is by assessing competencies in order to demonstrate the value of internships to a liberal arts and a political science curriculum. For example, the Council for the Advancement of Standards in Higher Education (CAS), just one of several higher education associations to have moved in this direction,[6] has articulated standard outcomes for internships[7] that are derived from general learning domains such as knowledge acquisition, cognitive complexity (critical thinking), personal growth and development, civic engagement, practical competence, and interpersonal competence (2015). These overlap the eight career readiness competencies spelled out by NACE (2021), namely: career and self-development; communication; critical thinking; equity and inclusion; leadership; professionalization; teamwork; and technology.[8] In NACE's schematic, these universal competencies represent clusters of knowledge, abilities, and skills that liberal arts students should master in preparation for post-graduation work.[9]

To estimate the impact or effectiveness of internship experiences, scholars have focused largely on individual-level learning outcomes that are measured by the actual or perceived development of competencies such as these (Maertz, Stoeberl, Marks 2013; Nghia and Duyen 2019). Some of the major findings about the instrumental value of experiential learning are summarized below, categorized by competency domain: educational outcomes and academic gains; knowledge and cognition; civics and ethics; self-development; and skills, career-related in particular.

Educational Outcomes and Academic Gains. A large subset of research is concerned with the effects of internships on students' performance in college. Noting first that participation in high-impact practices tends to be inequitable, with first generation, transfer students, and African American and Latino students least likely to have such experiences, Kuh, O'Donnell, and Schneider (2017) find that participation in "high-impact practices" (HIPs) such as internships enables deeper forms of learning and higher rates of student success, and these effects accrue to all students, but proportionally more for students from historically underserved groups (c.f. Kuh 2008; O'Neill 2010; Kuh et al. 2010; Kuh and O'Donnell 2013). Scholars such as Kuh (2008) and Kuh, O'Donnell, and Schneider (2017) empirically demonstrate the effects of experiential learning on student success, which manifests in an "undergraduate experience marked by academic achievement, engagement in educationally purposeful activities, satisfaction, persistence, attainment of educational objectives, and acquisition of desired learning outcomes that prepare one to live an economically self-sufficient, civically responsible, and rewarding life" (2017, 9). Whether these effects hold for political science internships specifically remains an open question, a point that McClellan, Kopko, and Gruber (2021) make in their study of high-impact practices in the discipline. Their analysis, based on National Survey of Student Engagement data (NSSE 2019, which documents that nearly half of all college student respondents completed internships of all kinds, either independently or through a program), demonstrates self-reported gains in practical competencies such as interpersonal and career skills, but unearths no significant impacts on other abilities such as analyzing and applying theories. They recognize that this finding could be due to the fact that all internship experiences were surveyed, regardless of their connection to a directed course of study.

Parker III et al. (2016) confirm that students who engage in internships tend to make greater three-year gains in grade-point averages (GPA) than their counterparts who do not engage in internships, and also find the positive impact on fourth-year grades to be significantly more pronounced at some types of schools than at others, particularly at Hispanic-Serving Institutions (HSIs). Because of the strong, positive effects on the academic performance of students who had lower grades prior to interning, they emphasize that institutions "must grant access to varying student academic levels as students who might benefit from the experience are possibly being denied the opportunity to gain from it" (2016, 108). Although earlier studies located marginal negative impacts of working outside of college on GPA (Ehrenberg and Sherman 1987), more recently Routon and Walker (2018) conclude from their large-n study of internship program completion and continuity in college attendance[10] that internship participation is associated with higher student grades. Knouse, Tanner, and Harris (1999) also found that students with internship experience had significantly higher average grades than their counterparts, as did Lowenthal and Sosland (2007) who found that the Washington, DC semester internship experience had a positive impact on participants' subsequent academic performance, especially for females and government majors, as compared to students who did not intern. Further academic performance benefits include a reduction in stress and improved adjustment to new life circumstances (Binder et al. 2015; Chemers, Hu, and Garcia 2001).

Knowledge and Cognition. Improved college performance is likely related to the cognitive development that interns can experience in well-structured internships. In their (small-n) study of political science research interns in Australia, Moon and Schokman (2000) write that students "learned vivid lessons concerning the issues of knowledge in the policy process and the relationship between theory and practice in politics. As a result, we conclude that the internships provided greater benefits than vocational relevance alone. They also enriched the students' political science education" (175). This conclusion is echoed in a number of studies (c.f. Simons et al. 2012), but it has not been established that interns acquire significantly more in-depth understanding of academic content compared to their counterparts who do not complete internships (Aldas et al. 2010). Regardless, in their (large-n) longitudinal study of undergraduates at US colleges and universities, Kilgo, Sheets, and Pascarella (2015) find that students who intern evidence greater satisfaction with cognitive activities and a higher need for cognition (how much one enjoys thinking).[11]

Civics and Ethics. For students of political science, connecting with constituencies that a public agency or nonprofit organization serves can deepen an intern's sense of purpose and community, and likely their participation in it (McCartney, Bennion, and Simpson 2013). As Alex-Assensoh and Ryan (2008) assert, increased engagement among students is an important resource for social capital and American democracy, and they find that among former Washington Internship Institute interns, students translate their learning-by-immersion into policy strategies they pursue in their own states or local communities. Lowenthal and Sosland (2007) document similar impacts of the DC semester on former interns, specifically in higher rates of involvement in service learning as well as campus and community activities post-internship, compared to those who do not intern. Kilgo, Sheets, and Pascarella (2015) note that interns also tend to develop a sense of socially responsible leadership, and Aldas et al.'s (2010) analysis of National Survey of Student Engagement (NSSE) data reveals that two-thirds (66%) of undergraduate seniors in an experiential-intensive course of study[12] reported that they felt able to contribute to the welfare of their community, compared to only 48% of all other respondents.

Self-Development. One of the ways that internships permit personal growth is by placing individuals in unfamiliar situations that tend to bring interests, values, and beliefs into sharper focus. Through interning, students can develop greater confidence in their abilities as well as awareness of their strengths and limitations (Anderson et al. 2002). Being able to decide against a possible career without major consequences is a distinct benefit; and conversely, successful internships can translate into more clearly defined post-baccalaureate plans. Comparative data analyzed by Bradberry and De Maio (2019; their study was also longitudinal[13]), Routon and Walker (2015), and Lowenthal and Sosland (2007) show that interns have a higher likelihood of attending or planning to attend graduate school or law school.

Career Readiness Skills. Apart from the discipline-specific knowledge that students might gain or reinforce through public affairs internships, the transferable career-readiness skills they acquire can also resonate academically as well as in their life's work. Among the soft skills developed through (in-person) internships are interpersonal skills such as teamwork or collaborating with peers to solve problems, and communication, including listening, and being able to address different audiences verbally and in writing. Students should be able to convey ideas clearly on paper and in emails, in person and online, and formally and informally (Foster Shoaf 2020; Routon and Walker 2015). Much of the same skill development also occurs in virtual or remote internships (Criso, Low, and Townsend 2021; Hora et al. 2021a; Jeske and Axtell 2018). An added value of these skills is enhanced employability, and several studies in different fields have documented a boost to former interns' chances of being hired after graduation compared to those who did not complete an internship (Gault, Leach, and Duey 2010; Harvey, Moon, and Geall 1997; Knouse, Tanner, and Harris 1999; Silva et al. 2016)—a condition that holds for students at Historically Black Colleges and Universities as well (Williams et al. 2020). However, except for Bradberry and De Maio (2019), who find that significant employment benefits accrue to political science interns specifically, most of these studies have been conducted outside the discipline, and further research is needed to confirm whether public affairs internships garner the same employability effects as they do for those who major in business and science.

When students experience the conditions that foster benefits such as these, their satisfaction can be long-lasting—as researchers who conduct longitudinal studies or studies of alumni have discovered. For instance, in their survey of graduates from a political science department, Raile et al. (2017) found that alumni respondents recommended that students be given more information about internships and more help obtaining them, and the researchers concluded that they had underestimated the perceived importance of internship experiences to alumni.

Unsurprisingly, as experienced internship coordinators know, not all experiences yield the desired outcomes that faculty propose and students seek, and the degree and scope of derived benefits vary widely among individual students—even those who land the same internship placement and start with the same basic skillset. While scholars and practitioners have catalogued a multitude of challenges and adverse conditions that can prevent learning and skill development (Hesser 2014; Lei and Yin 2019; Wang and Chen 2015), they have also demonstrated empirically that certain internship practices yield greater benefits than others, and these have come to be known colloquially as "best practices."

THE MEANING OF *BEST PRACTICES* IN INTERNSHIPS

Generalizable research on undergraduate interns has generated broad consensus about how to facilitate effective learning through certain methods and approaches, or what some collectively refer to as "best practices." Although a strict definition of best practices would be those standards that emerge from a research process that eliminates all other competing explanations for outcomes (Bretschneider, Marc-Aurele, and Wu 2005)—a standard that we neither claim to reach here nor locate in the literature—for the purposes of this discussion, we use the term loosely and define them as *activities that experienced educators broadly acknowledge as generating effective internship outcomes* and which are *based on empirical evidence* and *rooted in accepted standards.* It should be kept in mind, however, that most of what is known about internships is based on studies of in-person or face-to-face experiences that were prevalent by the mid-1900s, although as noted above, recent work has shown that virtual or remote internships can produce many of the same outcomes (Hora et al. 2021a; Jeske 2019; Jeske and Axtell 2016; and see Chapter 15 by Cabrera Rasmussen and Van Vechten). Conclusions about effective methods are also based on studies of students who have completed courses or coursework associated with internships, and usually by choice (i.e. they engaged in non-compulsory internships); Klein and Weiss (2011), for instance, find evidence that compelling students to intern can have negative rather than positive outcomes. Additionally, recent research also calls attention to biases based on a preponderance of White students among current and past populations of interns (Ericksen and Williamson-Ashe 2019; Hora, Gopal, and Wolfgram 2021; Hora et al. 2021b; Knouse, Tanner, and Harris 1999; Williams et al. 2020). All of these factors are worth considering when reviewing the current state of the literature on internships.

To engage in best practices is to assume that certain conditions must be present if "excellence in outcomes" is to be obtained (King 2014). Among the conditions that scholars have identified as either necessary and/or sufficient for quality internship programming,[14] *institutional capacity* in the form of commitment and sufficient resources rises to the top. Universities and colleges must articulate and pursue standards for well-executed, integrative learning experiences—standards that should be built

Table 1: Summary of Best Practices in Internships

COLLEGE/UNIVERSITY

Administrators & Staff; Faculty/Instructors

GENERAL OBJECTIVES/DESIRED OUTCOMES: **FULFILL EDUCATIONAL MISSION** OF GRADUATING A DIVERSE GROUP OF KNOWLEDGEABLE AND SKILLED STUDENTS WHO CAN ACHIEVE THEIR POTENTIAL AS PEOPLE, CITIZENS, AND WORKERS; BUILD INSTITUTIONAL REPUTATION FOR EDUCATIONAL EXCELLENCE; INCREASE STUDENT RETENTION, GRADUATION RATES, AND PRODUCTIVITY OF ALUMNI.

Maximize opportunities for student learning: "Identify relevant and desirable student learning and development outcomes" (CAS 2015); offer a wide range of placements so students can apply knowledge in different settings and with new people (Kuh 2008); offer on-campus internships (Fede et al. 2017); encourage traditional-length (min 5- to 12-wk) internships; recruit students at all levels to intern (Hora et al. 2020; Parker et al. 2016).

Develop impactful pedagogy: Intentionally design coterminous, credited curriculum (an internship class) so students can integrate, synthesize, and apply knowledge (Kuh 2008; Kolb 1984, Beard & Wilson 2013); purposefully design programs to critically explore relationships among concepts, theory, & knowledge gained both in courses and practical settings (CAS 2015). Generate reflective writing & reflective discussion about issues such as the distribution of power in society or organizational behavior, students' skills, attitudes, & interests, and observed professional & ethical behaviors (Ambrose et al. 2010; CAS 2015; Clark 2003; Stirling et al. 2017); have students keep & review a weekly journal, highlighting recurring themes or ideas (O'Neill 2010).

Offer complementary co-curricular activities: Develop or provide students with links to internship-related materials, e.g. guides for writing résumés, professional conduct, & reflection; practice and review mock interviews (Gavigan 2010; Eyler & Giles 1999; Kolb 1984).

Incorporate equity: Properly compensate & support campus coordinators (CAS 2015); ensure enough internships are available and appropriate for all demographic & developmental profiles of student population & institutional programs (CAS 2015; Parker III et al. 2016; Zilvinskis 2017); provide universal access to internship-related materials; address financial needs inclusively (Scott-Clayton 2017); disseminate info to achieve consistency; reach all who might potentially benefit from programs or financial aid; partner with site supervisors who understand goals & can provide feedback continually (Deschaine & Jankens 2017; Eyler 2009; Kennedy et al. 2015).

Assess student progress & program. Administer pre- and post-assessment surveys; collect written student evaluations (CAS 2015); conclude experience with final presentations or public reports (Reding & O'Bryan 2013); review program (CAS 2015).

Maintain external relations. Build relationships with providers through repeated personal contact (CAS 2015; Kuh 2008).

STUDENT

GENERAL OBJECTIVES/DESIRED OUTCOMES: **BUILD KNOWLEDGE, SKILLS, NETWORKS:** PREPARE FOR POST-GRADUATION WORK AND LIFE SATISFACTION AND SUCCESS: GAIN/TEST SUBJECT KNOWLEDGE AND SKILLS, SELF-KNOWLEDGE, INSIGHTS ABOUT POSSIBLE CAREER(S), ACQUIRE KNOWLEDGE ABOUT COMMUNITY, NETWORK

Apply and build discipline-related knowledge. Apply theoretical knowledge to new situations (Anderson 2014; Crebert et al. 2004; Hindmoor 2010; Kuh, Kinzie, Schuh, & Whitt 2010) discover relevance of learning through real-world applications (Kuh & O'Donnell 2013; Aldas et al. 2010). Intentionally gather info from professionals in the field through planned assignments such as on-site interviews (Gavigan 2010).

Develop and apply transferable competencies & skills. Invest significant effort and time to practice & develop skills, and seek constructive feedback in order to adjust behaviors: communication (speaking & writing), teamwork (diplomacy & cooperation), time management, critical thinking, computing/information technology, independence, and problem-solving, work-related expertise (Coker at al. 2017; Crebert et al. 2004; Griffin, Lorenz, & Mitchell 2010; Hocking et al. 2004; King 2014; Robles 2012). Take active role in charting short- and long-term plans, e.g. 4-year plan (Carey 2010; Crebert et al. 2004).

Table 1: Summary of Best Practices in Internships

Prepare for (engaged) citizenship. Contribute to welfare of community through meaningful work (Coker et al. 2017; Callanan & Benzing 2004); understand differences, develop appreciation of a diverse society including people of other racial and ethnic backgrounds (Coker et al. 2017; Schamber & Mahoney 2008); formulate new attitudes that lead to potential changes in civic behavior and participation (Eyler & Giles 1999; Mariani and Klinkner 2009; Simons et al. 2012).

Develop self-knowledge, more accurate self-concept, and ethical perspectives. Develop awareness of personal values, goals, and self-concept through reflection writing and discussion (Brooks et al. 1995; O'Neill 2010; Simons et al. 2012; Stirling et al. 2017); build resilience and confidence through persistence (Goodenough et al. 2020; Liu et al. 2011; Yeh 2010).

Discern one's career path (pursue career development). Develop cultural awareness of workplace; practice cooperation by working with as many different persons as possible, observe workplace etiquette and leadership (Crebert et al. 2004); change or add second major or minor (CAS 2015); explore "career fit" by investigating career choices without lifelong commitment, or validate a career path or discover what one doesn't want to do (Callanan & Benzing 2004; Dailey 2016; Gavigan 2010; O'Neill 2010; Greenhaus et al. 2000). Develop confidence about ability to enter workforce or attend graduate school (Acai et al. 2014; Bradberry and De Maio 2019; Cedercreutz & Cates 2010).

INTERNSHIP PROVIDER

GENERAL OBJECTIVES/DESIRED OUTCOMES: **DERIVE ORGANIZATIONAL BENEFITS:** SHORT-TERM: LABOR, KNOWLEDGE, WORK PRODUCT/PRODUCTIVITY; LONG-TERM: KNOWLEDGE, RELIABLE LABOR FORCE WITH REQUISITE CAPACITIES AND SKILLS TO PROCURE HIGHER PRODUCTIVITY RATES, BETTER REPUTATION, STRONGER TIES TO UNIVERSITY OR INTEGRATION WITH COMMUNITY

Develop human resources/present and future labor force: Trained, site supervisors must understand the student's learning goals & partner with the academic supervisor provide continuous monitoring and frequent feedback (Eyler 2009; Kuh and O'Donnell 2013). Develop useful artifacts such as internship evaluations indicating a prospective employee's readiness (Hart/AAC&U 2008). Communicate with campus to increase likelihood of knowledge transfers with future interns and campus as source of potential employees (Reagans & McEvily, 2003; Narayanan et al. 2010).

Promote work productivity and student learning: Assume the role of an educator (Sosland and Lowenthal 2017). Develop a work agreement with the intern, collaboratively, before work begins (Kuh 2013), and clarify work goals in a learning contract once the intern has been exposed to the organization; give interns significant, varied, goals-focused assignments that are clearly related to the academic goals of the program, student's interests, and worksite's expertise, and cover breadth and depth of issues (Clayton 2013; Eyler 2010; Kuh 2008; Kuh & O'Donnell 2013; Thessin & Donnelly-Smith 2010). Match students to appropriate projects, minimizing clerical tasks (Uzzi & Lancaster 2002); vary settings to increase student interaction with different people and situations (Brooks et al. 1995); make good use of the person's abilities (Narayanan 2010); give frequent, timely, and constructive feedback, including final, written evaluations that are reviewed with intern and shared with campus coordinators (Kuh & O'Donnell 2013; O'Neill 2010); give interns a platform to share or demonstrate their competence and progress, such as through a presentation to others, and recognize good work (Donnelly-Smith 2010; Kuh 2008; Kuh & O'Donnell 2013; Reding & O'Bryan 2013).

into programs from the beginning so that assessments can be performed regularly and subsequent adjustments can be made in a process of continual improvement. Sufficient resources include access to technical information and personnel adequate to support programmatic objectives and institutional missions. Institutions must adequately compensate faculty, administrators, or staff who are responsible for coordinating a program (see Chapter 10 by Gentry). Responsibility for meeting standards must be borne by faculty, who must be responsive to students' educational needs, and students, who must be prepared and motivated to learn and fulfill roles in suitable organizations. Collaboration among stakeholders is also key: as one scholar puts it, "Internships at their best are a partnership among students, campus professionals, faculty, and employers" (Carey 2010, n.p.).

The "partners," or stakeholders as they are referred to here, include the following: (a) institutional actors: faculty and instructors who deliver internship programs, but also administrators and staff; (b) student interns; and (c) employers, internship providers, or site supervisors—all of whom are motivated by different but complementary objectives. Table 1 summarizes the major types of tasks these stakeholders should assume if they are to create the conditions for internship success. The table synthesizes the evidence-based practices that researchers have identified as being positively associated with stakeholders' respective goals.[15]

College and University Stakeholders: Faculty, Instructors, Staff, and Administrators. At the college or university level, administrators, staff, instructors, and faculty collaborate to deliver the educational mission of their institutions and the learning goals of their colleges and departments, which revolve around graduating students who have the tools to achieve their potential as persons in society, in the economy and workplace, and as members of a political community (Jacoby 2009). They must do so equitably, enabling wide and inclusive access to learning opportunities. For some, the need to build and maintain their institution's reputation or "brand" of education could incentivize curricular innovation such as internship classes with embedded research, and for others this need might lead to more centralized, coordinated planning of internship opportunities, such as through a campus internship office (see Chapter 12 by Chávez Metoyer). Because institutions also benefit from having a stable student population, it behooves them to increase student retention and graduation rates as well as to ensure the productivity of their alumni by offering high-impact learning experiences such as internships (Anderson 2014; Kuh 2008; Zilvinskis 2017). Although many campuses centralize internship coordination in career centers, academic departments are often tasked with internship programming, or faculty develop programs to meet perceived student needs for experiential education. Across campus, programming must be well-coordinated and "integrated into the life of the institution" (CAS 2015, 7).

Students as Stakeholders. Student interns also have incentives to engage in "best practices" in their quest to obtain, earn, and build knowledge, intellectual and practical skills, and networks that will enable them to succeed post-graduation in their personal lives, in society, and in the economy. To succeed in their internship placements and beyond, they must take advantage of opportunities to become more competent communicators who can work with others as well as independently, problem-solve, and use their expertise, thereby developing a sense of civic competence, possibly an inclination for civic engagement, and an understanding of differences among people in a diverse political community (Yates and Youniss 1996). Through work, observation, and reflection, their perspectives, attitudes, and awareness might grow in ways that help them to flourish as political science majors, with the ability to discern and chart their career paths more deliberately. Through on-site tasks, they can build their capacity for skills and traits that will help them succeed as interns, students, and future contributors to the workforce (see Chapter 4 by McQueen, Jenkins, and Wiley).

Internship Providers and Site Supervisors as Stakeholders. Employers also are concerned with shaping a productive workforce both in the short- and long-term, and can benefit by giving interns the opportunity to develop and share their labor and growing expertise. They are also educators (Sosland and Lowenthal 2017). If employers work with campus coordinators to fulfill students' goals, providing continual supervision and feedback, and challenging students to excel, the arrangement can be mutually beneficial (Shindell 2019; see Chapter 8 by Lowenthal and Sosland). The literature is clear about the need for communication between campus educators and providers to establish expectations about how internships can fulfill their educational mission (Narayanan et al. 2010), and expectations should be made explicit in contracts signed by supervisors and the student before the work begins (Pecorella 2007; see also Chapter 5 by Simpson, Braam, and Winston). Throughout the internship the supervisor should be accessible and welcome questions (Hora et al. 2020). The internship provider should match students to appropriate and challenging projects, varying projects to increase interns' exposure to situations where they can problem-solve, maximizing interns' interaction with diverse people inside and outside the organization, making interns feel that they and their work are valued in the organization, and minimizing clerical tasks (Thessin and Clayton 2013; Eyler 2010; Donnelly-Smith 2010). As a trusted role model, a site supervisor can help interns navigate ethical issues (Titus and Ballou 2014). Hora et al. (2020) note that supervisor behaviors that include open communication, accessibility, and paying attention to interns' learning are significantly and positively associated with intern satisfaction and career development. Finally, alumni who serve as internship providers and mentors can also augment the institution's ability to deliver impactful learning (Raile et al. 2017).

Because of the curricular role that departments typically play in managing internships, it also makes sense for this review to cover, in more detail, specific "best practices" that political scientists can implement at the department level in their pursuit of desired outcomes. What does recent scholarship reveal about best practices in political science internship programming? Only a handful of broad assessments of effective political science practices have been conducted (Ahmad 2020; Collins, Gibbs and Schiff 2012; Hindmoor 2010), and other research explores narrower aspects of internships in the discipline. Table 2 presents a synthesis of evidence-based findings and conclusions relating to best practices in political science internships.[16]

BEST PRACTICES IN POLITICAL SCIENCE INTERNSHIP PROGRAMS

Virtually all scholarship related to effective internship practices emphasizes the critical role of faculty mentors and the importance of internship courses. Pecorella (2007) emphasizes that a "coterminous academic component"—an intentionally-designed internship class for which students earn credit—*must* accompany the internship experience. Simply earning credit isn't enough, for as he puts it, "In the absence of a structured academic component, the internship experience is too limited and, as a consequence, may actually prove antithetical to the values of liberal arts education" (2007, 80). Pedagogically, the class should be intentionally structured to incorporate readings and assignments that enable students to critically explore core political science concepts such as power, fairness, inequality, or justice, and to actively compare theoretical knowledge to practical experience (CAS 2015; Pecorella 2007). A singular text or set of readings could be assigned to the class, or students might be asked to develop and read from a short list of titles that relate directly to their individual internship work.

Because learning depends on active, critical reflection (Blount 2006; Carson and Fisher 2006), students must engage in reflective writing followed by discussion. A careful process of reflection obliges students to consider their skill development, possible changes in their attitudes and interests, and their observations about professional and ethical behaviors in the workplace (Stirling et al. 2017; CAS 2015; Ambrose et al. 2010; Clark 2003). Some of these issues can be covered in a daily log or weekly journal, with entries recorded as responses to prompts (Alm 1996; Gavigan 2010). Entries can then be translated into a biweekly or monthly summation in which they highlight recurring themes or ideas retrospectively (Anderson 2014; Gavigan 2010; O'Neill 2010; Colby et al. 2007), and also relate them to assigned texts or materials from related political science courses. These records can provide personal yardsticks for interns and enable campus coordinators to take stock of the kinds of issues each placement site tends to raise (Colby et al. 2007, 244). Students also need to complete a final research paper or project that provides a basis for assessing academic outcomes (Pecorella 2007; see also Chapter 16 by Clucas in this volume). Finally, a public forum in which students make a final presentation or report on their experiences, either at their internship site or on campus (or both), can promote self-reflection and learning, and also help publicize the program to prospective interns (Bradberry and DeMaio 2019; Donovan, Porter, and Stellar 2010; Reding and O'Bryan 2013).

In addition to developing an impactful internship curriculum, faculty sponsors must play different roles throughout an internship to fully implement best practices. Their one-on-one mentorship becomes especially critical if no internship courses are offered through the department or on campus. Berg scrutinizes the role of mentors in detail in Chapter 6 (of this volume), expanding upon Pecorella's (2007)

Table 2: Best Practices in Political Science Internships

DEPARTMENTAL LEVEL: FACULTY/INSTRUCTORS

GENERAL OBJECTIVES/DESIRED OUTCOMES: FULFILL EDUCATIONAL MISSION OF GRADUATING KNOWLEDGEABLE AND SKILLED POLITICAL SCIENCE MAJORS OR MINORS WHO CAN ACHIEVE THEIR POTENTIAL AS WORKERS, CITIZENS, AND PEOPLE; BUILD DEPARTMENTAL REPUTATION FOR EDUCATIONAL EXCELLENCE; INCREASE STUDENT RETENTION, GRADUATION RATES, AND PRODUCTIVITY OF ALUMNI.

Maximize opportunities for student learning:

- Identify a wide range of public affairs-oriented internship experiences
- Ensure enough public affairs internships are available for all demographic & developmental profiles of major/minor population (Zilvinskis 2017; CAS 2015)
- Find opportunities where students can experience different settings and encounter a diverse range of people & situations (Kuh 2008)
- Identify student development/learning outcomes directly related to political science coursework, engaging major questions in the discipline & subfields of interest (CAS 2015)
- Review possible learning outcomes with students to raise awareness of benefits to be gained through interning (Nghia & Duyen 2019).
- Match student interest to the form of the internship: civic ed/service-oriented or research-based (Donavan 2011)
- Design traditional-length (5- to 12 -week) internships (Gilmore et al. 2015)
- Develop internships with a focus on public affairs, governing, or policy (Fede et al. 2017)
- Provide systematic, proactive monitoring prior to, during, and immediately following the internship (Pecorella 2007)
- Give students the freedom to choose; refrain from compulsory internships (Klein & Weiss 2011)

Develop impactful pedagogy:

- Intentionally design and deliver a coterminous, credited internship class so students can "integrate, synthesize, and apply knowledge" (Kuh 2008; Beard & Wilson 2018; Kolb 1984)
- Partner with site supervisors to communicate department goals and academic major/minor expectations and requirements (Eyler 2009; Kennedy et al., 2015; Hoyle & Deschaine 2016)
- Finalize a work-learning contract that site supervisor will carefully review (Pecorella 2007)
- Use class time and assignments to critically explore relationships among concepts, theory, & knowledge reinforced or expanded in practical, public-affairs settings (CAS 2015).
- Generate reflective writing & reflective discussion about issues such as the distribution of power in society or organizational behavior
- Develop guidelines for reflection; generate reflective writing & reflective discussion about students' skills, attitudes, & interests, and observed professional & ethical behaviors (Stirling et al. 2017; CAS 2015; Moore 2013; Ambrose et al. 2010, Clark 2003)
- Have students keep & review a daily or weekly journal, highlighting recurring themes or ideas (Anderson 2014; O'Neill 2010; Gavigan 2010; Colby et al. 2007).
- Assign a final research paper; monitor progress in stages
- Conclude experience with final student presentations or public reports (Reding & O'Bryan 2013)
- Make sure students know their rights; faculty must know reporting protocols in case of on-site misconduct or harassment (Diamond-Welch & Hetzel-Riggin 2018; Yamada 2016)

Offer complementary co-curricular activities:

- Offer guides for interviews; practice and review mock interviews (Gavigan 2010; Eyler & Giles 1999; Kolb 1984)
- Develop or provide links to career development-related materials such as résumé-writing or workplace etiquette guides

Distribute resources equitably:

- Chairs should ensure internship coordination and close advising work is compensated through (fractional or whole) course releases
- Integrate internship course into political science curriculum (CAS 2015)
- Provide universal access to internship-related materials (CAS 2015)
- Use department resources to disseminate information about opportunities (for internships, related coursework, financial aid) to all majors and minors
- Address financial needs inclusively by developing opportunities for interns to receive grants or be paid (Scott-Clayton 2017; Yamada 2016)

Assess student progress & program:

- Administer pre- and post-assessment surveys, including student self-assessment
- Conduct mid-internship eval including an on-site visit if possible (Pecorella 2007)
- Collect written evaluations of student at conclusion of internship (CAS 2015)
- Collect final evaluations of program by students (CAS 2015)
- Review program periodically (CAS 2015)
- Maintain external relations: build relationships with providers through repeated personal contact, including alumni who can help strengthen relationships between department and community (CAS 2015; Kuh 2008)

pointed statement: "Rule number one, successful internships require systematic and proactive monitoring prior to, during, and immediately following the internship experience" (2007, 79). First, a faculty sponsor or coordinator must work with the student to capitalize on a completed self-assessment (see the Supplemental Internship Resources section for sample questions) in order to identify fitting placements, and soon after, a set of measurable learning goals that will be communicated to an internship provider before work begins (CAS 2015). The articulation of a student's academic interests, internship objectives, and career intentions, in addition to programmatic/departmental expectations, allow site supervisors to help design relevant projects and minimize menial work. Faculty sponsors should therefore help students develop a work-learning contract that will outline the intern's and worksite's educational partnership, preferably one that spells out a project that the organization needs (Hindmoor 2010) but connects to coursework, and is a realistic fit with the individual's capacities but also contains challenging tasks (O'Neill 2010).

Faculty should also facilitate an in-person evaluation with the student midway through the term, noting unmet objectives and progress made, and implement course corrections if necessary (Pecorella 2007). This check-in also enables the intern to raise concerns that may be difficult to voice to a supervisor directly. A site visit can allow consultation with the supervisor as well. At the conclusion of an internship, campus coordinators must collect final, written evaluations of the intern's performance, and in reviewing the results with the student, must reevaluate sites and their ability to fulfill prior commitments (CAS 2015). Artifacts from this process can be used in assessments of the department's internship program (CAS 2015).

Finally, some administrative responsibilities should be assumed by department faculty or instructors to ensure fairness, equal and universal access, safety, standardized practices, assessments of the program at the departmental or institutional level, and a program that is well-integrated in the university (CAS 2015). Faculty coordinators should know the legal parameters and ramifications for transgressions; they should know whom to contact if harassment or other legal issues arise (Diamond-Welch and Hetzel-Riggin 2018; and see Chapter 3 by Yamada in this book). Internship coordinators are responsible for helping students prepare to apply for and work in internships, which often means developing, distributing, or connecting to guides or videos for résumé and cover letter writing, email etiquette and professional conduct; to handbooks containing other information about practical or legal matters; or directing students to appropriate campus staff (Eyler and Giles 1999; Kolb 1984). If career centers do not offer mock interviews, faculty might also require prospective student interns to rehearse with their peers, an exercise that could include recording mock interviews and reviewing them together (Gavigan 2010).

A career center or other campus coordinator may be charged with identifying and screening political science-related/public affairs internship providers, developing and maintaining lists of reliable placements, and cultivating relationships with community members, but departments also have a long-term interest in taking those steps (True 2011). Renewable lists of placements should embrace a wide range of opportunities—including political office, urban or city government agencies, regional or special governments, public policy-oriented nonprofits, and law firms. If these lists are maintained by the department, the listings should be able to accommodate any student majoring or minoring in the department (CAS 2015; see Supplemental Internship Resources for sample items to include in a database).[17]

In some low-density opportunity areas (e.g., small towns) where few public agencies are located, there are several ways to accommodate political science students. Based on his study of a long-running internship program in a small city, Anderson (2014) recommends that students, wherever they are placed, concentrate on examining how an organization's structure, process, and outcomes enable or inhibit the attainment of public and political goals (2014, 865), and this approach could be taken at for-profit enterprises if the position is designed intentionally and well, especially if no public affairs positions can be found in the community (Chapter 14 by Božović and McCartney contains a guide for pursuing this option). Alternatively, virtual or remote internships represent educational opportunities that continue to expand in number, and on-campus internships with a policy focus could also be cultivated to accommodate students who have limited resources—but this practice is not without its critics.[18] Scott-Clayton (2017), for example, recommends creating internships that replace off-campus jobs "with more academically-compatible on-campus ones" (1), because these have the added benefits of increasing student retention and program completion, particularly for students who are cash-strapped or have limited transportation options. Likewise, Fede, Gorman, and Cimini (2018) conclude that "student employment that incorporates aspects of experiential education in a [...] university position with time spent in the community appears to be beneficial for undergraduates from a wide range of academic disciplines" (121).

Finally, unequal access to high-quality internship opportunities continues to disadvantage many students who would benefit from an internship but face high financial barriers or arbitrary academic hurdles (Jones, Win, and Vera 2020). As Hora (2019) writes,

> Too many students lack the financial resources, social connections and time to find and pursue an internship. Our research shows that, of the students who have not had an internship, 64% wanted to but could not because of: 1) the need to work at their current job, 2) a heavy course load, 3) a lack of opportunities in their field and 4) insufficient pay. That those obstacles disproportionately impact low-income and working students, for whom an internship may be an especially important vehicle for social mobility, should raise red flags for campus leaders (2019, n.p.).

Echoing these points, Mallinson (in Chapter 11, this volume) and Gelbman, Gentry, and Van Vechten (2015) also argue that inequalities among students can be reinforced when programs require internships without regard for the accessibility of sites, the quality of the experience, or the unintended consequences of diverting students from paid work. Instead of encouraging the "best and brightest" to complete internships, a practice that simply reifies disparities that graduates will carry into their careers, equity demands that institutions find ways to accommodate all students who desire to complete a high-quality internship; best practices involve taking deliberate steps to ease undue strains. Unless institutions and departments can marshal enough resources to offset these inequities by identifying paid internships, rewarding placements that are either close to or on campus, locating or supplying student scholarships, subsidies, or grants, then internships should not be a required curricular element.

As this review of the literature demonstrates, the implementation of a quality, effective, academic internship program from beginning to end requires careful preparation, intentionality, communication, sustained commitment, appropriate compensation and resources, and regular assessment on the part of *all* internship partners. Stakeholders—meaning universities or college administrations, departments, students, and providers—must partner to achieve the best possible outcomes, foremost among them *learning* that is deep, impactful, and lasts a lifetime. Success is ultimately shaped by a surplus of factors, and some of the conditions that influence success in different settings are examined in the chapters that follow. The evidence-based practices explored in subsequent pages are clearly rooted in a body of scholarship replete with empirical and practical insights that can help students—and their faculty mentors and site supervisors—realize the educational potential of internship experiences.

REFERENCES

Acai, Anita, Victoria Cowan, Stephanie Doherty, Gaurav Sharma, and Naythrah Thevathasan. 2014. "Exploring the Role of the University Student as an Experiential Learner: Thoughts and Reflections from the 2013 Cohort of 3M National Student Fellows." *Collected Essays on Learning and Teaching* 7 (2): 1–11. https://celt.uwindsor.ca/index.php/CELT/article/view/3978.

Ahmad, Tashfeen. 2020. "Improving Political Science Degree Programmes in the Twenty-First Century." *Review of Economics and Political Science* 5 (3): 231–247. https://doi.org/10.1108/REPS-02-2019-0023.

Aldas, Tulin, Victoria Crispo, Natalie Johnson, and Todd A. Price. 2010. "Learning by Doing: The Wagner Plan from Classroom to Career." *Peer Review* 12 (4): 24–28.

Alex-Assensoh, Yvette, and Mary Ryan. 2008. "Value-Added Learning." *Peer Review* 10 (2/3). https://www.aacu.org/publications-research/periodicals/value-added-learning.

Alm, Cynthia. 1996. "Using Student Journals to Improve the Academic Quality of Internships." *Journal of Education for Business* 72 (2): 113–115.

Ambrose, Susan A., and Laurie Poklop. 2015. "Do Students Really Learn from Experience?" *Change* 47 (1): 54–61. doi:10.1080/00091383.2015.996098.

Ambrose, Susan A., Michael W. Bridges, Michele DiPietro, Marsha C. Lovett, and Marie K. Norman. 2010. *How Learning Works: Seven Research-Based Principles for Smart Teaching.* San Francisco, CA: Jossey-Bass. https://firstliteracy.org/wp-content/uploads/2015/07/How-Learning-Works.pdf.

American Association of Colleges and Universities. 2021. "What is VALUE?" Association of American Colleges and Universities (AAC&U), Accessed July 10, 2021. https://www.aacu.org/value.

Anderson, Peggy, Marcia Pulich, and James Sisak. 2002. "A Macro Perspective of Non-Clinical Student Internship Programs." *The Health Care Manager* 20 (3): 59–68.

Anderson, Brian. 2014. "High-Impact Political Science Internships in a 'Low-Density Opportunity' Environment." *PS: Political Science and Politics* 47 (4): 862–866.

Beard, Colin, and James P. Wilson. 2018. *Experiential learning: A Practical Guide for Training, Coaching, and Education (4th Ed.).* Philadelphia, PA: Kogan Page.

Benavides, Abraham, Lisa A. Dicke and Amy C. Holt. 2013. "Internships Adrift? Anchoring Internship Programs in Collaboration." *Journal of Public Affairs Education* 19 (2): 325–353.

Berg, John. 2014. "Two Threats to Political Science Internships: Press Attacks and Incorrect Student Assumptions." Paper Prepared for Delivery at the Annual Meeting of the American Political Science Association, Washington, DC.

Binder, Jens F., Thom Baguley, Chris Crook, and Felicity Miller. 2015. "The Academic Value of Internships: Benefits across Disciplines and Student Backgrounds." *Contemporary Educational Psychology* 41: 73–82.

Blount, Alma. 2006. "Critical Reflection for Public Life: How Reflective Practice Helps Students Become Politically Engaged." *Journal of Political Science Education* 2 (3): 271–283.

Bradberry, Leigh A., and Jennifer De Maio. 2019. "Learning By Doing: The Long-Term Impact of Experiential Learning Programs on Student Success." *Journal of Political Science Education* 15 (1): 94–11.

Bretschneider, Stuart, Frederick J. Marc-Aurele, Jr., and Jiannan Wu. 2005. "'Best Practices' Research: A Methodological Guide for the Perplexed." *Journal of Public Administration Research and Theory: J-PART* 15 (2): 307–323.

Brooks, Linda, Allen Cornelius, Ellen Greenfield, and Robin Joseph. 1995. "The Relation of Career-Related Work or Internship Experiences to the Career Development of College Seniors." *Journal of Vocational Behavior* 46: 332–349.

Brownell, Jayne E., and Lynne E. Swaner. 2010. "Five High-Impact Practices: Research on Learning Outcomes, Completion and Quality." Washington, DC: Association of American Colleges and Universities.

Busteed, Brandon, and Zac Auter. 2017. "Why Colleges Should Make Internships a Requirement." Gallup [Blog], November 27. https://news.gallup.com/opinion/gallup/222497/why-collegesinternships-requirement.aspx.

Callanan, Gerard, and Cynthia Benzing. 2004. "Assessing the Role of Internships in the Career-Oriented Employment of Graduating College Students." *Education + Training* 46(2): 82-89.

Cannon, J. Andrew, and Mark J. Arnold. 1998. "Student Expectations of Collegiate Internship Programs." *Journal of Education for Business* 73 (4): 202–205.

Carey, Shelley J. 2010. "From the Editor." *Peer Review* 12 (4). https://www.aacu.org/publications-research/periodicals/editor-92.

Carson, Lyn, and Katherine Fisher. 2006. "Raising the Bar on Criticality: Students' Critical Reflection in an Internship Program," *Journal of Management Education* 30 (5): 700–723.

Cedercreutz, Kettil, and Cheryl Cates. 2010. "Cooperative Education at the University of Cincinnati: A Strategic Asset in Evolution." *Peer Review* 12 (4): 20–23.

Chemers, Martin M., Li-tze Hu, and Ben Garcia. 2001. "Academic Self-Efficacy and First-Year College Student Performance and Adjustment. *Journal of Educational Psychology* 93 (1): 55–64. https://doi.org/10.1037/0022-0663.93.1.55.

Clark, Sue C. 2003. "Enhancing the Educational Value of Business Internships." *Journal of Management Education* 27 (4): 472–484.

Clark, Alistair, and Tristan Martin. 2016. "An Audit of Transferable Skills Teaching in UK Politics Departments." *European Political Science* 15 (3): 389–403.

Coker, Jeffrey, Evan Heiser, Laura Taylor, and Connie Book. 2017. "Impacts of Experiential Learning Depth and Breadth on Student Outcomes." *Journal of Experiential Education* 40 (1): 5–23.

Colby, Anne, Elizabeth Beaumont, Thomas Ehrlich, and Josh Corngold. 2007. *Educating for Democracy: Preparing Undergraduates for Responsible Political Engagement.* San Francisco: Jossey-Bass.

Collins, Todd, H. Gibbs, Jen Schiff. 2012. "Career Preparation and the Political Science Major: Evidence from Departments." *PS: Political Science and Politics* 45 (1): 87–92.

Council for the Advancement of Standards in Higher Education (CAS). 2015. "Internship Programs: CAS Standards and Guidelines." In *CAS Book of Standards*, Fort Collins: CAS.

Crebert, Gay, Merrelyn Bates, Barry Bell, Carol-Joy Patrick, Vanda Cragnolini. 2004. "Developing Generic Skills at University, During Work Placement and in Employment: Graduates' Perceptions." *Higher Education Research and Development* 23 (2): 147–165. doi: https://doi.org/10.1080/0729436042000206636.

Criso, Rachael, Jillian Low, and Kelen Townsend. 2021. "Starting the Debate on Remote Versus In-person Internship Skills Gain." Unpublished manuscript. PDF file.

Dailey, Stephanie. 2016. "What Happens Before Full-Time Employment? Internships as a Mechanism of Anticipatory Socialization." *Western Journal of Communication* 80 (4): 453–480.

D'Aloisio, Anna. 2006. "Motivating Students Through Awareness of the Natural Correlation Between College Learning and Corporate Work Settings." *College Teaching* (54) 2: 225–229.

Dewey, John. 1938. *Experience and Education.* New York, NY: Collier Macmillan.

Diamond-Welch, Bridget, and Melanie Hetzel-Riggin. 2018. "Title IX Protections for College Legislative Interns: What Should You Know and What More Can Your Program Do." *Journal of Political Science Education*, 15 (2): 257–263. https://doi.org/10.1080/15512169.2018.1474116.

DiMaggio, Anthony. 2018. "Is Political Science Relevant? The Decline of Critical Scholarly Engagement in the Neoliberal Era." *Poverty and Public Policy* 10 (2): 222–252.

Doherty, Leanne. 2011. "Filling the Female Political Pipeline: Assessing a Mentor-Based Internship Program." *Journal of Political Science Education* 7 (1): 34–47.

Donavan, Janet. 2011. "Designing an Intellectually Challenging Internship Program." Prepared for Presentation at the Annual Meeting of the American Political Science Association, Seattle, Washington, September 1.

Donovan, Timothy, Richard Porter, and James Stellar, J. 2010. "Experiencing Success: Some Strategies for Planning the Program." *New Directions for Teaching and Learning* 124: 89–94. doi: 10.1002/tl.426.

Donnelly-Smith, Laura. 2010. "Vice President for Strategic New Business Development and Marketing, Siemens Healthcare." *Peer Review* 12 (4). https://www.aacu.org/publications-research/periodicals/making-most-out-internships-interview-christi-m-pedra-senior-vice.

Dworkis, Martin B., Samuel F. Thomas, and Ruth Weintraub. 1962. "Establishing an Administrative Internship Program." *Public Administration Review* 22 (2): 75–81.

Ehrenberg, Ronald, and Daniel Sherman. 1987. "Employment while in College, Academic Achievement, and Postcollege Outcomes: A Summary of Results." *Journal of Human Resources* 22 (1): 1–23.

Ericksen, Kirsten. S., and Sandra Williamson-Ashe. 2019. "Holistic Justice Instruction through High-Impact Educational Practices at Historically Black Colleges and Universities." *Urban Social Work* 3 (S1): S100-S114.

Eyler, Janet S. 2009. "The Power of Experiential Education." *Liberal Education* 95 (4): 24–31.

Eyler, Janet S., and Dwight E. Giles. 1999. *Where's the Learning in Service-Learning?* San Francisco, CA: Jossey-Bass.

Fede, Jacquelyn, Kathleen Gorman, and Maria Cimini. 2018. "Student Employment as a Model for Experiential Learning." *Journal of Experiential Education* 41 (1): 107–124. https://doi.org/10.1177/1469787417747057.

Fernald, Peter, and Gary Goldstein. 2013. "Advanced Internship: A High-Impact, Low-Cost, Super-Capstone Course." *College Teaching* 61 (1): 3–10.

Finley, Ashley, and Tia McNair. 2013. *Assessing Underserved Students' Engagement in High Impact Practices.* Washington, DC: Association of American Colleges and Universities.

Foster Shoaf, Nicole R. 2020. "Political Science Internships: A Path to 'Workforce Ready' Without Selling Out." Paper Presented at the Biennial Meeting of the APSA Teaching & Learning Conference, Albuquerque, NM.

Fry, Betty, Gene Bottoms, and Kathy O'Neill. 2005. "The Principal Internship: How Can We Get it Right?" Southern Regional Education Board, Atlanta, GA.

Gault, Jack, Evan Leach, and Marc Duey. 2010. "Effects of Business Internships on Job Marketability: The Employers' Perspective." *Education + Training* 52 (1): 76–88. https://doi.org/10.1108/00400911011017690.

Gavigan, Lisa. 2010. "Connecting the Classroom with Real World Experiences through Summer Internships." *Peer Review* 12 (4).

Gelbman, Shamira, Bobbi Gentry, and Renée Van Vechten. 2015. "Exploring Dimensions of Inequality in Political Science Internships." Paper Prepared for Delivery at the Annual Meeting of the American Political Science Association, San Francisco, CA.

Gentry, Bobbi, and Renée Van Vechten. 2018. "The What and How of Political Science Internships." Paper Prepared for Delivery at the Annual Meeting of the American Political Science Association, Boston, MA.

Goodenough, Anne, Hazel Roberts, David Biggs, James Derounian, Adam Hart, and Kenny Lynch. 2020. "A Higher Degree of Resilience: Using Psychometric Testing to Reveal the Benefits of University Internship Placements." *Active Learning in Higher Education* 21 (2): 102–115.

Greenhaus, Jeffrey H., Gerard A. Callanan, and Veronica M. Godshalk. 2000. *Career Management, 3rd ed.* Mason, OH: Thomson-South-Western.

Griffin, James E., Gregory. F. Lorenz, and David Mitchell. 2010. "A study of outcomes-oriented student reflection during internship: The integrated, coordinated, and reflection based model of learning and experiential education." *Journal of Cooperative Education and Internships* (44): 42–50.

Hanson, Janice. 1984. "Internships and the Individual: Suggestions for Implementing (or Improving) an Internship Program." *Communication Education* 33 (1): 53–61.

Hart, Peter. 2008. *"How Should Colleges Assess and Improve Student Learning? Employers' Views on the Accountability Challenge."* AAC&U/Peter D. Hart Research Associates.

Harvey, Lee, Vicki Geall, and Sue Moon. 1997. "Graduates' Work: Organisational Change for the Development of Student Attributes." *Industry and Higher Education* 11 (5): 287–296. https://doi.org/10.1177/095042229701100504.

Hennessy, Bernard C. 1970. *Political Internships: Theory, Practice, Evaluation.* University Park, PA: Penn State Studies.

Hesser, Garry. 2014. *Strengthening Experiential Education: A New Era.* Mount Royal, NJ: National Society for Experiential Education.

Hindmoor, Andrew. 2010. "Internships within Political Science." *Australian Journal of Political Science* 45 (3): 483–490.

Hirschfield, Robert, and Norman M. Adler. 1973. "Internships in Politics: The CUNY Experience." *PS: Political Science & Politics* 6 (1): 13–18.

Hocking, J. Barry, Michelle Brown, and Anne-Wil Harzing. 2004. "A Knowledge Transfer Perspective of Strategic Assignment Purposes and Their Path-Dependent Outcomes." *International Journal of Human Resource Management* 15: 565–586.

Hora, Matthew T. 2019. "Internships as a High-Impact Practice? *Inside Higher Ed*, September 23. https://www.insidehighered.com/views/2019/09/23/campuses-should-proceed-caution-when-it-comes-student-internships-opinion.

Hora, Matthew T., Adrian Huerta, Anita Gopal, and Matthew Wolfgram. 2021. "A Review of the Literature on Internships for Latinx Students at Hispanic-serving Institutions: Toward a Latinx-Serving Internship Experience." University of Wisconsin–Madison, Wisconsin Center for Education Research, WCER Working Paper No. 2021-2. https://wcer.wisc.edu/docs/working-papers/WCER_Working_Paper_No_2021-2.pdf.

Hora, Matthew T., Changhee Lee, Zi Chen, and Anthony Hernandez. 2021. "Exploring Online Internships amidst the COVID-19 Pandemic in 2020: Results from a Mixed-Methods Study." University of Wisconsin-Madison: Center for Research on College-Workforce Transitions. http://ccwt.wceruw.org/documents/CCWT_report_Exploring%20online%20internships%20amidst%20the%20COVID-19%20pandemic%20in%202020.pdf.

Hora, Matthew T., Matthew Wolfgram, Zi Chen, Jiahong Zhang, and Jacklyn John Fischer 2020. "A Sociocultural Analysis of Internship Supervision: Insights from a Mixed-Methods Study of Interns at Five Postsecondary

Institutions." WCER Working Paper No. 2020-8, University of Wisconsin-Madison. https://www.wcer.wisc.edu/publications/abstract/wcer-working-paper-no.-2020-8.

Hoyle, Jeffrey, and Mark E. Deschaine. 2016. "An Interdisciplinary Exploration of Collegiate Internships." *Education and Training* 58 (4): 372–389.

Jacoby, Barbara. 2009. *Civic Engagement in Higher Education: Concepts and Practices.* San Francisco, CA: Jossey-Bass. http://sla.fgu.edu.tw/attachments/article/124/FINAL%20FINAL%20CEIHE%20-%20NTNU%2012-8-14.pdf.

Jarvis, Peter, John Holford, Colin Griffin. 2003. *The Theory and Practice of Learning.* London: Routledge.

Jeske, Debora. 2019. "Virtual internships: Learning Opportunities and Recommendations." In *Total Internship Management: The Employer's Guide to Building and Sustaining the Ultimate Internship Program 3rd Edition,* ed. Robert Shindell, 171–177. Cedar Park, TX: Intern Bridge, Inc.

Jeske, Debora, and Carolyn Axtell. 2016. "Going Global in Small Steps: E-Internships in Small and Medium-Sized Organizations." *Organizational Dynamics* 45 (1): 55–63.

Jeske, Debora, and Carolyn Axtell. 2018. "The Nature of Relationships in e-Internships: A Matter of Psychological Contract, Communication and Relational Investment." *The Journal of Work and Organizational Psychology* 34 (2): 113-121. https://doi.org/10.5093/jwop2018a14.

Johnson, Matthew. 2016. "Communicating Politics: Using Active Learning to Demonstrate the Value of the Discipline." *British Journal of Educational Studies* 64 (3): 315–335.

Jones, James R., Tiffany Win, and Carlos Mark Vera. 2021. "Who Congress Pays: An Analysis of Lawmakers' Use of Intern Allowances in the 116th Congress," https://payourinterns.org/wp-content/uploads/2021/03/Pay-Our-Interns-Who-Congress-Pays.pdf.

Kennedy, Monica, Stephen Billett, Silvia Gherardi, and Laurie Grealish, eds. 2015. *Practice-based Learning in Higher Education.* London: Springer.

Kilgo, Cindy, Jessica Ezell Sheets, and Earnest Pascarella. 2015. "The Link Between High-Impact Practices and Student Learning: Some Longitudinal Evidence." *Higher Education* 69: 509–525.

King, Mary. 2014. "Ensuring Quality In Experiential Education." In *Strengthening Experiential Education: A New Era,* ed. Garry Hesser. Mt. Royal, NJ: National Society for Experiential Education.

Klein, Markus, and Felix Weiss. 2011. "Is Forcing Them Worth the Effort? Benefits of Mandatory Internships for Graduates from Diverse Family Backgrounds at Labour Market Entry." *Studies in Higher Education* 36 (8): 969–987.

Kolb, David. A. 1984. *Experiential Learning: Experience as the Source of Learning and Development.* Englewood Cliffs, NJ: Prentice Hall.

Knouse, Stephen B., John R. Tanner, and Elizabeth W. Harris. 1999. "The Relation of College Internships, College Performance, and Subsequent Job Opportunity." *Journal of Employment Counseling* 36 (1): 35–43. doi: 10.1002/j.2161-1920.1999.tb01007.x

Kuh, George D. 2008. "High-Impact Educational Practices: What They Are, Who Has Access to Them, and Why They Matter." Washington, DC: Association of American Colleges and Universities.

Kuh, George D. 2013. "Taking HIP's to the Next Level." In *Ensuring Quality and Taking High-Impact Practices to Scale*, ed. George D. Kuh and Ken O'Donnell. Washington, DC: AAC&U.

Kuh, George D., Ken O'Donnell, and Carol Geary Schneider. 2017. "HIPs at Ten." *Change: The Magazine of Higher Learning* 49 (5): 8–16. DOI: 10.1080/00091383.2017.1366805

Kuh, George D., Jillian Kinzie, John Schuh, and Elizabeth J. Whitt. 2010. *Student Success in College: Creating Conditions that Matter.* San Francisco: Wiley.

Lei, Simon, and Dean Yin. 2019. "Evaluating Benefits and Drawbacks of Internships: Perspectives of College Students." *College Student Journal* 53:181–189.

Liu, Yongmei, Jun Xu, and Barton A. Weitz. 2011. "The Role of Emotional Expression and Mentoring in Internship Learning." *Academy of Management Learning and Education* 10 (1): 94–110.

Lowenthal, Diane, and Jeffrey Sosland. 2007. "Making the Grade: How a Semester in Washington May Influence Future Academic Performance." *Journal of Political Science Education* 3 (2): 143–160.

Maertz, Carl, Philipp Stoebrl, and Jill Marks. 2013. "Building successful internships: lessons from the research for interns, schools, and employers." *Career Development International* 191 (1): 123–142.

Mariani, Mack, and Philip Klinkner. 2009. "The Effect of a Campaign Internship on Political Efficacy and Trust." *Journal of Political Science Education* 5 (4): 275–293.

McCartney, Alison Rios Millett, Elizabeth Bennion, and Dick Simpson. 2013. *Teaching Civic Engagement: From Student to Active Citizen.* Washington, DC: American Political Science Association.

McClellan, Fletcher, Kyle Casimir Kopko, and Kayla L. Gruber. 2021. "High-Impact Practices and Their Effects: Implications for the Undergraduate Political Science Curriculum." *Journal of Political Science Education* [Online], 1–19.

Moon, Jeremy, and Wykham Schokman. 2000. "Doing Politics: Political Science Research Internships and Political Science Education." *Politics* 20 (3): 169–175.

Moore, David Thornton. 2013. "For Interns, Experience Isn't Always the Best Teacher." *Chronicle of Higher Education* 60(12), A28–A30.

Murphy, Thomas P. 1973. *Government Management Internships and Executive Development.* Lexington, MA: Lexington Books.

Narayanan, V. K., Paul Olk, and Cynthia Fukami. 2010. "Determinants of Internship Effectiveness: An Exploratory Model." *Academy of Management Learning and Education* 9 (1): 61–80.

National Association of Colleges and Employers. 2021. "What is Career Readiness?" NACE. Accessed July 1, 2021. https://www.naceweb.org/career-readiness/competencies/career-readiness-defined/.

National Survey of Student Engagement. 2019. Engagement Insights: Survey Findings on the Quality of Undergraduate Education. Bloomington, IN: Indiana Center for Postsecondary Research.

Neapolitan, Jerry. 1992. "The Internship Experience and Clarification of Career Choice." *Teaching Sociology* 20 (3): 222–231.

Nghia, Tran Le Huu, and Nguyen Thi My Duyen. 2019. "Developing and Validating a Scale for Evaluating Internship-Related Learning Outcomes." *Higher Education* 77: 1–18.

O'Neill, Nancy. 2010. "Internships as a High-Impact Practice." *Peer Review* 12 (4). https://www.aacu.org/publications-research/periodicals/internships-high-impact-practice-some-reflections-quality.

Parker III, Eugene T., Cindy Kilgo, Jessica A. Ezell Sheets, and Earnest Pascarella. 2016. "The Differential Effects of Internship Participation on End-of-Fourth-Year GPA by Demographic and Institutional Characteristics." *Journal of College Student Development* **57** (1): 104–109.

Pecorella, Robert F. 2007. "Forests and Trees: The Role of Academics in Legislative Internships." *Journal of Political Science Education* 3 (1): 79–99.

Pellegrino, James W., and Margaret L. Hilton, eds. 2013. *Education for Life and Work: Developing Transferable Knowledge and Skills in the 21st Century.* Washington, DC: Committee on Defining Deeper Learning and 21st Century Skills; Center for Education; Division on Behavioral and Social Sciences and Education; National Research Council.

Perlin, Ross. 2012. *Intern Nation: How to Earn Nothing and Learn Little in the Brave New Economy.* New York: Verso Books.

Piaget, Jean. 1971. *Psychology and Epistemology.* Harmondsworth, UK: Penguin.

Raile, Eric D., Elizabeth A. Shanahan, Michael P. Wallner, Linda M. Young, Marja Avonius, Micaela Young, and Nacer Tayeb. 2017. "Using Alumni Views to Connect the Past, Present, and Future in Political Science." *PS: Political Science and Politics* 50 (3): 837–41. doi:10.1017/S1049096517000695.

Reding, Kurt F, and David O'Bryan. 2013. "Ten Best Practices for Business Student Internships." *Strategic Finance* 95 (4): 43–48.

Roberts, Jay. 2018. "From the Editor: The Possibilities and Limitations of Experiential Learning Research in Higher Education." *Journal of Experiential Education* 41 (1): 3–7.

Robles, Marcel M. 2012. "Executive Perceptions of the Top 10 Soft Skills Needed in Today's Workplace." *Business Communication Quarterly* 75: 453–465.

Routon, P. Wesley, and Jay K. Walker. 2015. "A Smart Break? College Tenure Interruption and Graduating Student Outcomes." *Education Finance and Policy* 10 (2): 244–276.

Routon, P. Wesley, and Jay K. Walker. 2018. *College Internships, Tenure Gaps, and Student Outcomes: A Multiple Treatment Matching Approach.* Rochester, NY: Social Science Research Network. SSRN Scholarly Paper. https://papers.ssrn.com/abstract=3192004.

Schamber, Jon F., and Sandra Mahoney. 2008. "The Development of Political Awareness and Social Justice Citizenship through Community-Based Learning in a First-Year General Education Seminar." *The Journal of General Education* 57 (2): 75–99. doi:10.1353/jge.0.0016.

Scott-Clayton, Judith. 2017. "Federal Work-Study: Past its Prime, or Ripe for Renewal?" Brookings Institution, Evidence Speaks Reports 2(16).

Shindell, Robert. 2019. *Total Internship Management.* Cedar Park, TX: Intern Bridge.

Silva, Patrícia, Betina Lopes, Marco Costa, Ana I. Melo, Gonçalo Paiva Dias, Elisabeth Brito, and Dina Seabra. 2018. "The Million-Dollar Question: Can Internships Boost Employment?" *Studies in Higher Education* 43 (1): 2–21.

Simons, Lori, Lawrence Fehr, Nancy Blank, Heather Connell, Denise Georganas, David Fernandez, and Verda Peterson. 2012. "Lessons Learned from Experiential Learning: What Do Students Learn from a Practicum/ Internship?" *International Journal of Teaching and Learning in Higher Education* 24 (3): 325–334.

Sims, Paul, Michael Sukowski, and Margaret Trybus. 2007. "Reaching the tipping point: the interconnectedness of a school leadership program." In *At the Tipping Point: Navigating the Course for the Preparation of Educational Administrators: The 2007 Yearbook of the National Council of Professors of Educational Administration*, ed. Linda Lemasters and Rosemary Papa. Lancaster, PA: DEStech Publications, 409–420.

Sosland, Jeffrey, and Diane Lowenthal. 2017. "The Forgotten Educator: Experiential Learning's Internship Supervisor." *Journal of Political Science Education* 13 (1): 1–14.

Stirling, Ashley, Gretchen Kerr, Ellen MacPherson, Jenessa Banwell, Ahad Bandealy, and Anthony Battaglia. 2017. "Do Postsecondary Internships Address the Four Learning Modes of Experiential Learning Theory? An Exploration through Document Analysis." *Canadian Journal of Higher Education*, 47 (1): 27–48.

Thessin, Rebecca A., and J. Clayton. 2013. "Perspectives of School Leaders on the Administrative Internship," *Journal of Educational Administration* 51 (6): 790–811.

Titus, Sandra, and Janice Ballou. 2014. "Ensuring PhD Development of Responsible Conduct of Research Behaviors: Who's Responsible?" *Science and Engineering Ethics* 20 (1): 221–235.

True, Michael. 2011. *Starting and Maintaining A Quality Internship Program, 7th Edition.* Grantham, PA: Messiah College Internship Center. http://www.internqube.com/uploads/4/8/0/7/4807298/starting_an_internship_program_-_7th_edition.pdf.

Van Vechten, Renée, and Bobbi Gentry. 2017. "Internships Across the Discipline: Community Colleges vs. Four-Year Colleges and Universities." Paper prepared for delivery at the Annual Meeting of the American Political Science Association, San Francisco, CA.

Wang, Shu-Tai, and Cheng-Chung Wang. 2015. "Path Analysis on the Factors Influencing Learning Outcome for Hospitality Interns—From the Flow Theory Perspective." *Journal of Education and Learning* 4 (3): 25–44.

Whitaker, Urban. 1989. *Assessing Learning: Standards, Principles and Procedures.* Philadelphia: Council for Adult Experiential Learning.

Williams, Tameka, Daniel K. Pryce, Tyler Clark, Hydeia Wilfong. 2020. "The Benefits of Criminal Justice Internships at a Historically Black University: An Analysis of Site Supervisors' Evaluations of Interns' Professional Development." *Journal of Criminal Justice Education* 31 (1): 124–140.

Yamada, David C. 2016. "The Legal and Social Movement Against Unpaid Internships." *Northeastern University Law Journal* 8 (2): 357–96. https://papers.ssrn.com/sol3/papers.cfm?abstract_id=2338646.

Yates, Miranda, and James Youniss. 1996. "A Developmental Perspective on Community Service in Adolescence." *Social Development* 5 (1): 85–111. doi:10.1111/j.1467-9507.1996.tb00073.

Yeh, Theresa L. 2010. "Service-Learning and Persistence of Low-Income, First-Generation College Students: An Exploratory Study." *Michigan Journal of Community Service Learning* 16:50–65.

Zilvinskis, John. 2017. "Measuring Quality in High-Impact Practices." *ProQuest LLC*, Ph.D. Dissertation, Indiana University.

ENDNOTES

1. In this chapter, the terms *experiential learning* and *internships* are used interchangeably (unless otherwise noted).

2. Survey responses tend to center on students' self-reported gains. Student-level data tend to be grade-point averages (GPA) and graduation rates. Mixed-methods studies pepper the literature in addition to a few comparative, longitudinal studies in the area of internships (not in abundance, however). Lowenthal and Sosland (2007) is a good example of a mixed-methods, comparative study of internships (in Washington, DC).

3. Kuh (2008) defines "historically underserved" as underrepresented minority, first-generation, transfer, and low-income students.

4. In their review of internship program webpages and course outlines, Stirling et al. (2017) find that most internship programs emphasize the first two stages rather than the linking of theory with practice, and they argue that political science departments should design programs that will promote more comprehensive coverage of these stages. As described by Auerbach in Chapter 7, research internships are promising examples of such programming.

5. These criteria are articulated in Lowenthal and Sosland (2007).

6. Others include the Association of American Colleges and Universities (AAC&U), the National Society for Experiential Education (NSEE), the National Association of Colleges and Employers (NACE), and the Council for the Advancement of Standards in Higher Education.

7. Although standards for internship programs have been developed at the professional association level and periodically revisited "through a consensus model of member associations and other experts" (for CAS that has been a 30-year process; see Introduction, CAS 2015), extant work exploring the impact of these standards remains thin, and coverage of political science internships has been infrequent.

8. AAC&U also enumerate 16 Essential Learning Outcomes "that all students need for success in work, citizenship, and life" (2021, n.p.): "The VALUE rubrics include Inquiry and Analysis, Critical Thinking, Creative Thinking, Written Communication, Oral Communication, Quantitative Literacy, Information Literacy, Reading, Teamwork, Problem Solving, Civic Knowledge and Engagement—Local and Global, Intercultural Knowledge and Competence, Ethical Reasoning and Action, Global Learning, Foundations and Skills for Lifelong Learning, and Integrative Learning."

9. For example, critical thinking, which they define as the ability to "identify and respond to needs based upon an understanding of situational context and logical analysis of relevant information," would manifest in behaviors such as making decisions and solving problems using sound, inclusive reasoning and judgment; gathering and analyzing information from diverse sources and individuals to fully understand a problem; accurately summarizing and interpreting data with an awareness of personal (and other) biases that may impact outcomes; and so forth (2021).

10. Their sample includes over 442,000 students from 619 institutions of higher education in the United States. They estimate internships' impacts on academic performance, human and social capital gains, satisfaction with the college experience, and post-graduation goals and plans. Using a method of propensity score matching, they conclude that "many of the benefits of internship participation would be underestimated if the effects of discontinuous college tenure were not accounted for" (Routon and Walker 2018, 1).

11. According to Kilgo, Ezell Sheets, and Pascarella (2015, 513): "The overall sample in the study consisted of incoming first-year students at 17 four-year colleges and universities located in 11 different states from four general regions of the United States. Of the original sample of 4,193 students who participated in the late summer/early fall 2006 testing, 2,212 participated in the spring 2010 follow-up data collection [four years later], for a response rate of 52.8%. These students represented approximately 10% of the total population of incoming first-year students at the 17 participating institutions."

12. Students at the Wagner College on Staten Island, NY, learn through the "Wagner Plan," which is designed to cultivate "lifelong learners and active members of their professional communities" (Aldas et al. 2010, n.p.). Students in each class annually experience learning through research projects, service learning, field trips, and internships.

13. Bradberry and DeMaio write: "Of our survey respondents who entered Cal State University Northridge as first-time freshmen (FTF), 77% of the Model United Nations (MUN) students and 58% of the Judicial Internship Program (JIP) students graduated in 4 years or less. These numbers are well above the university average of 15% for FTF graduating in 4 years or less, and the national average of 40% for all institutions and 35% for public institutions [...] However, it not correct that the students admitted are predominantly students with

the highest GPAs. In fact, in MUN, there is no GPA requirement to apply. [...]Among the applicants for both programs, there is a variation in GPAs, majors, courses taken, and their overall level of preparation. [...] As a result, while we are not claiming a causal relationship or that participation in MUN or JIP alone leads to higher graduation rates, it is undisputed that these programs provide: external motivation for students to stay on track; positive peer influence, camaraderie, and support; and mentorship from faculty coordinators, judges, diplomats, and other professionals—all of which students are far less likely to receive in a traditional classroom setting" (2019: 103).

14. We note that the language used in CAS standards is "*shall*" versus "*must,*" deliberately conveying a sense of necessity; here we opt to use "should" and "must."

15. The objectives identified in the tables are both explicitly and implicitly recognized as incentivizing action around experiential education (CAS 2015; Hocking, Brown and Harzing 2004; Kuh 2008; NACE 2021; True 2011).

16. Many of these focus on political science interns specifically, but some include social science majors, and others are studies of undergraduates that have been cited in the political science internship literature.

17. Note that students who are not majoring or minoring in political science should also be able to access these opportunities (and many do, especially if these placements might enable them to achieve their learning goals), but the department's primary obligation is to deliver a curriculum for its majors.

18. Conflicts of interest, limited scope, and limited exposure to the community (external to campus) are possible constraints that make on-campus positions less desirable than off-campus ones.

CHAPTER 3

Major Legal Considerations Pertaining to Internships

David C. Yamada, Suffolk University

The burgeoning intern economy developed largely in the absence of federal guidelines or clarifying legal precedents until recently, creating significant ambiguity around interns' rights, internship providers' responsibilities, and institutions' potential liabilities. During the past decade, litigation has helped clarify the relationship among students, their university or college, and their internship providers under current employment and education laws. This chapter surveys the major legal developments concerning internships, including compensation, harassment, and discrimination issues, with the core question being whether an internship is treated as an employment relationship under the law. With this briefing, relevant stakeholders can seek advice of their local counsel for further clarification about legal rights and responsibilities concerning interns as they aim to implement higher quality, accessible internship opportunities, especially for students who are interested in politics and public policy.

INTRODUCTION

The worlds of politics and public policy have long been associated with unpaid and low-paid labor, and well before internships became common. Volunteering to support candidates for office is an American civic tradition, with tasks ranging from passing out campaign literature to drafting position papers. Furthermore, countless young people have found their ways to city halls, state capitals, and Washington DC to gain experience in government and policy making.

While these more casual arrangements continue, many such opportunities have been formally recast as internships. During the past four decades, this trend has dovetailed with the growth of an American "intern economy," marked by increasing expectations that students in degree programs should seek out internships to complement their classroom learning (Perlin 2012; Yamada 2002). Professional work experience, credentials for future education and employment, and networking opportunities are commonly touted as the benefits of doing internships. Increasingly, colleges and universities have partnered with internship providers to create affiliated programs, thereby allowing institutions of higher learning to offer academic credit in return for practical experience.

Until relatively recently, this intern economy grew without external oversight, becoming, in essence, a *de facto* required, intermediate stage of post-secondary education, bridging the worlds of classroom learning and entry-level professional employment. The legal status of those designated as interns, and the corresponding liability-related responsibilities of both internship providers and universities associated with internship programs, were not well defined (Yamada 2002). This was especially so with regard to potential protections and liabilities under minimum wage and employment discrimination statutes.

The past decade, however, has witnessed growing attention being paid to the legal implications of internships, including lawsuits and policy initiatives that are sharpening our focus on how the intern economy relates to employment and education law (Perlin 2012; Yamada 2016a; Yamada 2016b). These developments have had considerable "on the ground" impacts, putting organizations that hire interns and post-secondary educational institutions that facilitate internships on notice that liability exposure cannot be ignored. They also have raised important questions of what legal protections should extend to those working in internship capacities. These matters are notably pertinent to internships in fields that are popular options for students studying political science and related disciplines.

This chapter examines the primary legal issues surrounding internships, especially in the realms of employment law and education law, with special attention paid to internship settings popular with students studying political science, public policy, and public administration. While intended primarily to inform educational stakeholders and internship providers who are directly involved with administering and overseeing internships, it will also be useful to students who are exploring their internship options and wondering what, if any, legal protections might cover them if certain situations arise. In addition, the chapter will examine some of the deeper legal and social policy issues pertinent to the growing intern economy.

Accordingly, the second section examines the basic employment and education framework around internships, and the subsequent section discusses best practices concerning internships in the contexts of both liability exposure and access to internship and accompanying career opportunities in the fields of politics and public policy. The chapter concludes with some closing observations about the intern economy, attendant social policy issues, and creating opportunities for participation in public life.

Before proceeding, please note three disclaimers:

First, the forthcoming discussion heavily emphasizes federal employment and education law. While it is beyond the scope of this chapter to provide a comprehensive primer on all applicable legal developments, it is important to note that on occasion state and local laws and ordinances may enter the picture. That said, readers who seek an explanation of major legal issues pertinent to internships commonly sought by political science students will find it here.

Second, it follows that the content provided here is for informational purposes only and should not be interpreted or relied upon as legal advice. Especially for those responsible for creating and administering internship programs, consultation with counsel well versed in employment law and education law relevant to interns is strongly urged. This word of caution is provided for more than the standard obligatory reasons. The legal implications of internships can be very tricky, and the law itself continues to evolve. Many of the legal issues discussed here have been subjects of litigation only relatively recently, which suggests a body of law still in development. As suggested above, state legislation and local ordinances may address intern rights issues as well. Future executive orders, legislation, and ordinances may materially impact the legal status of interns. At the federal level, especially, a new presidential administration may result in major changes.

Finally, I readily disclose that I have been both a scholar and an advocate on these issues. My research and scholarship on the legal implications of unpaid internships began some 20 years ago, and it quickly led to a firm conclusion that protections for interns require significant expansion (Yamada 2002; Yamada 2016a; Yamada 2016b). This includes a more inclusive application of minimum wage laws and the closure of disturbing loopholes in employment discrimination and sexual harassment laws. Accordingly, during the past decade, I have participated in legal advocacy and public education initiatives supporting stronger protections for interns, including proceedings discussed here.

LEGAL FRAMEWORK

It is important to clarify at the outset that there is no official legal definition of "intern." Although fields such as medicine formalized the status of intern long ago, there is no general corollary in the structure of employment law. This is among the reasons why cases addressing intern employment rights have been litigated in recent years.

The main legal issues surrounding internships include: (1) potential obligations of internship providers to pay interns pursuant to minimum wage laws; (2) potential protections and liability exposure concerning interns under employment discrimination laws; and (3) obligations to prevent and respond to sex discrimination and sexual harassment under federal education law in internship programs affiliated with educational institutions.[1] These legal issues are relevant to interns, internship providers, and colleges and universities that are facilitating internships or sponsoring internship programs.[2]

As the discussion below will explain, distinctions among internships in the private, non-profit, and public sectors can carry legal significance. Therefore, it may be helpful to identify popular types of internship placements for political science students associated with these sectors. Examples of private sector internship placements include political and public affairs consulting firms, public opinion polling firms, media companies of all types (though some are non-profits), and corporate departments devoted to regulatory matters. Examples of non-profit internship placements include advocacy groups, political campaigns, policy shops and think tanks, labor unions, and community development and charitable agencies.[3] Public sector internship placements include virtually any local, state, regional, or federal governmental entity.

Minimum Wage and Overtime Laws

Are interns entitled to the minimum wage and overtime pay under the Fair Labor Standards Act of 1938 (FLSA 1938), the federal law that prescribes wage and hour standards? The answer is a highly qualified *maybe* for internships with private sector, for-profit organizations, and *highly doubtful* for internships with non-profit and public-sector entities.

During the early 2010s, a flurry of lawsuits sought court rulings that interns are entitled to compensation under the FLSA and corresponding state laws (Yamada 2016a). Most of these legal claims were brought against private sector, for-profit employers. This distinction is significant, given that internships in political and policy settings are predominantly in the non-profit and public sectors. As such, we need to parse out the potential application of labor standards statutes to different categories of organizations that hire interns.

Private sector internships

In 2018, the US Department of Labor (DOL), under the Trump Administration, issued new guidelines for determining when a private sector, for-profit internship provider is exempt from paying an intern at least the federally mandated minimum wage, as well as overtime pay when warranted (DOL 2018). These guidelines were contained in a revised memorandum designated as Fact Sheet #71: Internships Under The Fair Labor Standards Act. In the document, the DOL endorses a "primary beneficiary test" that asks whether the internship provider or the intern derives the primary benefits of the internship experience. If the latter, then the intern is not an employee under the FLSA and thus is not entitled to compensation.

To make this determination, the DOL cites the following factors to be weighed, with no single one regarded as controlling:

1. The extent to which the intern and the employer clearly understand that there is no expectation of compensation. Any promise of compensation, express or implied, suggests that the intern is an employee—and vice versa.
2. The extent to which the internship provides training that would be similar to that which would be given in an educational environment, including the clinical and other hands-on training provided by educational institutions.

3. The extent to which the internship is tied to the intern's formal education program by integrated coursework or the receipt of academic credit.
4. The extent to which the internship accommodates the intern's academic commitments by corresponding to the academic calendar.
5. The extent to which the internship's duration is limited to the period in which the internship provides the intern with beneficial learning.
6. The extent to which the intern's work complements, rather than displaces, the work of paid employees while providing significant educational benefits to the intern.
7. The extent to which the intern and the employer understand that the internship is conducted without entitlement to a paid job at the conclusion of the internship (DOL 2018).

The primary beneficiary test inures to the benefit of internship providers that do not wish to pay their interns, especially those who partner with educational institutions and who require interns to acknowledge that they are neither getting paid nor are entitled to paid employment once the internship concludes. It also puts the burden of questioning the lawfulness of an unpaid internship on individual applicants, and few are likely to do so in view of the risks involved.

The DOL's 2018 guidelines incorporate the primary beneficiary test as adopted in *Glatt v. Fox Searchlight Pictures, Inc.* (2015), a class action lawsuit brought by unpaid interns who worked for a motion picture distributor and sought compensation under both the FLSA and New York Labor Law. The lead plaintiff, Eric Glatt, had interned in the accounting department of the movie *Black Swan*. The US Court of Appeals for the Second Circuit rejected an earlier legal test adopted by the DOL under the Obama Administration that required internship providers to meet a more stringent set of standards to be exempt from paying interns. Among other things, this earlier test required internship providers to demonstrate that they received "no immediate advantage from the activities of the intern" in order to earn an exemption. Instead, the Court adopted the primary beneficiary test, which is widely considered as making it easier for internship providers to claim exemptions from paying their interns.

Non-profit and public sector internships

At present, the legality of unpaid internships in the non-profit and public sectors is more clear-cut. The DOL interprets the FLSA as to generally permit unpaid internships in the non-profit and public sectors. In the aforementioned Fact Sheet #71, the DOL explains minimum wage exemptions under the statute for non-profit and public sector internship providers:

> The FLSA exempts certain people who volunteer to perform services for a state or local government agency or who volunteer for humanitarian purposes for non-profit food banks. [The Wage and Hour Division of the DOL] also recognizes an exception for individuals who volunteer their time, freely and without anticipation of compensation, for religious, charitable, civic, or humanitarian purposes to non-profit organizations. Unpaid internships for public sector and non-profit charitable organizations, where the intern volunteers without expectation of compensation, are generally permissible (DOL 2018).

Employment Discrimination Laws

Employment discrimination laws are among the major sources of potential legal protections for interns and liability exposure for internship providers. Successful discrimination claims may entitle a claimant to a variety of relief, including the possibility of emotional distress and punitive damages. However, in order to claim these protections, interns must be considered employees under the statutory definitions of employee status. Accordingly, the following section will: (1) summarize the major federal employment discrimination statutes and their respective protected classes; (2) examine the critically important threshold legal standards used to determine whether interns are employees under these laws; and (3) discuss the major employment discrimination claims that may protect interns and create liability risks for internship providers.

Major Federal Employment Discrimination Laws

The following are summaries of the major federal laws enforced by the US Equal Employment Opportunity Commission (EEOC):

Title VII of the Civil Rights Act of 1964 (Title VII 1964)

Title VII prohibits an employer from discriminating against an employee or job applicant on the basis of "race, color, religion, sex, or national origin" (Title VII 1964). It includes the Pregnancy Discrimination Act, which prohibits employment discrimination on the basis of pregnancy or childbirth. Title VII covers employers with 15 or more employees.

Of special note are two forms of discrimination: sexual harassment and LGBTQ discrimination.

Sexual harassment. Title VII's prohibitions against sex discrimination include sexual harassment. Sexual harassment claims typically arise in two ways. The first is called a "quid pro quo" (*this for that* in Latin) claim, whereby a condition of employment—such as a raise or promotion—is directly tied to an employee's submissionto unwelcome sexual advances. This may come in the form of an inducement, a threat, or both.

The second, and more common, type of sexual harassment claim is the creation of a hostile work environment. In *Harris v. Forklift Systems, Inc.* (1993), the US Supreme Court articulated the current legal test for determining what constitutes an unlawful hostile work environment under Title VII, identifying two prongs that must be proven. First, the target of harassment must subjectively perceive the work environment to be hostile or abusive. Second, the work environment must be objectively hostile or abusive, i.e., as seen through the eyes of a "reasonable person."

To determine the latter objective prong, factors that may be considered "include the frequency of the discriminatory conduct; its severity; whether it is physically threatening or humiliating, or a mere offensive utterance; and whether it unreasonably interferes with an employee's work performance." Tangible behaviors may include, but are not limited to, repeated sexual vulgarities, innuendo, or humor directed at an individual; unwelcome sexual overtures, and inappropriate physical touching.

LGBTQ discrimination. In a major case decided in 2020, *Bostock v. Clayton County, Georgia*, the Supreme Court held that Title VII's prohibition against sex discrimination covers sexual orientation and gender identity (*Bostock v Clayton County* 2020). The Court held that "(a)n employer who fires an individual merely for being gay or transgender defies the law." Prior to this decision, discrimination in employment against LGBTQ individuals was legal in over half of the states. Bostock puts all employers on notice that discrimination on this basis is now an unlawful employment practice under federal law.

Equal Pay Act of 1963 (EPA 1963)

The EPA requires men and women to receive equal pay for equal work, within the same workplace. Although the EPA is part of the Fair Labor Standards Act, whose provisions are normally enforced by the DOL, it is enforced by the EEOC.

Age Discrimination in Employment Act of 1967 (ADEA 1967)

ADEA prohibits an employer from discriminating against an employee or job applicant on the basis of age. This law was designed to protect older workers against job bias. Thus, an individual must be age 40 or over to be a protected party. ADEA applies to employers with 20 or more employees.

Title I of the Americans with Disabilities Act of 1990 (ADA 1990)

The ADA prohibits an employer from discriminating against qualified individuals with a disability in all aspects of the employment relationship. The ADA is most frequently invoked in claims alleging an employer's failure to provide a reasonable accommodation for a disability. It applies to employers, including state and local governments, with 15 or more employees.

Rehabilitation Act of 1973

The Rehabilitation Act protects federal employees against disability discrimination, similar to how the

ADA protects private sector employees and other public employees.

Genetic Information Non-Discrimination Act of 2008 (GINA 2008)

GINA protects employees against discrimination on the basis of genetic information. The statute applies to employers with 15 or more employees.

Anti-Retaliation Protections

Every one of the aforementioned federal employment discrimination laws includes an anti-retaliation provision that prohibits employer retaliation against those who report, file complaints about, and/or cooperate in investigations and proceedings concerning alleged discrimination. Retaliation allegations are raised as standalone legal claims.

Are Interns Protected Under Employment Discrimination Laws?

In order for interns to be protected by federal employment discrimination laws, they must fall within the statutory definition of employee. Once again, let us quickly provide a summary answer to this question before going into details: (1) Paid interns are likely to be considered employees covered by federal employment discrimination laws, especially if they are compensated directly by their internship provider; and (2) unpaid interns are unlikely to be considered employees covered by these laws.

The relevant employment discrimination laws are notably unhelpful in determining whether those hired in non-standard work relationships are covered by their protections. Title VII, ADEA, ADA, and GINA all define "employee" as "an individual employed by an employer." This circular definition offers little clarification on whether interns are covered parties. When statutory definitions are so unhelpful, we must turn to judicial interpretations and administrative determinations for guidance.

The easy cases are when interns are hired, supervised, and directly paid by their internship host. In such instances, they will be deemed an employee of that entity under these laws and can bring claims under them. In essence, their status will be treated as a traditional, short-term, and/or part-time employment relationship.

As to whether unpaid interns are protected by these laws, the leading federal court decision addressing this issue, decided in 1997, suggests that they are not. *O'Connor v. Davis* involved an undergraduate social work student, Bridget O'Connor, who alleged that she had been sexually harassed by a staff psychiatrist, James Davis, during an internship at a psychiatric care clinic in New York (*O'Connor v. Davis* 1997). O'Connor claimed that Davis's harassing behavior, which included repeated sexual vulgarities and overtures, began early in her internship and continued thereafter. She brought her concerns to her supervisor at the clinic, who did nothing to remedy the situation.

In an opinion addressing whether O'Connor could bring suit under Title VII, the US Court of Appeals for the Second Circuit observed that compensation "is an essential condition to the existence of an employer-employee relationship." Accordingly, because the psychiatric care clinic did not directly pay O'Connor (though she was paid by the federal work-study program), the Court found that she was not employee within the meaning of Title VII and thus could not bring a claim for sexual harassment.

Although subsequent litigation on this question has not been abundant, a federal district court in *Wang v. Phoenix Satellite Television US, Inc.* (2013) approvingly cited *O'Connor v. Davis* in holding that Xueden Wang, a graduate student in journalism who did an unpaid internship with a media company, could not bring a sexual harassment claim under the New York City Human Rights Law. Although Wang's claim alleged, among other things, that she had been subjected to repeated sexual overtures and unwelcome touching by her supervisor, the court held that because she "received no remuneration for her services," her "hostile work environment claim must fail."

In the *Wang* case, at least, the fallout from the court's decision helped to prompt legislative change. In 2014, New York City amended its Human Rights Law to cover unpaid interns.

In fact, in addition to New York City, a small number of states and municipalities now confer varying protections against discrimination and sexual harassment to unpaid interns under their own employment laws. These include California, Connecticut, Illinois, New York, Oregon, New York City, and Washington DC. For institutions of higher education and internship providers, these state and local legal developments underscore the importance of consulting with local employment counsel to ensure compliance.

Finally, it is important to note the Congressional Accountability Act of 1995 (CAA 1995), discussed in greater detail below. Among other things, the CAA's protections against discrimination and harassment apply to unpaid interns.

Major Types of Employment Discrimination Claims[4]

Intentional Discrimination

Intentional discrimination claims involve either an individual employee or group of employees alleging discrimination, such as a failure to hire or promote, wrongful termination, or segregated work assignments motivated by protected class membership. This is the classic form of a discrimination claim. In such instances, an allegedly discriminating party's intentions are typically inferred by their actions.

Hostile Work Environment (Harassment)

The creation of a hostile work environment on the basis of protected class status is considered a form of intentional discrimination. As discussed above, most of the major case law has developed in the context of sexual harassment. In addition, harassment on the basis of other protected classes covered by federal discrimination laws is also unlawful.

Sexual harassment is especially pertinent to the intern context, given periodic news reports of harassing behavior coming out of legislative settings and political campaigns. Furthermore, with many students choosing to be out about their sexual orientation or gender identity, harassment of LGBTQ individuals merits attention as well.

Disparate Impact Discrimination

Disparate impact discrimination occurs when a facially neutral employment policy or practice has the effect of excluding or minimizing opportunities for those of legally protected classes, and the policy or practice cannot be defended on grounds of job-relatedness and business necessity.

A facially neutral policy or practice applies to everyone, such as a requirement that all applicants for certain positions take an aptitude test with a minimum pass rate. If the aggregate results of administering that test demonstrate a wide statistical variation in pass rates among groups on the basis of race, sex, or other protected classes, then it may be an unlawful employment practice. In order to continue using that test, the employer must show that it is an effective and reliable screening device for hiring individuals to those positions.

Failure to Provide a Reasonable Accommodation

The ADA's protections against disability discrimination include an employer's obligation to provide a reasonable accommodation for an employee's qualifying disability. This may include, for example, physical alterations to the work environment (such as a wheelchair ramp or adjusted desk height) or accommodations for written employment tests (such as extra time). Title VII's protections against religious discrimination require employers to make reasonable accommodations for religious faith. Under both the ADA and Title VII, an employer may respond to a reasonable accommodation request by claiming the defense of undue hardship, asserting that the requested accommodation is too expensive or too disruptive.

Many colleges and universities have experienced dramatic increases in requests for disability-related accommodations. Whether this trend applies to internship settings is not clear, but it should be noted as a possibility.

Retaliation

Retaliation allegations are raised as standalone legal claims. They are among the most common counts included in discrimination lawsuits.

For example, suppose an intern covered by Title VII reports sexual harassment by their supervisor to the organization's human resources (HR) office. HR proceeds to investigate the complaint, which includes interviewing the intern's supervisor. The supervisor, angered over the accusation, responds by taking away useful assignments from the intern and giving them a poor evaluation. From a legal standpoint, the intern may have both sexual harassment and retaliation claims against the organization.

Congressional Accountability Act of 1995 (CAA 1995)

Especially relevant to this volume, it is important to correct a common ongoing misconception that Congress and the rest of the federal legislative branch are broadly exempt from protective employment statutes. The Congressional Accountability Act of 1995 filled this gap in federal workplace protections by requiring Congress and associated agencies to comply with most federal employment statutes that apply to the private sector and other governmental agencies and institutions. The covered statutes include the Fair Labor Standards Act and the employment discrimination laws discussed above. Significantly, the CAA's protections against discrimination and harassment extend to unpaid interns. Claims under the CAA are to be filed with the Office of Congressional Workplace Rights.

Title IX of the Education Amendments of 1972 (Title IX 1972)

Title IX prohibits sex discrimination in "any academic, extracurricular, research, occupational training, or other education program or activity" administered by post-secondary institutions that receive federal financial assistance. The Office for Civil Rights at the US Department of Education enforces Title IX. Claimants who successfully prove intentional discrimination may recover monetary damages. Given the widespread use of federal financial aid and grant programs, this statute applies to almost every accredited college and university.

Pertinent to this chapter, Title IX obliges schools to take preventive and responsive measures concerning sex discrimination at affiliated internship program placements. Sexual harassment is a considerable focus of current Title IX enforcement efforts.

However, pursuant to the federal appeals court ruling in *O'Connor v. Davis* (1997) discussed above, internship providers probably do not face Title IX liability for on-site discrimination or harassment. The court held that hosting the internship did not turn the psychiatric hospital where an unpaid intern experienced sexual harassment into a potentially liable administrator of an education program under Title IX, and thus the hospital was not proper defendant under the statute.

BEST PRACTICES: TWO DIMENSIONS

The important question of what constitutes best practices in the legal context of internships has two, perhaps conflicting, dimensions. Depending on values, ethics, and priorities, best practices for internship providers and educational institutions in terms of minimizing liability exposure may not necessarily mesh with best practices for students and others in terms of maximizing opportunities and providing working conditions safe from mistreatment.

The Bare Minimum: Liability-Reducing Practices for Internship Providers and Educational Institutions

If one defines best practices for internship providers and educational institutions solely through the lens of minimizing liability exposure, then assessments of the relevant legal risks and design of preventive and responsive policies and procedures quickly become evident. The following points, building on the discussion in Part II, shape the parameters of this minimalist approach.

- For-profit internship providers may be exempt from paying interns under the federal minimum wage law if they can satisfy the Primary Beneficiary Test favored by the US Department of Labor. To minimize their liability exposure, they can arrange their internship offerings to meet as many of the factors under the primary beneficiary test as possible. This includes requiring interns to acknowledge that no compensation will be provided and that they are not entitled to paid employment after the internship is over.

- Non-profit and public sector internship providers are likely exempt from paying interns under the Fair Labor Standards Act, under the DOL's current interpretation of the law. To minimize their liability exposure, some internship providers in these sectors require interns to acknowledge in writing that they are volunteers.
- Paid interns are very likely to be covered by federal employment discrimination laws. To minimize their liability exposure, internship providers should treat paid interns as employees for purposes of policies and programs concerning diversity education, sexual harassment prevention and response, and similar in-house measures.
- Unpaid interns are unlikely to be covered by federal employment discrimination laws. Internship providers who do not pay their interns are thus much less likely to face liability exposure under these statutes.
- Educational institutions are obliged under Title IX to protect students enrolled in their internship programs from sex discrimination and sexual harassment at the host sites. To minimize their liability exposure, colleges and universities should consult guidelines from the US Department of Education, Office for Civil Rights. Specific measures may include orientation briefings for interns; training and education programs for program administrators, affiliated faculty, and affiliated internship providers; and policies and procedures for reporting, investigation, and resolution.

The Better Way: Ethical Practices to Expand Opportunities and Protections for Interns

If internship providers and educational institutions want to go beyond what the law requires in ways that expand opportunities and protections for interns, then a protocol of best practices starts to look much different. This may, frankly, expose them to greater liability exposure, but arguably, it is the right thing to do.

Paying interns

If internship providers and educational institutions wish to maximize opportunities for students and others of all economic backgrounds and diversity groups to obtain internship experiences, then they should support and facilitate paid internships. These priorities are especially significant for internships in politics and public policy, which long have been among the "glamour industries" in which unpaid internships are common, along with media, entertainment, and fashion (Yamada 2002). Internships in these fields open doors to opportunities that shape and influence public debate, opinion, taste, and culture. Restricting vital entry points to individuals who can afford to work for free creates, in effect, a pipeline narrowed by economic class disadvantages and exclusion of historically disadvantaged groups.

A prime example of an exclusionary practice is the White House internship program (https://www.whitehouse.gov/get-involved/). Touted as a "highly competitive" program, it requires a minimum work commitment of 45 hours per week, yet under Democratic and Republican administrations alike, it has provided no compensation and no housing assistance. By limiting participation to those who can afford to provide free labor while living in one of the nation's most expensive housing markets, this marquee opportunity reinforces unequal access to experiences that can have formative career impacts. Hopefully this practice will change in the face of growing criticism of unpaid internships in high-profile settings.

Paying interns has the added benefit of creating an authentic employment relationship. Paid internships are free of the faint (or not-so-faint) smell of exploitation that comes with providing and expecting free labor. At the same time, in return for compensation and other benefits of a job, an intern is expected to provide quality work. In a good way, this harkens back to the days before internships became so common, when most young people gained early work experience and honed their work ethic in entry-level jobs unrelated to their career aspirations.

Paid internships also release internship providers from feeling semi-obliged to offer an enhanced "experience" to interns. Instead, the internship can focus on doing the work at hand, whether it means writing a draft of a position paper, collecting signatures to qualify a ballot measure, or being assigned to take food orders for the day.

It should be acknowledged that unpaid internships have their strong defenders (Yamada 2016a). During the early 2010s, when lawsuits challenging unpaid internships attracted national media coverage, critics of the litigation defended unpaid internships as training experiences and characterized interns seeking back pay as "entitled." Colleges and universities have lobbied the Department of Labor not to engage in aggressive enforcement of minimum wage laws against internship programs.

Offering paid internships can occur in several ways:

- The internship provider pays its interns directly, as it would any other employee, and treats internships as fixed-length employment arrangements;
- An affiliated institution of higher education or a third party (such as a foundation or other philanthropic entity) provides funding to cover stipends for interns who otherwise would not be paid; or,
- The federal work-study program is accessed to pay students to work in non-profit and public-sector internships, or, on some occasions, in for-profit internships directly related to a student's course of study.

Internship providers and higher education institutions have used these various arrangements for many years, without apparent difficulty, but with potential liability exposure as summarized in the following subsection. Each arrangement presents its own legal and bureaucratic requirements. (For example, a student may earn academic credit for a work-study job, but subject to limitations detailed by federal regulations.) Once formalized, however, the logistics are simply repeated for future new interns.

For conventional internship providers and associated parties in public policy settings, the funding mechanisms should be easy enough to work out. Political campaigns and lobbying activities, however, may present additional bureaucratic machinations, especially if interns are not paid directly by the internship provider. Interns working in a lobbying capacity may also have to comply with applicable regulations and reporting requirements.

Protecting interns

Even before the #MeToo and Black Lives Matter movements sharpened our focus on important issues of mistreatment, bias, and exclusion, these concerns had been prominent in fields where internships are popular, including politics and public policy. For example, legislative and political campaigns have not been strangers to reports of sexual harassment and similar inappropriate conduct directed towards interns.

Accordingly, it would behoove all internship providers, including those that are popular destinations for students of political science, as well as educational institutions sponsoring internship programs, to commit to preventing discrimination and harassment and creating welcoming environments for diversity of all kinds.

As the legal discussion above suggests, the best way to ensure that interns will be protected under federal employment discrimination laws is for internship providers to pay them directly, as employees. By contrast, not paying interns, or providing compensation through third-party sources, may preclude or complicate interns' attempts to access these statutory protections, unless the internships are located in the small number of states or municipalities that extend their own anti-discrimination protections to unpaid interns, as discussed above (see "Are Interns Protected Under Employment Discrimination Laws?").

Even if internship providers and/or associated educational institutions determine that discrimination laws may not protect their interns, through employee handbooks and student policies they may contractually agree to safeguard interns against discriminatory behavior and assume liability where appropriate. This would, of course, carry legal obligations, but it would constitute an act of social responsibility that messages a genuine commitment to inclusion and diversity.

Finally, educational institutions that host or sponsor internship programs should take their Title IX responsibilities seriously, including educating both interns and affiliated internship providers about sexual harassment protections.

CONCLUSION

As the foregoing discussion indicates, legal issues concerning internships have come under closer scrutiny during the past decade or so. From the standpoint of paying interns and protecting them from discrimination and harassment, judicial decisions have clearly sided with a restrictive view on what legal safeguards may be available to them. As presented here, this leads us to a duality of "best practices" for educational institutions and internship providers, with one approach attempting to minimize liability exposure and another attempting to maximize opportunity and safety.

In urging the latter option, I reiterate my observation in an earlier writing that "the status of interns connects to broader social concerns about the future of work and the contingent workforce, the funding of higher education (including the dramatic rise of student loans), and the challenges of creating a sustainable, entry-level job market for those attempting to enter professions and vocations" (Yamada 2016b, 948). Simply attaching the label of "intern" to what otherwise would likely be considered a fixed-length, entry-level job now potentially excuses employers from paying the minimum wage and from facing liability for discrimination and harassment. Colleges and universities are complicit in this dynamic by charging full tuition for academic credit, earned by working without pay for internship providers that are reaping the benefits.

We know that in the realms of politics and public policy, good internships can be remarkable, even life-changing, experiences. However, the popularity of unpaid internships in these fields and the current legal state of affairs advantage those who can afford to work for free and who may not need protections against discrimination and harassment. If we want to promote truly diverse flows of talent into civic life, then this is not how to do it.

In sum, the intern economy has become a place where core precepts of equal opportunity, compensation for work rendered, and protections against workplace mistreatment have been sacrificed in return for experience, networking, and connections for those who can afford it—increasingly with judicial approval. Hopefully, updated chapters in future editions of this book and similar volumes will reflect changes in the law that embrace basic legal safeguards for those designated as interns.

REFERENCES

Perlin, Ross. 2012. Intern Nation: How to Earn Nothing and Learn Little in the Brave New Economy. New York: Verso.

Yamada, David C. 2002. "The Employment Law Rights of Student Interns." *Connecticut Law Review* 35 (1): 215-57. Available at: https://papers.ssrn.com/sol3/papers.cfm?abstract_id=1303705.

Yamada, David C. 2016a. "The Legal and Social Movement Against Unpaid Internships." *Northeastern University Law Journal* 8 (2): 357-96. Available at: https://papers.ssrn.com/sol3/papers.cfm?abstract_id=2338646.

Yamada, David C. 2016b. "'Mass Exploitation Hidden in Plain Sight': Unpaid Internships and the Culture of Uncompensated Work." *Idaho Law Review* 52 (3): 937-51. Available at: https://papers.ssrn.com/sol3/papers.cfm?abstract_id=2905779.

Primary statutory and legal materials

Fair Labor Standards Act of 1938

The full text and a summary of the Fair Labor Standards Act (29 USC §201) and other helpful information are available at the website of the US Department of Labor, Wage and Hour Division: https://www.dol.gov/agencies/whd/flsa.

Federal Employment Discrimination Laws

The full texts and summaries of the federal employment statutes discussed here—including the Age Discrimination in Employment Act of 1967 (29 USC §621), Americans with Disabilities Act of 1990 (42 USC §12101), Equal Pay Act of 1963 (29 USC §206), Genetic Information Non-Discrimination Act of 2008 (42 USC §2000), Rehabilitation Act of 1973 (29 USC §701), and Title VII of the Civil Rights Act of 1964 (42 USC §2000e)—and other helpful information are available at the website of the US Equal Employment Opportunity Commission: https://www.eeoc.gov.

Congressional Accountability Act of 1995

The full text and summary of the Congressional Accountability Act (2 USC §1301) and other helpful information are available at the website of the US Office of Congressional Workplace Rights:
https://www.ocwr.gov/about-ocwr/overview/about-caa-reform-act.

Title IX of the Education Amendments of 1972

Full information about Title IX (29 USC §1681) training and enforcement can be obtained at this US Department of Education website: https://sites.ed.gov/titleix/.

Case Law and Other Materials

Bostock v. Clayton County, Georgia, 140 S.Ct. 1731 (2020).

Glatt v. Fox Searchlight Pictures, Inc., 811 F.3d 528 (2015).

Harris v. Forklift Systems, Inc., 510 U.S. 17 (1993).

O'Connor v. Davis, 126 F.3d 112 (2d Cir. 1997).

Wang v. Phoenix Satellite Television US, Inc., 976 F.Supp.2d 527 (S.D.N.Y 2013).

US Department of Labor (2018). Fact Sheet #71: Internships Under The Fair Labor Standards Act, available at: https://www.dol.gov/sites/dolgov/files/WHD/legacy/files/whdfs71.pdf.

ENDNOTES

1. Because of the potential fluidity of legal standards for interns, these questions are as close to an issues checklist as is comfortably provided in a volume whose shelf life will likely exceed its immediate publication for some time. Universities and internship providers should use these questions to guide their consultations with legal counsel, as well as take into account the matters raised in the section named "Best Practices" in this chapter.

2. As to terminology used in this chapter: first, it uses the term "internship providers" rather than employers, because the latter term presumes a legal relationship that may not be present, for reasons discussed. Second, some educational institutions may refer to internships as externships, but in this context there is no legal distinction between the terms.

3. While for the purposes of this chapter these entities are all included under the banner of non-profit organizations, the Internal Revenue Service makes significant distinctions between them in terms of tax-exempt status.

4. This summary is based on the author's experience of teaching a survey-level law school Employment Discrimination course for some 20 years. It is designed to provide an informative overview.

CHAPTER 4

Integral or Irrelevant: What Makes a Desirable Political Science Intern?

Shannon D. McQueen, West Chester University
Clinton M. Jenkins, Birmingham-Southern College
Susan L. Wiley, The George Washington University

Although the benefits of interning are well known, we know less about the qualities and skills of interns that sponsoring organizations value highly. We examine this question using site supervisor feedback about a major urban research university's political science internship program. We analyze quantitative data from site supervisor evaluations of student interns to determine which qualities are valued highly, and find that dependability, work ethic, attendance, usefulness to the organization, and level of initiative are most desirable. We also analyze open-ended responses regarding intern tasks, and both positive and negative aspects of intern performance. This research offers greater insights into the role of internships in undergraduate education, as well as the skills and traits that are perceived to closely affect interns' performance. Our conclusions are relevant to political science educators as well as political science students seeking internships or preparing to search for a job.

INTRODUCTION

Interning is an integral part of the student experience across universities and can have long lasting post-graduation effects. For example, in 2019 the National Association of Colleges and Employers (NACE) found that "graduating seniors who applied for a full-time job and participated in an internship received 1.17 job offers, while those who did not intern received 16% fewer job offers" (Koc et al. 2019). However, we know less about what qualities internship employers value in a political science college intern. This information is crucial to the success of our students, and needs to be examined through an academic lens.

In this chapter we explore political science internships from the supervisors' point of view. Using data collected between 2013 and 2018 from nearly 400 site supervisors who oversaw interns participating in-person in a for-credit program at The George Washington University (GWU), we analyze the skills and traits reported as being utilized, which of these were valued in their interns, and which of these that supervisors would like to see improved or developed further. Fundamentally, we offer an evidence-based look at the qualities endemic to political science internships that are conducted in person.

We find that political science internships tend to require substantial amounts of writing, communication, and research. Additionally, site supervisors lamented a lack of attention to detail and lack of initiative, but when interns did exhibit those positive traits their supervisors praised them. According to our respondents, the ideal undergraduate political science intern tends to have a strong team-oriented attitude, produces quality work with attention to detail, and demonstrates significant independent initiative. These results have implications for how political science faculty design curricula and which skills are emphasized in preparing their students for future careers.

WHAT WE KNOW ABOUT COLLEGE INTERNSHIPS AND SKILLS

Internships are associated with tangible academic gains (Healy and Mourton 1987; Knouse et al. 1999; Routon and Walker 2015, 2018), civic skill development (Eyler and Halteman 1981; Mariani and Klinkner 2009), and employment advantages such as faster integration into the labor market (Klein and Grauenhorst 2014) and greater employability (Nunley et al. 2016; Silva et al. 2016; Teichler 2011). Thus, substantial research has documented that internships provide clear benefits to students across a wealth of areas. Yet much of what we know about the desirability of skills is anecdotal. Some scholars suggest that "... no single set of personal attributes and experiences seems to assure success as an intern... The type of person who seems to function well as an intern is one who is self-confident, tactful, mature and open and responsive to his situation; he is not necessarily an outstanding student, nor has he had prior practical political involvement" (Hedlund 1973, 24). Others note the importance of qualities such as maturity, tact, and energy, and sense of political curiosity (Hennessy 1970).

Previous work focusing on site supervisors has identified their importance to the success of an internship (Benavides et al. 2013; Sosland and Lowenthal 2017). Regular feedback from site supervisors can increase the quality of the intern's learning experience, although many site supervisors fail to do so frequently or systematically (Waters and Gilstrap 2012). In exploring the traits internship supervisors seek in interns, NACE found that they look for strong critical thinking, teamwork, work ethic, and oral/written communication skills (Koc et al. 2019). Additionally, NACE (2020) surveyed employers regarding the attributes they seek in college graduates, highlighting the five most desired attributes: problem-solving skills, ability to work in a team, strong work ethic, analytical/quantitative skills, and communication/writing skills (NACE 2020). Their study includes a wide spectrum of students, but it is not clear that the same set of skills is also most desirable for political science majors.

We build on this work by analyzing five years' worth of site internship supervisor evaluations from the internship-for-credit program at one university. We first provide an overview of the prominent skills that interns utilize or rely on in their internships, ranging from researching to event planning, as well as the traits that site supervisors perceive as essential to performing related tasks. Second, we identify qualities that site supervisors would like to see developed further in their interns: most notably these include writing and communication, taking initiative, and paying attention to details.

DATA AND METHODS

We analyze site supervisor evaluations of participants in the GWU Political Science Department's internship-for-credit program.[1] To receive academic credit, a student must be a declared political science major with at least junior standing,[2] have a confirmed internship, and have taken a minimum of three introductory political science courses. Each student who has registered for the internship course must complete a learning contract signed by the internship sponsor outlining the nature of the internship, the substantive work to be completed, the student's learning objectives, and a proposed paper topic. The final paper, which is due on the last day of classes, is expected to complement the intern's duties and should be based on some issue or problem that concerns the agency or office in which the student works. Students are expected to meet with or email the Director of Undergraduate Studies every three or four weeks to recap their work and report any problems. Finally, internship sponsors are asked to submit an evaluation of the intern's performance.

Our analysis rests on a dataset constructed from 372 intern evaluation forms collected during fall and spring semesters, 2013 to 2018; most internships (76%) were conducted in the spring.[3] The forms are emailed to all site supervisors at the end of each semester, and include both qualitative and quantitative measures of intern performance. We use the quantitative data to provide summary statistics about interns' work and we analyze qualitative data with Atlas.ti.[4] Utilizing an In Vivo coding methodology,[5] we identify and analyze the occurrence of certain phrases including the overall performance of the intern, positive and negative comments, and internship activities. Because there was very little variation in the results based on the category of the sponsoring organization or students' sex, we present the results aggregated for all evaluations.[6]

RESULTS

Location and Time

GWU students interned at a range of organizations that can be grouped into five major categories: nonprofit or advocacy organizations, think tanks or research organizations, international governments, the United States government, and businesses or corporations.

Figure 1. Number of Interns by Type of Internship

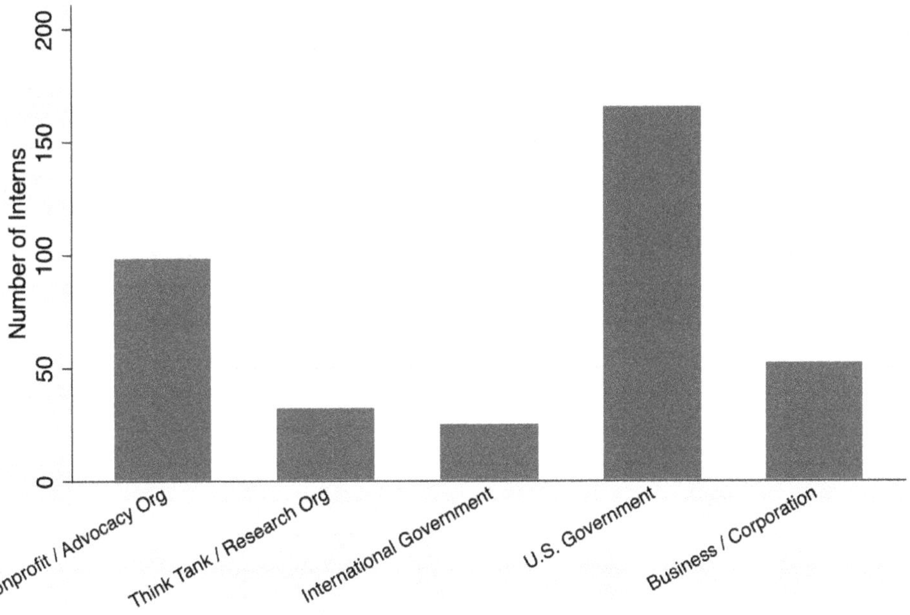

As depicted in figure 1, slightly under half of all internships involved the US government, which includes "Hill internships" in Congressional offices (members or committees), as well as more unconventional placements, such as the Office of the First Lady. About 25% of internships are conducted at nonprofit organizations, including partisan establishments such as the Republican Governors Association, and advocacy groups such as Planned Parenthood, the Human Rights Campaign, or Refugee International. Around 14% of internships take place through businesses or corporations such as law offices or media consulting groups, and even fewer are completed through think tanks or international governing bodies. No statistically significant differences were found when analyzing type of internship placement by sex (female/male).

Overall Performance

Turning now to intern performance, we first provide an overview of how site internship supervisors rated interns on eight different skills or traits. In particular, we observe ratings of interns' performance with respect to their dependability, work ethic, attendance, usefulness, ability to work effectively with others, quality and quantity of work produced, and level of initiative. These were assessed on a scale of 1 (poor) to 5 (excellent). Most interns received 5s or 4s on these assessments, indicating generally very high levels of satisfaction. Each of the assessed qualities had a mean score between 4.6 and 4.9.[7]

All supervisors agreed that the internship was a good learning experience for the student and that academic credit was merited. No supervisor rated an intern's performance as unsatisfactory, possibly because the internship program was structured to facilitate high levels of communication among participants. Additionally, all respondents were interested in having another GWU student intern for them in the future. The item that yielded the most response variation asked if the site supervisors shared their evaluation with the intern. On that question the site supervisors split evenly, with 50% reporting that they shared the evaluation and 49% reporting that they did not share it.

Skill Utilization

To gain insight into the skills that interns employed during their internships, we turn to a question that asked site supervisors to provide a description of a project or situation for which a student was responsible and to comment on their performance.[8] We coded their open-ended responses to identify the type of work the interns completed, noting each respondent's comments or phrases that referred to a specific activity. We then grouped these phrases to identify the specific skills used.[9] Based on these responses, we created a typology of intern work that encompasses five main skill categories: writing and communication, event planning, supervision skills, research and analytic skills, and service. The categories and their frequencies are depicted in table 1.[10]

About 55% of all interns completed work with substantial writing or communications components. This category covers a wide range of projects, all of which involved summarizing, sharing, and/or communicating information. Specific types of work included giving presentations; writing policy, legal, and research briefs; crafting a proposal for a new podcast; and developing advocacy documents. For example, one intern at a consulting firm developed a new business plan for the firm, "including a marketing plan, budget forecast, and people plan."

Table 1: Student Engagement in Internship Activities

Activity Category	Percentage*	*n*
Communication and Writing	55.6%	207
Research and Analytics	43.3%	161
Constituent and Customer Service	11.8%	44
Event Planning	9.9%	37
Management or Leadership of Others	8.3%	31

* *Percentage of 372 total interns*

The next most common internship activity was research and data management/analysis. Around 43% of interns engaged in these activities, which involved compiling, researching, or analyzing a range of topics. One intern analyzed congressional and think tank hearings, while another built a "national data base [sic] of good news arising from the Tax Cuts and Jobs Act." Research included client-focused work for consulting firms, topic-centered research for think tanks and nonprofits, and advocacy planning for interest groups or other non-profits.

Fewer than 12% of all interns used event planning, supervision, and service-based skills. Event planning often involved assisting with preparations for large events, which was the case for an intern who coordinated and marshaled the crowd at a climate march, and another intern who organized "Press Breakfasts" on Capitol Hill. After one intern was so successful in helping plan a forum in Brussels, their organization sent them to assist with the event in person. Supervision skills refers to leading a team or directly supervising others, as was the case with one intern who managed the recruitment, organization, and training of hundreds of volunteers for a congressional campaign, and another who trained new interns and volunteers on how to contact voters. Finally, the service category contains any work done to connect to or satisfy clients or constituents. Most of these comments came from Hill intern supervisors, whose interns engaged in constituent services, such as leading Capitol tours or handling constituent concerns.[11] For example, one supervisor wrote that the intern "learned about the public policy process, client management, communications, Hill advocacy, conducting research and more." Another noted that the student had learned "the basis of political advocacy from taking research or policy positions and [how to] translate those into advocacy actions." The skills that internship supervisors described tended to reflect the specific focus of the organization, such as networking, writing, communication, research, data analytics, or policy analysis.

Room for Improvement

To gain insight into the sorts of attributes site supervisors view as valuable but believe their interns did not possess, we asked the site supervisors to provide recommendations to improve students' performance. We coded their answers by noting which competencies the site supervisors mentioned, identifying 11 broad categories of abilities that respondents wanted to see developed.[12]

Table 2 depicts the percentage of interns who received comments relating to each area of improvement. When supervisors critiqued the intern, they frequently commented on the need for improved written and oral communication skills. Many comments suggested that interns should hone their writing skills and look for opportunities to improve. Other comments in this category noted something more interpersonal, such as a lack of ability to communicate well, to listen to supervisors, or to share progress. For example, one site supervisor suggested that the intern "listen carefully when work instructions were being given," and another noted how the intern "lacked communication skills" as they did not update supervisors on their progress with projects.

Table 2: Intern Supervisor Comments Regarding Areas of Improvement

Comment Category	Percentage*	*n*
Lacked communication and writing skills	16.1%	60
Lacked initiative	13.4%	50
Lacked attention to detail	9.9%	37
Lacked topical or specialized knowledge	8.9%	33
Needed increased confidence	6.7%	25
Lacked time management skills	5.4%	20
Lacked interpersonal skills and ability to work with others	4.8%	18
Did not manage their own workflow	3.8%	14
Lacked engagement	2.7%	10
Did not respond to corrections	1.3%	5
Worked slowly	1.1%	4

* *Percentage of 372 total interns*

About 13% of interns received a recommendation to take initiative, to act and engage with the work independently. These comments suggest site supervisors desire a certain level of autonomy and self-direction in interns. One site supervisor succinctly noted the importance of taking initiative, and recommended the intern "take ownership of tasks and develop a working knowledge of topics she is not already invested in when they are assigned to her. Doing so would signal to employers that she not only cares about the work she is doing, but she is capable of taking on larger work and thinking about more complex issues." Many supervisors connected a lack of initiative to a lack of overall engagement with the internship experience, such as one supervisor noting the intern "could be more engaged with the work. I felt she missed out on some awesome projects because she didn't volunteer for or identify organizational tasks." Here, the student's lack of initiative was seen as a lack of investment in the work.

The finding that interns often lack initiative is not unexpected. Students likely feel nervous or vulnerable in unfamiliar semi-professional settings, making them less likely to take risks or demonstrate initiative in their work. One supervisor acknowledged this connection, noting, "With more working experience, she will acquire more self-confidence and will be able to take more initiative." Nearly 7% of interns received comments that referred to a student's lack of confidence. Furthermore, a student's prior experience within the classroom can influence their desire to take risks. In some classrooms, opportunities to take initiative can be rare, while the ability to complete a task and follow directions is emphasized. Asking to be put on a certain project or considering directions beyond the assigned tasks constitute new skills for students to learn.

Another common critique of interns was attention to detail. Many supervisors appraised the intern's lack of editing skills or attention to smaller details. For instance, a supervisor noted that the intern is, "very bright but she lacks attention to detail and organization." Other supervisors supplied specific examples, such as encouraging the intern to carefully check citations for projects, better edit their own writing, or "pay attention to minute formatting details." Some supervisors did note the contextual nature of this critique. One supervisor reported that the intern, "can be a bit sloppy in checking pieces for accuracy (he usually figures out his own mistakes) but most of that is accounted for because of the fact that ... the stats that I ask for are needed relatively quickly and he is put under pressure." Thus, in addition to developing better editing skills, interns may not be used to working in fast-paced work environments, resulting in more "little" mistakes.

Around 20% of all comments were positive, regardless of what type of organization one worked for, or the sex of the intern. Some respondents were so impressed by an intern's work that they extended the internships or offered their intern a job. For example, one supervisor noted that the intern "has been a great addition to our policy staff and has contributed in many ways. He has a can-do attitude, and we have invited him to stay on as a paid intern through the summer. He will help to staff our annual conference and trade show in early June."

Interestingly, many of the positive comments discussed level of initiative. This further suggests, as much as site supervisors' lament for more initiative taking, that self-motivation is both a skill and attribute of interns that is highly valued. For example, one site supervisor noted they would "hire the student here in a heartbeat! He was a pleasure to work with and showed a lot of initiative." Another site supervisor specifically noted that "the student doesn't just complete tasks, he goes above and beyond every time he delivers an assignment. He has completely restructured our team site as asked, while at the same time contributing fresh ideas and methods on his own for how to improve it. I can always rely on the quality of his work." Again, there do not appear to be any substantial differences in the frequency or types of critiques based on the sex of the intern.[13]

RECOMMENDATIONS AND CONCLUSION

Supervisors commonly identify three skills when considering what makes a valuable intern. Primarily, interns with strong written and oral communication skills, both in producing work and communicating interpersonally within the work environment, received frequent positive comments from site supervisors. Additionally, site supervisors often praised interns who showed initiative. Students who enthusiastically asked for more assignments, demonstrated their independence, and brought their ideas to a project were considered exceptional interns. Exhibiting initiative may seem self-evident to the seasoned professional, but many students struggled to exercise it in an internship setting. Finally, site supervisors appreciated when interns consistently produced high-quality work—in particular, when the intern exhibited attention to detail, a team-oriented spirit, and functioned well as part of a team. Thus, it is not only work products that are valued, but the attitudes that students bring with them into the internship.[14] These results correspond to the 2020 NACE report of desired attributes for job candidates more broadly, as the ability to work on a team, possessing a strong work ethic, and communication skills are attributes that over 77% of employers desire on students' résumés (NACE 2020).

Based on these results, we make a series of recommendations for political science programs and educators that should enhance the internship experience for both the interns and the sponsoring organizations. Some of these suggestions require low effort and minimal infrastructure, while others may require more intensive effort and additional support.

Because communication—both content-oriented and interpersonal—appears vital to students engaging in internships, our first recommendation is that political science educators expand opportunities for practicing communication skills in their courses. Ideas for communication skill development include requiring more in-class presentations of student work, providing space for interpersonal interactions with peers in class, and integrating structured meetings with professors for students to practice providing updates on extended projects. Mastery of these skills is likely to translate into better teamwork and ability to work with supervisors throughout an internship.

Second, we recommend that faculty integrate into their courses more assignments that mimic those that students are asked to produce in an internship or workplace. For instance, interns are often tasked with writing memos, developing proposals or recommendations, or writing briefs, all of which vary significantly from the standard "academic paper" often assigned. While standard academic writing is a crucial skill that demands frequent exercise, practicing alternative types of writing may help interns meet worksite expectations quicker, enabling them to focus on acquiring new knowledge and developing other skills at their places of work.

Third, inviting students into the editing process by assigning longer-term projects with draft milestones (and providing prompt feedback) is one way to help students develop greater attention to detail. Breaking down a major assignment into stages over a semester may have the added advantage of modeling for students the systematic planning of major projects. Five percent of all site supervisors expressed a desire for students to improve on planning and time management, and almost 4% more expressed a wish for students to manage their own workflow.

Fourth, political science faculty should design curricula and assignments that empower students to take greater initiative in and ownership of their research projects. For example, students should be given opportunities to devise their own research questions, plan a project to investigate their questions, and carry out their research and analysis. Faculty might also consider providing students with options for how to present information for a given assignment (podcast, verbal presentation, handouts, videos, and so forth) to emphasize student choice and control. If group work is assigned, students might also develop their supervision abilities. In general, assigning more team-oriented, self-designed research projects can help students prepare for the type of work they may do in an internship or in the workforce, post-graduation.

Fifth, beyond the classroom, we recommend that advisors, whether they occupy that role formally or informally, proactively communicate to students the skills and traits that internships may require of them. This approach can help frame students' expectations about their internships, helps them anticipate their employers' expectations about their performance, and can prompt them to focus on developing attributes in preparation for an internship. Reviewing a simple "10 Tips for Interning" handout with prospective interns is one way to share this information. A sample document is available in the Supplemental Internship Resources section.

Our sixth and final recommendation reiterates a strong point made by others in this volume: making expectations clear at the outset is critical for long-term success, particularly with respect to the skills that an intern seeks to develop. While clear expectations won't make intern performance anywhere near perfect, it may result in fewer site supervisors wishing for greater "x, y, or z" in an intern's performance.

These recommendations are intended to help faculty prepare students for both internships in political science and professional work in related fields, and we believe that it is safe to assume that site supervisors of political science interns value the same sorts of skills in non-political science interns and in their professional employees as well.[15] Communicating, taking initiative, and paying attention to details are likely to be assets for all students in all sorts of internships and professional settings.

We did, however, identify one set of skills that site supervisors of political science interns may uniquely value: the writing of memos and briefs, and writing generally. These kinds of documents and writing styles often differ from those common to business, corporate settings, or even the natural sciences, so students with majors other than political science may find them to be of limited value. However, we assert that there is merit in offering political science students the opportunity to develop these skills, regardless of their intended career.

Overall, the results of our analysis confirm what most academic internship advisors already know: interns often do an impressive amount of work (with significant variation across interns and internships, of course). Political science interns tend to use five major types of abilities most frequently—communication and writing; research and analysis; constituent or customer service, event planning; and supervision of others—and over three-quarters of the projects named by site supervisors involve writing/communication and research-based skills. Given the great potential for students to excel as interns and future drivers of the workforce, we recommend that political science instructors use the classroom to help students sharpen their transferable skills so that they can meet and exceed the expectations of their site supervisors and future employers.

REFERENCES

Benavides, Abraham D., Lisa A. Dicke, and Amy C. Holt. 2013. "Internships Adrift? Anchoring Internship Programs in Collaboration." *Journal of Public Affairs Education* 19 (2): 325–353.

Eyler, Janet, and Beth Halteman. 1981. "The Impact of a Legislative Internship on Students' Political Skill and Sophistication." *Teaching Political Science* 9 (1): 27–34

Healy, Charles. C., and Don L. Mourton. 1987. "The Relationship of Career Exploration, College Jobs, and Grade Point Average." *Journal of College Student Personnel* 28 (1): 28–34.

Hedlund, Ronald. 1973. "Reflections on Political Internships." *PS: Political Science & Politics* 6 (1): 19–25.

Hennessy, Bernard C. 1970. *Political Internships: Theory, Practice, Evaluation.* The Pennsylvania State University Series, no. 28. University Park, PA: Pennsylvania State University.

Koc, Edwin, Joshua Kahn, Andrea Koncz, Angelena Salvadage, and Anna Longenberger. 2019. "2019 Internship & Co-Op Survey Report Executive Summary." National Association of Colleges and Employers (May): 1–9. https://www.naceweb.org/uploadedfiles/files/2019/publication/executive-summary/2019-nace-internship-and-co-op-survey-executive-summary.pdf.

Knouse, Stephen B., John R. Tanner, and Elizabeth W. Harris. 1999. "The Relation of College Internships, College Performance, and Subsequent Job Opportunity." *Journal of Employment Counseling* 36 (1): 35–43. doi: 10.1002/j.2161-1920.1999.tb01007.x.

Mariani, Mack, and Philip Klinkner. 2009. "The Effect of a Campaign Internship on Political Efficacy and Trust." *Journal of Political Science Education* 5 (4): 275–93. doi: 10.1080/15512160903272160.

National Association of College and Employers (NACE). 2020. "Key Attributes Employers Want to See on Students' Resumes." National Association of Colleges and Employers. https://www.naceweb.org/talent-acquisition/candidate-selection/key-attributes-employers-want-to-see-on-students-resumes/.

Nunley, John M., Adam Pugh, Nicholas Romero, and R. Alan Seals. 2016. "College Major, Internship Experience, and Employment Opportunities: Estimates from a Résumé Audit." *Labour Economics* 38 (January): 37–46.

Routon, P. Wesley, and Jay K. Walker. 2015. "A Smart Break? College Tenure Interruption and Graduating Student Outcomes." *Education Finance and Policy* 10 (2): 244–76. doi: 10.1162/EDFP_a_00160.

Routon, P. Wesley, and Jay K. Walker. 2018. "College Internships, Tenure Gaps, and Student Outcomes: A Multiple Treatment Matching Approach." *Education Economics*, 27 (4): 383–400. doi: 10.1080/09645292.2019.1598336.

Silva, Patricia, Betina Lopes, Marco Costa, Dina Seabra, Ana I. Melo, Elisabeth Brito, and Gonçalo Paiva Dias. 2016. "Stairway to Employment? Internships in Higher Education." *Higher Education* 72 (6): 703–21. doi: 10.1007/s10734-015-9903-9.

Sosland, Jeffrey K., and Diane J. Lowenthal. 2017. "The Forgotten Educator: Experiential Learning's Internship Supervisor," *Journal of Political Science Education*, 13 (1): 1–14.

Teichler, Ulrich. 2011. "Bologna—Motor or Stumbling Block for the Mobility and Employability of Graduates?" in *Employability and Mobility of Bachelor Graduates in Europe*, eds. Schomburg, Harald, and Ulrich Teichler, 3–41. Rotterdam, The Netherlands: Sense Publishers.

Waters, Regina and Christina Gilstrap. 2012. "Intern Performance Reviews: The Supervisor's Perspective." *NACE Journal* 72 (4): 27–31.

ENDNOTES

1. The Political Science department and GWU strive to make the internship class as accessible as possible. Credit may be earned for a paid or unpaid internship, and the GW Career Services Center has funds available for students who are foregoing Federal Work-Study in order to intern. There are also transportation funds available to students who are interning. PSC 2987, Internship in Political Behavior, the department's for-credit internship program, is offered fall, spring, and summer terms. PSC 2987 is variable (1, 2, or 3 credits): for one credit the student must intern a minimum of eight hours per week and write a 10-page paper. For two credits a student must intern a minimum of 10 hours per week and write a 12-page paper. For three credits a student must intern a minimum of 15 hours per week and write a 15-page paper. The class is graded on a pass/fail basis. Up to three credits of PSC 2987 may be earned towards the political science major. During a typical academic year between 120 and 130 majors register for PSC internship credit, around 20% of whom are declared political science majors. Many other political science majors become interns without registering for credit. The Political Science Department maintains a list of available internships, as does Career Services.

2. There are three reasons for the upper-class requirement. First, logistically speaking, neither the internship program nor the internship class can be staffed by the faculty needed to accommodate the large number of majors who would like to intern for credit within the department. Second, first-year and sophomore students are not eligible for internship credit to encourage a greater focus on adjusting to the demands of college. The third reason for requiring junior standing is so that the student will have acquired enough knowledge of the discipline to be able to apply it to the internship. Other internship-for-credit opportunities are available from other programs in the university for those second-year students most motivated to complete an internship.

3. This research was approved by the Institutional Review Boards of The George Washington University and Birmingham-Southern College.

4. Atlas.ti is a qualitative analysis software suite that enables researchers to use a variety of tools to analyze qualitative data found in formats such as audio clips, text documents, images, social media data, and more. More information can be found at: https://atlasti.com/product/what-is-atlas-ti/.

5. In Vivo is a qualitative form of content analysis that highlights the language of the respondents. Codes are created from the transcripts themselves, rather than established in advance by the researchers.

6. There is considerable variation in the number of hours students spend interning. The majority of students interned under 500 hours, with a mean of 300 hours (s.d. 159 hours). Students working over 500 hours may have interned for longer than the length of a semester or interned for an extremely demanding organization, such as the White House Office of Public Engagement. Based on institutional guidelines for academic credit, students interning for one credit averaged 120 hours within the semester; for two credits the average was 150 hours; students earning three credits averaged 225 hours. Most students work about 18 hours per week per 16-week term.

7. There are no significant differences in evaluations based on sex of the intern.

8. Site supervisors often requested students to engage and utilize more than one skill or trait in their internship. Very often, those whose work involved a research component were also required to share or summarize findings. When internship supervisors mentioned more than one skill, the individual comment was coded for each respective skill. For example, one intern prepared and then publicly presented updates for a major corporation's leadership on election integrity work, using both research and communication skills. Another followed several conferences on think tanks, and ultimately wrote a report of their findings. Thus, there would be two distinct skills identified and tracked in the supervisor's response.

9. To develop categories for this data, all responses were initially coded based on the skill listed in the internship evaluation. Then, responses were grouped based on coding themes that emerged from the data. Codes were refined to best reflect the themes in the supervisor evaluations. After an initial independent coder explored the code themes in the documents, the larger group verified the patterns found in the analysis. About 17% of all open-ended responses provided by supervisors referred to interns' activities. Many site supervisors used terms such as "research" and "project," suggesting a heavy research component for many internships. Additionally, words like "team," "us," "staff," and "helped" underscore the importance of interpersonal and teamwork skills within the internship.

10. This list was created by first coding the type of activity that the supervisor noted the student completed within the evaluation. Based on all responses, we then grouped similar activities together based on our subjective assessments of the nature of each task to identify common categories. One of the coauthors served as the primary coder making the initial groupings; these were then verified by the coauthors.

11. In assessing skills by sex (binary male/female categories are used in the analysis), there do not appear to be any differences. A Chi-Square test of independence between sex of the intern and internship activity revealed a p-value of 0.157, meaning that we cannot conclude the variables are associated.

12. We followed a coding process similar to that in the previous section.

13. A Chi-Square test of independence between sex of the intern and criticism revealed a p-value of 0.172, meaning that we cannot conclude that variables are associated.

14. Similar to others (Knouse et al. 1999), we find no differences in evaluations of intern performance based on sex of the intern.

15. For the most part, we believe this to be a noncontroversial assumption, as we have no reason to believe that there exist large differences between what is valued by political science internship site supervisors, site supervisors of others, and professional employee supervisors.

CHAPTER 5

Preparing Students for Internships

Dick Simpson, Scott Braam, and Myron Winston
University of Illinois at Chicago

Preparing political science students for a successful internship experience involves helping them find an appropriate internship placement, assessing their goals, clarifying expectations, and providing a forum for discussion and reflection that allows them to anticipate issues that could develop during their work experience. A successful internship does not occur by accident. Success requires intentionality and planning on the part of the faculty and flexibility on the part of the student.

INTRODUCTION

A significant function of a successful internship program is helping students find a good placement and preparing them for undertaking that internship. Often students will find an internship entirely upon their own with no coaching. It seems that just as often, students have little idea about the internship they wish to pursue or how to land one that complements their major or advances their career prospects. In this chapter we address these and other issues, the solutions for which have proven to be essential to the internship program at University of Illinois at Chicago (UIC).

Our discussion covers preparing students for finding an internship as well as the process of placing students with organizations, a system that is well-developed in our case. We address how to assess students' academic goals and aspirations (which are key to landing an internship) and we also outline effective steps for navigating the application process.

Professional development is a component of the internship course at UIC, which has been designed to facilitate discussion and reflection on all aspects of the internship experience. We explain how an internship curriculum can serve as a vehicle for debriefing, writing about, and examining complementary theoretical and practical lessons, an approach that helps to maximize student learning throughout the internship experience—but especially as a means to prepare students for experiential work.

We conclude by discussing the techniques and methods that constitute best practices and sharing evidence for their efficacy—approaches intended to help participants avoid mistakes and render the internship a successful learning experience, even prior to their first day at the worksite.

IMPROVING INTERNSHIP PROGRAMS

Internship programs in many political science departments remain underdeveloped. Collins, Knotts, and Schiff (2012) conducted a survey to determine the degree of career preparation that occurs within the political science major, discovering that most departments rely on voluntary internships and few require internships or other specific courses designed to address professional development.[1] They found that roughly only 10% of political science departments required internships while some 97% of department chairs reported that a political science major could receive academic credit for an internship. In a national study of internship practices, Gentry and Van Vechten (2018) surveyed political science departments in 2015 and 2016, finding that nearly all departments in four-year institutions award academic credit for internships (89.6%), but that less than half of community colleges do (43.8%).[2] These results imply that internships are a common means to facilitate experiential learning and that virtually all political science departments rely on them for the professional development of their students. However, the suggestion that most interns have neither a class, nor required readings, nor a discussion forum signals the ineffectiveness of this approach. Students can be confronted with a wide array of internship opportunities—in fact the job posting site, Chegg Internships, advertised 13,310 positions for summer 2021[3]—but opportunity alone does not guarantee an equally good experience or maximal learning.

PREPARING STUDENTS: AN OVERVIEW OF THE PROCESS

Student preparation is a critical determinant for both finding a fitting internship and obtaining the professional development that an internship experience should offer. At UIC, we have developed processes to place students at appropriate sites and prepare them for success. Over the three decades we have taught the internship class, we have assembled paper files of more than 100 community organizations, government organizations, political campaigns, civic groups, and law firms which have hosted our interns in the past or have specifically requested interns. Although we have not yet digitized our files, any interested students (including those looking for potential jobs after graduation) can come to the political science office to peruse the files for possible internships, or we provide direct suggestions to inquiring students. The larger college also maintains its own database of internships that students can consult and advertises opportunities through their own outreach efforts.

We meet individually with prospective student interns, in person during non-pandemic times or remotely or electronically otherwise, first determining whether they have already obtained an internship. The only criterion we insist upon in order to receive course credit is that it be related to public affairs: government, politics, or the law in some way. By this measure, working for a homelessness agency by itself would not qualify, whereas working for a community or civic group trying to change government policies around poverty, hunger, or homelessness would. If they have secured a suitable internship which qualifies for credit and in which they can work at least 10 hours a week for the 15-week semester, we approve their internship and grant them permission to register for the class. At that time, we recommend that they read the first book assigned for the course—preferably before they begin their internship.

If students don't already have an acceptable internship, we assist them in their search. In our interview with prospective interns, we first ask where they live within our large Chicago metropolitan area, as that will often determine which elected official or community organization will be most interested in accepting them and will be the easiest to access geographically, i.e., with a short commute. We also determine whether they have a preferred type of internship in mind. Information from our files, our one-on-one meeting, and independent exploration of websites helps students narrow their search. We recommend that they select at least three, but preferably five, possible sites. Once they have assembled a short list of possibilities, the students themselves must make the phone calls to request an interview and complete the applications.

Students don't always obtain the internship at the top of their list, so it is important that they apply to more than one place. However, we have found that if students are willing to be flexible about their placement and make a sufficient number of contacts with potential sites, all of them will land an internship within a few weeks. Even faculty in universities that are located in smaller towns or rural areas where there are fewer internship possibilities are usually able to place students, although significantly more effort might be required on theirs and the students' parts to identify potential placements. Because some internships that have moved online are likely to remain online, geography is no longer a barrier in all cases (see Chapter 15 by Cabrera Rasmussen and Van Vechten).

We find that much of the work of preparing interns for work can be done within an internship class once students have secured a placement. Students not concurrently enrolled in a course can also benefit from the materials which we make widely available. When it is not possible for a political science department to offer an internship class because there are too few students or too few faculty or staff resources to do so, then meeting with students individually during their internship semester, or even better, meeting with groups of internship students several times during the semester, can work as well. Overall, we have found that placing students in a class or workshops where they read course materials together and discuss their internships as they evolve, either weekly or several times a month, produces deeper learning.

FINDING AN INTERNSHIP

Many students have no idea how to search effectively for an internship and require faculty assistance; a good internship program helps match students to the best available possibilities. This begins with an assessment of a student's academic goals, professional aspirations, and personal interests. Personal evaluations can be performed with a faculty member, as described in Chapter 8 by Lowenthal and Sosland (see sample self-assessments in Supplemental Internship Resources, hereafter "supplementals"), or students can also self-assess independently with tools available through career placement or service learning centers on most university campuses, as Reeher and Mariani (2002) suggest. Essentially, students should identify possible placements that deal with the subjects and issues that interest them but not allow their preconceptions, biases, or political beliefs to hold them back from trying something unfamiliar—a pathway that could help them develop a better understanding of our multidimensional and fluid political world.

We recommend building a department file of potential internship sites, whether maintained in hard copy or managed electronically. Records can be built over time with feedback from previous interns and should be updated systematically. At some universities students are encouraged to write letters to future potential interns containing candid perspectives and "insider" information about their work experiences. Also, student reflection papers submitted at the end of the course often provide instructors with a clear idea of which internship sites have been most to least productive or have provided the best opportunities and supervision, information that can be added to the growing files. The least productive sites can be flagged or removed from the files as potential future placements. If permanent internship files are not maintained in a political science department, we would advise students to consult campus service learning or civic engagement centers for their internship advice; they often have relationships with community and civic organizations that welcome university support.

APPLYING FOR AND LANDING AN INTERNSHIP

Frequently, students do not know how to apply successfully for an internship and would benefit from an internship coordinator's assistance or advice. During the preliminary one-on-one meetings in which we help students identify three to five prospective sites, we coach students on how to navigate the application and interview process.

Among the points we stress are that the internship application, phone contact, and internship interview represent opportunities to make a good, first impression; therefore, students will need to pay close attention to detail when completing written applications. Parris and Adams (1994) suggest the following steps for applying for an internship:

- Read requirements and follow directions carefully
- Establish a checklist of requested information
- Make note of deadlines
- Request official transcripts if required
- Begin writing a letter of interest (a cover letter)

- Make sure that all materials are typed neatly with no spelling or grammatical errors
- Make sure that you have followed all directions
- Make copies of all materials for your personal files
- Send all requested materials in one packet three to four weeks before the deadline
- Follow up within a week to confirm that your application packet was received

Clearly, when done well, the application process requires considerable lead time to assemble and polish a high-quality application packet.

The most common error, as with job searches, is that students simply assume that sending a single email to the generic office address or submitting an application electronically will garner a reply. Students need to be informed that this not the case. At worst, offices tend not to follow up unsolicited email applications. In Chicago politics for instance, the saying from political machine politicians is: "We don't want nobody; nobody sent." That is, in politics a recommendation from a trusted source is often what opens doors, which is why students should take advantage of networking events both on- and off-campus (or online, such as town halls or district events) to make connections with elected officials, staff members, and alumni who can facilitate introductions to internship coordinators. At best, email recipients do not answer quickly because of other priorities, thereby delaying the process.

To avoid the worst-case scenarios, we advise students to call the organization, ask for the internship coordinator, and request an internship interview (in person or electronically), following up if they don't hear back within a few days. We stress the need to talk to actual people at potential internship sites, not to rely on one-way communication via emails or websites.

INTERVIEWING FOR AN INTERNSHIP

Faculty often wrongly assume that students know how to behave and dress professionally. Personal appearance is one aspect of professional etiquette, which we discuss as being important not just during the application process but throughout the internship experience.

Although most internships are unpaid, students should still approach the internship interview with the same respect that one would have for a full-time job. The following "do's" apply when interviewing for an internship:

- Dress professionally, even in the event of a remote interview. Professional attire is the standard for interviewing (see supplementals).
- Be prompt. Students should show up for the interview on time or before the appointed time.
- Be respectful and courteous at all times, even if you are asked challenging questions.
- Research the official or agency with which you are seeking an internship so that you can (a) demonstrate that you are informed, and (b) ask meaningful questions.
- Clarify what your hours and main responsibilities would be and how the internship will be performed: in-person in an office, completely remotely, at events that require transportation, or some combination of these.
- Have copies of your résumé and, if possible, letters of recommendation on hand when interviewing in case you are asked to supply them.

In 30 years, we have never had a case in which students who diligently pursued an internship with our coaching didn't land one, although it may not have been their first choice. Regardless of their placement status, by the end of the first individual mentorship meeting or class, students should be equipped to navigate these initial stages of an internship and launch their search with the best possible chances for success.

PREPARING STUDENTS FOR SUCCESS THROUGH AN INTERNSHIP COURSE

Many students have already found an internship before the class begins, but all students are required to have secured an internship by the end of the second week of class and to submit a letter from their internship supervisor spelling out the conditions of the internship and tasks to be performed. Some programs require a more formal contract (see other chapters in this volume and supplementals for samples), or an agreement spelling out the goals and expectations of both the internship provider and the student, as well as the student's anticipated learning opportunities, which could include attending staff or public meetings, undertaking research projects for the internship site, or attending events. We warn our students that they cannot get course credit without opportunities to learn, even if they can expect to answer phones or file paperwork.

Students should be given the opportunity to reflect on their activities and observations throughout the internship, integrating political science with practice. While it is possible to meet with individual students regularly, it is certainly more efficient to hold weekly hour-long class sessions. Our internship classes range in size from five to 25 students and we generally agree that about 15 students is the ideal class size. Another advantage of a class is that students can learn from their peers and work through shared, practical dilemmas, such as how to address mistakes or avoid costly ones.

The internship class at UIC incorporates different methods, materials, and assignments to achieve a sense of dynamism: readings, journaling, oral reports, book discussions, and, most importantly, discussions about site activities. Each week students report successes and problems that suggest to fellow interns (and us) various strategies for improving their experiences. As a class we also attend special events held on Constitution Day, the National Student Issues Convention, and the Urban Forum, and reflect on those shared experiences in class.[4] Finally, students are separated into three or four subgroups with peers who work in similar settings (public offices, political campaigns, law offices, and the like) for targeted discussions and readings.

The class is structured around discussions involving everything from making a great first impression to the use of pressure and confrontation strategies to protest political power; we consider political processes such as organizing, funding, and winning political campaigns. To facilitate dialogue and deeper understanding, students are required to read and analyze five books during the semester: three as a class collectively; one that students select individually that directly relates to their internship; and one with a subgroup, which they report on to the entire class so that those working on campaigns, for instance, learn from peers working in another area, such as law. Teaching a text to the entire class builds student confidence and presentation skills. Students use these readings to help frame their final reflection paper as well. For instance, they might reflect on the implications of campaign donations, examining the assertion made in the campaign-related text about the need for candidates to call or meet with prospective donors personally to raise larger amounts, and weighing it against the reality that their candidate refused to do so and was underfunded in comparison to the opponent.

The shared class readings cover three main topics. Office etiquette and professionalism are thoroughly addressed in Reeher and Mariani's *The Insider's Guide to Political Internships* (2002).[5] Simpson and O'Shaughnessy's *Winning Elections in the 21st Century* (2016)[6] encompasses electoral politics, campaigns, public officials, and civic agencies. Saul Alinsky's *Rules for Radicals* (1971)[7] introduces students to non-electoral political activism via community-based organizations.

Because students typically work for Republican or Democratic campaigns, pro- or anti-mayoral blocs of the Chicago city council, organizations favoring or opposing particular legislation, prosecutors or public defenders, and corporate or public interest lawyers, they can use class time to directly compare their diverse experiences inside a common framework of readings and lectures, interaction that enriches and deepens their internship experience. The faculty coordinator and students agree to keep confidential what is said in class and written in final reflection papers.

PREPARING STUDENTS FOR SUCCESS ON-SITE

Many students are new to professional settings and therefore may need training in workplace protocols.

As Reeher and Mariani (2002) stress, successful students, even when they are unpaid, treat their internships as a professional job, while students who "phone it in" tend to have negative internship experiences without gaining the contacts and skills needed for career success. Since worksite success depends partly upon being comfortable and confident, the class helps build confidence and lets students know that it's okay to approach their supervisors to volunteer for greater responsibilities or to ask to attend staff meetings where they can learn more.

We begin the first class session with a review of a few do's and don'ts of internships.

1) Seek to become an assistant to a particular staff member so they can mentor you on the job and so you can learn particular skills and assume real responsibilities if you have not been assigned them initially.
2) Insist that while you are happy to duplicate papers or do data entry, your university (and/or professor) requires you to attend staff meetings, attend court proceedings, city council meetings, or staff planning sessions, or learn particular skills to earn course credit. If handling mail in a public official's office, for instance, the work could progress to drafting letters or emails in response to constituent letters, press releases, website announcement, or drafting a candidate's public remarks. Meaningful work should be spelled out in a work plan or course contract as much as possible (see supplementals for samples.)
3) You should not be afraid to ask questions. "Fake it until you make it" does not fly in a professional work environment. Pretending to understand something, while you clearly do not, will lead to awkward moments and generally more work.

If students find their work consistently unfulfilling then they should talk with their supervisors or seek out faculty for advice. Reeher and Mariani (2002) point out that students have agency, and while they will not always get exactly what they want, they can take steps to make their internship a positive, educational experience. Interns should also be urged to have fun, work hard, try to stay positive, and do their best. In the rare cases when an internship doesn't work out, they should be moved to a new internship by the course instructor without penalty. Whether they are in an internship class or doing an internship under the general supervision of a faculty member, it is important that students report regularly on their progress and any problems. They should be mentored by the faculty member as well as their on-site supervisor.

OTHER ISSUES RELATING TO PREPAREDNESS

As the course progresses, we focus on the students' experiences, attitudes, and observations during their internships. We review strategies for success in future endeavors, preparing them for myriad challenges that await them by focusing on skills such as managing expectations, exercising patience, and accepting the incremental nature of tackling new tasks. These aspects of internships will persist beyond the pandemic, which has forced many students into online internships, as will being able to work remotely in the "new normal" of the post-pandemic period.

Millennial and Gen Z students tend to value authenticity, organic style, and individuality over "fitting in," but there are limits to the value of these qualities in different workplaces (Francis and Hoefel 2018).[8] We encourage students to be themselves but emphasize that they need to understand and respect the existing social norms and rules of an internship worksite. For instance, we note that personal appearance ought not to provide a distraction to others.

One psychological phenomenon we address in class is the "imposter syndrome," a common, powerful, and often paralyzing feeling of self-doubt that plagues first-time job applicants: they feel they don't belong. Chrousos and Mentis (2020) explain that those with imposter syndrome have an innate fear of being discovered as a fraud or non-deserving, despite their demonstrated talent and achievements. Imposter syndrome has been found to be more prevalent in high achievers, women, and underrepresented racial, ethnic, and religious minorities (Chrousos and Mentis 2020).[9] One way students might move past this normal feeling is to "dress the part" or "dress for the job they want." If they know they appear professional, they are more likely to project confidence and professionalism.[10] Discussing the issue in class can also be useful in overcoming student fears.

CONCLUSION

How do we know that these techniques to prepare and guide student interns work? The first level of evidence are the evaluations of different faculty members who have taught our internship class, students' reflection papers on the experience, and the evaluations of internship site supervisors who employ our interns in positions year after year. In addition, we have reviewed student course evaluations stretching over several decades. They show that regardless of whether tenured faculty or advanced graduate students teach the UIC Internship course, if these methods are followed, students rank the course highly and intern supervisors are equally positive in their student evaluations.

In addition, a significant number of our interns are offered full-time jobs and supervisors frequently write highly positive recommendations for students going on to graduate or law school. About 10% to 20% of our students each semester receive job offers by the end of their internship. Some land scholarships, including major ones like the Truman or Marshall Fund scholarships. A large number of our interns go on to law school or graduate school. Finally, many former interns now hold important positions in government, the private sector, and non-profit organizations.[11]

The more regularly an internship program is offered, either each semester or once a year, the easier it is to recruit students into the program, build up a series of placement sites that take interns, and improve the internship experience over time. The internship program at UIC benefits from 30-plus years of successful coordination with over 100 host sites and organizations and our internship course is well-developed. For departments that do not offer a class to complement for-credit internships, we suggest at least an orientation workshop for all interns during the first week of class, and reiterate that faculty mentorship needs to occur during the semester (see Chapter 6 by Berg) rather than at the end of the course when students submit a final reflection and evaluations are complete.

Our experience is that of a solid, well-rounded internship program, whose core elements include one-on-one counseling sessions, thorough preparation of students for all stages of the internship experience, and an intentionally structured classroom experience. Our goal is to provide a meaningful and value-added learning experience for students, and experience teaches that this "formula" works well across time and generations. The internships we help develop for students are, in many ways, a capstone to their political science major.

REFERENCES

Alinsky, Saul. 1971. *Rules for Radicals.* New York: Vintage Press.

Chrousos, George P., and Alexios-Fotios A. Mentis. 2020. "Imposter Syndrome Threatens Diversity." *American Association for the Advancement of Science* 367 (6749): 749–750.

Collins, Todd, H. Gibbs Knotts, H. Gibbs, and Jen Schiff. 2012. "Career Preparation and the Political Science Major: Evidence from Departments." *Political Science & Politics 45* (1): 87–92.

Francis, Tracy, and Fernanda Hoefel. 2018. "True Gen: Generation Z and its Implications for Companies." *McKinsey & Company,* 1–10. https://www.mckinsey.com/industries/consumer-packaged-goods/our-insights/true-gen-generation-z-and-its-implications-for-companies#.

Gentry, Bobbi, and Renée Van Vechten. 2018. "The What and How of Political Science Internships: Best Practices in the Discipline." Paper presented at the Annual Meeting of the American Political Science Association, Boston.

Parris, Alyssia J., and Howard G. Adams. 1994. *Your Internship is as Good as You Make It: A Practical Guide to Student Internships.* Danbury, CT: Union Carbide.

Reeher, Jack, and Mack Mariani. 2002. *The Insider's Guide to Political Internships: What to Do Once You're in the Door.* Boulder, CO: Westview Press.

Simpson, Dick, and O'Shaughnessy. 2016. *Winning Elections in the 21st Century.* Lawrence, KS: Kansas University Press.

Slank, Shanna. 2019. "Rethinking the Imposter Phenomenon." *Ethical Theory and Moral Practice* 22 (1): 205–218.

ENDNOTES

1. The authors find that voluntary internships and traditional faculty advising still dominate departmental approaches to the task of preparing undergraduate students for the job market.

2. Based on a 2015 national survey of four-year institutions (n=115; response rate of 20.5%) and a 2016 follow-up survey of community colleges (n=51; response rate of 6.7%). The latter statistic is consistent with the results of a 2018 APSA Community College Faculty Survey, whereby 39.7% (n=112) reported that their institution offers internships for credit. Survey was administered to 2,634 faculty in the US; 298 responded to the online survey between March 26 and May 2, 2018, for a response rate of 11.2%.

3. "Find Political Science Internships." *Chegg Internships*, Accessed April 20, 2021, https://www.internships.com/political-science.

4. The National Student Issues Convention is held every October. As of 2020, more than 10 universities and community colleges send more than 300 students to participate in designing a student issues agenda and meet directly with public officials to press for local, state, and national government action on student concerns. The UIC Urban Forum is held annually at the University of Illinois at Chicago with 700 students and community leaders who meet with major urban scholars and public officials. The theme of the 2021 Urban Forum was racial and income inequality in Chicago and nationally.

5. The guide does not address race, ethnicity, and culture in a meaningful way—something that is of the utmost importance, especially in the current political context. The guide focuses on federal political internships rather than aldermanic, mayoral, or other local and community-based organizations, civic/activist groups, and law internships, which are most popular among our students. Their guide is technologically and historically outdated, written before smart phones, social media, COVID-19, Zoom and similar online platforms, and the Obama and Trump presidencies, rendering parts of the book obsolete.

6. Simpson and O'Shaugnessy (2016) offer a definitive guide to elections, political campaigns, elected officials, and civic organizations. In the interests of full disclosure, it is written by one of the chapter authors and is a primary text for the internship course at UIC.

7. Alinsky (1971) highlights the substantive and symbolic power of political activism through pressure and confrontation strategies. We find that it spurs genuine debate and engages students in robust discussion.

8. Francis and Hoefel (2018) argue that the current college-age generation feels comfortable not having only one way to act themselves. The search for authenticity generates greater freedom of expression and greater openness to understanding different kinds of people. We encourage students to be individuals and at the same time to understand and respect social norms.

9. Slank (2019) argues that individuals who experience imposter syndrome are rational. We agree with Chrousos and Mentis (2020) that institutions and departments should take steps to allay these fears, as the political science pipeline could suffer.

10. Chrousos and Mentis (2020) state that professors, principal investigators, and peers should encourage students and fellow social scientists to focus on factual evidence regarding their academic performance and to set realistic expectations. One way that we address this is in the discussions around managing expectations and exhibiting professionalism in internships.

11. It is worth noting that our interns often hold campus leadership positions such as student body president or student member of the university's board of trustees.

CHAPTER 6

Mentoring Interns

John C. Berg, Suffolk University

Mentoring of interns is essential to assure that internships are an academic experience in which students learn about political science to justify the academic credit they receive. Mentoring is done mostly through personal communication, both oral and written, and can be facilitated by incorporating into the internship program components such as journals, class meetings, learning contracts, self-evaluations, and site visits. This chapter also briefly considers how to conduct mentoring in special situations, including those that are geographically distant from campus or are ephemeral, namely political campaigns.

INTRODUCTION

The main job of any political science intern's faculty sponsor is to help the intern learn political science. Mentoring is essential to that task. Personal interaction is the essence of mentoring, but the impact of such interaction can be maximized through an internship program's structure.

Not all internships are rewarded with academic credit. However, if an institution does give credit and charges tuition for those units, it incurs an obligation to provide the same degree of learning that would be available in a classroom course. Doing so involves more than just specifying the time that students must spend on course-related activities; interns must be provided with the stimuli and tools to understand what they are learning and how their experience fits into an academic discipline.

Consider the case of Sonia Smith, a journalism student at Georgetown who wrote about her internship at the online magazine *Slate*, which did not pay her as an intern but required her to receive academic credit. She enrolled in a one-credit course, "Internship in Business," missed the single class meeting, never met the instructor, and wrote a short reflection paper at the end to pass the course. She enjoyed the internship, but no matter what she paid for the course, she did not get her money's worth (Smith 2006).

Despite these shortcomings, Smith enjoyed and learned from her experience. Some interns do not: they may be limited to menial work, harassed by their supervisors, exploited for their free labor, or simply ignored (Perlin 2012). They may also concentrate so much on carrying out their assigned tasks that they do not recognize how their work relates to political science. If universities value internships because scholarly research has legitimized them as "high-impact practices" that lead to greater student retention (Kuh 2008), then universities must ensure that students learn.

David Thornton Moore (2013) has argued that while university administrators advertise their school's commitment to experiential learning, including internships, they have done little to define what is academically valuable about these programs or how that value is to be attained. Moore attempts to fill this need with an intensive analysis of the curriculum and pedagogy of internships. Specifying what academic knowledge and theoretical understanding students gain from internships and how they are guided to such learning makes it possible to justify giving academic credit. Moore emphasizes that faculty mentors have a role to play in both of these areas.

WHAT IS MENTORING?

Vasgird and Phillips (2019) offer a general definition of mentoring, albeit one intended for senior researchers mentoring their junior colleagues, writing:

> A mentor is someone who shares knowledge and serves as an experienced and trusted advisor. . . the role of a mentor has expanded and often includes supervisor, collaborator, professional development coach, advocate, and friend. . . Perhaps most importantly, a mentor is someone who takes a sincere interest in the future growth and development of a trainee. (Vasgird and Phillips 2019, np)

The task of a faculty member mentoring an intern is more limited than this in some ways, but broader in others. It is more limited in that it focuses on what the student does as an intern, a role that is usually part-time and of limited duration. A mentoring relationship developed through an internship program may sometimes grow to cover all aspects of the intern's professional life, continuing for years past graduation, but mentoring essentially relates to the internship directly.

On the other hand, while a mentor should certainly be interested in the student's future growth and development, guiding the intern's learning must be the immediate priority. Faculty are obligated to promote understanding of the academic discipline, in this case political science.

Intern mentoring, therefore, can be defined as *the interaction of a faculty sponsor with an intern in order to facilitate learning*. Mentoring can be contrasted with *monitoring*, or *actions taken to ensure that the internship is meeting certain standards*, such as the number of hours worked or the quality of that work. Mentoring is always supportive; monitoring tends to involve verification and enforcement. Although the two are theoretically distinct, in practice the distinction is blurred because internship coordinators typically perform both roles. For instance, a site visit can be purposed simultaneously to review whether learning goals are being met and to check on the student's attendance and job performance.[1] In the American system of higher education more generally, faculty are expected to both teach (mentor) and grade (monitor) their students, despite the inherent tension between these two roles. This chapter focuses specifically on mentoring; however, it should be noted that many mentoring activities overlap with monitoring functions.

Research on faculty mentoring of political science interns is thin. Although Pecorella (2007) uses the word *monitoring* instead of mentoring, he asserts the importance of "continual faculty sponsor-intern discussions throughout the experience, incorporating questions, challenges, and, if necessary, faculty-intern confrontations over the nature of the internship experience" (2007, 84).[2] Doherty's (2011) scholarship focuses on mentoring in a specific context, namely, a program designed to make women students feel more confident about seeking political office by placing them with women legislators who serve as their mentors. In the case she describes, legislators were selected for their desire to play this role, and many intern supervisors also regard themselves as mentors (Sosland and Lowenthal 2017). However, mentoring by a faculty member is distinctive in that it usually involves focusing on generalizable job skills and holistic career readiness, as well as advancing a better understanding of politics.

Research in related disciplines offers useful insights about the nature of intern mentoring, such as that of Rothman (2007), who, like Sosland and Lowenthal (2017), studied the role of site supervisors. She performed a content analysis of suggestions from 345 business students about ways supervisors could improve the intern experience, finding a consensus that good supervisors defined tasks clearly, communicated well, and made their expectations transparent (2007). In political science, faculty mentors should define the nature and type of academic learning that should occur through internship activities (such as the relation between information and power, or the role of veto points in the legislative process) and communicate those expectations to the intern.

In the area of education, Crutcher and Naseem (2016) reviewed over 30 empirical studies on mentoring new teachers published in education journals since 2000, and they determined that effective mentoring practices involved "(a) critical reflection and feedback, (b) modeling, (c) collaboration, and (d) knowledge about the needs of novice teachers" (2016, 40). Their conclusions equally apply to political science internship faculty, whose focus should be on the general needs of up-and-coming political scientists, as well the specific needs of students that they discern through one-on-one consultations.

Finally, Kaslow and Mascaro (2007) digest a great deal of research and capitalize on their personal experience with mentoring clinical psychology doctoral students who work in academic hospitals. They define mentoring as "a unique and distinctive personal relationship in which more experienced faculty members, clinical supervisors, or professionals who are trusted advisors and wise people engage in a variety of interactions with the interns and postdoctoral fellows whom they mentor" (2007, 192). They clearly distinguish mentoring from supervising, noting the same person may do both, but the functions differ: "The mentor has greater investment in the personal and career development of the protégé than is the case in supervision where the focus is primarily the development of competence" (2007, 192). In other words, the mentor seeks to help mentees develop a better understanding of their personal and professional goals and how to attain them.

Mentoring should also be beneficial to the mentor as well as the mentee. Vasgird and Phillips (2019) identify the personal and professional yields for experiential learning mentors:

> (M)entors typically find satisfaction in sharing their knowledge and experience, and renew their enthusiasm for the profession. It can help the mentor develop and enhance professional networks, extend their professional contributions, and contribute to the advancement of the field. Mentors can gain the opportunity to learn about new research areas, build a strong research program, gain new friendships, and affect the future by leaving a part of their expertise and values in every trainee. (Vasgird and Phillips 2019, np)

Essentially, faculty mentors develop a legacy through their interns, and have the potential to energize their own work by expanding their own networks and scope of their research.

All of these studies provide useful suggestions for what mentors should do. However, since faculty mentors are responsible for assuring that academic learning takes place, their roles should also be considered in relationship to the curriculum and pedagogy of internships.

THE CURRICULUM OF INTERNSHIPS

Although many political science internship programs require an affiliated classroom course, the curriculum we are concerned with is that of the internship itself: what students are expected to learn from their work experience. We can consider this in terms of *learning goals*.

In some programs every intern will have the same goals. This is particularly appropriate if all the interns have similar placements, such as with different members of a state legislature. At the other end of the spectrum, interns may have different learning goals relevant to their individual placements. In such cases, the relationship between placement and learning goals can work in two directions: an intern may accept an internship because it sounds interesting, and may need help developing a credit-worthy set of learning goals for that placement; or an intern may have a prior idea of what they would like to learn, and need help selecting an appropriate placement by which to do so. The faculty mentor can help in both of these situations by helping students clarify their goals and by exploring what learning is likely to transpire in a given placement. The mentor should also help the intern stay focused on the political science content of what they are learning. A learning agreement (sometimes called a learning contract, as highlighted in Chapter 8 by Lowenthal and Sosland) can be used to help articulate goals; such agreements are discussed more thoroughly below.

During the placement search, mentors should help students distinguish between the nature of an organization as a whole and what is involved in a particular internship position. Students may make two kinds of wrong assumptions. First, they may assume that everyone in a particular kind of organization—a business, a public relations agency, a media outlet—does the sort of work that is implied by the organization's overall purpose. In truth (and as faculty are aware), organizations often encompass multiple functions that are political in nature, such as lobbying or regulatory compliance. Second, while interns tend to be drawn to organizations they have heard of, some of the most substantive placements can be with small nonprofits or grassroots campaigns, among others, which tend to be understaffed and willing to give interns substantial responsibility in return for their much-needed labor.

Many campuses now have a centralized internship office that maintains a database of possible placements (see chapters by Chávez Metoyer and Simpson, Braam, and Wilson). While such an office can be a useful resource, the staff is unlikely to have as complete an understanding of the academic goals of an internship program as the faculty sponsor does, so an important mentoring task is to help students evaluate these placements. When students come to the program with placements they have landed on their own, perhaps through family or other personal connections, mentorship involves helping the student evaluate these as learning opportunities. Finally, some students will feel so lucky to be offered any type of placement that they will want to accept it immediately. Here the mentor can compel the student to pause and consider their options by requiring formal approval before the placement can be accepted for credit. The placement agreement form in the supplemental resources section is one way of formalizing such an approval.

Once an intern has been placed and has been at work for a week or two, it is time to develop more structured learning goals. Moore (2013) suggests that these can be sorted into six categories: facts and information, concepts, skills and competencies, social and organizational knowledge, personal development, and values and ethics. The learning agreement form included in the supplemental resources section includes fewer categories: *facts, skills*, and *ethics*. Requiring interns to complete this form only after a discussion with the faculty mentor encourages them to think about their goals more analytically, and many students will need help distinguishing these academic goals from work tasks. For example, a legislative intern may write: "make sure all constituent requests are answered promptly." While doing so would certainly require some learning, the focus here is on the work achievement; instead, the mentor can help the intern consider what *factual knowledge* (e.g., knowing which state office is in charge of which function) and *skills* (e.g., effective telephone communication) are involved, and also scrutinize the *theoretical connections* to political science (the function of constituent service in representative government, in this example).

Leaving aside these general matters, mentors must ensure that political science content is recognizable in the intern's learning goals. If politics is defined as the authoritative allocation of values (Easton 1953), the mentor can help the intern understand how such an allocation is occurring through the internship activities. For example, in the common situation where an intern is working on constituent services, the mentor might ask what values the constituent is seeking, who has the authority to provide those values, and what the role of the elected official is. To consider how this works more specifically, we now turn to pedagogy.

THE PEDAGOGY OF INTERNSHIPS

Following a detailed discussion of the pedagogical differences between the classroom and field experience, Moore (2013) condenses this discussion into a number of issues. Three of them are particularly relevant to the pedagogy involved in mentoring. First, the kinds of knowledge involved are distinct: students in the classroom are taught abstract categories, with examples used to illustrate them. On the other hand, interns in the field encounter these abstractions as real human experiences, sometimes painful ones, such as a constituent facing eviction, or a restaurant owner seeking legislative relief to avoid bankruptcy. The mentor can help the student relate the concrete to the abstract. Second, professionals in the field are likely to think differently from academics, with an orientation toward how to get things done, rather than how to understand them or about the lessons that can be drawn from them. The mentor can help the intern see how understanding and effectiveness are related. Finally, the concepts and relationships are presented in some logical order in the classroom; in the field, they can come up at any time, without their theoretical context being apparent. The mentor can help the student see how an event is part of a process (Moore 2013).

Mentoring requires systematic contact between mentor and intern, because mentors can also help interns deal with practical problems that could arise at any point during a semester. For some students, an internship will be their first experience working in an office; others will have office experience, but not on a professional level. Experienced interns may be surprised to encounter new types of problems. Internships may begin with drudgery, such as hours of filing, and interns need help figuring out how to secure more meaningful tasks. They may also need advice about dealing with difficult workplace colleagues. More seriously, interns may encounter abusive supervisors or harassment at their worksites; fortunately, this is not common, but interns need active support when it happens.

Mentors learn about these issues through four types of personal contact: *meetings*, either one-on-one in the mentor's office or as part of a group, such as in an internship class; *journals* kept by the intern and read and responded to by the mentor; *written reports* usually generated at the midterm and always at the end of the internship; and *site visits* by the mentor to meet with both intern and supervisor. Each is considered separately below.

Meetings

Many internship programs require that all interns attend class weekly or biweekly. A course usually includes a curriculum that includes readings and assignments; even so, it is also desirable to include some time for the interns to compare notes on their experiences since the last meeting. Simply put, interns benefit from learning from each other and often share complementary experiences. In addition, if an intern is encountering problems, other interns may have suggestions about how to handle them. From the point of view of mentoring, the instructor can use such discussions to help interns make theoretical generalizations and broader comparisons. If appropriate, students can also be asked to relate theoretical concepts from assigned reading to observations about their experiences as interns. To use an example from personal experience, asking students to read Max Weber's essay about bureaucracy and then evaluate the degree to which their placement organization is bureaucratic can lead to fruitful discussions, both of Weber's concept and about their own situations (1993 [1922]).

Ideally, the internship should carry the same academic credit as any other course, and the concurrent seminar should count as another course. If this is not possible, adjustments need to be made to prevent placing unreasonable time demands on the intern. A part-time internship should involve 12–15 hours a week at the placement for the student to integrate as fully as an intern can into the office; 10 hours per week is a minimum, but anything less generally limits the learning potential. Other adjustments might involve the number or length of the class meetings. Based on 40 years of intern supervision, I have found that none of these adjustments will work as well as counting the program as a two-course package, but they may be necessary.

In cases where a paired internship class is not feasible, the instructor should meet personally with interns on a regular basis. The purpose of these meetings should be the same as that of the mentoring portions of a weekly class, discussed previously. One way to do this would be to focus on discussion of the student's internship journal, discussed in the next subsection.

Journals

All internships should require a journal even if there are class meetings, because writing about one's experience contributes to understanding that experience. Some instructors assign a journal that is no more than a simple log. Chizeck says, "Minimally a journal should document the hours spent on site and give a description of the activities and events the student encounters," and adds that "a journal is really the minimum writing to be expected from a student" (2004, 8). As an experienced internship mentor, I believe that requiring only a log abandons most of the learning potential of a journal, and I agree with Chizeck who maintains that a more substantive journal is a more useful teaching tool. Thus, by providing guidance about what should be explored in the journal and how to discuss it, the mentor needs to ensure that journal writers connect practice with theory and also reflect on these linkages. A sample set of guidelines is included in the supplemental resources section.[3] Included in it are a weekly assessment of progress toward the intern's learning goals, but there are some advantages to avoiding an exclusive focus on such goals. Many interns find themselves in unanticipated circumstances or engaged in aspects of the internship they had been unaware of initially. The guidelines encourage interns to reflect more deeply on any elements they found interesting, a process that can open the door to new learning and corresponding learning goals. This will be discussed further in the section on learning contracts, below.

Written guidelines for journaling are a good start. However, the essence of journal-based mentoring is the instructor's feedback. Such feedback should be frequent, ideally once a week, and should help point the intern toward deeper reflection on what has been observed, its meaning, and how their understanding relates to the intern's learning goals. For example, the mentor might pose questions for the intern to reflect on in the next journal entry. For the intern, it is best to write the journal as soon as possible after the experience, and rapid and consistent feedback from the instructor helps cement the learning.

Learning Contracts

The document that sets both realistic and aspirational goals for the internship—recognizing that these are likely to evolve during the course of the internship—is commonly labeled a "Learning Agreement" or "Learning Contract" (see supplementals).[4] In the Suffolk University program, a separate *Placement Agreement* was used at the very beginning of the internship to signify agreement about hours, schedules, and general responsibilities, whereas the *Learning Contract* (or *Learning Agreement*) was used to articulate learning goals. Using two separate documents helps make the distinction between these purposes clear to the intern and the supervisor.

The initial choice of placement should reflect learning goals in a general way. However, until the intern settles into the job and understands both what the organization does and their own role in it, specifying goals can be difficult. For this reason, it is advisable to make the learning contract due two weeks after the internship has started, and to allow (or periodically require) adjustments to the goals as the internship continues. As noted above, the mentor helps students discern the differences between work goals (e.g., "get an email newsletter sent to everyone on the mailing list") and learning goals ("learn what role electronic communications play in relations between constituents and their representative"), and once the document is complete, the mentor should review the learning agreement and directly and quickly address any such confusion, either in writing or in person.

Goal attainment is also more likely when self-aware interns establish their own learning goals, and mentors can be a big help in keeping those goals top of mind by providing instructions for interns' self-reporting. The form included in the supplemental resources section asks students to think about their skills, factual knowledge, and ethical awareness, and then to develop goals for further learning in each area. These goals then serve as the basis for interns' written and oral mid-term and final self-evaluations.

Intern Self-Evaluations

Most internship programs require a final written report from the intern. It's useful to require a midterm report as well so that the mentor can intervene to help the student correct any problems that may not emerge through journaling or class discussions. An example of instructions for mid-term and final self-evaluations, extracted from my course syllabus, can be found in the supplemental resources section. Internship courses can be used to require oral presentations of both reports, which can help a student meet the oral communication goals of an institution or department and also enable opportunity for peer evaluation and feedback. An important role for the faculty mentor is to help interns improve on the midterm report by clarifying their attainment of learning goals and modifying those goals as appropriate. This can be achieved by the final report; however, if placed at the end of the semester, not all students will read the instructor's comments and it will be too late to implement suggestions. A final opportunity for mentoring comes during site visits, which ideally should be part of every internship.

Site Visits

Surveying internship programs at a medium-sized state university in the late 1980s, Chizeck (2004) found that social science programs featured "little faculty involvement" (5). Site visits, however, can add value both to an internship program and the process of mentoring, and should be included wherever possible. Without them, faculty mentors can find it difficult to understand the potential of a placement site or help the intern evaluate the learning opportunities at a specific site.

Site visits advance monitoring as well as mentoring; they help prevent the rare situation when a student claims to be doing an internship but isn't; and a final site visit gives the supervisor a chance to give a more nuanced evaluation of the intern's performance instead of simply filling out a written form (such as the prompt in the supplemental resources section). Much more importantly, site visits allow the faculty mentor to observe and evaluate several aspects of the intern's environment: the physical setting, the social atmosphere in the office or on site, and the personal relationship between intern and supervisor. Based on these observations, the mentor can discuss with the intern how to increase the value of the experience and suggest improvements both to the intern and supervisor. For these reasons, best practices include site visits at the midterm and end of the internship. If time permits, a site visit at the beginning can be used to negotiate and sign the placement agreement.[5]

It is worth mentioning other advantages of site visits. With respect to the educational institution, site visitations convey to students that internships are opportunities offered by their university, not simply outside activities they are doing on their own, and this understanding will bear fruit later through alumni relations. Site visits can also strengthen relationships between the academic program and the site supervisors. In my experience, students and supervisors frequently express their gratitude for faculty members' visits. For the individual faculty member, these efforts can provide openings for research, as well as wider familiarity in general with the various political settings where interns work.

Special circumstances

Some types of internships pose special problems for monitoring. This section addresses two such circumstances: geographically distant internships, and internships in political campaigns.

On-site internships in Washington, DC and in other countries have been growing in popularity. However, unless a university possesses the resources to maintain its own center in one or more of these places, it is easier for the institution to contract with an established organization that provides on-site placement assistance, supervision, and evaluation. In DC, the Washington Center and American University are very different examples of such programs (see also Chapter 13 by Chin), as are Educational Programmes Abroad (known in the US as EPA Internships) and the International Partnership for Service-Learning in the countries where they operate. These organizations provide supporting documentation, such as supervisor evaluations and confirmation of the work done, and in some cases grant transferable credit from an accredited institution. However, the home-campus-based faculty mentor should maintain contact with the intern throughout the internship and require at least a weekly journal submission. If possible, a mid-term site visit increases substantially their ability both to mentor and assess, but it is the rare university administration that can be convinced that such visits are worth the expense.

Electoral campaigns remain popular sources of political internships. Rife with learning opportunities, they do present a few potential dilemmas that need to be addressed early in the process. First, campaigns are largely volunteer-driven, and campaign staff often consider interns as just another kind of volunteer. It is often difficult to convince campaign staff to set aside special opportunities for interns, and virtually impossible to enforce any agreements that are made. To deal with this, the mentor needs to help the intern understand that their responsibilities will correspond to their capabilities and the willingness to work that they demonstrate. This is true in many placements, but much more so in a campaign.

Second, campaigns end—abruptly—on election night. A final meeting between the intern and supervisor will be almost impossible to arrange just before the election (everyone will be too busy) and just as difficult after the election when the offices are closed and staff have moved on, either to a vacation or their next job. The faculty mentor should work with the intern to find a supervisor who will be available to provide a personalized assessment when the election is over, filling out and returning any evaluation forms, and meeting with the intern and sponsor—off-site or virtually if necessary—to discuss that evaluation.

CONCLUSION

Mentors play an essential role in ensuring the academic quality of internships. Today, university administrators, career services staff, and students tend to view internships only in relationship to career development, or as providing an inside track to a future job (Berg 2014; Perlin 2012). It is the mentor's job to show the student that an internship can be so much more, and that if the intern wants academic credit, it *needs* to be more. Fortunately, doing so is not difficult. In general, students enjoy writing about their experience and discussing what they learned with their peers. When faculty mentors insist on regular journaling, class discussions, personal meetings, and evaluative reports, and also provide consistent, targeted feedback, interns gain a greater understanding of the political science discipline, which is a vitally important goal of any political science course.

REFERENCES

Berg, John C. 2014. "Two Threats to Political Science Internships: Press Attacks and Incorrect Student Assumptions." Paper presented at the American Political Science Association, Washington, DC.

Chizeck, Susan. 2004. "Academic Standards for Internships." *NSEE Quarterly* 29 (1): 1–12.

Crutcher, Paul A., and Samina Naseem. 2016. "Cheerleading and cynicism of effective mentoring in current empirical research." *Educational Review* 68 (1): 40–55.

Denda, Kayo, and Jennifer Hunter. 2016. "Building 21st Century Skills and Creating Communities: A Team-based Engagement Framework for Student Employment in Academic Libraries." *Journal of Library Administration* 56 (3): 251–265.

Doherty, Leanne. 2011. "Filling the Female Political Pipeline: Assessing a Mentor-Based Internship Program." *Journal of Political Science Education* 7 (1): 34–47.

Easton, David. 1953. *The Political System: An Inquiry Into the State of Political Science.* New York: Knopf.

Kaslow, Nadine J., and Nathan A. Mascaro. 2007. "Mentoring Interns and Postdoctoral Residents in Academic Health Sciences Center." *Journal of Clinical Psychology in Medical Settings* 14 (3): 191–196.

Kuh, George D. 2008. "High-Impact Educational Practices: What They Are, Who Has Access to Them, and Why They Matter." Washington, DC: American Association of Colleges and Universities.

"mentor, n." 2021. *OED Online,* March, Accessed May 20. Oxford University Press. https://www-oed-com.ezproxy.redlands.edu/view/Entry/116575?rskey=Y6UDDG&result=1.

Moore, David Thornton. 2013. *Engaged Learning in The Academy: Challenges and Possibilities.* London: Palgrave Macmillan.

Pecorella, Robert F. 2007. "Forests and Trees: The Role of Academics in Legislative Internships." *Journal of Political Science Education* 3 (1): 79–99.

Perlin, Ross 2012. *Intern Nation: Earning Nothing and Learning Little in the Brave New Economy.* London: Verso.

Rothman, Miriam. 2007. "Lessons Learned: Advice to Employers from Interns." *Journal of Education for Business* 82 (3): 140–144.

Smith, Sonia. 2006. "Biting the Hand That Doesn't Feed Me: Internships for College Credit Are a Scam." *Slate,* June 8. http://www.slate.com/articles/news_and_politics/hey_wait_a_minute/2006/06/biting_the_hand_that_doesnt_feed_me.html.

Sosland, Jeffrey K., and Diane J. Lowenthal. 2017. "The Forgotten Educator: Experiential Learning's Internship Supervisor." *Journal of Political Science Education* 13 (1): 1–14.

Vasgird, Daniel, and Trisha Phillips. 2019. "Responsible Conduct of Research, Basic Course: Mentoring." CITI Program (online).

Weber, Max. 1993 (1922). "Bureaucracy." In *Critical Studies in Organization and Bureaucracy*, ed. Frank Fischer and Carmen Sirianni, 4–19. Philadelphia: Temple University Press.

ENDNOTES

1. Conversely, the documents and personal conversations used to mentor (discussed later in this chapter) are also a source of information about the intern's performance, and in the case of internships which earn letter grades, may be one of the considerations evaluated for that grade. This is not unique to internships.

2. If we rely on the definition of "mentor" in the *Oxford English Dictionary* (2021) as "a person who offers support and guidance to another," then *mentoring* is a more accurate term for what Pecorella calls monitoring.

3. This document is adapted from guidelines developed by the late Helen Graves of the University of Michigan-Dearborn. She created it for Canadian Parliament internship positions, and I used her rubric in my teaching for over 40 years.

4. I prefer the term "agreement," because I find that the term "contract" implies too legalistic an arrangement.

5. Some faculty may want their students to build or have a sense of agency over this aspect of the process, leaving the direct learning contract negotiations up to them.

CHAPTER 7

Constructing a Research Internship Program To Promote Experiential Learning

Arthur H. Auerbach, University of Southern California

Whereas most traditional undergraduate internship programs have allowed students to gain valuable work experience, the Jesse M. Unruh Institute of Politics at the University of Southern California (USC) expanded its internship program to include a distinctive research internship program in which students work with professionals from both the private and public sectors on specific public policy issues. As students engage with outside research internship providers, they become more expert in policy areas that are relevant to the public at large. In-depth research combined with on-campus professionalization components allow interns a unique experience that serves them well upon graduation.

INTRODUCTION

Although most undergraduates tend to think of internships programs as being the same across institutions, varying goals, tasks, and expectations can yield dramatically different experiences between institutions and even among students on the same campus. This chapter explores a unique research internship program at the University of Southern California (USC) that incorporates close interaction between students and internship providers, in-depth student research based on a structured research agenda, a series of professionalization workshops, and work that culminates in a student-led professional presentation to internship providers and peers. The combination of these elements has proven to be a highly effective instructional strategy for the students and genuinely rewarding for the internship providers.

The Value Of Research Internships

University training programs have relied on internships to immerse students in real-world experiences for over a century (Lehman and Quick 2011; Kelly and Bridges 2005; Kelly and Gaedeke 1990; Kim, Kim, and Bzullak 2011). Experiential learning programs can operate as a bridge between theory and practice, as Fry, Bottoms, and O'Neill (2005) acknowledge in their definition of internships:

> A well-designed internship expands the knowledge and skills of candidates while also gauging their ability to apply new learning in authentic settings as they contend with problems that have real-world consequences. Built right, an internship becomes a sturdy vessel upon which new practitioners can navigate the swift, unpredictable currents that separate classroom theory and on-the-job reality (Fry, Bottoms, and O'Neill 2005, 3).

In addition to traditional internships, research is also considered essential to the undergraduate experience, enabling students to master core competencies of higher education, developing attributes that every graduate of every degree will possess (Barrie 2007; Partridge and Sandover 2010). Engaging students in meaningful research has been shown to improve student experience and retention (Brew 2010; Locks and Gregerman 2008; Partridge, Lee, and Sandover 2010), and can lead to the development of research skills that pave the way to postgraduate studies. Whether students are working within an office addressing real-world issues or at home conducting in-depth academic research on the very same issues, the advantages of a policy research internship program are well substantiated. In light of the multiple benefits of both undergraduate research and the value of traditional internship programs, it made sense to combine these into one program, the California Research Internship Program at USC.

California Policy Research Internship Program

The California Research Internship Program stemmed from the traditional internship program that is offered through the Jesse M. Unruh Institute of Politics. For several decades, the Unruh Institute has facilitated political internships in and around the Los Angeles area. Staff assess the students' experience and interests, and then match the students, based on their qualifications, to internship providers who partner regularly with the Institute.[1] After résumés and cover letters are prepared by the students, with staff assistance as needed, the Institute applies to one or more internships on behalf of the students. After a brief interview and acceptance by a provider, students are then enrolled in the internship class and can receive academic credit for their on-site and academic work.

Whereas this model works for many students, over time the faculty and staff at the Institute came to recognize that some students' educational needs were not being met. Specifically, many hoped to conduct intensive research in a public policy area such as education, the environment, or criminal justice, among others, and most had neither the ability nor interest to travel away from campus to fulfill a traditional internship.

A number of additional factors were considered when weighing whether to create such a program. First and foremost, a research internship program would require external internship providers who were willing to work with our students. Finding internship providers did not pose a problem as there were several hundred associated with our traditional internship program that we could draw on, many of whom were alumni or were connected to the university through its long history in the Los Angeles community, and the prospect of receiving 500–600 hours of research on their specific area of interest created a powerful incentive for participation. We contacted a sample of our providers and they expressed significant interest.

The second consideration was faculty involvement. In 2010, this challenge was met when the Department of Political Science agreed to assign a faculty member to run the Institute's internship programs—both the traditional program and the planned research program—within their teaching load. Faculty participation ensured the that rigorous research agendas would be created in coordination with internship providers and that there would be a mechanism put in place for supplying routine guidance to participating students throughout the semester.

The final element of success was staff support. In order to create robust internship programs, the Institute agreed to hire a dedicated staff member both to place students in traditional internships and to help coordinate the research program. Today the staff member monitors the progress of students' research, tracks their research hours, and communicates information about upcoming meetings and events. Ultimately, the strong combination of student and internship partner interest with faculty and staff support has allowed the research internship course to flourish.

The Internship Providers

The first major step in creating the research internship program was to identify one or more internship providers who would be willing to work with our students on intensive research projects over the course of a semester. Initially, the answer to this question was quite simple. In 2009, USC was approached by Project Vote Smart (PVS) to have USC students assist in their research.[2] For 18 months, the partnership met the needs the Unruh Institute wanted to fulfill, but the relationship came to an end when PVS staff were recalled from the USC campus as a means of consolidating their organizational resources. The search for a research internship provider resumed.

The following year, the Institute reached out to California Strategies, LLC, to gauge their interest in partnering with USC. The Institute had a long-time relationship with several persons at the firm, a lobbying outfit with offices in Los Angeles and throughout the United States. Their work covers a number of policy areas including energy, environmental regulations, green technology, health care, land use, and water use. After a series of conversations, California Strategies agreed to come on board as our sole research internship partner. Three of the firm's principal partners would work with three groups of student interns (five students per group) on different policy areas. The idea was that the partners would meet with their students on a monthly basis for progress checks, and students would have continual access to their partners via e-mail and/or phone conversations. Students and partners would hold an initial meeting to craft a research agenda, and a faculty member would join in. This structure was followed for the 2012–13 academic year, but at the end of spring 2013, the model was slightly altered out of concern that the program was overburdening California Strategies as our sole research partner.

For AY 2013–14, it was decided that California Strategies would remain a policy research partner and that two more would be added. The first of these was Parent Revolution, a nonprofit that works to transform underperforming public schools by empowering parents to advocate for their children's education. Parent Revolution was a good fit for our program as education policy is a popular policy topic among USC students. The second was the National Association of Latino Elected and Appointed Officials (NALEO). NALEO is a non-profit organization that works to facilitate the full participation of Latinos in the American political process, and their work includes issues such as civic engagement and immigration reform. Working with three advocacy groups not only has enhanced the diversity of policy issues that students can explore but also has avoided overburdening any one provider by rotating them as needed. Thus, the current model allows for greater long-term sustainability.[3]

Selecting the Interns and Setting the Research Agenda

The research internship program accepts applications from students during the first three weeks of the semester. Students are selected based upon several criteria, including: area of interest, year in school, grade point average, and availability to meet for designated meetings. In the application, students are asked to rank their policy interests in order to help the staff place them into one of two research groups, which usually consist of five to six students apiece. After students are selected into the program and accept their policy group placement, they are permitted to register for the class. Students are able to register for two, three, or four units: the larger the number, the more research hours and length of the final policy paper. For 2 units, interns must do 100 hours of research and complete an eight- to ten-page policy paper; for 4 units the intern must do 200 hours of research and write a 12- to 15-page policy paper.

In week four of the semester, interns are required to attend a research skills seminar run by the staff at one of the USC libraries.[4] The librarians discuss various on-line search engines and other library resources that the students can use during their research internship. Since the students are already aware of the policy area in which they will work, they are able to ask relevant questions. Interns also conduct field research as part of their research agenda. Research partners will often connect students to policy experts in regulatory agencies and/or within a particular industry. Thus, the combination of traditional library research, on-line sources, and additional resources supplied by policy partners lays the foundation for research skill development.

The first face-to-face meeting between the partners and the students occurs shortly after the research skills seminar. The partners plus faculty member, staff, and students come together to collaborate and craft a research agenda for the semester; creating a full research agenda actually takes place over several weeks through continuing consultation among them. The overarching goal is for students to conduct individual research that helps answer a broader research question. As noted above, students' research agendas often include a field research component, and they are afforded latitude to design their field research as they and the internship provider see fit; typical methods include personal interviews or large-scale surveys. After the initial student-and-partner meeting, students then consult with the faculty member and Unruh staff twice a month to refine the research and ensure that adequate direction on the project is being provided. At these meetings, each student gives an update both orally and in writing about their progress, and participation in the semi-monthly research meetings counts towards a portion of the students' course grade. Approximately halfway through the semester, the partners and students meet a second time at the Mid-Semester Exchange. At this gathering the partners hear about the progress of the research being conducted and offer additional suggestions and direction for the students.

Final Presentation and the Final Policy Report

As the semester nears its conclusion, students prepare to make a final presentation of their research and accompanying policy recommendations. To prepare, each research team undertakes two formal run-throughs with the faculty member and Unruh staff. The final presentations are conducted in a professional manner, with student teams collaboratively preparing 30- to 40-minute lecture slide presentations in which they summarize their research to an audience that includes their internship provider, advising faculty member, the other students in the program, and the Unruh staff. It is not uncommon for research partners to invite special guests to the presentation, particularly persons for whom the research may be relevant, and audience members are encouraged to pose questions that students answer during the final 30 minutes. Students also prepare a two-page synopsis for audience members.

In addition to the final presentation, students individually are required to write a final policy report that includes an abstract, introduction, findings, and conclusion (i.e., policy recommendations). Students also integrate their individual research into a comprehensive policy report, which counts for a separate portion of the students' grades.

Professionalization Components of the Course

Research interns not only conduct research on their respective policy areas, but also they are required to participate in several professionalization events to help prepare them for life after graduation. Initially, the research interns were required to participate in two workshops that were mainstays of the traditional internship program. The first was an interview skills workshop in which professionals from political offices, political consulting firms, and non-governmental organizations were invited to sit on a panel to discuss the process of interviewing. After a 30-minute moderated discussion, a short series of three-minute mock interviews took place between the professionals and the students so that the students could get a sense of how interviews are actually conducted. By the end of the evening, every student had undergone two mini-interviews in which they received feedback on each. This process successfully provided a look into the process of real-world interviewing.

Students were also required to attend a mid-semester Jobs Forum Workshop in which professionals from various employment sectors interacted with interested students in an intimate setting. Following a 45-minute (in-person) moderated panel discussion, the participants would break out into different parts of the room where students could ask questions and have them answered in an informal and comfortable environment. The overarching goal was simple: to educate students about how to gain employment.

In 2018, additional professionalization workshops were created to give students greater choice. Today, in any given semester, five to six workshops are offered and the students are required to attend any two (including those described above). Students can more easily accommodate this flexible structure, and it better meets the needs of those who have taken the course in prior semesters.[5]

A third element of professionalization is our mentoring program. The Unruh Institute is fortunate to have enlisted many professionals from both the public and private sectors who volunteer to work with our students. These individuals often participate in panel discussions on campus regarding various political issues of the day; they also mentor students in small group settings and talk about their work. The Unruh staff distribute lists of professionals and accompanying biographies to both our traditional and research interns, and the interns choose the top three they would like to meet. Then, three to four students are selected to meet with each fellow and the time and location are coordinated. Nothing more is required of the students other than to speak with the professionals for 30 minutes and learn from them about pursuing post-graduation employment.

Finally, interns are required to attend two political events during the semester and submit a short memorandum on each event regarding the nature of the topic, who spoke, what was said, and their personal perspective about what they heard. The Center for the Political Future,[6] as well as other campus organizations, sponsor numerous lunchtime and evening political events with panelists who discuss and debate issues of the day. The research interns are permitted to attend any political event on campus as a means of exposing them to topical issues. Students whose schedules cannot accommodate any on-campus events are free to attend off-campus events. The goal is to ensure that students are not learning solely within the classroom but are engaging live policy issues that affect them and others.

THE VALUE OF RESEARCH INTERNSHIP EXPERIENCE

Student evaluations have revealed a number of notable features of the research internship program.[7] The evaluation form was administered fall 2018 through spring 2020 and examined various aspects of the class, including design elements of the course, development of skills such as critical thinking and communication, and application of the course to students' academic or career goals. Reported results are based on responses from 14 out of 53 interns who fully completed the evaluations over five semesters, for an overall response rate of 26.4%.

Regarding course design, students were asked about their level of agreement with three statements: (1) "The course objectives were well explained"; (2) "The course assignments were related to the course objectives"; (3) "I understood what was expected of me in this course." On a four-point scale where "0" represented low agreement and "4" represented strong agreement, students gave the course design high marks, ranging from 3.17 (mean score in spring 2018) to 3.89 (in fall 2019). The overall impact of the course was estimated through respondents' level of agreement with three other statements: (1) "I learned perspectives, principles and practices that I expect to apply in new situations"; (2) "This course challenged me to think critically and communicate clearly about the subject"; (3) "This course provided me with information that may be directly applicable to my career or academic goals." Again, respondents generally agreed that the program is achieving these learning objectives (mean score of 3.33 from fall 2018 through spring 2019, and 3.67 in fall 2019 and spring 2020). Taken together, these data suggest that the program is designed well and that students find it creates the potential for applied learning in both the short-and long-term.

The responses to open-ended questions were further enlightening. In particular, nearly every evaluator commented that the most valuable aspect of participating in the research program was the opportunity to conduct in-depth research on a particular policy area. Undergraduates are often asked to conduct research on a number of topics during a semester, but the research program allowed students to focus on a policy area of their choice for the entire semester while employing a variety of research techniques. Table 1 lists several of the research projects that have been completed in recent years along with the types of research utilized in each.

Table 1: California Policy Research Internship Program Projects, 2018–2021

Academic Year	Internship Provider and Team Project	Online Research	Survey Data	Personal Interviews	Field Work
Spring 2021	California Health Project: "Depolarizing America"	X	X	X	
Fall 2020	Crown Castle 5G: "Conquering the Digital Divide"	X	X		
Spring 2020	Los Angeles DCFS*: "Creating a Culture of Success"	X			
Fall 2019	Nature Conservancy: "Managed Retreat, City of Long Beach"	X		X	
Spring 2019	Los Angeles Mayor's Office: "LA Urban Biodiversity"	X			X
Spring 2019	California Strategies, LLC: "California High Speed Rail"	X		X	

Table 1: California Policy Research Internship Program Projects, 2018–2021					
Fall 2018	LA Councilmember Mike Bonini: "Reimagining District 11"	X			X
Spring 2018	LA Councilmember Paul Krekorian: "Homeless Crisis in Los Angeles"	X			
* Los Angeles County Department of Child and Family Services					

To elaborate on one of these projects, in the spring 2021 semester, USC students were asked to tackle one of the most challenging issues of our time: depolarizing the American populace. We partnered with the California Health Project (CHP), a non-governmental organization that strives to produce constructive engagement across political divides to promote the democratic process. The research agenda required USC students to create and deploy a survey, to which over 100 USC students ultimately responded, and to conduct in-depth interviews of undergraduates about how polarization might be resolved. The survey, developed in partnership with CHP, will serve as a template for future projects.

In the course evaluations, students also commented on the value of the professionalization workshops. In particular, both the networking events and the résumé workshop were identified as particularly helpful. The benefits of the networking events are clear, as students are able to connect with practitioners in an informal setting and also acquire tools to connect effectively with other professionals. The résumé workshop helps students refine critical documents, increasing the likelihood of finding a job after graduation.

In addition to the course evaluations, the research internship program undergoes annual review by faculty and staff in an effort to make changes as needed. Such a revision took place after the program had been operating for several years: in response to student evaluations, as noted above, the menu of workshops was expanded. The program continues to be refined in response to feedback from students as well as providers.

CONCLUSION

As with any new program, its creation invites challenges. First, success relies on those who are essentially willing to volunteer their time. In our case, we must lean heavily on internship providers to satisfy core program requirements, which include building and executing a manageable research agenda every semester; meetings with and mentorship of a group of students; and shepherding of projects that are time-intensive. For anyone attempting to set up a program, an inadequate supply of partners limits the range and scope of projects available to students.

Second, insufficient support for faculty and adequate staffing can also pose insurmountable hurdles, especially for resource-stressed campuses that may be unable to compensate a coordinator for such an undertaking. Third, student interest in a research internship program might be lacking. Given the evidence that both research experiences and internships have the potential to improve student gains, especially among historically underserved groups (Kuh 2008; Kuh et al. 2007), universities have incentives to pursue undergraduate research programs like ours.

The research internship program at USC offers a great deal more benefit than simply having students conduct research. Undergraduates embrace the opportunity to interact with working professionals on public policy issues that are relevant to the public at large and also satisfy their curiosity. Students not only gain the experience of making professional presentations based on their research but also offer meaningful policy recommendations that are beneficial to the internship providers. Perhaps one of the greatest advantages of the research program is that students assume an active role in designing and carrying out the research, activities that foster ownership of their work. As we know from our graduates, the unique experiences enabled by the California Policy Research Internship Program are ones that will stay with students long after graduation.

REFERENCES

Barrie, Simon. 2007. "The Conceptual Framework for the Teaching and Learning of Generic Graduate Attributes." *Studies in Higher Education* 32 (4): 439–48.

Boud, David, and Nicky Solomon. 2001. *Working-based Learning: A New Higher Education?* Buckingham, UK: The Society for Research into Higher Education and Open University.

Brew, Angela. 2010. *National Teaching Fellowship Final Report: Enhancing Undergraduate Engagement Through Research and Inquiry*. Australian Teaching and Learning Council.

Brow-Ferrigno, Tricia and Rodney Mult. 2004. "Leadership Mentoring in Clinical Practice: Role Socialization, Professional Development and Capacity Building." *Educational Administration Quarterly* 40: 468–94.

Fry, Betty, Gene Bottoms, and Kathy O'Neill. 2005. *The Principal Internship: How Can We Get It Right?* Atlanta, GA: Southern Regional Education Board.

Kelly, Craig, and Ralph Gaedeke. 1990. "Student and Employer Evaluation of Hiring Criteria for Entry-Level Marketing Positions." *Journal of Marketing Education* 27 (3): 64–71.

Kelly, Craig, and Claudia Bridges. 2005. "Introducing Professional and Career Development Skills in the Marketing Curriculum." *Journal of Marketing Education* 27 (3): 212–8.

Kim, Eyong, Kijoo Kim, Michael Bzullak. 2011. "A Survey of Internship Programs for Management Undergraduates in AACSB-Accredited Institutions." *International Journal of Educational Management* 26 (7): 696–709.

Kuh, George D. 2008. *High-Impact Educational Practices: What They Are, Who Has Access to Them, and Why They Matter.* Washington, DC: Association of American Colleges and Universities.

Kuh, George D., Jillian Kinzie, Ty Cruce, Rick Shoup, Robert M. Gonyea. 2007. "Connecting the Dots: Multi-Faceted Analyses of the Relationships between Student Engagement Results from the NSSE, and the Institutional Practices and Conditions That Foster Student Success." Center for Postsecondary Research, Indiana University Bloomington (Revised January 7).

Lehman, Lynn, and Marilynn Quick. 2011. "Crossing the Line: A Qualitative Study of Administrative Interns' Experience." *International Journal of Education Leadership Preparation* 6 (4): 1–15.

Locks, Angela, and Sandra Gregerman. 2008. "Undergraduate Research as an Institutional Retention Strategy." In *Creating Effective Undergraduate Research Programs: The Transformation from Student to Scientist*, eds. Roman Taraban and Richard Blanton, 11–32. New York: Teachers College Press.

Partridge, Lee, and Sally Sandover. 2010. "Beyond 'Listening' to the Student Voice: The Undergraduate Researcher's Contribution to the Enhancement of Teaching and Learning." *Journal of University Teaching & Learning Practice* 7 (2): 1–19.

ENDNOTES

1. The Unruh Institute works with over 200 internship providers in the Los Angeles area alone.

2. PVS is a non-partisan, non-governmental organization that works to educate the American public about the political stances of candidates running for public office, in essence fact-checking the truth behind candidates' statements by comparing these to their records.

3. In fall 2017, it was decided that the program would be reduced to two research groups (five to six students apiece) due to limited faculty and staff time. The Unruh staff work to accommodate students' top choice of research group, but that is not always possible.

4. Only the research interns are required to attend this seminar (i.e., not the traditional interns).

5. Students in the traditional internship program can take POSC 395 for up to 8 units. Many students elect to take the course as a series of two-unit classes in order to expand their internship experiences.

6. The Center for the Political Future (https://dornsife-center-for-political-future.usc.edu/) was founded at USC by Professor Robert Shrum and Mike Murphy in 2018, "combining rigorous intellectual inquiry, teaching, and practical politics as a means of advancing civil dialogue and research that transcends partisan divisions." The Unruh Institute is a component of the Center that focuses on experiential learning for students.

7. The use of anonymous student course evaluations was approved by the USC Institutional Review Board on September 9, 2020, study identification number UP-20-00844. The statistics reflect evaluation forms submitted by fourteen respondents out of 53 interns who participated in the program over five semesters (spring 2018 through spring 2020).

CHAPTER 8

Assessment in Internships: A 360-Degree Review for Students, Supervisors, and Professors

Diane J. Lowenthal and Jeffrey K. Sosland
American University

In this chapter we focus on the value of assessment for internships and experiential education. While most educators incorporate assessment of the internship and focus solely on the student, we take a broader and more holistic approach here, adapting an approach known as the "360-degree review" for interns, their supervisors, and professors. We share recommendations for effective assessment of internships and related internship courses.

INTRODUCTION

Internships have become a near-essential component of undergraduate education. At the same time, assessment in higher education has increasingly gained attention (DiLoretto, Pellow, and Stout 2017) and in fact is required by state and regional accrediting bodies (Gaston 2018). In this chapter we delineate best practices in assessment of internships and advocate adapting the 360-degree feedback approach to internship assessment.

The phrase "360-degree feedback" became popular in the 1990s as a more integrated and comprehensive approach to employee assessment (Edwards and Ewan 1996). By 2016, Bracken, Rose and Church wrote that 360-degree feedback was "embedded in many of our human resources (HR) processes applied at individual, group, and organizational levels. The practice of 360° Feedback has been around so long now that we are all comfortable with it." (2016, 761). It is also important that students gain an understanding and competency with this approach to prepare them for assessment in the workplace.

Our approach adapts 360-degree feedback to assessment for and of different internship stakeholders as shown in figure 1.[1] Naturally, we expect the intern to be assessed by the internship supervisor (IS) and by the faculty advisor who establishes course requirements such as journals and informational interview papers. However, it's valuable to expand assessment beyond the intern's performance. We also expect the student to assess the internship supervisor and the broader experience at the internship, as well as the faculty advisor through the use of enhanced course evaluations. Finally, we recommend that the faculty advisor provides feedback to the internship supervisor and vice versa. The more feedback that occurs among the stakeholders, the better the experience will be for the current intern, future interns, and the experiential education program.

Through various means, including the internship contract and midterm and exit assessments, the faculty member should work with the internship supervisor and the student to promote academic and career development. In this chapter we argue that the internship stakeholders can maximize their ef-

Figure 1: 360-Degree Assessment: Key stakeholders assess each other

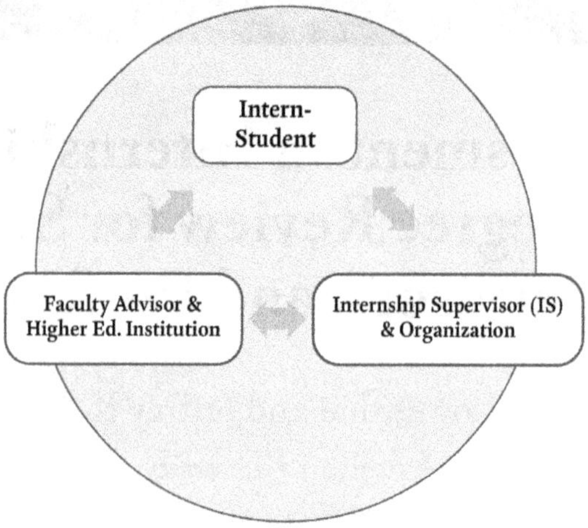

fectiveness when operating within a comprehensive assessment approach and strong educational infrastructure that is formed by online student self-assessment, an internship contract, student course assessment, and faculty and IS assessment of the intern (also see figure 2).

The 360-Degree Review for Internship Stakeholders: The Roles of Students, Supervisors, and Professors in Experiential Learning

The primary stakeholders of an internship program include the intern (student), faculty advisor (professor), and the internship supervisor (IS) or the boss at the internship site: all three play essential roles in this experiential learning process. The college or university and the internship organization are also important stakeholders; these institutions should provide the resources and educational infrastructure to ensure appropriate assessment of the primary stakeholders.

Internship Supervisor (IS)

Essentially an IS is an educator and the IS plays a pivotal part in assessing students who are earning academic credit. Ideally, the IS supervises, instructs, and mentors while retaining a formal educational responsibility to evaluate the student intern. By supervising a real work experience for student interns, an IS not only facilitates professional networking opportunities but also develops a student's individual work skills and provides practical knowledge that animates classroom theory. Ultimately, an IS often will become a source for letters of recommendation, if not a first job offer. In exchange, an IS obtains needed labor, paying little or no wages; the IS also receives the new perspective and energy infused into the workplace by interns. The organization that hosts interns also benefits from increased visibility on college campuses and an enhanced organizational image in the larger community (True 2013). Although the IS is naturally oriented toward the organization, one can also play an important role in ensuring that the internship is not a part-time or summer job, but rather, an opportunity for students to gain valuable experience in a field while simultaneously taking a required course or seminar.

The academic credit for the internship is for learning, not just for doing (Batra 2001; Kent and Swift 2000). According to US law and as discussed by David Yamada in this volume, the primary point of a college internship is not lining up a first job, but rather, furthering the student's higher education (US Department of Labor 2010).[2] The IS can be instrumental in making sure genuine learning happens.

In fact, effective internship supervisors see themselves as educators and can fulfill this role best when college-run internship programs are well-run and empower the motivated IS with proper guidance. Our previous research on internship supervisors finds that they are serious educators and important assessors.[3] As an experienced IS noted: "I absolutely feel as an internship supervisor that I am an educator. I teach interns the system, how to do their job effectively. I give constructive criticism during their internship. And I hope that I teach that what you learn in class is not always applied the way you expect in the real world. I teach students not just the skills they need to do this job, but skills that will help them in any position they might have in the future."[4] In a strong partnership with the faculty advisor and credit-granting academic institutions, internship supervisors will continue to be excellent and memorable educators of students and important assessors of their internship work.

Faculty Advisors

Faculty advisors have been recognized as playing a complementary role in ensuring students are learning from their internships. Moore (2013) uses an analogy to make a critical point about the importance of faculty guidance during an internship, explaining that a literature professor would not assign a novel to students without sharing some literary theory, critical methods, as well as historical context. In other words, the professor must give students tools to study fiction effectively. Similarly, faculty advisors for an internship are responsible for sharing the appropriate tools for effectively learning from the internship experience: the students should be taught to examine, to analyze, and to critique the experience (Moore 2013). Simply reading a novel or holding down an internship can be accomplished without faculty providing the tools mentioned here. Yet, having a nuanced understanding of a novel or an internship and obtaining academic credit for developing such an understanding are quite different. Numerous studies have shown that, done correctly, experiential learning during an internship "leads to deeper, more nuanced understanding of [the] subject matter" (Eyler 2009, 27).

In fact, the faculty advisor is the lead stakeholder or quarterback for the internship 360-degree review, the internship experiential learning, and grade decision-making. Cantor (1995) defines experiential learning as "activities that engage the learner directly in the phenomena being studied" (1995, 1). As we have previously explained, experiential learning takes place in the world outside the classroom with a practitioner's guidance and an educator's oversight (Lowenthal and Sosland 2007). Fundamentally, experiential learning is an extension of classroom studies for which the student receives credit and it is the professor who has the final say on whether a student should receive that academic credit. To emphasize the academic nature of experiential learning and the central role for the faculty advisor, Whitaker (1989) lists five academic standards for ensuring quality assurance when awarding credit for experiential learning:

1. Credit should be awarded only for learning, and not for experience.
2. College credit should be awarded only for college-level learning.
3. Credit should be awarded only for learning that has a balance, appropriate to the subject, between theory and practical application.
4. The determination of competence levels and credit awards must be made by appropriate subject matter and academic experts.
5. Credit should be appropriate to the academic context in which it is accepted. (Whitaker 1989, xvii)

Internship learning is not an ad hoc process. Effective experiential learning requires the educator to create an infrastructure that relates the internship to the course topics (Sosland and Lowenthal 2017). The faculty advisor assigns analytical assignments designed to enhance students' internship experience and to provide the framework within which to reflect, conceptualize, analyze, test, and apply ideas encountered outside the classroom. This educational infrastructure includes a faculty member providing thoughtful instruction, oversight, and evaluation for academic credit. The faculty member should establish clear learning objectives, which are spelled out in a syllabus or in an individualized study contract. Kent and Swift (2000) contend that "the key ingredient to internship success is effective faculty supervision" (36). Throughout the course of the semester, the faculty advisor should make certain the student is capable of performing at least a minimum of repetitive, clerical, or secretarial tasks (Batra 2001); ultimately, however, the full experience should be credit-worthy.

Even when the interns' duties are well defined and subject to evaluation, without help from faculty mentors and internship supervisors, students may not recognize the connection between the work they do in the internship and their academic work. For faculty, internships add value to their teaching when theories presented in class are connected to the interns' work environment. Cook, Parker, and Pettijohn argue that there is "general agreement that the internship experience help[s] students relate academic theories learned in the classroom to work-place experiences" (2004, 184). This connection is forged when students reflect on whether material covered in class or through individualized study relates to their internship responsibilities. Specifically, faculty may ask what theories individual interns are acting upon while performing daily tasks at their worksites. Alm recommends that students keep journals and question the "differences between what I [the intern] observed in the field and what I learned in class" (1996, 114). Keeping a journal helps students to reflect on their experiences and to make explicit connections between these two realms.

For effective 360-degree assessment, faculty should include varied assignments that provide opportunities for students to demonstrate what they have learned in their internships and faculty should elicit feedback from the internship supervisor and others at the internship site when possible. (We elaborate on potential assignments in the recommendations section of this chapter.) Faculty assessment of all internship course requirements remains a central part of the internship assessment process.

Aside from a faculty member's course-related responsibilities, there is also value in student assessments of faculty and the internship class in final course evaluations. In addition to standard prompts, internship course faculty should request that specific internship-related questions be asked by their institutions. This feedback should enable faculty to learn from students' insights and experiences and to adjust course content, such as by improving assignments and activities so that an internship course and the internship are coordinated and integrated experiential learning experiences (Beard 2007). Sample questions that could elicit this information include some of the following (posed with a standard agree-disagree Likert scale):

Questionnaire items relating to the value of the internship to the class:
The internship experiential learning is interesting and stimulating.
The internship experiential learning encourages students to think.
The opportunity for group discussion of internships is valuable.

Questionnaire items relating to self-assessment:
I gained a better understanding of myself through this class.
I increased my awareness of my own interests and skills.
I developed confidence in myself.

Questionnaire items relating to professional skills and attitudes
I developed the specialized skills needed by professionals in this field.
I learned about career opportunities.
I developed a clearer sense of professional identity.[5]

Student Intern

Researchers have identified a variety of problems and solutions related to student interns. Some problems result from poor planning by the institution or inadequacies in administering the internship course; some are due to the interns themselves and their failures; and others may result from the internship supervisor.

Hite and Bellizzi (1986) suggest that internship programs need to be well planned and executed or students will have a negative experience. They note three key reasons for a suboptimal experience: unclear standards, misunderstandings or misrepresentation regarding the merits of the job, and misinformation by the organization regarding the duties required. For example, misunderstandings arise when a student fails to fully research an organization or to ask critical questions during the internship interview process, thus failing to ascertain if there is a good *fit* between the organization's expectations and the student's skills and preferences. In addition, the university may plan and administer internships poorly, and the programs may be misunderstood by the organizations involved. This is the case where the organization wrongly regards interns as a free source of labor for clerical tasks and ignores the experiential learning objectives, as dramatized in Hollywood movies, popular magazine articles, and notable court cases that focus on abused or exploited interns (Hlavac and Easterly 2013; Scheiber 2015). In such cases, students can spend an entire semester engaged in menial tasks unrelated to their academic studies, such as answering the phone, filing, or doing a single repetitive task. Such an arrangement clearly does not warrant academic credit. Other common problems that plague a poorly organized internship effort include too many interns and insufficient work for each individual, inadequate workspace, an IS who is routinely out of the office or busy with other responsibilities, organizations that fail to prioritize assigning tasks to interns, and work that is unrelated to the intern's academic studies. Ultimately, poor planning can result in an unfortunate combination of boredom and frustration for the student.

Internships also fail because students lack specific skills expected of them by their IS. Without these skills, it is difficult if not impossible for IS's to fulfill their educational responsibilities. In fact, some potential interns "are not adept at speaking or writing" (Hartman et al. 2005, 348). Generally, according to Hartman et al. (2005), employers seek interns who understand the organization's mission and possess strong interpersonal skills, motivation, initiative, a strong work ethic, and an appreciation for teamwork. Employers complain that, unfortunately, many students lack one or more of these valuable skills. Moreover, some potential interns have fundamental problems that frustrate the IS, including those who lack maturity or are ignorant of workplace etiquette. Overall, many undergraduates and "new graduates have unrealistic expectations of the professional world" (Hartman et al. 2005, 348; Waters and Gilstrap 2012); they simply do not know how to survive, much less thrive, in an office environment. There are several ways these pitfalls can be addressed.

One approach is to incorporate student self-assessment from the outset. Prior to commencing their internship search, and with the help of faculty, students need to ask themselves some basic questions about their skill set, their strengths and weaknesses (in particular as they relate to their "career readiness"), and their goals for the internship. Students should also be challenged to think about big questions, including, "How do I find a job that I like or maybe even love?" "How do I balance my career with my family?" "How can I make a difference in the world?" and, "What do I want to grow into?" (Burnett and Evans 2016). By continuing self-assessment during the semester, students can gain clarity about what they want from an internship and they are better positioned to be successful in their search—and ultimately in their internship course and career. (A list of self-assessment questions can be found in the Supplemental Internship Resources.)[6]

Because professional skill development is pivotal for student success, it is also up to the faculty advisor and internship supervisor to help develop "career readiness" skills, such as effective critical thinking/problem solving, oral communication, written communication, teamwork/collaboration, digital technology, leadership, professionalism/work ethic, career management and global/intercultural fluency (NACE 2019).[7] This could occur through mentorship (see Chapter 6 by Berg) or an internship class (see Chapter 5 by Simpson, Braam, and Winston).

Furthermore, the National Association of Colleges and Employers (NACE) recommends specific best practices for large and small organizations to promote coordination, mentoring, and in-house training during the internship. According to NACE's compendium of best practices (2020), internship work should be related to an intern's major, be challenging, and be recognized as valuable to the organization. The IS or the host organization should hold an orientation for interns so that, from the start, everyone is on the same page. Interns should receive a source (handbook or website) for answering frequently asked questions and delineating organizational rules. Ideally, an organization should have one person handling all matters relating to the organization's internship program, even if interns are supervised by a number of different persons in the organization. The host organization should offer in-house training for skills, which will benefit both the intern and the organization. Similarly, the organization should organize guest speakers and events that expose interns to the organizational culture. Finally, NACE indicates that an exit interview should be conducted to provide feedback from the student to the IS and vice versa (an assessment of the intern). Together, these best practices contribute to what NACE characterizes as a "premier internship program" (2020, 1).

The recommended practice of sharing feedback and evaluation is central to a student's internship experience; however, these practices are not always followed. In one of the few studies of internship supervisors, Waters and Gilstrap (2012) focused on internship performance reviews, finding that when an IS provides "periodic and constructive feedback to interns," the IS feedback has an important and positive impact on the intern's learning experience (Waters and Gilstrap 2012, 27; also see: Sosland and Lowenthal 2017). Even so, they found that few internship supervisors held one-on-one meetings with students. They also noted that the intern's academic institution often mandates that the IS complete a written assessment, yet their research found that the IS rarely reviews this valuable feedback with the student. Not surprisingly, interns want this one-on-one feedback from their IS (Rothman 2007).

Simply improving the assessment and feedback process, a duty that is central to the role of an effective internship supervisor, would improve the experience measurably for students. As explored elsewhere in this book, another way to improve communication is through the use of a college-provided contract to spell out duties and expectations on both sides. This tool effectively limits the abuse of free labor and formalizes the assessment process. When the intern, IS, and faculty advisor agree on a plan for the internship, they take an important step in establishing a 360-degree feedback strategy. Not only are expectations set, but also lines of communication are opened to ensure a clear pathway for assessment.

RECOMMENDATIONS

The recommendations we share below are based not only on our experience with internships, but also on a focus group and follow-up conversations with other faculty advisors. Collectively, the faculty have taught thousands of student interns over decades and across academic fields and subfields.[8] Figure 2 illustrates the recommendations for assessment over the course of the semester, and figure 3 includes additional details about assessment undertaken by the stakeholders.

Assessment Resources Promoting Internship Preparation

First, faculty advisors must help students with the internship search and other pre-internship preparations, including student self-assessment. The faculty advisor should assure a good fit between students' skills and professional desires on the one hand, and the needs and capabilities of the IS and the orga-

Figure 2: 360-Degree Assessment Process

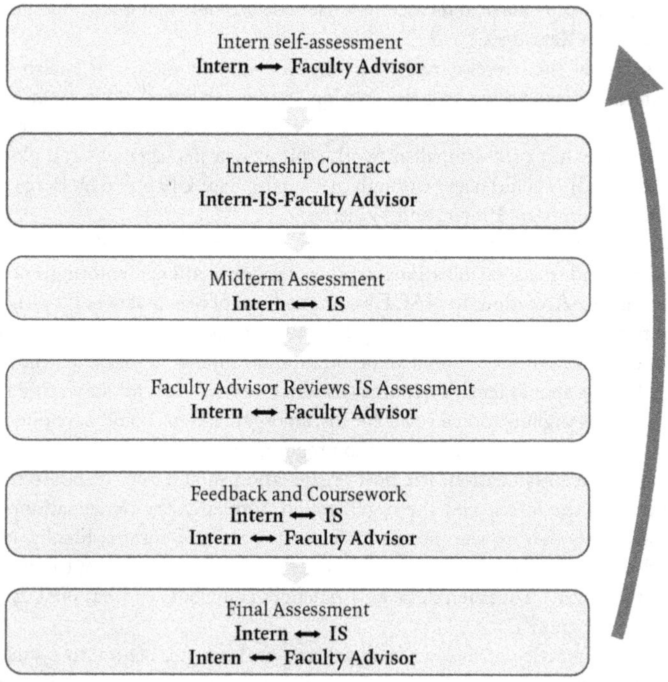

nization on the other. In actively assisting students during their search, faculty should coach them on effective cover letters and résumés, as well as aid in identifying the types of organizations or firms to which they should apply. For all of the above to be effective, this process incorporates guiding students through self-reflection assessment to determine who they are and what their aspirations are, including insights into individual strengths and weaknesses, specifically those relating to skills.

Internship database. The educational institution should make available to students a database of internship opportunities that includes a brief description of personal responsibilities at each organization and previous interns' evaluations. The internship search in itself can be an excellent learning opportunity and the skills it helps develop will be useful throughout a student's professional career. One insight that emerged from the focus group was that a faculty advisor, using class discussion and assignments, must motivate students to reflect carefully upon their internship and career goals, passions, and priorities. Students should be motivated to ask themselves: "What do I want from my internship experience?"

Focused search for a placement. To answer this question and to prepare for job interviews, students should carefully do their homework in connection with the search. They must uncover as much information as possible about the organization. Faculty ought to push students to look up the organization's website, annual reports, previous interns' assessments, and other materials using databases available through the university. The faculty advisor should emphasize that the intern is interviewing the organization as much if not more than the reverse.

Preparing students to work in professional settings. Both the faculty advisor and the internship supervisor should do more to prepare interns for the professional and social expectations they will face during the internship. The interview is a critical opportunity for the intern to gather information about the prospective employer's expectations. The IS ought to address duties and the scope of the work, the number of other interns who will also be working in the office, and what a typical day would likely involve. The intern should be prepared to answer questions such as, "Do you have the skills and background required for this internship and will you fit into the organization's culture?" More specifically, interns should be prepared to answer the following standard interview question: "Tell me about yourself and why should I hire you?"

The faculty advisor should also brief students on key skills and workplace norms in order to increase their odds of success. Before the internship begins, the faculty advisor should explain professional conduct (see also Chapter 5): be reliable, punctual, and courteous; wear proper office attire; take initiative; be attentive to detail; and always behave as a team player. As noted earlier, students must possess the prerequisite skills and knowledge so that the IS can spend the time and energy to teach other important workplace skills, such as professionalism and teamwork/collaboration. Faculty advisors and internship supervisors know what is expected of interns and should share that knowledge in a strategic way to increase the opportunities for success. Again, without an honest and thorough self-assessment, this part of the process is less likely to be either educationally or professionally successful.

Transparency and the Internship Contract

Second, the contract will also serve as a basis for the performance assessment the IS will complete in the middle and at the end of the term. To clarify expectations by all stakeholders and to minimize future misunderstandings, the college internship program should require the intern, internship supervisor, and faculty advisor to sign an internship contract (see samples in the Supplemental Internship Resources section). As described above, so that everyone has the same understanding and expectations about what will take place during the semester, students should have a detailed discussion with the IS concerning their duties before signing the contract. The discussion and contract will help all sides avoid misunderstandings and disappointment later in the term. As our focus group participants discussed, the IS—not the student or professor—should be the one who writes up the responsibilities in the internship contract. The internship contract should specify that a majority of an intern's time on the job must be devoted to substantive activity that relates to their college coursework. In addition, the contract must clearly state the days of the week and the total number of hours per week the student will spend at the internship. The IS must understand that the student has other academic obligations to fulfill and that the internship is (generally) only part-time. Unless the expectations of the internship are clearly spelled out in the internship contract, it is not possible to do a fair and complete assessment of the intern or the internship organization.[9]

Connecting Classroom Theory to Internship Practice

Third, a partnership between the IS and faculty advisor will facilitate connections between theory and practice. The IS should be encouraged (before taking on interns) to plan for training and setting up interns to succeed. Ideally, the training would include an orientation for all interns in the organization, an official handbook of rules, and information about professional development training resources that are available. This point was strongly agreed to among faculty advisors, but it was understood that smaller organizations might be limited in their capacity to implement all elements recommended by NACE. If the organization is too small to follow all best practices, then the faculty advisor will need to fill the void when it comes to job preparation. On site, the IS should also develop assignments for the intern that provide mutual benefits to the organization and to the intern. During the internship, the faculty advisor should act as a liaison between the student and the IS, when necessary. Being in contact with both the student and the IS, the faculty advisor is in a strong position to troubleshoot before problems become irreconcilable. The focus group discussed the value of site visits by the faculty advisor, especially for first-time internship organizations or supervisors. The faculty advisor should make course material, such as the syllabus, available to the IS to better understand what the intern is covering in class and in the intern's major and to assist the IS in connecting the internship experience to the classroom work. Ultimately, the IS's assessment of the intern should help the faculty advisor determine the student's grade.

Formal Assessments and Informal Check-ins

Formal assessments are essential not only at the end of the internship, but also midway through the semester. The IS should complete a written assessment and the intern should have an opportunity to discuss the assessment with the IS and (separately) with the faculty advisor. As faculty we know the value of receiving constructive feedback and responding in a professional environment. That is exactly the type of skill we hope students will develop in an internship. When students have the opportunity to respond to midterm feedback, we have found improvement in specific skills and overall performance (Lowenthal and Morrill Bijeau 2016). NACE offers sample assessment forms for the internship supervisor to use when evaluating the student.[10]

Beyond the formal assessments, we recommend that faculty check in with Internship Supervisors, ideally in the first half of the term. Sometimes the IS may wish to avoid putting certain concerns in writing or may not have time to write up complete assessments for outstanding interns. An email, phone call, or virtual check-in allows the IS and the faculty advisor to connect and share feedback about specific students as well as the broader internship experience. Regular communication between the IS and the faculty advisor effectively closes one part of the loop in the 360-degree feedback pathways introduced in figure 1.

Finally, the student should have the opportunity to assess the internship (IS and organization) as well as the faculty advisor/course to close the remaining spaces in the 360-degree feedback loop. Students can provide valuable information to the IS and internship site about their experience. They can share details about successful and unsuccessful aspects of the internship; when possible, internship organizations may revise their plans for future interns based on such feedback. Students can also share valuable feedback with the faculty advisor. Students might share details about the course, the instructor, and the assignments (in course evaluations). They might also offer information about their experience with the internship supervisor and the organization. This information is useful to the faculty advisor who can use it to reshape an internship course or recommend (or not recommend) to students with similar interests.

Fortunately, technology can make the assessment process more efficient and less cumbersome. We have used Symplicity and many others use Handshake, but additional options are available. Regardless of brand, the technology allows for collaboration on the internship contract (by the intern, IS, and faculty advisor), standardized assessments at set points during the term, automated communication (such as reminders) about assessments, a single system tracking all of the information, and the option to analyze the internship data. In addition, the system is paperless and environmentally friendly.

Figure 3: 360-Degree Assessment Checklist

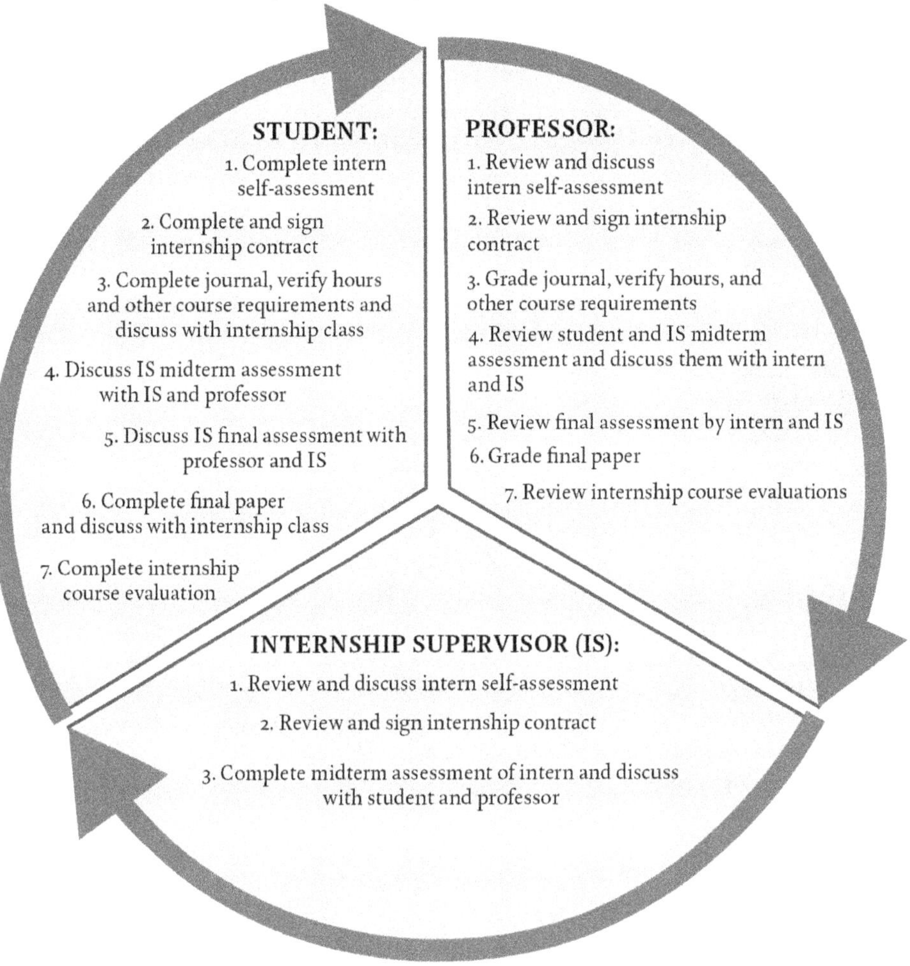

STUDENT:
1. Complete intern self-assessment
2. Complete and sign internship contract
3. Complete journal, verify hours and other course requirements and discuss with internship class
4. Discuss IS midterm assessment with IS and professor
5. Discuss IS final assessment with professor and IS
6. Complete final paper and discuss with internship class
7. Complete internship course evaluation
PROFESSOR:
1. Review and discuss intern self-assessment
2. Review and sign internship contract
3. Grade journal, verify hours, and other course requirements
4. Review student and IS midterm assessment and discuss them with intern and IS
5. Review final assessment by intern and IS
6. Grade final paper
7. Review internship course evaluations
INTERNSHIP SUPERVISOR (IS):
1. Review and discuss intern self-assessment
2. Review and sign internship contract
3. Complete midterm assessment of intern and discuss with student and professor

CONCLUSION

After two decades, 360-degree feedback in the workplace has been found to be valuable for employees and employers. While studies indicate that significant changes in behavior can occur as a result of well-implemented 360-degree assessments, others caution that such assessments can backfire if not implemented well (Edleson 2012). Internships are an ideal vehicle for providing more comprehensive and multi-sourced feedback because students are in internships to learn more about the positions and organizations where they are interning. Taking advantage of the opportunity to obtain varied and meaningful feedback from the internship site and the faculty advisor should enhance the overall learning experience.

REFERENCES

Alm, Cynthia. 1996. "Using Student Journals to Improve the Academic Quality of Internships." *Journal of Education for Business* 72 (2): 113–115.

Batra, Madan. 2001. "Faculty Supervision of Internships." *Journal of the Academy of Business Education* 2 (1): 12–22.

Beard, Deborah F. 2007. "Assessment of Internship Experiences and Accounting Core Competencies." *Accounting Education* 16 (2): 207–20. Available at: https://doi.org/10.1080/09639280701234625.

Bracken, David W., Dale S. Rose, and Allan H. Church. 2016. "The Evolution and Devolution of 360° Feedback." *Industrial and Organizational Psychology* 9 (4): 761–794.

Burnett, William, and David J. Evans. 2020 (2016). *Designing Your Work Life: How to Thrive and Change and Find Happiness at Work.* New York: Alfred A. Knopf.

Cantor, Jeffrey. 1995. *Experiential Learning in Higher Education: Linking Classroom and Community, ASHE-ERIC Higher Education Report No. 7.* Washington, DC: Association for the Study of Higher Education (ASHE).

Cook, Sherry, R. Stephen Parker, and Charles E. Pettijohn. 2004. "The Perceptions of Interns: A Longitudinal Case Study." *Journal of Education for Business* 79 (3): 179–185.

DiLoreto, Melanie A., Christie Pellow, and David L. Stout. 2017. "Exploration of Conceptions of Assessment in High-Stakes US Culture." *International Journal of Learning, Teaching and Educational Research* 16 (7): 1–9.

Edleson, Harriet. 2012. "Do 360 Evaluations Work? Yes, But Too Often They Aren't Administered or Followed Up Properly. Here's How to Boost Their Value." *Monitor in Psychology* 43 (10): 58.

Edwards, Mark R., and Ann J. Ewen. 1996. *360 Degree Feedback: The Powerful New Model for Employee Assessment & Performance Improvement.* New York: Amacom.

Ernest, Paul. 1998. "A Postmodern Perspective on Research in Mathematics Education." In *Mathematics Education as a Research Domain: A Search for Identity*, eds. Anna Sierpinska and Jeremy Kilpatrick (71–85). New York, NY: Springer Science & Business Media.

Eyler, Janet. 2009. "The Power of Experiential Education." *Liberal Education* 95 (4): 24–31.

Gaston, Paul L. 2018. *Assessment and Accreditation: An Imperiled Symbiosis. Occasional Paper No. 33.* Urbana, IL: University of Illinois and Indiana University, National Institute for Learning Outcomes Assessment (NILOA).

Hartman, Diane, Jan Bentley, Kathleen Richards, and Cynthia Krebs. 2005. "Administrative Tasks and Skills Needed for Today's Office: The Employees' Perspective." *Journal of Education for Business* 80 (6): 347–357.

Hite, Robert, and Joseph Bellizzi. 1986. "Student Expectations Regarding Collegiate Internship Programs in Marketing." *Journal of Marketing Education* 8 (3): 41–49.

Hlavac, George, and Edward Easterly. 2013. "Considerations Surrounding Internships." *NACE Journal* 74 (2): 6–12.

Kent, Russell, and Cathy Owens Swift. 2000. "Business School Internships: An Update." *Journal of Business Education* 1 (1): 31–43.

Lei, Simon, and Dean Yin. 2019. "Evaluating Benefits and Drawbacks of Internships: Perspectives of College Students." *College Student Journal* 53: 181–189.

Lowenthal, Diane, and Amy Morrill Bijeau. 2016. "Interning and Learning: Evaluations for Experiential Education." *Pennsylvania Drive-In for Internships*. Hershey, PA.

Lowenthal, Diane, and Jeffrey Sosland. 2007. "Making the Grade: How a Semester in Washington May Influence Future Academic Performance." *Journal of Political Science Education* 3 (2): 143–160.

Moore, David Thornton. 2013. "For Interns, Experience Isn't Always the Best Teacher." *Chronicle of Higher Education* 60 (12): A28–A30.

National Association of Colleges and Employers (NACE). 17 June 2020. "15 Best Practices for Internship Programs." Available at: http://www.naceweb.org/internships/15-best-practices.aspx.

National Association of Colleges and Employers (NACE). 9 June 2019. "Career Readiness for the New College Graduate, A Definition and Competencies." Available at: https://www.naceweb.org/uploadedfiles/pages/knowledge/articles/career-readiness-fact-sheet-jan-2019.pdf.

Rothman, Miriam. 2007. "Lessons Learned: Advice to Employers from Interns." *Journal of Education for Business* 82 (3): 140–144.

Scheiber, Noam. 2015. "Employers Have Greater Leeway on Unpaid Internships, Court Rules." *The New York Times*, July 2. Available at: https://www.nytimes.com/2015/07/03/business/unpaid-internships-allowed-if-they-serve-educational-purpose-court-rules.html?searchResultPosition=1.

Sheehan, Kim Bartel. 2001. "E-Mail Survey Response Rates: A Review." *Journal of Computer-Mediated Communication* 6(2). doi: 10.1111/j.1083-6101.2001.tb00117.x.

Sosland, Jeffrey K., and Diane J. Lowenthal. 2017. "The Forgotten Educator: Experiential Learning's Internship Supervisor." *Journal of Political Science Education* 13 (1): 1–14. Available at: https://doi.org/10.1080/15512169.2016.1165106.

True, Michael. 2013. *InternQube: Professional Skills for the Workplace.* Mechanicsburg, PA: Intrueition, LLC.

US Department of Labor. 2018 (2010). "Fact Sheet #71: Internship Programs Under The Fair Labor Standards Act." Available at: http://www.dol.gov/whd/regs/compliance/whdfs71.pdf.

Waters, Regina, and Christina Gilstrap. 2012. "Intern Performance Reviews: The Supervisor's Perspective." *NACE Journal* 72 (4): 27–31.

Whitaker, Urban. 1989. *Assessing Learning: Standards, Principles and Procedures.* Philadelphia: Council for Adult Experiential Learning.

ENDNOTES

1. Figure 1 serves as a foundation on which we build a more comprehensive approach to assessment (depicted in figure 3). This schematic represents our original work, and we became aware of a similar figure in Lei and Yin (2019) after we developed it.

2. Refer to the supplemental resource, Rules for Interns, for a list of criteria (FLSA fact sheet updated 2018).

3. Elements of this chapter were presented at the American Political Science Association's Annual Meeting, August 30, 2014, Washington, DC. A year later, the coauthors were awarded the APSA Political Science Education Section's "Best Presentation Award in 2014" for this work. In 2016 parts of this research were published in the *Journal of Political Science Education* in the article, "The Forgotten Educator: Experiential Learning's Internship Supervisor." The authors were recognized for this article with the "2019 National Society for Experiential Education (NSEE) Award of Excellence in Outstanding Experiential Education Research." With permission from Taylor & Francis, this chapter contains material borrowed from Sosland and Lowenthal (2016).

4. This quote comes from our 2009 pilot study.

5. American University, "Student Evaluation of Teaching (SET); Bank of Questionnaire Items," June 18, 2020, https://www.american.edu/provost/oira/set/qbank.cfm.

6. See supplemental materials for self-assessment worksheets, or Burnett and Evans (2020).

7. NACE offers sample assessment forms that include many career readiness skills. NACE Internship performance Assessments (midterm and final). See: https://www.naceweb.org/uploadedfiles/files/2017/career-readiness-resources/nace-cr-resources-intern-evaluations.pdf.

8. Eleven faculty advisors participated in the focus group on December 12, 2014. The participants had extensive experience in the internship realm, averaging over 10 years of experience each; several had more than 25 years of experience.

9. For sample internship contract, see Sosland and Lowenthal (2017) and see supplemental resources.

10. NACE, "Intern Performance Evaluation Template" (Courtesy of Career and Internship Center, University of Washington): https://www.naceweb.org/uploadedfiles/files/2019/career-readiness-resources/nace-cr-resource-university-of-washington.pdf.

CHAPTER 9

Community Colleges and Internships in Political Science: Challenges and Opportunities

Christina Sciabarra, Bellevue College

Bobbi Gentry, Bridgewater College

This chapter reviews opportunities and challenges associated with community college student internships and outlines steps for building and maintaining internship opportunities. Using data from a national survey of internship practices in US colleges and universities, we examine how students are served by internships and identify the kinds of resources that are needed to support community college student internships compared to four-year programs. Finally, we offer practical advice and recommendations for establishing and expanding internship opportunities on a community college campus.

INTRODUCTION

Because interns are able to explore careers and build professional skills while they support the work of organizations and elected officials, experiential learning should happen early and often throughout a student's academic career.[1] Internship opportunities can benefit all types of students in higher education, including those who attend community college. Community college students are often older and more diverse collectively compared to students enrolled at four-year institutions[2]; they tend to have heavier family or work responsibilities outside their academic studies but also are able to bring a wider range of experiences and perspectives to bear on the work they perform in internships. Given the student population and the distinctiveness of their goals, which typically include either earning a terminal two-year degree, career-oriented certificate, or transferring to a four-year institution,[3] running an internship program at community colleges involves unique challenges.

The purpose of this chapter is to consider the opportunities and challenges associated with political science internships on a community college campus. In the first part we address the potential benefits of developing opportunities for community college students. To contextualize our recommendations, which appear in the final section, we also present data from a 2017 national survey of faculty at community colleges about their experiences with political science internships—data that provide concrete knowledge about the variety of experiences across the US. We end with a set of practical recommendations for establishing and expanding internship opportunities at community colleges.

ENGAGING STUDENTS AND CREATING OPPORTUNITIES

A common myth regarding community college students is that they are somehow less motivated or capable than students who complete introductory level courses at four-year colleges and universities. Students select community college for a number of reasons including lower tuition, class sizes, open admissions, and flexible schedules (Chen 2021a), and 31.5% of students who begin at community college transfer to four-year institutions within six years (Barshay 2020; Shapiro et al. 2017). According to Shapiro et al. (2017), lower-income students represent a significant portion of the community college population (42%), and they transfer to four-year institutions at much lower rates than students with higher incomes (25.9% and 39.9% respectively; 2017, 23). Although there is more work to be done to retain all students and to ease their transfer into four-year institutions, community college students studying political science can be regarded as potential political science majors who will complete bachelor's and graduate degrees and actively engage in the political world.

WHAT COMMUNITY COLLEGE STUDENTS BRING TO INTERNSHIPS

A Wealth of Experience

The average age of a community college student is 28, which implies that they have more life experiences than the traditional age college student.[4] Many have worked in professional settings before enrolling in college and many of the skills they have developed should serve them well in political science internships. Many students have had their own small businesses, worked in sales, or are simply long-time workforce participants who know how to work on a team, complete administrative tasks, communicate efficiently, and behave with professionalism. They can join an office and immediately start conversing with constituents, writing correspondence, tracking data, or helping with organizational tasks, and their roles can expand quickly as they learn more context-specific information. Students can bring perspectives that may be missing from an organization's staff or help reach communities whose input is needed in order to meet the mission, vision, and project goals of an organization.

Diverse Perspectives

Diversity is often viewed as a defining feature of community colleges as they are often more ethnically and racially varied than four-year universities.[5] At the same time, there is little doubt that a workforce that includes people of diverse backgrounds, meaning more Black, Indigenous, and People of Color, LGBTQ+, disabled, and women students, is needed. Community college students are generally well-positioned for joining the public affairs career pipeline. In addition, given the general lack of diversity in the field of political science (Davis, McGrath, and Super 2019; Mershon and Walsh 2016), inviting students into professional settings early in their educational journeys increases the likelihood those students will continue studying and also major in political science. Community colleges provide fertile ground for recruiting and mentoring students early on in their post-secondary education and ensuring greater diversity of scholarship in the discipline (Chen 2021b).

BENEFITS FOR STUDENTS

Academic Gains

Kuh (2008) emphasizes in his work that certain kinds of academic activities, termed "high impact practices" (HIPs), have a significant impact on students of all types by creating opportunities for deep learning, which in turn helps them stay and complete their degrees. Internships are among the HIPs that are strongly associated with self-reported academic gains, higher grade point averages, and retention rates (Finley and McNair 2013).[6] More powerfully, research has shown that HIPs have a pronounced effect on historically underserved students in identified groups: African American, Latinx, and students with relatively low ACT scores (2013, vi). High-quality internships have the potential to help boost students' academic achievement while simultaneously preparing them for the workforce.

Career Exploration

Many students enroll in community colleges to explore subjects and figure out what they want to do (Freedman 2015).[7] Those who have been in the workforce may have not considered work in politics, policy, or public administration, and political science classes offer an opportunity to explore these aspects of public affairs. If coursework is coupled with an internship allowing students to see what it really means to work on a campaign, support constituent services for an elected official, provide administrative support for a municipal organization, or run social media for a non-profit focused on food security, for example, they can connect their academic learning with building practical skills and better envision a career path.

Résumé Building

Community college students often fall into two general groups: traditional and non-traditional, each with unique perspectives that are reflected in their educational paths and résumés.[8] Traditional first-year students, those moving directly from high school to college, have résumés that are often limited or lacking in professional skills and are peppered with volunteer work, minimum wage employment, and student group leadership. While these experiences often help build important strengths and skills, their competencies can obscured by the types of work that are often viewed as low-level and also unrelated to political science. Non-traditional students (characterized by part-time enrollment, working full-time, identifying as a single caregiver, not having a traditional high school diploma, or financial independence; see Carter 2016) who are employed often have a wealth of skills, but no experience in political science-related fields. Both types of students can benefit from internships, especially those which incorporate undergraduate research. Work in the field helps build interest in transferring to a four-year institution and, eventually, pursuing graduate school or professional positions related to their major.

Skill Building

Although many community college students possess professional skills, these may not be related to their professional goals and/or their major in political science. For example, a number of military veterans who want to study international politics struggle to convert their military experience into civilian skills. Working for a non-profit organization or on a political campaign is often very different from anything students have done before, and talking to and working with constituents, following federal guidelines, and managing social media are valuable skills they can apply in a variety of work settings, especially those in public affairs. Internships represent an opportunity for students to begin building or polishing a set of professional skills that will ultimately result in their selection for more internships and opportunities as students, and post-graduation employment.

Pre-Professional Development: Creating a Professional Network

Community college students bring varying types of interpersonal networks with them to college and their political science courses (Radford, Cominole, and Skomsvold 2015). Traditional students and high school students are connected to youthful segments of the local community and can quickly tap into a large group of people who are generally under 21. Non-traditional students may have similar connections, but depending on their age, tend to have a denser network of local businesses, civic organizations, and members of the community who are over the age of 21. Internships help students create and expand their networks to include potential referees and writers of letters of recommendation, mentors to practice informational interviews with, and contacts who can connect them with other professionals in the field.

Confidence Building

Students sometimes struggle to acknowledge that they are at a community college and feel as if they are not deserving of opportunities because they are not at a four-year university. This stigma can cause students to doubt their abilities, see themselves as "less than" their peers at four-year schools, and develop unproductive attitudes that can result in their dropping out of college (Holden et al. 2021). Internships signal to students that they are deserving; and in the process of building skills, growing their résumés, and developing their professional networks, students can build confidence and the realization that they are capable of success both in and out of the classroom.

CREATING INTERNSHIP OPPORTUNITIES FOR STUDENTS

Many community colleges lack the resources needed to help students create internship opportunities and many campuses employ a single person to provide career services for the entire college. Keeping in mind the limited resources and personnel on community college campuses, the following section offers guidance for faculty and administrators seeking to create opportunities for students.

Finding Partners and Opportunities

Elected Officials and Government Offices. Fortunately, elected officials and most government offices offer formal internship opportunities. Faculty members can also work with governmental offices and their staff to reserve specific internship placements for political science-oriented students or find other ways for them to prioritize students from community colleges. One promising place to look for opportunities can be with newly elected officials as they need to build a program from scratch and often need help getting started.

Nonprofit Organizations. Nonprofit organizations range from large international establishments with multiple offices all over the world to small local offices with few staff members and limited funding. Larger organizations often maintain an established internship program with a clear process and hiring criteria. Many local nonprofits also support interns, and if they do not, may be willing to convert volunteer positions into internships that carry more responsibility. Sometimes these organizations provide the best opportunities for community college students to achieve both their learning and career-related goals because they need help to implement projects but often lack the human resources to do so.

The following suggestions are largely directed at how to create these opportunities for students. In the absence of a listing of potential internship providers, faculty can have students start looking for opportunities at sites (or through apps) such as Handshake, Idealist, Indeed, WayUp, Volunteermatch, Internships.com, and the local United Way.

Recruiting Organizations and Creating Opportunities

You can take the following steps to create internship opportunities for your political science students if no internship programs exist on your campus.

- Consider the courses you teach and the organizations working on issues related to your area. Conduct research and locate a few organizations doing interesting work that you think would benefit students by helping them build skills and connect with the course material.
- Do your research before contacting the organization. Be familiar with their mission and vision and have an idea of how your course(s) connect(s) with their mission. Try to develop a sense of how your students could support their work.
- Contact the organization and talk to the internship coordinator. If the organization doesn't have one, search for a volunteer coordinator or start with top leadership. We recommend emailing and calling as well as using LinkedIn as it sometimes takes a few tries to get connected if you are not a donor.

- Start with an invitation to meet. It's often helpful to invite someone from the organization to address your class as a guest speaker. This signals not only that you value their work but also that there is a connection to coursework. You should clarify what skills and knowledge students need in order to support the organization.
- Come to the meeting with a few ideas about ways your students might support or get engaged with the organization. You could start with a service-learning project idea and explore whether it could be expanded into a longer-term internship.
- Help the organization outline the responsibilities of the intern and what they will provide and commit to regarding the student.
- Clarify the importance of student learning goals, being sure to emphasize that applied learning is the key to a successful internship. Emphasize that students' individual learning goals should be outlined at the beginning of their internships, preferably in a learning contract (see Supplemental Internship Resources for samples).
- Check with your legal department or assigned legal counsel to see if any organizations or activities could be off-limits based on state limitations regarding political actions.

A number of new types of internships are emerging that allow students to work from home or permit flexible hours. Micro-internships are short projects or specific assignments that allow students to gain the positive elements from an internship in a shorter amount of time, which could increase access for more students. Virtual internships are also expanding due to the changing nature of work and remote collaboration, a change that accelerated as offices shifted to remote work because of the COVID pandemic (see Chapter 15 by Cabrera Rasmussen and Van Vechten). Making students aware of what's possible and encouraging students to seek them out and apply for them are important first steps.

Preparing and Supporting Students

You can recruit students even before developing specific placements by checking to see who might be interested in an internship and what they would be looking for in desired experiences. If you are unable to recruit students ahead of time, then making them aware of the opportunities you have negotiated will often bring out students who would like to participate. The following list describes key steps and activities for preparing students for the internship and supporting them during the experience.

- Ensure that the position's responsibilities are clear to the student and that they are ready to meet the organization's expectations and commit the time to doing so. If you aren't sure they are committed then wait to move forward, as a student who does not perform well could damage your relationship with the organization either temporarily or permanently.
- Direct the student to visit the campus career center to create a résumé or to have an existing one reviewed. Their résumé should cover the skills and knowledge you discussed with the organization.
- Ensure the student practices for the interview. Students are often unprepared to participate in professional interviews and need help preparing to talk though their résumé and share stories that illustrate their strengths and experience. Remind the student to research the organization and consider how it connects with what they have learned in classes as well as their professional goals.
- Check in with your Title IX office and let them know about the internship. See if there are any documents they should review or supply to the student, and make sure that students receive training about their rights and protections. Students are protected by Title IX while participating in academic programs and it is important to equip them with the knowledge of their rights and what to do if they experience bullying, harassment, or other forms of discrimination (see Chapter 3 by Yamada for a discussion of Title IX protections for interns as courts have interpreted them).

- Determine whether the internship positions you develop can be awarded with academic credit. Consult career center staff or your program chair. It is important to make sure that new positions can be created and that students receive academic credit when possible. Even if those credits are not likely to transfer to a four-year institution, their transcripted work may be of interest to future employers.
- Depending on the type of the internship, the organization may require I-9 verification. Typically, international students are eligible to participate in internships that are directly related to their degrees. Work with your international education office to ensure the internship meets all Curricular Practical Training requirements, as failure to do so could place students at risk of having their visas rescinded. If a student is volunteering for an organization and receiving academic internship credit, it is unlikely an I-9 would be required. You can also help students find internship opportunities in their home countries or with their consulates or embassies in the US. If this is the case, be sure to advertise widely and reach out to undocumented students as they can participate in this opportunity with reduced fear of persecution.
- Ask students to outline three to five learning objectives they plan to reach by the end of the internship; have them articulate these goals in a learning contract (see Chapter 5 by Simpson, Braam, and Winston to learn more about these documents, and Supplemental Internship Resources for sample documents) and share them with their employer. These goals can be knowledge or skills and they should be connected to specific tasks or plans for meeting them. Help the student craft measurable goals and have them think about both quantitative and qualitative ways to capture their experiences and how they are meeting their goals.
- Check in with students throughout the internship about their progress towards their goals and about what they are learning from the experience. (See Chapter 6 by Berg for more information about faculty mentor responsibilities.)

Whether students intend to end their formal education with an associate degree or transfer to a four-year institution, internships have clear academic and career-related benefits. As scholarly research has documented, internships can help students explore career paths they are interested in, build and practice skills, and reflect on their learning to make essential connections between theory and practice (Maertz, Stoeberl, and Marks 2014). They build students' confidence as well as their academic profiles and résumés. Community college students who seek a terminal degree can especially benefit from an internship experience that provides concrete connections to a career after college. Keeping in mind the many ways that internships offer community college students uncommon learning experiences, we now delve into a descriptive analysis of community college internships.

EVIDENCE FROM A SURVEY OF COMMUNITY COLLEGES[9]

Survey data collected in 2017 point to specific opportunities and challenges that community colleges face. First, the number of community college students that participate in internship opportunities is relatively low. In 54% of community colleges "only a few" students participate in political science internships, and just under one-third of programs (32%) do not offer internships for credit. With low internship participation rates like these, we suspect that there are significant opportunities to create and grow internship programs on community college campuses.

Another major challenge is that internships are under-resourced and not well-coordinated. Nearly half (45%) of community college faculty agree that more resources are needed to compensate faculty or staff who coordinate and oversee internships (n=22). One-third of programs offer no extra compensation for those who coordinate internships in their department (33%, n=16), and students do not receive advising about internships in about one out of three programs (31.3%, n=15). Over a third of internship programs are located outside of the political science department, but a designated person on campus actively assists students with internship placements (38.3%, n=18). A majority of community college faculty agreed with the statement that "there is little to no effort to coordinate internships on our cam-

Figure 1. Percentage of Students Who take Internships for Credit at Community Colleges

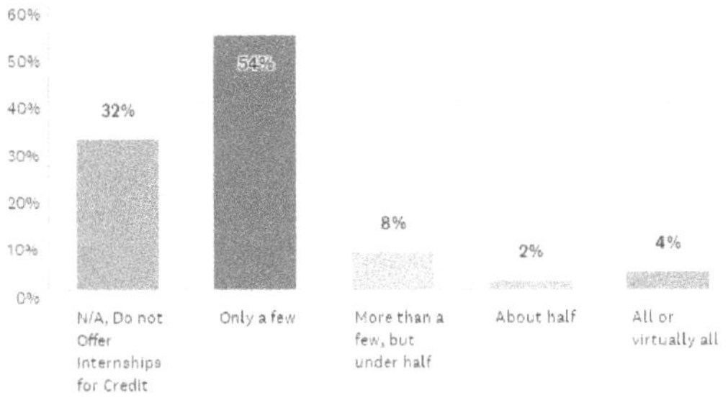

pus" (52%, n=26). These important structural dimensions would need to be addressed in order to create reliable opportunities for students with discipline-specific internship interests.

From a comparative perspective, more four-year faculty mention that students get help *finding* internships outside of the department (40.7%, n=48) than do community college faculty (29.2%, n=14). *Placement* for internships occurs outside of the department more frequently at community colleges (38.3%, n=18) than at four-year institutions (33.1%, n=36).

When asked about specific challenges faced by programs, the most common responses were: communication across campus (9.8%, n=4); finding internships for students (9.8%, n=4); lack of paid options for students (7.3%, n=3); lack of student interest (7.3%, n=3); and preparation of students for internships (7.3%, n=3).[10]

Community college faculty also shared their perspectives about the relative educational importance of internships. About half agreed that internships are "very important" for helping students prepare for the workforce (51.1%, n=24), for helping them become more informed citizens (44.7%, n=21), and for allowing them to identify their career preferences (51.1%, n=24). There is some disagreement about the value of internships in preparing students for study at four-year institutions with only 17.4% (8) saying that internships are very important, and 30.4% (14) saying that internships are somewhat important. Perhaps these low figures can be attributed to the fact that in about a quarter of cases (23.4%, n=11) students cannot transfer credit to a four-year institution, meaning that four-year institutions will not count internship credits earned at community colleges. On the other hand, over a third of faculty do not know if students can transfer credit for internships to four-year programs (40.4%, n=19).

BUILDING A COMMUNITY COLLEGE INTERNSHIP PROGRAM: RECOMMENDATIONS

Community colleges serve a wider segment of the general public than do four-year institutions and their primary commitments are education, training, and workforce development,[11] making them prime locations for the development of internships. Expanded political science internship opportunities would also allow community colleges to fulfill their general civic purpose of helping create a more informed citizenry and preparing students to be effective learners and leaders.[12] In light of the many benefits that internships can bring about, we offer a short list of recommendations that bring attention to key aspects of making internships work on community college campuses.

Recommendation 1: Coordinate across Campus. One of the main differences between community colleges and four-year institutions is that student advising is almost always done outside of the department at community colleges. Oftentimes the ones recommending courses to students are professional advisors, not professors in academic departments. This means that students who might want to do an internship for credit would need to know about opportunities and then need to inform their advisor about their interests. In other words, students' needs are best served when faculty, advisors, and internship coordinators collaborate to spread the word about internship opportunities and to build demand among students for experiential learning.

Recommendation 2: Secure More Institutional Resources. Resources are necessary to create a robust internship program at any institution, but this is especially the case at community colleges. Resources for community colleges could include compensation for a faculty member to run an internship program, for staff members to assist with program coordination, or for personnel to collect, maintain, and distribute information on available internship opportunities. We recommend pressuring administrators to make internships an educational priority by allocating resources for their support on every campus.

Recommendation 3: Seek or Create Paid Options for Students. For low-income students, those with caregiving obligations, working parents, and students in other precarious or demanding situations, an internship without pay is simply not feasible (Hora et al. 2019). Transportation also incurs direct costs and affects the accessibility of internship locations, not to mention the indirect costs associated with internships. Pay is essential for assuring access to experiential learning opportunities. In the case of unpaid positions, internship coordinators should consider asking internship providers to offer stipends to interns. Fundraising intended specifically for internships and experiential learning opportunities could also be organized. Donors to community colleges—including employers that host interns—could be sought out to offer institutional funding for career development.

Recommendation 4: Focus on Community Partnerships. Due to the nature of community college education, maintaining contact with former students and alumni can be difficult. Focus should therefore be on building and maintaining strong community partnerships rather than relying on alumni for connections as many four-year institutions do. Community colleges are well-placed to build partnerships due to their missions to support their community and to educate workers who will contribute to the US economy.[13] Consider potential partnerships with organizations whose work reflects the learning objectives of the discipline: civic engagement, political participation, and public service, among others.

CONCLUSION

Because their unique mission is to develop the workforce of tomorrow, community colleges are well-positioned to offer for-credit internships that prepare their diverse student populations for a range of careers, including public service. As this chapter points out, internship opportunities can and should be created to achieve equitable outcomes, and doing so requires coordination, communication, and deliberate effort by faculty, staff, and even students themselves.

At the community college level and beyond, political science students can be important contributors to discussions about access, diversity, and inclusivity, and experiential learning can help make that and other benefits possible. Community college internships create opportunities for students not only to learn about themselves and their community, but also to work on solutions to civic, political, and societal problems. Internships represent opportunities for community college students to understand power dynamics, explore ways to address issues in their community, and empower them as citizens and leaders, whose voices are necessary for systemic change.

REFERENCES

American Association of Community Colleges. 2021. "Fast Facts 2021." Accessed from: https://www.aacc.nche.edu/research-trends/fast-facts/.

Barshay, Jill. 2020. "Why so Few Students Transfer from Community Colleges to Four-Year Universities." *The Hechinger Report.* https://hechingerreport.org/why-so-few-students-transfer-from-community-colleges-to-four-year-universities/.

Carter, Jarrett. 2016. "The Term 'Non-Traditional Student' Is Extinct." *Higher Ed Dive,* October 3. https://www.highereddive.com/news/the-term-nontraditional-student-is-extinct/427467/.

Chen, Grace. 2021a. (2018). "Why More Students are Choosing Community Colleges over Traditional Four-Year Schools." *Community College Review,* updated July 14. https://www.communitycollegereview.com/blog/why-more-students-are-choosing-community-colleges-over-traditional-four-year-schools

Chen, Grace. 2021b. "The Value of Mentoring Programs at Community Colleges." *Community College Review,* January 27. https://www.communitycollegereview.com/blog/the-value-of-mentoring-programs-in-community-college.

Community College Research Center. 2021. "Community College FAQs." Teachers College, Columbia University, Accessed July 1, 2021. https://ccrc.tc.columbia.edu/Community-College-FAQs.html.

Davis, Megan, Erin McGrath, and Betsy Super. 2019. *2017–18 APSA Departmental Survey: Enrollments and Curriculums.* Washington, DC: American Political Science Association, May 21. https://www.apsanet.org/Portals/54/APSA%20Files/Data%20Reports/Enrollment%20Data/APSA%20Departmental%20Survey_Enrollment%20and%20Curriculum_FINAL.pdf?ver=2019-05-21-113745-243.

Finley, Ashley, and Tia McNair. 2013. *Assessing Underserved Students' Engagement in High Impact Practices.* Washington, DC: Association of American Colleges and Universities.

Freedman, Liz. 2015. "The Developmental Disconnect of Choosing a Major: Why Institutions should Prohibit Choice until Second Year." *The Mentor,* Vol. 15. Accessed July 1, 2021. https://journals.psu.edu/mentor/article/view/61278/60911.

Holden, Chelsey L., Lindsay E. Wright, Angel M. Herring, and Pat L. Sims. 2021. "Imposter Syndrome Among First- and Continuing-Generation College Students: The Roles of Perfectionism and Stress." *Journal of College Student Retention: Research, Theory and Practice* [Online] (June): https://doi.org/10.1177/15210251211019379.

Hora, Matthew T., Matthew Wolfgram, and Zi Chen. 2019. "Closing the Doors of Opportunity: How Financial, Sociocultural, and Institutional Barriers Intersect to Inhibit Participation in College Internships." Wisconsin Center for Educational Research, University of Wisconsin, Madison. http://www.wcer.wisc.edu/publications/working-papers.

Kuh, George D. 2008. *High-Impact Educational Practices: What They Are, Who Has Access to Them, and Why They Matter.* Washington, DC: Association of American Colleges and Universities (AAC&U).

Maertz, Carl P., Philipp Stoeberl, and Jill Marks. 2014. "Building Successful Internships: Lessons from the Research for Interns, Schools, and Employers." *Career Development International* 19 (1): 123–142.

Mershon, Carol, and Denise Walsh. 2016. "Diversity in Political Science: Why it Matters and How to Get It." *Politics, Groups, and Identities.* 4 (3): 462–466.

National Student Clearinghouse Research Center. 2017. "Two-Year Contributions to Four-Year Completions, 2017." NSC Research Center, March 29. Accessed July 1, 2021. https://nscresearchcenter.org/snapshotreport-two-yearcontributionfouryearcompletions26/.

Radford, Alexandria W., Melissa Cominole, and Paul Skomsvold. 2015. *Demographic and Enrollment Characteristics of Nontraditional Undergraduates: 2011-2012.* National Center for Education Statistics, US Department of Education, Web Tables NCES 2015-025. https://nces.ed.gov/pubs2015/2015025.pdf.

Schmiede, Angela. 2016. "Timing is Everything: When to Do an Internship." WayUp Community [blog], November 18. https://www.wayup.com/guide/community/timing-is-everything-when-to-do-an-internship/.

Shapiro, Doug, Afet Dundar, Faye Huie, Phoebe Khasiala Wakhungu, Xin Yuan, Angel Nathan, and Youngsik Hwang. 2017. "Tracking Transfer: Measures of Effectiveness in Helping Community College Students to Complete Bachelor's Degrees, Signature Report No. 13." Herndon, VA: National Student Clearinghouse Research Center.

St. Amour, Madeline. 2019. "Working College Students." *Inside Higher Ed*, November 18. https://www.insidehighered.com/news/2019/11/18/most-college-students-work-and-thats-both-good-and-bad.

Van Vechten, Renée B. , Bobbi Gentry, and Shamira Gelbman. 2015. "Best Practices in Political Science Internships." Questionnaire. May 1.

Van Vechten, Renée B. and Bobbi Gentry. 2017. "Internships Across the Discipline: Community Colleges vs. Four-Year Colleges and Universities." Presented at the Annual Meeting of the American Political Science Association, September 1, San Francisco, CA.

Van Vechten, Renée B., and Bobbi Gentry. 2017. "Best Practices in Political Science Internships (Community Colleges)." Questionnaire. July 21.

ENDNOTES

1. Or, as Angela Schmiede phrased it in 2016, "If it makes sense for your situation, intern early and often."

2. According to the Institute of Education Sciences (IES) situated in the National Center for Education Statistics, in 2019 "the distribution of US resident undergraduate students (full- and part-time) by racial or ethnic groups varied among public, private nonprofit, and private for-profit institutions and between two- and four-year institutions" (2021). Among four-year public institutions the racial/ethnic breakdown of the total undergraduate population enrolled in fall 2019 was: 55% white, 11% Black, 20% Hispanic (Latinx), 8% Asian, 1% Native American or Pacific Islander, and 4% Multi-ethnic (2 or more). In comparison, among two-year public institutions, 47% were white (8% lower), 14% were Black (3% higher), 28% were Hispanic/Latinx (8% higher), 6% were Asian (2% lower), 1% were Native American or Pacific Islander (no difference), and 4% were Multi-ethnic (two or more; no difference). Among undergraduates at four-year public institutions, 90% were under age 25, 7% were 25-34, and 2% were 35 and over. Among students in two-year public institutions, 80% were under 25 (10% lower), 14% were 25-34 (7% higher) and 7% were 35 and over (5% higher). Source: IES. 2020. "Characteristics of Postsecondary Students." US Department of Education, National Center for Education Statistics, Integrated Postsecondary Education Data System (IPEDS), Spring, Fall Enrollment component. See *Digest of Education Statistics 2020*, table 306.50 (for race/ethnicity) and table 303.50 for (age). https://nces.ed.gov/programs/coe/indicator/csb. See also CCRC (2021).

3. According to Barshay (2020), about 80% of community college students say they want to earn a bachelor's degree. However, according to IES, "After 150% of the normal time required for the completion of a program at a two-year degree-granting institution, 14% of students had transferred to another institution (transfer out data are required to be reported only by those institutions for which preparation for transfers is a substantial part of the institutional mission)." Source: IES. 2021. "Undergraduate Retention and Graduation Rates." US Department of Education, National Center for Education Statistics, Integrated Postsecondary Education Data System (IPEDS), May. https://nces.ed.gov/programs/coe/indicator/ctr.

4. Figure is provided by the American Association of Community Colleges. Cited in: Pannoni, Alexandra and Emma Kerr. 2020. "Everything You Need to Know about US Community Colleges: FAQ." *US News and World Report*, July 14. https://www.usnews.com/education/community-colleges/articles/2015/02/06/frequently-asked-questions-community-college.

5. See: IES. 2020. "Characteristics of Postsecondary Students." US Department of Education, National Center for Education Statistics, Integrated Postsecondary Education Data System (IPEDS), Spring, Fall Enrollment component. https://nces.ed.gov/programs/coe/indicator/csb.

6. According to the American Association of Colleges and Universities, high-impact practices include: first-year experiences, common intellectual experiences, learning communities, writing-intensive courses, collaborative assignments and projects, undergraduate research, diversity/global learning, ePortfolios, service learning, community-based learning, internships, capstone courses and projects. See https://www.aacu.org/resources/high-impact-practices.

7. Fifty percent of all undergraduate students are undecided upon entering college and 75% change their major at least once before graduation (Freedman 2015).

8. According to Carter (2016), 74% of all undergraduates (enrolled during academic year 2011-12) "possessed at least one characteristic of a non-traditional student," making the term practically obsolete. In any case (and depending on how narrowly one defines them), the terms are still commonly used.

9. For a full discussion of the data collection, please see: "Internships Across the Discipline: Community College vs. Four-Year Programs" by Van Vechten and Gentry, presented at the APSA Conference in 2017. In this chapter, data from two surveys are compared (Van Vechten, Gentry, and Gelbman 2015; Gentry and Van Vechten 2017). The first survey about internships was distributed via Survey Monkey to four-year institutions in 2015, and a nearly identical questionnaire regarding internships at community colleges was administered via Survey Monkey in summer 2017. We targeted department chairs or faculty who supervise internships. Our survey included a mix of 35 open and closed-ended questions, and sought general information about departments, internship practices, faculty perceptions, and resources available to students and faculty in community colleges. With a total of 38 valid, anonymous responses, the response rate for this survey was low, at 6.7%. Among the 51 respondents, the west (68.4%, n=26) was overrepresented, and equal numbers were from the Midwest, northeast, and south (4 each, 10.5%). Community colleges with large populations also led our sample; 35% (n=13) numbered over 15,000 students. Another 27% had populations between 5,001 and 15,000, and 27% had between 2,501 and 5,000. Between these two indicators, we believe the geographic variable could be more

problematic in terms of introducing bias, as educational practice is largely tied to state law (and we assume California respondents dominate our sample, given the state's outsized presence with 114 campuses at that time). "Best Practices in Political Science Internships (Community Colleges)," University of Redlands IRB approval: 2017-15-REDLANDS.

10. As an open-ended question, faculty could identify multiple challenges; therefore the percentages can add up to more than 100%.

11. The American Association of Community Colleges (AACC) acknowledges community colleges "as the premier workforce development providers in America," and as "the learning resource needed to sustain America's economic viability and productivity." Source: "Building a Nation of Learners by Advancing America's Community Colleges." 2021. AACC, Accessed July 10, https://www.aacc.nche.edu/about-us/mission-statement/.

12. Ibid.

13. Refer to the AACC statement cited above. Another reference point is found in the California Education Code, which spells out the mission of community colleges as offering academic and vocational instruction at the lower division, and states: "A primary mission of the California Community Colleges is to advance California's economic growth and global competitiveness through education, training, and services that contribute to continuous work force improvement." Source: California Education Code Section 66010.4 (a), Accessed July 12, 2021. https://leginfo.legislature.ca.gov/faces/codes_displayText.xhtml?lawCode=EDC&division=5.&title=3.&part=40.&chapter=2.&article=2.

CHAPTER 10

Faculty Perceptions and Compensation for Internships

Bobbi Gentry, Bridgewater College

Given the lack of general information about how internships are institutionally supported across the academy, the purpose of this chapter is to examine political science faculty perceptions about internships and how faculty are compensated for their internship-related activities. Based on over 160 departmental survey responses, this chapter explores similarities and differences among institutions based on type, region, public or private institutional status, number of faculty in the department, and size of the undergraduate student population. Data suggest that about one-third of faculty are not compensated for their supervision of internships, and wide variation prevails among those who receive institutional support. The need to value internships through both compensation and recognition in promotion and tenure is clear.

Although institutions and students value internships, does that value translate into resources for faculty pay and resources for building sustainable internship programs? Faculty compensation and resources matter because they clearly demonstrate the priorities of an institution. Compensation and institutional support impact a department's ability to deliver high-quality internship mentoring. As supervisors of internships, faculty assume key responsibilities to make sure that internships fulfill their academic purpose and that students are undertaking a meaningful educational experience at every step.

LITERATURE REVIEW

Pecorella (2007) encourages faculty in their roles as internship supervisors (or coordinators) to help students make connections between theory and practice. If faculty actively coordinate and oversee the internship at all stages, then the academic elements can be incorporated continually, such as through discussion and assignments that require students to read and reflect on their experience. Institutional barriers, including the lack of institutional investment in programs, impact student access to these learning experiences and also the quality of their experiences (Hora et al. 2019a). On the other hand, when internships are an institutional priority, students can encounter a richer array of resources that take shape in support services such as "interview coaching and résumé audits" (Hora et al., 2019a, 5), which can be delivered by career center staff or faculty. In addition to other forms of support for student interns, Finley and McNair suggest that faculty advising and the time they dedicate to internship programming directly impact student participation in internships (2013, 5). By extension, lack of faculty attention constrains students' ability to take full advantage of experiential learning, or to experience internships as a developmental process for acquiring, developing, and mastering new skills. Without guidance, students' ability to recognize the value of challenges and problem-solving, explore career options, and build new knowledge and skills may be limited.

Faculty support for student interns is also strongly associated with student satisfaction with their internship experience. Hora et al. (2019b) find higher student satisfaction and perceived value of an internship when their supervisor acts as a mentor and when "the relationship between their internship and their academic program" is strong and clear (2019b, 13). Faculty mentors, and sometimes site supervisors, can offer the support and mentorship needed to clearly connect interns' concrete learning goals and work to academic outcomes. However, in order to do so, faculty need time and resources to offer the kind of intense mentoring that produces high levels of student satisfaction and academic learning. To this point, mentors directly impact the developmental process, and this includes site supervisors who assume a mentoring role (McHugh 2016). Additionally, McHugh finds that being paid (or not) for an internship can also affect students' satisfaction with their experience. Specifically, students who have paid internships reported "higher levels of perceived supervisor support, supervisor mentoring, and task goal clarity" (McHugh 2016, 374). Finally, McHugh finds that when an academic program requires students to participate in an internship in an unpaid capacity, they are less satisfied with the experience (375).

Against this backdrop, this chapter considers the compensation of political science internship coordinators, a condition that represents either an institutional investment in experiential learning, or, where absent or lacking, a potential barrier to it. Survey data are used to describe and evaluate compensation structures in US colleges and universities. In addition, faculty perceptions about the overall value of internships and internship needs on their campuses are explored.

STUDY DESIGN

Two waves of surveys were deployed to assess internships within the discipline, and the same questionnaire (with small adjustments) was administered to two groups in order to establish whether and how institutional differences might exist across internship programs (Van Vechten, Gentry, and Gelbman 2015; Van Vechten and Gentry 2017). The first target sample included a wide variety of four-year institution types ranging from R1's with doctoral programs to small liberal arts colleges. The second was comprised of community colleges. A total of 121 participants responded to the first survey in 2015 and 51 responded to the second wave in 2017; for this file we had 166 viable cases. Response rates were 20.5% for the 2015 survey of four-year institutions, and 6.7% for the 2016 community colleges iteration. Community colleges from the West and with populations over 15,000 students were overrepresented among the respondents. The recruitment email was sent three times to department chairs or faculty in charge of internships.[1] Responses were pooled for analysis.

Our respondents were, by and large, faculty members with an "up close and personal" vantage point on students' internship experiences. As such, their perceptions should not be taken as representative of political science faculty more generally. On the other hand, their close connection increases confidence in the accuracy of the information they provided about their departments' internship programs. Furthermore, the respondents' intimate knowledge and experience with undergraduate internships was likely responsible for the survey's high item completion rates. For closed-ended questions, completion rates ranged from about 75% (91 responses) to 99% (120 responses). The open-ended questions unsurprisingly elicited somewhat lower completion rates, but most still garnered at least 100 responses.

The survey instrument contained a mix of 38 closed- and open-ended questions that collected information about internship practices in undergraduate political science programs at US colleges and universities, as well as gauged respondents' perceptions and attitudes regarding the value of and challenges associated with internships at their institution. Rather than report on the survey results in their entirety, this study zeroes in on those items that most clearly elucidate respondents' sense of the role internships play in their department and their effects on students' academic and professional achievements. Table 1 lists the relevant survey questions and their corresponding completion rates.

Table 1. List of Questions about Faculty Compensation and Internships	
Question	Number of Responses to selected questions (N)
If a faculty member in your department is responsible for coordinating or advising student internships, how is this person compensated? (open-ended)	166
Currently, Political Science majors benefit from a robust internship program on our campus. (T/F)	151
There is little or no effort to coordinate internships on our campus. (T/F)	145
Our department intends to expand internship offerings or create an internship program in the near future. (T/F)	92
We need more resources to adequately compensate faculty and/or staff for their current involvement in coordinating or overseeing internships. (T/F)	96
Internships tend to reinforce inequalities between students who are financially well-off and can afford to intern without pay, and those who cannot afford to work without pay. (T/F)	97

RESULTS

Among the more striking results that emerged were clear differences in perceptions about whether internships help students excel as political science majors. While over half of the respondents (59.9%, n=94) agreed that internships are an important part of excelling as a political science major, less than half (41.2%, n=68) thought internships were not important or somewhat important in this respect.

Figure 1. Faculty Perception of Internships As Important to Excelling as a Political Science Major

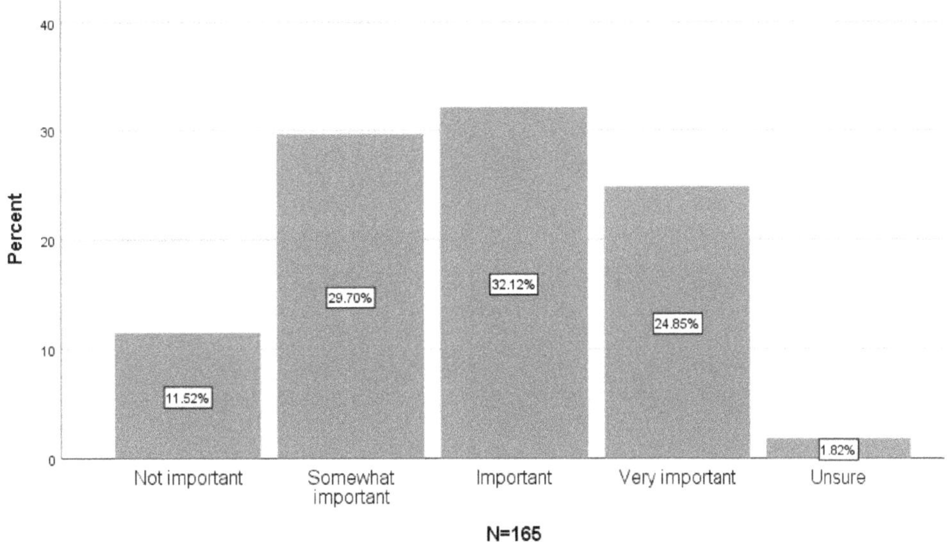

Faculty vary in their perceptions of how internships benefit students. More than three-quarters (84.3%, n=140) of faculty agreed that internships help students identify their career preferences. Only two participants responded that internships were not important in helping students identify their career preferences (1.2%). Overall, faculty see internships as a way for students to explore their career preferences before they leave the institution.

Figure 2. Faculty Perception of Internships as Helping Students Identify Career Preferences

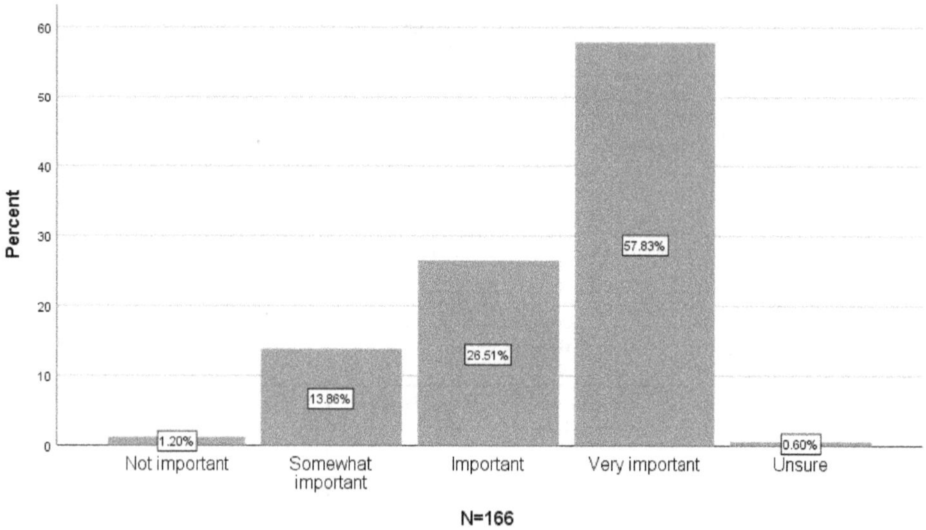

A larger concern identified in the overarching literature on internships is unequal access for students of lower-income backgrounds who are not able to intern because of the need to earn money or for anyone who is a caregiver or has significant family obligations (Hora et al. 2019a; Hora et al. 2019b; Perlin 2011). A specific survey question about whether internships reinforce inequalities among students provided some puzzling results. Faculty were split on whether or not they regarded this statement as true or false: "Internships tend to reinforce inequalities between students who are financially well-off and can afford to intern without pay, and those who cannot afford to work without pay." One in five respondents responded that they were unsure about this statement, which was the highest number of unsure responses in the dataset (20.4%, n=37). Overall, more faculty believed that internships do not reinforce inequalities (52.73%, n=58) than those who believed that they do reinforce inequalities (47.3%, 52), and there are no significant differences based on institution type.

Figure 3. Faculty Perception that Internships Reinforce Inequalities

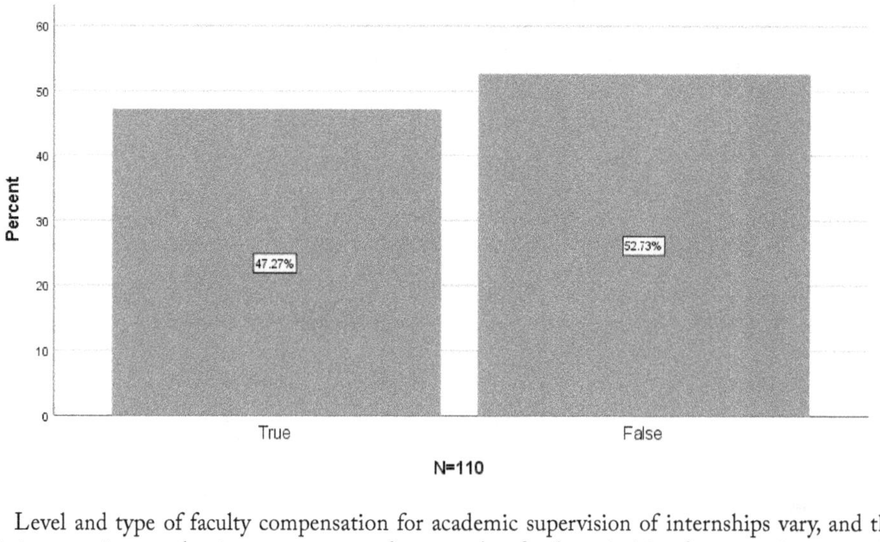

Level and type of faculty compensation for academic supervision of internships vary, and these variations can impact the time, resources, and energy that faculty prioritize for managing internships over their other responsibilities. Fewer than half of political science programs compensate faculty in some way (46.4%); however, in over one-third of programs the faculty internship supervisors are not compensated. Among the types of compensation mentioned[2] are the ability to accrue credits towards a course release, extra financial compensation in the form of a bonus or stipend, or including internship-related duties specifically in a job description (e.g., chair position or faculty member). In some cases, administrative responsibilities such as coordinating internships are handled in other offices, such as a specific internship office or career services, but supervised by faculty.

Figure 4. Faculty Compensation for Internship Supervision

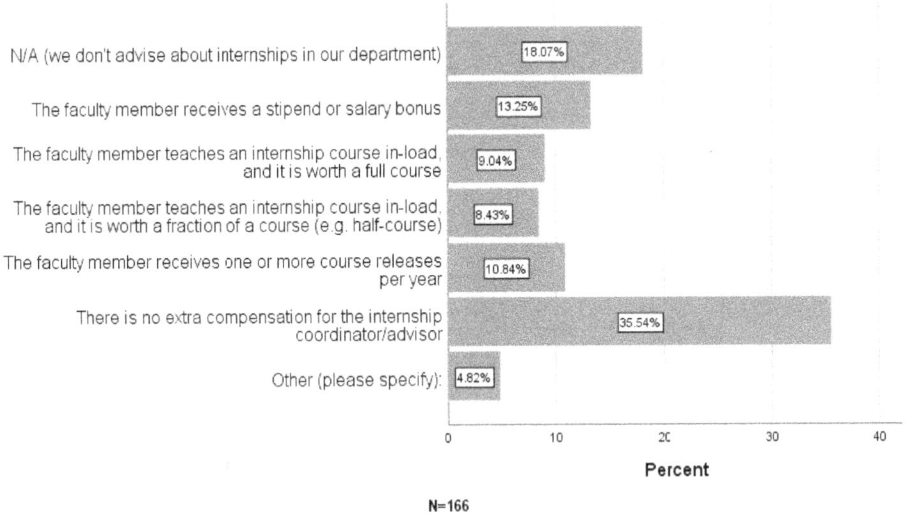

Overall, the most frequent response was that there is no extra compensation for those who coordinate internships (35.5%, n=59).[3] Of the departments with internship programs, two-thirds provide additional compensation for faculty supervisors, and the most frequent choice is a stipend or salary bonus (13.3%, n=22). If the value of internships is not prioritized with institutional resources for faculty supervision, then this does not bode well for the sustainability of internship programs.

Table 2. Compensation Differences by Institution Type

Compensation Type	Institution Type			
	Doctoral Program	MA-Granting	Liberal Arts	Community College
No Compensation	31.6% (6)	36.8% (14)	51.2% (21)	60% (18)
Course Release	10.5% (2)	26.3% (10)	9.8% (4)	6.7% (2)
Fraction of Course in Load	15.8% (3)	10.5% (4)	7.3% (3)	13.3% (4)
Full Course in Load	31.6% (6)	13.2% (5)	7.3% (3)	3.3% (1)
Stipend	10.5% (2)	13.2% (5)	24.4% (10)	16.7% (5)

As illustrated in table 2, stark differences exist among institutions with respect to compensation for coordinating or supervising internships (n=128). Many institutions (46.1%) offer no compensation. Doctoral programs are more likely to count an internship course as in-load. MA-granting institutions are more likely to allow a course release, whereas liberal arts institutions are most likely to provide a stipend to faculty, as are community colleges. Community college faculty are least likely to be compensated for their work (60% uncompensated), followed by liberal arts institution faculty (51.2% uncompensated). Departments with doctoral programs are more likely to compensate faculty in some way, but almost a third of them (31.6%) do not compensate faculty for supervising student interns. A few of these differences among institutions are large, and significantly so. Overwhelmingly, faculty are not being compensated for their work on internships.[4]

Size of the department also matters. Overall, most departments do not compensate faculty (46.8%, n=59), and very few departments offer compensation as a fraction of a course in load (10.3%, n=13). For small departments of 1 to 3 faculty members and large departments with over 25 faculty, no compensation is the norm. There may be various reasons for this. For small departments, resources might not be available. For larger departments, there may be a dedicated internship program or staff member who oversees internship programming. However, departments above 11 members tend to compensate faculty with a course release (33.3%, n=5). For departments of 16 to 25 faculty members, a full course in-load is the most likely form (26.7%, n=4).

Table 3. Compensation Differences by Number of Faculty in the Department

Compensation Type	How Many Faculty are in Your Department?				
	1–3	4–10	11–15	16–25	Over 25
No Compensation	66.7% (10)	53% (35)	13.3% (2)	20% (3)	60% (9)
Course Release	6.7% (1)	10.6% (7)	33.3% (5)	20% (3)	13.3% (2)
Fraction of Course in Load	13.3% (2)	7.6% (5)	13.3% (2)	13.3% (2)	13.3% (2)
Full Course in Load	0%	6.1% (4)	26.7% (4)	26.7% (4)	13.3% (2)
Stipend	13.3% (2)	22.7% (15)	13.3% (2)	20% (3)	0%
N=126					

Department size does seem to impact compensation type. In departments considered small (1 to 3 faculty) and extremely large (over 25 faculty), 66% and 60% percent of programs, respectively, offer no compensation to faculty. More than half (53%) of medium-sized departments (4 to 10) do not compensate faculty. Interestingly, programs with 11 to 15 faculty offer a course release (33.3%) or a full course in-load (26.7%), whereas programs with 16 to 25 faculty are more likely to offer a full course in-load (26.7%), among other options. Department size might be related to available resources including faculty time to teach a course. For example, small departments might need faculty to teach courses within the curriculum and do not have the flexibility in their course rotation to offer an internship course.

Table 4. Faculty Compensation and Faculty Perception of Internship Program Robustness

Robust Internship Program	Compensation Type				
	No Compensation	Course Release	Fraction of Course	Full course in Load	Stipend
True	48.9% (22)	75% (12)	40% (4)	93.3% (14)	70.6% (12)
False	51.1% (45)	25% (4)	60% (6)	6.7% (1)	29.4% (5)
N=103; Chi Square=13.29; p=.010					

Faculty compensation does appear to be related to faculty perceptions about whether the internship program is robust on their campus. Overall, 62.1% (64) of faculty believe that they have a robust internship program. However, in programs with no compensation or only internship responsibilities count as a fraction of a course in-load, 51.1% (45) and 60% (6) respectively do not believe that their institution has a robust internship program. This result demonstrates that faculty who are compensated are more likely to regard their own programs more positively.

Table 5. Faculty Compensation and the Need for More Resources					
Need More Resources to Compensate	Faculty Compensation				
	No Compensation	Course Release	Fraction of Course	Full course in Load	Stipend
True	79.1% (34)	54.5% (6)	42.9% (3)	38.5% (5)	38.5% (5)
False	20.9% (9)	45.5% (5)	57.1% (4)	61.5% (8)	61.5% (8)
N=87; Chi Square=12.61; p=.013					

How faculty are compensated directly impacts their perception that more resources are needed for faculty compensation. Across the board, 60.9% of faculty surveyed believe that more resources are needed to compensate faculty and/or staff. Faculty in programs that already provide compensation by counting courses in-load or providing stipends are more likely to say that they do not need more resources. Not surprisingly, departments with internship programs that do not compensate faculty represent a large majority who say that more resources are needed (79.1%, n=34).

Table 6. Faculty Perception of Need for more Resources by Institution type					
Number of Faculty in the Department		Institution Type			
	Need more resources to compensate?	Doctoral Program	MA-Granting	Liberal Arts	Community College
1–3	True	—	—	0% (0)	70.6% (12)
	False	—	—	100% (2)	29.4% (5)
4–10	True	100% (1)	71.4% (10)	59.3% (16)	100% (7)
	False	0% (0)	28.6% (4)	40.7% (11)	0%
11–15	True	50% (1)	71.4% (5)	0% (0)	100% (2)
	False	50% (1)	28.6% (2)	100% (5)	0% (0)
16–25	True	77.8% (7)	50% (1)	50% (1)	50% (2)
	False	22.2% (2)	50% (1)	50% (1)	50% (2)
Over 25	True	71.4% (5)	100% (4)	0% (0)	0% (0)
	False	28.6% (2)	0% (0)	100% (1)	100% (1)

Controlling for the number of faculty, there is an interactive relationship between institution type and the need for more resources.[5] Most respondents agree that more resources are needed to run internship programs. For instance, respondents at universities without a doctoral program agree that more resources are needed, including 71.4% (10) of programs with 4–10 faculty, 71.4% (5) of programs with 11–15 faculty, 50% (1) of programs with 16–25 faculty, and 100% (4) of programs with over 25 faculty. However, respondents at liberal arts institutions with small (1–3 faculty) and medium (11–15 faculty) believe that they do not need more resources to compensate faculty or staff in running internships.

While institution type does matter, location (Chi-Square=10.80, p= .546) and whether an institution is public or private are not statistically significant factors (Chi-Square=6.64, p=.156). How faculty are compensated has no statistical association with financial support for students (Chi-Square=1.65, p=.801) or faculty perceptions about whether or not internships reinforce economic inequalities (Chi-Square 9.47, p=.304). Lastly, faculty compensation is not associated with whether a department intends to expand its internship program in the future (Chi-Square=3.72, p=.881).

WAYS TO RETHINK INTERNSHIPS

Faculty can be compensated in a variety of ways, including a stipend, a course release, or accumulating a number of internships to count for a course in load. However, less than half of all programs compensate faculty for internship coordination or supervision. This lack of pay and lack of emphasis on the value of internship work could manifest in lower amounts of time and energy that the faculty mentor invests in the internship. Although resources for internship opportunities can be coordinated by an internship or career services office, the academic nature of for-credit internships demands faculty oversight and sufficient compensation.

Because unequal access to internships endures, internships for which students pay tuition are neither affordable nor feasible. Yet, if we rethink internships to emphasize accessibility and do away with tuition for internships, then what does that mean for faculty compensation? Faculty mentor students throughout the process and oftentimes counsel many interns. One way to rethink compensation is for each internship to count towards a course in load, at least fractionally. One example would be to set the minimum number of students required for a course as the number of internships that counts for a course in load. For instance, if the minimum number of students is eight, then eight internships are needed to have a course count in load. Faculty would accrue these internship credits towards a course in load until they reached the required number for a course to run. This option is more workable for smaller institutions with fewer internships throughout the year, in comparison to large institutions with many interns that would potentially require more faculty resources and supervision; in that case, it would make sense to provide compensation for a position rather than as an add-on to current internship responsibilities.

Internship mentoring should also be included in faculty considerations for promotion and tenure. Whereas individual mentoring can count in the teaching elements of promotion packets, contributions for mentoring should be counted as service to the institution. Mentoring students requires connecting theory to practice, a teaching skill; and being a faculty mentor is a service to the institution because it increases retention, improves recruitment, and improves job prospects for new graduates (Hora et al. 2019b; Kuh 2008; McClellan et al. 2021; McHugh 2016).[6]

CONCLUSIONS

This research exploring how faculty perceive the relative value of political science internships and how they are compensated for their internship-related work sheds light on some of the similarities and differences among institutions. The results raise deeper questions and suggest several different directions for expanding this work.

Faculty receive compensation in many different ways, but over one-third of faculty are not compensated for their work with internships. Lack of compensation has the potential to negatively affect internship offerings, level of faculty oversight, connections with alumni, and new internship opportunities in the community. Community college faculty are especially interested in additional resources for delivering internship programs to their students to help them prepare for careers and connect their academic learning to experience.

Faculty across the board agree that more resources are needed to facilitate internships. Institutional investment in both support for students and compensation for faculty are impactful for student learning and perceived educational value (Hora et al. 2019b). There are opportunities to work with alumni relations to develop scholarships, community partnerships, and investments in career-related internships.[7] Faculty should communicate the value of internships to administrators, who in turn can convey these priorities to prospective donors. Internships remain valuable to institutions of higher education because they shorten the time for recent graduates to find a job (Knouse and Fontenot 2008), are a long-term investment in soon-to-be-alumni, and are a high-impact practice that is a retention tool (Kuh 2008).

Apart from the faculty perceptions and compensation issues addressed here, constructing a more holistic picture of internships would require additional information about compensation levels, institutional initiatives, or possibly strategic planning for making major investments in experiential learning. Many faculty agree that adequate compensation would help ensure appropriate levels of internship supervision, which directly affects students' preparation for internship work (Hora et al. 2019a), student learning outcomes (McHugh 2016), and perception of the value of internships (Hora et al. 2019b). However, as our survey results show, although many in the political science profession believe that internships are an important learning experience for many students, about half do not acknowledge that internships reinforce inequalities among students. These perceptions will shape the future of internships in our discipline as much as others who recognize the potential for change will. The hope is that knowledge will better equip us to focus on student learning outcomes in academic internship experiences and create more equity for students and faculty.

REFERENCES

Finley, Ashley, and Tia McNair. 2013. *Assessing Underserved Students' Engagement in High Impact Practices.* Washington, DC: Association of American Colleges and Universities.

Hora, Matthew T., Matthew Wolfgram, and Zi Chen. 2019a. "Closing the Doors of Opportunity: How Financial, Sociocultural, and Institutional Barriers Intersect to Inhibit Participation in College Internships." Wisconsin Center for Educational Research, University of Wisconsin, Madison. Retrieved from: http://www.wcer.wisc.edu/publications/working-papers.

Hora, Matthew T., Zi Chen, Emily Parrott, and Pa Her. 2019b. "Problematizing College Internships: Exploring Issues with Access, Program Design, and Developmental Outcomes in Three U.S. Colleges." Wisconsin Center for Educational Research, University of Wisconsin, Madison. Retrieved from: http://www.wcer.wisc.edu/publications/working-papers.

Knouse, Stephen B., and Gwen Fontenot. 2008. "Benefits of the Business College Internship: A Research Review." *Journal of Employment Counseling* 45 (2): 61–66.

Kuh, George D. 2008. *High Impact Educational Practices: What They Are, Who has Access to Them, and Why they Matter.* Washington DC: American Association of Colleges and Universities.

McClellan, Fletcher, Kyle Casimir Kopko, and Kayla L Gruber. 2021. "High-Impact Practices and Their Effects: Implications for the Undergraduate Political Science Curriculum." *Journal of Political Science Education* 0:0, pages 1–19. doi: 10.1080/15512169.2020.1867562.

McHugh, Patrick P. 2016. "The Impact of Compensation, Supervision and Work Design on Internship Efficacy: Implications for Educators, Employers and Prospective Interns." *Journal of Education and Work* 30 (4): 367–382.

Pecorella, Robert F. 2007. "Forests and Trees: The Role of Academics in Legislative Internships." *Journal of Political Science Education* 3 (1): 79–99.

Perlin, Ross. 2011. *Intern Nation.* London: Verso.

Van Vechten, Renée B., and Bobbi Gentry. 2017. "Best Practices in Political Science Internships (Community Colleges)." Questionnaire. July 21.

Van Vechten, Renée B., Bobbi Gentry, and Shamira Gelbman. 2015. "Best Practices in Political Science Internships." Questionnaire. May 1.

ENDNOTES

1. In the first survey, respondents were nearly evenly split between public and private institutions, with 50.9% from the former (n= 59) and 49.2% from the latter (n=57). A plurality (43.3%) identified their institution as a liberal arts college, another 35.8% PhD programs in political science, and two respondents (1.7%) were at two-year community colleges. All of the major geographic regions of the United States were represented, including 28.3% of respondents from the Midwest, 26.7% from the Northeast, 32.5% from the South, and 11.7% from the West. The overwhelming majority of respondents (87.4%) worked in standalone political science departments, with most of the remainder in combined or catch-all social science departments. More than half (57%) of their departments were small, with ten or fewer faculty members; at the other extreme, large departments of 25 or more faculty accounted for just 12.6% of the sample. One potential source of bias in our sample was department size, which (unsurprisingly) is strongly associated with the type of institution. All but seven of the private institutions represented in our survey had an undergraduate population of under 5,000 (87.7%, n=50), whereas almost all of the public institutions in our sample had populations over 5,000 (88.1%, n=52). In the second survey of community colleges, among the 38 respondents, the West (68.4%, n=26) was overrepresented, and equal numbers were from the Midwest, Northeast, and South (4 each, 10.5%). Community colleges with large populations also led our sample; 35% (n=13) numbered over 15,000 students. Another 27% had populations between 5,001 and 15,000, and 27% had between 2,501 and 5,000. Between these two indicators, we believe the geographic variable could be more problematic in terms of introducing bias, as educational practice is largely tied to state law (and we assume California respondents dominate our sample, given the state's outsized presence with 114 campuses).

2. If they were compensated, respondents were asked to explain how in an open-ended, follow-up item.

3. Among the respondents, there are political science departments that do not have an internship program and therefore have no need to compensate faculty to run an internship program (18.1%, n=30).

4. Interestingly, institution type does not affect faculty perceptions of internships as reinforcing inequalities between students, even though institution type does affect inequalities among faculty.

5. While a relationship was present between institution type and need for more resources, it was not statistically significant at the $p<0.05$ level.

6. Internship programs that connect with their alumni network are also opportunities for alumni to give back and build a positive relationship with the institution.

7. Applications such as Alumni Fire or Handshake are new programs that institutions are using to connect to alumni, which can be leveraged by departments for internship purposes.

CHAPTER 11

Funding for Interns

Daniel J. Mallinson, Pennsylvania State University, Harrisburg

Unpaid or underpaid internships can create serious practical and equity concerns for our students, especially first generation and low-income students. Internships in public service professions are often unpaid, and those who desire college credit often face a double financial barrier. This chapter discusses a scaffolded approach to internships and draws on survey data to suggest how faculty and institutions can address these needs through one of several innovative departmental models. The roles of both the federal government and APSA in elevating the discussion of internship funding are also explored.

INTRODUCTION

"I am looking for help finding an internship. I know it can help me in my career, but I can't work unpaid. Do you know of good paid internships?" Probably anyone who has worked with political science students looking for internships has heard this conversation starter. Serving students who cannot afford to complete an unpaid internship tends to be the norm for the vast majority of faculty working in higher education. Given that unpaid internships are more prevalent in what some have called "glamorous fields" (Curiale 2009) such as politics, entertainment, communications, and journalism (Joyce et al. 2018), funding can be a major hurdle for political science students and supporting faculty. The intent of this chapter is to discuss how faculty, departments, and political science as a profession can help students secure paid internships or provide support for unpaid opportunities. It begins by discussing what advisors should know from the students' point of view. Three models are discussed: unpaid for-credit, unpaid no credit, and paid internships. Next, the chapter presents a scaffolding approach that faculty can use to help students work their way up to high-profile, paid internships. Next, models of institutional efforts for supporting interns are discussed. Finally, the chapter addresses the roles of both the federal government and the American Political Science Association (APSA) in elevating paid internships in the public sector.

STUDENT INTERNSHIP MODELS

Before delving into internship funding models, it is first useful to consider the direct costs of geographically distant internships. High quality internships are often found in locations far from students' homes. This means that students must find and pay for housing in addition to their other basic living expenses (Edwards and Hertel-Fernandez 2010). Consider the highly desired internship location of Washington, DC. As of March 2021, the average rent in Washington, DC was $2,000 per month for a one-bedroom apartment.[1] For a three-month summer internship, students could easily pay $6,000 in rent alone in 2021. If a student chose to live outside of the District, they could pay lower rent, but would likely also pay more for the daily commute to their internship. Additionally, students must eat, which could amount to hundreds or even thousands of dollars (see Chapter 13 about DC internships by Chin for a more detailed breakdown of costs).

Finally, the student might seek course credit for their internship. In 2021, the average cost for a college credit in the United States was $559.[2] The average in-state tuition for public universities was slightly lower ($396 per credit) and the average cost for out-of-state students and those at private universities was much higher ($1,101 and $1,492, respectively). Thus, the total cost for tuition and living expenses for a summer internship could conceivably have reached $10,000 in 2021. If a student were paid the average wage for a Washington, DC internship in 2021, $15 per hour, they would gross only $7,200 over the course of a 12-week experience, before taxes.[3] Or, in the case of unpaid internships, as is most often the case in public sector internships (Edwards and Hertel-Fernandez 2010; NACE 2019), the students must fully absorb the expenses. While the DC internship experience and placements outside the US are among the most financially costly, especially compared to local and state government experiences, this quick calculation illustrates the financial reality for many students.

Further, the DC example does not consider other financial complications that students, especially those from less advantaged backgrounds, face. Consider the student who lives completely independently and must either sublet or absorb the cost of a year-round apartment during the summer months. Or consider the student who supports an extended family, or even immediate family (such as a child, spouse, or parent), financially. The barriers to completing internships, especially unpaid, mount quickly and can result in unequal access to these vital career development opportunities.

Before addressing the roles of faculty and departments in increasing internship equity, it is important to understand the three different models of internships from the perspective of students: unpaid and for credit; unpaid with no credit; and paid internships (whether for credit or no credit). Each has benefits and drawbacks.

Unpaid, For Credit

Unpaid internships with a paired academic component can serve both the internship-granting institution and the intern well. While unpaid internships correlate negatively with future salary and employment, they do help students with networking and either confirming or rejecting their career goals (Crain 2016). Further, partnerships between academic programs and employers are necessary for ensuring high-quality experiences (Joyce et al. 2018). And earning credit appears to make students feel more accountable and care more about their performance at the internship (Saltikoff et al. 2018).

Students in most cases, however, pay tuition for this support. This is sensible given that faculty are supervising and assessing students, meaning that university resources are expended in the students' completion of a credited internship. From the students' perspective, however, this is a double financial blow: not only do they receive no compensation for their work, but they must also pay tuition. For those students who are responsible for paying their own way through college or receive limited support from others, the double financial burden creates a hurdle both to perceiving that an internship is possible and completing one for academic credit (Shade and Jacobson 2015). One way to avoid the pitfall of paying for credits, particularly in the summer when financial aid does not apply, is to complete the requirements for zero credits. This allows the internship to appear on the transcript without extra tuition charges.

Unpaid, No Credit

Unpaid internships without an accompanying academic component can free students from the financial burden of tuition. However, these also retain a strong potential for exploitation and undermining the core educational purpose of an internship. This is not to argue that all unpaid internships are necessarily exploitative, but such an outcome is possible because unpaid laborers and "volunteers" at both for- and non-profit organizations, including governments, often lack legal and institutional protections (Allan 2019; Baines, Cunningham, and Shields 2017; also see Yamada this volume). Without the faculty supervision that accompanies a for-credit internship, students are essentially on their own to navigate issues such as discrimination or exploitive practices, should they arise (Sosland and Lowenthal 2017).

Paid (Credit or No Credit)

Paid internships have many advantages; aside from providing an income stream that is usually indispensable, there is evidence that they lead to better career outcomes in the long run. Students who have had paid internships tend to be more employable (Hunt and Scott 2017), eventually receiving more job offers and higher starting salaries than those who either completed an unpaid internship or no internship (NACE 2019). The major downsides of paid internships are that some institutions do not award credit for paid internships, and across the board they are highly competitive, attracting strong candidates with experience and developed skill sets. This is where strategic thinking on the part of the advisor and the student can be advantageous. Faculty can be strategic partners in scaffolding internships in ways that increase equity and students' competitiveness. Scaffolding involves building toward complex tasks, and because faculty regularly employ such techniques in their courses, they can easily transfer them to internship advising.

More specifically, scaffolding occurs when "a teacher…offers explicit support and guidance to help a learner to perform a difficult task beyond [their] own capacity" (Kazak, Wegerif, and Fujita 2015, 1269). Faculty are used to helping students structure the learning of complex tasks including research methods (Fisher and Justwan 2018) and civic skills (Saks McManaway and Lorentz 2020). Career skills, including those necessary for obtaining competitive paid internships, can be integrated directly into a discipline's curriculum, i.e., to create a scaffold (Mertz and Neiles 2020): networking, searching for opportunities, keeping track of early application deadlines, identifying transferable skills gained from coursework and service to student organizations, résumé preparation, informational interviews, and more. Scaffolding can also provide a useful structure for faculty working directly with students. For this approach to be effective, it is useful for advisors to think of a student's time in a program holistically and proactively rather than simply to provide semester-to-semester course advising (Varney 2007).

Unpaid internships, whether for credit or not, can also be viewed as ladders that students can climb to paid internships. These experiences help build skills that render students more competitive for paid, and possibly more prestigious, opportunities later in their academic careers. Faculty should be cognizant of making strategic decisions regarding funding, however, when helping a student build an internship plan. Student employment increased markedly from the 1970s to 2000s (Scott-Clayton 2012), and the double financial burden of a for-credit unpaid internship is most acutely felt during the summer months, when students are less likely to be living on campus or have scholarship support. With advance planning, some students can complete an internship during a semester when they are completing less-intensive coursework, a strategy that can help students balance demands on their time and also maintain a solid GPA.

Planning should also acknowledge the advance deadlines that are often established by paid internship programs. For example, the Finnegan Foundation Fellowship in Pennsylvania state government is awarded through a competitive essay contest, with a typical deadline that occurs in the February prior to a summer internship. The Pennsylvania House Fellowship, awarded by the General Assembly on a rolling basis, has a March 1 deadline for summer, May 1 deadline for fall, and October 1 deadline for spring semester. The federal government's Pathways program for undergraduates, graduate students, and recent graduates sets various deadlines depending on the agency that is hiring. Students must gain experience navigating job applications through USAJobs for these positions and must apply during an (often short) application window. The White House and the US State Department's unpaid internship programs require students to apply at least a full eight months before their summer experience owing to an intensive interview process and a federal background check. Fortunately, students can sign up for alerts from these programs to help them stay aware of application windows and deadlines. The Virtual Student Federal Service, which provides eight-month (also unpaid) virtual internships in a variety of federal departments, only accepts applications during the month of July, after which applicants are screened and matched with agencies. Faculty can encourage students to be proactive in building their experiences, being organized, and preparing early for desired opportunities.

Career services staff represent another strategic partner in this scaffolding approach. Institutions of higher education have been expanding their career services, although students have not necessarily been increasing their use of such resources (Fadulu 2018; McGrath 2002). The best approach to career services support, however, is not simply passive referral by faculty, but active collaboration between faculty and career counselors (Ledwith 2014; Mallinson and Burns 2019). Whereas such collaboration often requires largely uncredited service time on the part of faculty, political science programs benefit from collaborative career courses, seminars, and positive, personal working relationships between career counseling staff and faculty (Mallinson and Burns 2019; McDow and Zabrucky 2015).

Moon and Schokman (2000) offer another possible model that faculty can directly integrate into their courses: a political science research assistantship embedded within a class on policy process and analysis (see also Chapter 7 by Auerbach in this book). The course they designed at the University of Western Australia includes five weeks of coursework on the policy process, followed by an eight-week internship wherein students provide policy research for a political organization. The internship portion is unpaid, but students build foundational skills and add to a portfolio of coursework that can help them secure external internship opportunities later in their career.

INSTITUTIONAL MODELS

Even with such scaffolding, however, equity concerns remain. Institutional support for disadvantaged students can help even the playing field (Hindmoor 2010), but results from a national survey of political science departments make evident that there is wide variation in financial support for interns across political science departments (Van Vechten, Gelbman, and Gentry 2015; Van Vechten and Gentry 2017).[4] Only 23% of responding departments provide interns with financial support, yet even that percentage masks a lower level of direct support from departments. Figure 1 shows the types of support reported. Of the 39 programs that provided specific details regarding their funding support, two indicated that

Figure 1. Types of Internship Support Reported by Departments

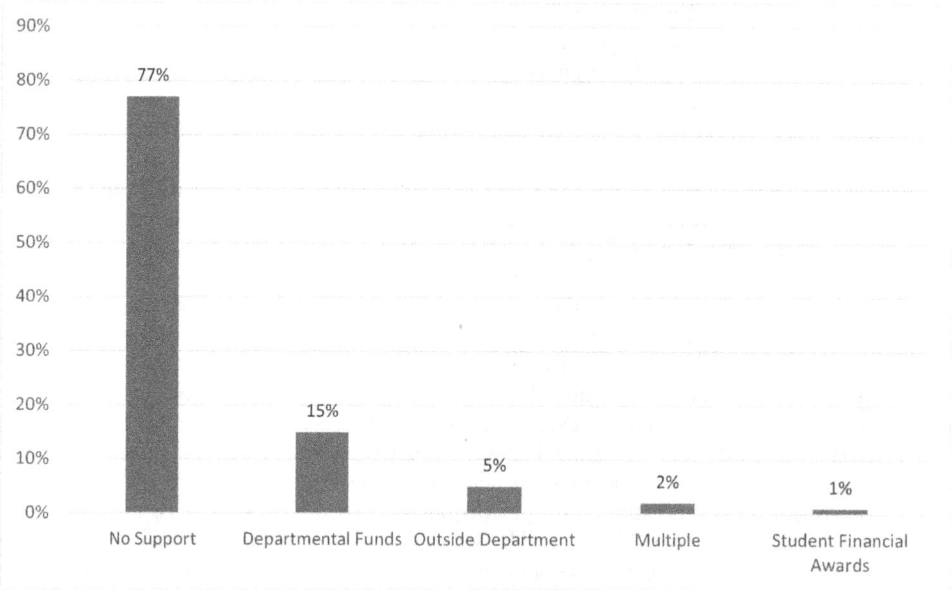

there is no additional support beyond normal student financial awards, and nine reported that the source of additional support was outside of the department; most often this was in the form of college- or university-wide grants. Other sources included academic centers, the career center, and service-learning.

Three departments reported a multi-pronged approach to financial support across the institution. The most comprehensive included the application of student financial aid to Washington, DC internships, competitive university-wide summer internship grants, and departmental scholarships for summer internships with the Washington Internship program. Two others reported a mixture of small department scholarships (one described as "pocket money") and university financial aid.

Direct departmental financial support of student interns fell into three categories: small grants, scholarships, and endowments. Small grants ranged from $500 to $1,500 to help defray costs. Some departments tie the funding to having an unpaid internship and others specifically provide travel support if travel to the internship is required. In terms of scholarships, seven departments reported either considering internships in their criteria for departmental scholarships or providing a limited set of scholarships or single scholarship explicitly for internships. Three of those departments designate the scholarships specifically for Washington, DC experiences. Finally, seven departments indicated that they had endowed or private funds that provide funding support in the form of small grants or scholarships, but the presence of an endowment suggests that these funds are protected/designated specifically for internships. As these survey responses show, there is no "one-size-fits-all" approach to providing financial help for students, but they suggest three basic approaches. The following three institutional funding models will expand on these findings to suggest best practices for supporting interns financially.

Model 1: Philanthropy-Based Subsidies

Regardless of whether departments wish to provide small grants or full scholarships for unpaid interns, developing philanthropic sources of funding can offer stable support via an endowment. Relying on departmental funds or periodic giving that fluctuates with the financial circumstances of the institution and the economy means that funding may fall through for interns in a given fiscal year. One way that political science departments have approached raising scholarship funds, including those directed at internships, is to name the funds for popular, impactful, and long-standing members of the faculty. Examples include the McClellan Fund at Elizabethtown College (https://www.etown.edu/depts/ppls/index.aspx), Wendell "Roy" Gruenewald Intern Scholarship at Ball State (https://www.bsu.edu/academics/collegesanddepartments/political-science/admissions-financial-aid/scholarships#accordion_gruenewaldintern), and the Jerome Mileur Internship Fund/Scholarship at the University of Massachusetts at Amherst (https://polsci.umass.edu/undergraduate-programs/internships).

The University of South Dakota's Farber Fund (https://www.usd.edu/arts-and-sciences/farber-fund) is also a notable example of a faculty-named fund that combines flexibility with purpose. It is named after a long-standing member of the political science department, Dr. William Farber, who retired in 1976. Although current students have no personal connection to the namesake, the fund now provides over $170,000 annually for internship stipends, study abroad, and research. The fund's growth benefits from its flexibility, in that its broad range of potential uses means that many students are supported by the fund during their studies. This is not to say that grateful alumni would not donate to an internship-only fund, but as this example shows, a broader designation can help develop a critical mass, as not all students in a program will complete an internship and their personal connection to an earmarked fund would be more limited. Essentially, the more students potentially helped by a fund, the more a program could anticipate future contributions from them. Additionally, endowed funds give departments spending flexibility, enabling them to vary the proportion of funds used for internships, depending on demand. Thus, political science departments could consider establishing a fund that features both flexibility and purpose, including the support of unpaid interns.

Alumni may also wish to self-name funds for internships, like the Gordon and Norma Guyer Public Policy Internship Award at Michigan State University (https://polisci.msu.edu/undergraduate/scholarships.html). A notable example of an alumna-named fund that directly addresses gender equity concerns in internships is the Barbara Lee Fellowship (https://www.simmons.edu/undergraduate/academics/undergraduate-research-and-fellowships/opportunities-simmons/barbara-lee) at Simmons University (Doherty 2011). Drawing on its location in Boston, Massachusetts, the fellowship pairs women interns with women state legislators. As of 2011, the program provided a stipend of $1,750 and students could earn internship credits. Doherty (2011) reported that the program was effective in increasing women students' view of their viability in politics and the program had great success in seeing alumni pursue careers in public service. This is a good example of how pay, credit, and faculty support can be combined to address gender disparities in internships as well as public service.

Finally, some departments also have funds that memorialize the legacy of students, such as the Adam Gregory Thomas Legislative Internship Scholarship at the University of Nevada, Reno (https://www.unr.edu/political-science) and the Sara Katherine Ullman Memorial Internship Award at Ohio University (https://www.ohio.edu/cas/political-science/financial-aid). Other funds honor local public officials, like the Grand Valley State University's Paul B. Henry Congressional Internship (https://www.gvsu.edu/polisci/scholarships-33.htm). Political science departments can work with their development offices to cultivate philanthropy and should keep internship support in mind as a possible use of funds donated by alumni or in honor of individual (or multiple) faculty or students.

Model 2: Center-Based Subsidies

While not available at all institutions, academic centers or institutes, which are typically organized around a common subject (e.g., The McCourtney Institute for Democracy) and not housed within an academic department, have long been increasing in number across higher education. They became ubiquitous at research institutes in the 1980s (Stahler and Tash 1994) and can be viewed as having more of an impact on an institution's research enterprise than its educational mission (Bunton and Mallon 2007). Still, some institutes and centers offer funding for internships and, as purported funding magnets for institutions, they could be leveraged as another means beyond departments for cultivating internship support. The William J. Hughes Center at Stockton University (https://stockton.edu/hughes-center/), for example, provides $1,000 of funding to one student per semester who attends the Washington Center Internship program (https://twc.edu/). The Hughes Center is highlighted because it is at a smaller public regional comprehensive university, not an R1. While the Center has limited funds compared to a large research institution, it still provides support for internships. Likewise, the Institute of Public Affairs and Civic Engagement at San José State University offers the $2,000 IPACE scholarship (https://www.sjsu.edu/polisci/scholarships/ipace.php) to one political science intern who is concurrently enrolled in an internship course for credit.

The Institute for Public Administration (https://www.bidenschool.udel.edu/ipa) at the Biden School of Public Policy & Administration at the University of Delaware is an example of what an institute at a larger school, with a big name attached, can do. The Institute provides fellowships for legislative, judicial, and local government internships.[5] Not only do students receive a stipend, but they also receive carpool travel assistance to Dover and internship course credit. Granted, not all schools can do this, but political science programs on campuses with large policy-, democracy-, and governance-oriented centers should push them to provide opportunities like these, especially if they are named for prominent public servants.

Model 3: Tuition Waivers

Whereas the first two models focus on providing stipends to students, a third form of support involves lessening the cost of obtaining credit for either unpaid or paid internships. To achieve this, universities and colleges could waive the tuition costs for qualifying experiences or enable students to add a course to a transcript with variable credits attached. The state of Massachusetts offers students at its public universities a need-based waiver of tuition and housing subsidy for the Washington Center Internship experience (https://www.mass.edu/osfa/programs/washingtoncenter.asp). Chapman University waives tuition for credited international internships, which typically require significant additional costs for relocation and living (https://www.chapman.edu/international-studies/center-for-global-education/travel-courses/tuition-waiver.aspx). Vanderbilt University has a program to waive tuition for a one-credit summer internship (https://www.vanderbilt.edu/career/career-exploration/internships/). Alternatively, students could fulfill all the academic requirements to have their internships transcripted with fewer units attached. The transcript would show zero or more units on a student's transcript, up to the maximum allowed before a tuition charge is triggered. An institution could go further by awarding fractional credits to faculty based on the time they spend with students, rather than the number of units that students accumulate. Doing so reduces tuition costs for the students while also protecting and providing compensation for faculty time. Tuition reductions come at a direct cost to the institution, of course, but some institutions are willing to bear this as an investment in their students.

FEDERAL SUPPORT

Proposals for changing how the federal government supports public sector internships are of particular importance to political science programs. Only 6% of House interns were paid in 2017 (members of Congress can choose to pay them through their own budgets), although 46% of US Senators reported paying their interns either an hourly wage or fixed stipend (Vera and Jenab 2017). The House Paid Internship program was created in 2019, and in 2020 the Committee on House Administration issued new regulations for paid internships (Committee on House Administration 2021). House members receive a yearly allowance of $25,000 to pay interns (Senators receive $50,000 via their program), and these funds can be used to pay both DC and district office interns. These dedicated funds should increase the number of paid internships on the Hill, which may, in turn, make them even more competitive. The rules do not set specific wages for all offices, as the House Intern Pay Act would, and the allowance can be spent on equipment (such as laptops that connect directly to the US House network) and stipends in any amount (minimum of $100 per intern). Further, interns cannot work for a member for more than 120 calendar days and must be able to demonstrate that they are part of a formal education program.

In 2010, a report by the Economic Policy Institute proposed a new federal Student Opportunity Program that would "serve as a pipeline to college completion and employment for high-achieving, low-income students, helping them to acquire the skills, contacts, and experience that will improve their future labor market potential and encourage them to pursue careers in public service" (Edwards and Hertel-Fernandez 2010, 2). The program is based on the model of Federal Work Study (FWS), with schools receiving funds based on the number of enrolled students that qualify using the Free Application for Federal Student Aid (FAFSA). The program would have income-based eligibility limits, but schools would determine which unpaid internships could count as quality employment, set award amounts, enroll students, and dispense monies. The authors argue that many institutions could do this through their existing FWS infrastructure, but some may need to develop additional staff support. Indeed, many colleges do this already, with the important caveat that using FWS money requires both the student to qualify based on income and the internship itself to qualify, which precludes internships with political campaigns.

The report also offers two alternative (or additional) implementation strategies. First, colleges and universities could compete for funds from the US Department of Education for the purpose of developing their own "internship support programs for low-income students" (7). Second, the federal government could directly incentivize and support internships in federal executive agencies. Edwards and Hertel-Fernandez (2010) suggest that this be administered by the Office of Personnel Management. In addition to directly funding students who are completing unpaid public sector internships, the authors suggest that Congress should make money available for federal, state, and local governments to improve their internship experiences for students. A major benefit of federal funding for such an initiative would be to expand opportunities for high-quality internships beyond Washington, DC and other major metropolitan areas. Supporting both students and internship providers in state and local governments would allow students to complete high-quality internships closer to home, which could, in turn, reduce their living expenses. The combination of reduced costs to complete an internship and a stipend for their labor would make internships more accessible to low-income students.

THE PROFESSION AND INTERNSHIPS

What is the American Political Science Association's (APSAs) role in the internship landscape? This handbook is an important marker of the Association's, and particularly the Political Science Education section's, commitment to internships. APSA has also been working to make equity and inclusion an important emphasis, but the profession, and the public service professions that it serves, will not diversify quickly or adequately if the pipeline of talent faces structural barriers for some (women, BIPOC, first generation students) and advantages for others (White, male, multi-generation students and those wealthy financially and/or well-connected). Because internship funding lies at the heart of equity concerns for the public service career pipeline (Doherty 2011; Hindmoor 2010), APSA should consider taking the following three steps.

First, APSA should expand on the effort of this book in making internships, particularly cultivating paid internships, a priority. APSA could look to the model internship guidelines developed conjointly by the Network of Schools of Public Policy, Affairs, and Administration (NASPAA) Urban Management Education Committee and the International City/County Management Association (ICMA) Advisory Board on Graduate Education for Master's in Public Administration students. In regard to compensation, the guidelines state as follows:

> Internships are in many cases one of the methods for the student to finance his/her education. While it is not always feasible, every effort should be made to create "funded" internships. The old adage "you get what you pay for" is true for many internships. Local governments that contribute financially to the support of the internship are more likely, over time, to make meaningful use of the intern, to provide the intern with good supervision, and to demand more from the intern in terms of professional productivity. The more the intern is treated as a temporary or part-time employee, the more valuable the internship will be to the student and the local government. Providing financial support to the internship is also likely to increase the pool of potential interns from which the local government can choose. (Benavides, Dicke, and Holt 2013, 352)

This type of collaborative statement between an academic organization (NASPAA) and one representing potential internship providers (ICMA) establishes an expectation that departments can leverage when establishing collaborations with internship providers (Benavides, Dicke, and Holt 2013).

Second, encouraging more research on political science internships, particularly around pay, would be valuable. There is a broader literature on career and equity disadvantages of unpaid internships, but much of that work is done outside of political science and has substantial limitations (Rothschild and Rothschild 2020). This is not to say there is no literature on political science internships, but much of it focuses on learning outcomes (e.g., Lucas 2020; Mariani and Klinkner 2009). Even articles offering guidance on how to better institutionalize internships do not discuss pay (Foster Schoaf 2020). In fact, a recently published article on internship supervisors points to knowledge gaps on internship pay through its future research questions: "Do unpaid internships get more substantive responsibility and thus learn more than paid interns? Do internship supervisors treat paid interns differently from unpaid interns?" (Sosland and Lowenthal 2017). The survey included in this volume provides insight into how some departments handle internship support, but additional institutional research would be helpful for departments that want to follow best practices. Specifically, several models are outlined above, but there is need for systematic knowledge about how to develop these kinds of programs. Best practices for university fundraising and development can provide guidelines for cultivating resources for supporting interns, but understanding the details of how political science departments have established and maintained their support could have value across the discipline.

Third, APSA, perhaps through the Political Science Education member section, is positioned to champion federal initiatives like the Student Opportunity Program and expand programs like the House Paid Internship Program to executive agencies. As a professional organization, APSA represents members who are often reliant on unpaid internships to help their students progress professionally. Given the possibility for abuses of interns and the equity concerns of relying so heavily on unpaid opportunities, APSA could add its voice to calls for better intern pay within the public sector.

REFERENCES

Allan, Kori. 2019. "Volunteering As Hope Labour: The Potential Value Of Unpaid Work Experience For The Un-And Under-Employed." *Culture, Theory and Critique* 60 (1): 66–83. doi: 10.1080/14735784.2018.1548300.

Baines, Donna, Ian Cunningham, and John Shields. 2017. "Filling The Gaps: Unpaid (And Precarious) Work In The Nonprofit Social Services." *Critical Social Policy* 37 (4): 625–645. doi: 10.1177/0261018317693128.

Benavides, Abraham D., Lisa A. Dicke, and Amy C. Holt. 2013. "Internships Adrift? Anchoring Internship Programs in Collaboration." *Journal of Public Affairs Education* 19 (2): 325–353. doi: 10.1080/15236803.2013.12001736.

Bunton, Sarah A., and William T. Mallon. 2007. "The Impact of Centers and Institutes on Faculty Life: Findings from a Study of Life Sciences Faculty at Research-Intensive Universities' Medical Schools." *Innovative Higher Education* 32 (2): 93–103. doi: 10.1007/s10755-007-9041-0.

Collins, Todd A., H. Gibbs Knotts, and Jen Schiff. 2012. "Career Preparation and the Political Science Major: Evidence from Departments." *PS: Political Science & Politics* 45 (1): 87–92. doi: 10.1017/S1049096511001764.

Committee on House Administration. 2021. "House Paid Internship Program." US House of Representatives. https://cha.house.gov/member-services/house-paid-internship-program.

Crain, Andrew. 2016. "Exploring the Implications of Unpaid Internships." *NACE Journal*, November 1. https://www.naceweb.org/job-market/internships/exploring-the-implications-of-unpaid-internships/.

Curiale, Jessica L. 2009. "America's New Glass Ceiling: Unpaid Internships, the Fair Labor Standards Act, and the Urgent Need for Change." *Hastings Law Journal* 61 (6): 1531–1560.

Doherty, Leanne. 2011. "Filling the Female Political Pipeline: Assessing a Mentor-Based Internship Program." *Journal of Political Science Education* 7 (1): 34–47. doi: 10.1080/15512169.2011.539911.

Edwards, Kathryn Anne, and Alexander Hertel-Fernandez. 2010. *Paving the Way Through Paid Internships: A Proposal to Expand Educational and Economic Opportunities for Low-Income College Students.* Washington, DC: Economic Policy Institute and Dēmos.

Fadulu, Lola. 2018. "Why Aren't College Students Using Career Services?" *The Atlantic.* Last Modified January 20, 2018. Accessed August 21, 2020. https://www.theatlantic.com/education/archive/2018/01/why-arent-college-students-using-career-services/551051/.

Fisher, Sarah, and Florian Justwan. 2018. "Scaffolding Assignments and Activities for Undergraduate Research Methods." *Journal of Political Science Education* 14 (1): 63–71. doi: 10.1080/15512169.2017.1367301.

Foster Schoaf, Nicole. 2020. "Political Science Internships: A Path to 'Workforce Ready' without Selling Out." *APSA Preprints.* doi: 10.33774/apsa-2020-hknr6.

Hindmoor, Andrew. 2010. "Internships Within Political Science." *Australian Journal of Political Science* 45 (3): 483–490. doi: 10.1080/10361146.2010.499186.

Hunt, Wil, and Peter Scott. 2017. "Participation in Paid and Unpaid Internships Among Creative and Communications Graduates." In *Higher Education and Social Inequalities*, eds. Richard Waller, Nicole Ingram and Michael R. M. Ward, 190–207. New York, NY: Routledge.

Joyce, Peter, Sandra Staklis, Ami Thakkar, and John Vavricka. 2018. *Making Paid Internships the Standard: A Global Lens.* Research Triangle Park, NC: RTI International.

Kazak, Sibel, Rupert Wegerif, and Taro Fujita. 2015. "Combining Scaffolding for Content and Scaffolding for Dialogue to Support Conceptual Breakthroughs in Understanding Probability." *ZDM* 47 (7): 1269–1283. doi: 10.1007/s11858-015-0720-5.

Ledwith, Katherine E. 2014. "Academic Advising and Career Services: A Collaborative Approach." *New Directions for Student Services* 148: 49–63. doi: 10.1002/ss.20108.

Lucas, Kevin. 2020. "Internships for Credit: Linking Work Experience to Political Science Learning Objectives." *APSA Preprints.* doi: 10.33774/apsa-2020-mrs8n.

Mallinson, Daniel J., and Patrick Burns. 2019. "Increasing Career Confidence through a Course in Public Service Careers." *Journal of Political Science Education* 15 (2): 161–178. doi: 10.1080/15512169.2018.1443820.

Mariani, Mack, and Philip Klinkner. 2009. "The Effect of a Campaign Internship on Political Efficacy and Trust." *Journal of Political Science Education* 5 (4): 275–293. doi: 10.1080/15512160903272160.

McDow, Lauren W., and Karen M. Zabrucky. 2015. "Effectiveness of a Career Development Course on Students' Job Search Skills and Self-Efficacy." *Journal of College Student Development* 56 (6): 632–636.

McGrath, Gary L. 2002. "The Emergence of Career Services and their Important Role in Working with Employers." *New Directions for Student Services* 2002 (100): 69–84. doi: 10.1002/ss.71.

Mertz, Pamela S., and Kelly Y. Neiles. 2020. "Scaffolding Career Skills into the Undergraduate Curriculum Utilizing a Backward Design Approach." In *Integrating Professional Skills into Undergraduate Chemistry*

Curricula, 43–55. American Chemical Society.

Moon, Jeremy, and Wykham Schokman. 2000. "Political Science Research Internships and Political Science Education." *Politics* 20 (3): 169–175. doi: 10.1111/1467-9256.00127.

NACE. 2019. *The 2019 Student Survey Report*. Bethlehem, PA: National Association of Colleges and Employers.

Rothschild, Philip C., and Connor L. Rothschild. 2020. "The Unpaid Internship: Benefits, Drawbacks, and Legal Issues." *Administrative Issues Journal* 10 (2): 1–17.

Saks McManaway, Kimberly, and Kevin G. Lorentz. 2020. "Service Guarantees Citizenship: Portfolio Work, Populism, and Scaffolding in Introductory American Government Classrooms." *Journal of Political Science Education* [Online]: 1–14. doi: 10.1080/15512169.2020.1796688.

Saltikoff, Nathalie, Alifeya Albers, Laura Rossi-Le, and Eric Hall. 2018. *Unpaid Internships and Early Career Outcomes*. Bethlehem, PA: NACE Center for Career Development and Talent Acquisition. https://sites.sju.edu/careers/files/2018-nace-unpaid-internships-and-early-career-outcomes.pdf.

Scott-Clayton, Judith. 2012. "What Explains Trends in Labor Supply Among US Undergraduates, 1970–2009?" *National Bureau of Economic Research Working Paper Series*. doi: 10.3386/w17744.

Shade, Leslie Regan, And Jenna Jacobson. 2015. "Hungry For The Job: Gender, Unpaid Internships, And The Creative Industries." *The Sociological Review* 63 (S1): 188–205. doi: 10.1111/1467-954x.12249.

Sosland, Jeffrey K., and Diane J. Lowenthal. 2017. "The Forgotten Educator: Experiential Learning's Internship Supervisor." *Journal of Political Science Education* 13 (1): 1–14. doi: 10.1080/15512169.2016.1165106.

Stahler, Gerald J., and William R. Tash. 1994. "Centers and Institutes in the Research University: Issues, Problems, and Prospects." *The Journal of Higher Education* 65 (5): 540–554. doi: 10.2307/2943777.

Van Vechten, Renée B., Bobbi Gentry, and Shamira Gelbman. 2015. "Best Practices in Political Science Internships." Questionnaire. May 1.

Van Vechten, Renée B. and Bobbi Gentry. 2017. "Best Practices in Political Science Internships (Community Colleges)." Questionnaire. July 21.

Varney, Jennifer. 2007. "Proactive Advising." In *Academic Advising Approaches: Strategies That Teach Students to Make the Most of College*, eds. Jayne K. Drake, Peggy Jordan and Marsha A. Miller, 137–154. San Francisco, CA: Jossey-Bass.

Vera, Carlos, and Daniel Jenab. 2017. *Why Paid Internships are a Must in Congress*. Washington, DC: Pay Our Interns.

ENDNOTES

1. Rent Café, "Washington DC Rental Market Trends," Accessed March 20, 2021, https://www.rentcafe.com/average-rent-market-trends/us/dc/washington/.

2. EducationData.org, "Cost of a College Class or Credit Hour," Accessed March 20, 2021, https://educationdata.org/cost-of-a-college-class-or-credit-hour.

3. Indeed.com, "How much does an intern make in Washington, DC?" Accessed March 20, 2021, https://www.indeed.com/career/intern/salaries/Washington--DC.

4. This national survey was conducted in two waves, with the first surveying four-year institutions ranging from R1's to liberal arts colleges in summer 2015. The second wave in summer 2016 included community colleges. A total of 172 departments responded. This chapter draws from two of the 48 questions about department internship practices.

5. For legislative internships, see: https://www.bidenschool.udel.edu/ipa/student-opportunities/legislative-fellows; for judicial internships visit: https://www.bidenschool.udel.edu/ipa/student-opportunities/judicial-fellows; and for local government go to: https://www.bidenschool.udel.edu/ipa/student-opportunities/management-fellows.

CHAPTER 12

Working with Campus-wide Internship Coordinators and Centers

Cynthia Chávez Metoyer, California State University, San Marcos

Because internships take place outside the classroom, many institutions have developed policies, protocols, and related documentation to ensure that students, faculty, and the institution know their responsibilities and are prepared to deal with difficult situations. These requirements occasionally change and may not be well-known to faculty. Rooted in personal experience and observations at California State University, San Marcos, the author suggests how to best leverage the services of a campus-wide academic internship office or coordinator. Likely benefits and disadvantages of working with a campus internship office are identified to generate conversation about how political science departments might work effectively with a campus internship office where they exist or could be established.

INTRODUCTION

Both academic and non-academic internships can provide students opportunity for personal and professional growth. Unlike non-academic internships, academic internships are not simply about gaining hands-on experience; rather, they integrate disciplinary knowledge and theory learned in the classroom with practical application and professional development in a workplace setting. Since most four-year institutions operate under shared governance in which the faculty retain primary authority over curricula, academic internships are commonly offered through disciplinary departments that determine eligibility criteria, academic work expectations, grading rubrics, and hours requirements that are based on institutional credit-hour policies.[1] Generally, faculty are responsible for *supervising* student interns; as with any other credit-bearing course, faculty determine the required assignments, assess student progress, and assign a grade or course credit for academic internships. On some campuses, faculty are also responsible for *monitoring* or *managing* the administrative aspects of internships, which includes collecting emergency contact information and liability waivers from students, finding suitable internship sites, and conducting site visits to ensure site safety. On some campuses like mine, however, the administrative aspects of academic internships are managed by a campus-wide coordinator or center, what I will refer to in this chapter as a *campus internship office*.[2] Its name and location within the institutional structure vary by campus and depend upon both the positioning of academic internships in the curricular experience of the campus (whether internships are required or optional, for example), and the campus's philosophy regarding experiential educational learning.

At some universities and colleges, the campus internship office is a stand-alone office; at others it is commonly positioned within Academic Affairs, Student Affairs, or Community Engagement.[3] When the campus internship office is situated within Academic Affairs, there tends to be a focus on learning outcomes, teaching practices, and the role of faculty supervisors. When located within Student Affairs, the focus is generally on providing career readiness resources, including job postings, interview skills, and job search strategies. When placed within a Community Engagement Division, benefits for the community and fostering community partner relations tend to be highlighted. Regardless of its placement in the organizational structure, the internship office is usually established to develop a more organized, coordinated approach to managing internships and to enhance experiential learning.[4]

Research on academic internships has focused primarily on student learning outcomes in two areas: one, the impact of internships on academic and/or career success; and two, the effectiveness of internships for career readiness (Binder, et al. 2015; Callanan and Benzing 2004; Erdogan and Stuessy 2015; Kappe and Flier 2012; Knouse, Tanner, and Harris 1999; Lei and Yin 2019; Taylor 1988). This rich and growing body of literature includes research on equity gaps, student access, and the differential impact of paid and unpaid internships on future career success (Blau and Lopez 2020; Fairtlough, et al. 2014; Fuller and Schoenberger 1991; Heidelberg 2019; Hernandez et al. 2014; Liu, et al. 2020; Mclean, et al. 2018; see also chapter by Mallinson). Additionally, professional organizations such as the National Association of Colleges and Employers (NACE), the Cooperative Education and Internship Association (CEIA), and the Association of American Colleges & Universities (AACU) regularly conduct employer surveys and research on the impact of internships on professional skills, gaps in education, employment trends, and hiring statistics.[5]

Despite the important contributions these organizations have made to our understanding about internships, practical guidance about *how* academic departments can best work with a campus internship office or coordinator (when one does exist) remains unclear. The aim of this chapter is to offer some practical insight into working with a campus internship office. Based on my experience as the Faculty Director of a campus internship office for six years,[6] 15 years of experience as the Political Science Department's internship coordinator, and a brief survey I conducted of 23 California State University campuses,[7] I offer my informed observations and suggest how to best leverage the services of a campus internship office. The purpose of this chapter is to generate conversation about how political science departments might work effectively with an existing campus unit that manages internships, or where one is being planned, by identifying possible benefits and pitfalls. What follows is a brief discussion about how and why my university established a campus internship office and its functions; an examination of the potential advantages and drawbacks of a campus internship office; and practical considerations for working with a campus internship office.

WHY A CAMPUS INTERNSHIP OFFICE? CSUSM'S STORY

California State University, San Marcos (CSUSM) is one of 23 campuses in the California State University (CSU) system. CSU system-wide policies establish oversight, guidelines, and procedures for nearly every aspect of the 23 campuses; these are derived from and shaped by state legislation, regulations, Board of Trustees resolutions, and executive directives. In 2011, the Chancellor's Office issued Executive Order 1064, requiring each campus to establish student internship policies and procedures to maximize students' educational experience as interns, to mitigate potential risks to participants, and to minimize the university's liability exposure.

In response to EO 1064, President Karen S. Haynes charged a Student Placement Task Force in September 2013 to examine CSUSM's practices and to identify how these might be structured to best serve the students, faculty, and community stakeholders.[8] The Task Force defined "student placement" as student work related to their CSUSM educational experience (both academic and co-curricular) at a community organization, including clinical practice, service learning, senior experience, internships, and field research. The Task Force learned that individual programs were well-organized, with a few exceptions; however, from a university-wide perspective, student placement was inconsistently organized, uncoordinated, and confusing. More specifically, the Task Force found that while certain programs had clearly outlined procedures (namely clinical practice, service learning, and senior experience), internships and international service learning placements lacked clearly defined processes. Further, the Task Force discovered strong evidence that the campus community was confused by different types of placements and, consequently, defaulted to referring to all types of placements as "internships" (Student Placement Task Force 2014). After interviewing various campus stakeholders and surveying models at other institutions, the Task Force concluded that campus-wide coordination of internships was needed.

In April 2014, the Task Force was renamed the Implementation Team for Student Placement and its membership was expanded to include additional faculty and staff representing each of the divisions and academic colleges.[9] In short, the Implementation Team was responsible for operationalizing recommendations to ensure compliance with EO 1064 which, among other things: a) required that each campus's student internship policy spell out how to best support academic internship offerings across programs; b) identified a suitable online database for collecting and managing the student placement process;[10] and c) determined where to locate the campus internship office both physically and within the organizational structure.

In an effort to understand student placement practices across campus, members of the cross-divisional Implementation Team provided various perspectives and also interviewed stakeholders engaged in experiential learning.[11] Following this consultative process, the task force recommended that an office be established specifically to serve both students and faculty. Thus, the Office of Internships was established in 2015 for two main purposes: to provide robust administrative and operational support for faculty and students engaged in the high-impact practice of for-credit, academic internships; and to assist with sustaining existing internship sites and developing new community partnerships with entities interested in offering academic internships. The newly established Office of Internships was situated within the Community Engagement Division,[12] reflecting CSUSM's philosophy that experiential educational learning involves both faculty-directed learning and community partners who serve as co-educators offering professional work experience and mentoring new generations as they enter the workforce.

CSUSM's Office of Internships is co-led by a full-time Administrative Director and a Faculty Director, who has re-assigned time from teaching duties.[13] The Administrative Director's main responsibilities are to manage the business operations and develop new community partners, whereas the Faculty Director's primary role is to assist faculty members with the curricular aspects of academic internship courses. The Office is responsible for developing and managing an online database for collecting required documentation from students and community partners, providing a student safety orientation, evaluating and approving community partner applications, and overseeing an emergency readiness plan.

In earlier years, an Office of Service Learning was responsible for collecting the required placement documentation from faculty who had gathered it from their students. These were tracked manually with a spreadsheet, a process that was both inefficient and time consuming, particularly if the required documents were not submitted simultaneously. As a result, student contact information was not readily available should an emergency occur when the university office was closed. Thus, the online database was a game-changer as it integrated all required student placement forms and community partner information into one system.[14] Not only did this allow students to complete and submit the required documents electronically, but personal, emergency, and site supervisors' contact information became readily accessible to supervising faculty and Office of Internships staff. Additionally, the online database became the repository for procurement documentation of approved internship sites: it generates data for campus reporting (e.g., total hours invested in the community; numbers of students by major; etc.), and it is a user-friendly system that students can utilize to search for prospective internship opportunities with whom the university has a partnership agreement.[15]

CAMPUS INTERNSHIP OFFICE: POTENTIALS AND PITFALLS

A designated campus internship office makes possible the centralizing of information and resources for students, faculty, and the institution. When it assumes responsibility for coordinating the administrative aspects of internships, the faculty's workload lightens considerably; when it is adequately staffed, the office can make numerous other benefits possible for all stakeholders. However, as with all institutional arrangements, there are also pitfalls to consider. The benefits and drawbacks of working with an internship office are explored below.

Potential Benefits

Clerical and Operational Support

One important purpose of a campus internship office is to give students, faculty, and community partners access to academic internship opportunities and supply the resources and tools to support them. With regard to students, this usually includes articulating eligibility criteria and relevant policies and/or protocols, supplying information on how to find an internship and sources of internship opportunities,[16] providing assistance with navigating the placement process, fielding questions, and managing safety concerns and policy violations. With respect to faculty, this may include collecting all required documentation from students and community partners directly; articulating faculty responsibility and relevant protocols and/or policies; interfacing with other university offices when necessary, such as with international studies to secure curricular program training approval for international students; offering classroom presentations; providing teaching resources such as sample syllabi and learning plans, hours logs, and/or assignment ideas; and offering topical workshops to encourage best practices. Where community partners are concerned, a campus internship office provides guidelines for posting internships on the university's site as well as information about working with students, and is the place where all queries can be directed.

Risk Assessment and Compliance

Over a decade ago, the literature on high-impact practices documented the positive benefits for students who participate in internships,[17] and colleges have since pushed for students to engage in them.[18] However, a critical mass of students participating in internships can pose management issues for colleges and universities, who, for better or worse, have become increasingly risk averse in the last several decades (Bialostok, et al. 2012; Moran 2015; Strikwerda 2014). As reviewed in Chapter 3 by David Yamada, colleges and universities are expected to act with reasonable care to ensure a positive, safe, and valuable learning experience for students. Identifying and effectively mitigating risks that could (or do) exist, especially those that could cause avoidable or undue harm, concern all stakeholders. Colleges and universities, therefore, generally should require documentation for students involved in any academic internships, including emergency contact information, site supervisor information, and a liability waiver, as well as establish clear safety expectations and protocols in order to reasonably prevent foreseeable harm to students.

In the absence of a campus internship office, the responsibility for mitigating risk associated with internships defaults to individual faculty and academic departments. If risk assessment is outside the scope of their regular work duties, they may be altogether unaware of this responsibility, or they may establish their own practices, forms, and protocols which may not adhere to state, federal, or university guidelines. Without a designated campus internship office, varying processes and practices related to student placements are likely to exist across campus, and they may even contradict one another. However, a campus internship office makes possible the establishment of a consistent, campus-wide risk assessment plan aimed at identifying potential hazards, assessing the likelihood of unsafe occurrences, and developing protocols for dealing with emergency situations.

Generally, these responsibilities are shared with other entities on campus (offices of risk management, procurement and contracts, legal counsel, and so forth) who collectively determine *what* information should be collected from students and community partners; *how* the information will be collected and managed; *when* the information will be collected; and *what* the consequences are for not submitting documentation (for example, whether a registration hold will be placed on a student's account). If given adequate institutional oversight of student placements, a campus internship office can protect students from potentially exploitative or inappropriate situations by vetting prospective community partners and educating them about campus expectations for interns, and requiring that student interns complete a workplace and safety orientation before they begin their internships.

A related potential benefit of having a campus internship office is effective compliance management. In addition to internal policies that could extend to liability insurance coverage, conflict of interest, student conduct, and standards for internship postings, colleges and universities are bound by external regulations such as those issued by the US Department of Labor (DOL) and the US Equal Employment Opportunity Commission regarding discrimination, sexual harassment, and reasonable accommodations for disability and religion (again, see Yamada in this volume). Because existing policies can be modified or new ones introduced, it is helpful to have a single office dedicated to staying up-to-date and keeping other campus stakeholders informed of new developments.

Crisis Management

Whereas *risk* management is a strategic effort to identify and assess the likelihood and impact of possible dangers that commonly occur in a workplace,[19] and also to clarify the steps needed to eliminate or mitigate those dangers, *crisis* management is concerned with responding to, managing, and recovering from an unexpected occurrence. It is impossible to fully anticipate the nature and extent of disruptive threats and emergencies or to foresee when they will occur. But crises do happen: natural disasters, active shooters, mass violence, terrorist threats or attacks, bomb threats, widespread power outages, hazardous materials releases, and disease outbreaks are just some of the possible scenarios to consider. Most colleges and universities have a crisis (or emergency) management plan that establishes a chain of command outlining the authority and related responsibilities of campus officials and staff for many of these scenarios. A crisis management plan attempts to protect the health and welfare of the campus community, mitigate operational disruption, and minimize physical or environmental damage.

While a campus internship office is unlikely to spearhead a crisis management response for the entire college or university, communication with potentially affected students, their emergency contacts, and staff at the internship site could be critical. For example, when two planes crashed into the World Trade Center's North and South Towers on the morning of September 11, 2001, not only did New York University (NYU) officials have to evacuate students from their dorms because of hazardous materials contamination, it was also important to confirm whether any NYU students were involved in experiential learning activities in the towers. Thankfully, no NYU students were on-site (Lucia and Murphy 2001).

The COVID-19 pandemic is another example that highlights the usefulness of a campus internship office with respect to crisis management. In spring 2020 when colleges and universities across the nation abruptly pivoted from in-person to remote delivery of classes, questions emerged regarding off-campus experiential learning activities. Could students continue working physically at their off-site placement if it remained open, but their classes were online? If so, under what circumstances? Was it safe? Did students need to sign a liability waiver that specified the risks associated with COVID-19? Did internship sites need to provide additional documentation to prove they were following public health orders? What would happen if the internship site closed, or if interns were uncomfortable continuing to work onsite? Were there particular requirements for a remote internship? Together with university leaders and guided by state and public health orders, our campus internship office team navigated through the flurry of questions and concerns to develop a singular set of university guidelines for students participating off-campus experiential learning.[20]

In short, not only would a campus internship office retain a list of all student interns along with their location and emergency contact information, but also its staff could brainstorm possible crisis scenarios both to identify potential threats and game out the tasks, communications, and information needed to coordinate with appropriate players to best manage the crisis.

Community Engagement

During the last two decades, a national movement has emerged to renew the civic mission of US colleges and universities to better meet societal needs. This has resulted in a growing emphasis on community engagement in higher education. The Carnegie Foundation defines community engagement as the "collaboration between institutions of higher education and their larger communities (local, regional/state, national, global) for the mutually beneficial exchange of knowledge and resources in a context of partnership and reciprocity" (Public Purpose Institute 2021). Colleges and universities today tend to be perceived not as traditional, sole, expert producers of knowledge, but rather, as collaborators in knowledge production, or as stakeholders among many other knowledge partners in the community (Bovill 2020; Gibbons et al. 2012).

Internships offer an important pathway for colleges and universities to engage with their community, helping to vitalize a community by addressing its needs (Bracic 2018; Jacob 2015).[21] Engagement demands energy, planning, and communication between the university and community partners, and the acknowledgement that community partners are also educators and experts who foster students' personal, academic, and professional growth by involving them in meaningful workplace activities. Absent a campus internship office, the responsibility of developing and sustaining meaningful internships with community partners usually falls to faculty. While faculty play an important role in identifying prospective community partners and fostering good relationships with them, many faculty do not have the time to actively seek out new partners and conduct site visits. Neither can faculty be expected to manage the administrative aspects of community partnership development.

On many campuses, risk management and/or contracts-related offices are involved in overseeing community partner agreements. Their primary objective vis-à-vis community partners is to garner formal agreements that clarify the responsibilities of all parties and spell out how liability and workers' compensation issues will be handled. But what these offices generally do not do is cultivate new community partners to meet the curricular needs of the various academic departments; rather, their role is to assess and approve prospective community partners as part of their contract and risk management duties. However, with community engagement as a central objective, a designated campus internship office can take responsibility for outreach and cultivating partnerships with prospective community organizations in order to meet stakeholders' ever-changing needs.

Main Point of Contact

Another potential benefit of a campus internship office is the ability to operate as the main point of contact for all inquiries and resources concerning academic internships. A campus internship office can serve as a one-stop shop where students, faculty, and external community members can get all their internship-related questions answered. This does not eliminate consultation and/or coordination with other offices, but when needed, the campus internship office team can consult with other offices to get answers instead of making the "client" bounce around between campus offices. A case in point is when a student reports to her faculty member that she was sexually harassed at her internship site. Whom does the faculty member contact to report the incident, and is there a correct order to the reporting? The Department Chair, College Dean, Dean of Students, Title IX coordinator, and Risk Management are all possibilities. Whereas each of these parties might have a legitimate need to be informed of the matter, the faculty member may not be aware of all who should be contacted. But when there is a designated campus internship office, the faculty member only needs to contact that one office to report an incident. The campus internship office bears the responsibility for informing all necessary parties or advising the faculty member on appropriate action to be taken.

Receiving information and instructions from multiple locations can be quite confusing, especially during a rapidly evolving crisis with decisions being made in real time. Pointing again to the example of the global pandemic, multiple faculty on my campus expressed their appreciation for the up-to-date communications they received from our office as well as the ability to get questions answered in a timely manner. Particularly at the start of the stay-at-home orders in early March 2020 when new information was pouring in, senior leadership would announce a flurry of decisions in the morning—only to supersede them later that day with new decisions. Our office was able to facilitate the flow of information specifically regarding academic internships and communicate it to relevant faculty. As the main point of contact for internship-related activities, a campus internship office is also able to identify patterns of concerns that need to be addressed by senior leaders. Thus, a campus internship office can serve as an information hub to disseminate information and channel concerns.

Data Collection

A final potential advantage is the collection, compilation, and analysis of quality data about experiential learning within higher education institutions. Just as colleges and universities track degree completion, admissions, and recruitment numbers, it is useful to collect reliable and accurate data on academic internships, such as: the number of students enrolled in an internship course; number of hours invested in the community; numbers of students participating in internship by departments, colleges, and internship sites; and demographic student information, to name a few. As managers of student placements, a campus internship office is aptly situated to collect such data.

Collecting and analyzing student placement information can help colleges and universities better understand the impact of experiential learning on student success, graduation, and retention rates; provide insight on where to invest resources and determine what areas or processes need improvement; and equip decision-makers with accurate data to respond to problems more effectively. Valid and reliable data collected and analyzed over time help us make connections that lead to insights and programmatic improvements.

Possible Pitfalls

When our university initially established a campus internship office many faculty, including me, questioned this proposal. How would this impact internship offerings at the department level? Would this increase faculty workload? How would it be funded? Through a series of town halls and faculty meetings, these concerns were allayed.

Curriculum Control

Might a campus internship office infringe upon faculty control of the curriculum? Most four-year institutions endorse the American Association of University Professors (AAUP's) Statement on Government of Colleges and Universities (1966), which asserts that the faculty possess primary authority over the academic area, including such matters as the curriculum, standards of faculty competence, and standards of student achievement. Therefore, while internship courses are subject to university policies that govern administrative practices such as a credit-hour policy and safety and risk management guidelines, faculty control the academic content of internships. Faculty members are the ultimate developers, implementers, and evaluators of the internship curriculum, and by design, a campus internship office should not encroach upon the curricular component of internship courses. On the other hand, a campus internship office can be built to function like other university offices, offering support and services for a targeted group of students and their faculty.[22] In short, it is generally agreed that the campus internship office operates not as creator of the curriculum but as guardian of standards and procedures.

Increased Workload

With the founding of a campus internship office and the new procedures it establishes, faculty may be concerned that they will be saddled with additional work. After all, it is not unusual for senior leaders to announce a new policy or make a decision that creates more work for faculty and staff. There was some skepticism regarding how the centralized process would impact faculty workload when the internship office was established at CSUSM. The new directors met with departments offering internship courses to clarify their respective roles and explain how the shared database and online internship placement process would work. To build and manage a campus database, the internship office would be responsible for collecting the required documentation directly from the students, thereby removing this task from faculty's plates.

Reluctance to Share Community Contacts

A campus internship office is likely to provide campus-wide access to internship opportunities through a shared database. If faculty members have cultivated relationships with organizations and maintain their own list of internship opportunities for their majors, they may resist contributing to a shared database because they are worried that other students might "steal" those coveted internships and leave their majors without placements. A few faculty members at CSUSM initially expressed such concerns. However, their reluctance to utilize a shared database was eased following a series of discussions with the campus internship office directors that offered the following rationale in response to their concerns.

1. Internships are not necessarily specific to a major. The organization determines what skills and criteria they are looking for in an intern, and these are specified in a job description. The organization may choose to specify a desired major or majors, but it is not within the purview of any campus member to make this determination. Organizations conceivably can offer multiple internship opportunities. For example, a political science faculty member may have fostered a partnership with an elected official, but in addition to a political science intern, the elected official might want to hire an audit intern (accounting major). The accounting major did not "steal" the internship from the political science major because they were not competing for the same internship. Competition for placements will indeed occur, but usually it happens among students in cognate disciplines. For example, students from media studies, visual and performing arts, and marketing would likely meet the *basic* qualifications to be a social media intern. Even so, it's highly unlikely that all students would meet the *specified* qualifications; a political science, music, or finance major, to name a few, likely would not. Moreover, the internship must meet the disciplinary requirements of students' respective departments.[23] Nevertheless, it behooves political science faculty to cultivate relationships with local elected officials, public agencies, law offices, and appropriate non-profit organizations to create a pipeline for their students and to refine the qualifications, as internship opportunities are not "owned" by any one department.

2. Internship opportunity scarcity. Of the 1,302 community partners in the database as of spring 2020, only 194 of them hosted 413 interns, meaning that 85% of community partners had at least one unfilled internship opportunity. Supply continues to meet and outstrip student demand.[24] Furthermore, an important charge of the campus internship office is to continually develop new community partnerships. The CSUSM model encourages faculty to request that the campus internship office initiate a partnership agreement with an organization they would like to work with, and students can find an internship on their own and request it be added to the database at any time.[25] Prospective community partners independently can apply to become a community partner through the website. Moreover, the Administrative Director actively reaches out to prospective community partners through networking events such as Chamber of Commerce meetings, career fairs, and local business engagements. Since 2015 when the office was established, the number of community partners has grown to 1,400 (in 2021), a 243% increase.

On balance, the potential benefits of a campus internship office outweigh possible pitfalls: a campus internship office is positioned to build consistency across departments and colleges in terms of best practices, documentation and compliance, communication, and data collection.

PRACTICAL CONSIDERATIONS: HOW TO START WORKING WITH AN INTERNSHIP OFFICE

To get started working with a campus internship office, it is important to understand its defined roles and responsibilities as compared to those of faculty and/or academic departments.

Student internship policy. Check to see if your campus has a university and/or college internship policy. Campus policies provide general guidance, a larger frame within which departments may establish specific internship procedures. A campus policy will likely define an internship consistent with US Department of Labor (DOL) standards and include guidance around health and safety, prohibited activities, and the requirements and responsibilities of all parties involved. While DOL standards do not prohibit unpaid internships, your university may. If there is no internship policy regarding compensation for internships, you will want to ensure your requirements are consistent with DOL standards (Department of Labor 2018; also see Chapter 3 by Yamada).

Roles and responsibilities. An important objective of a campus internship policy is to prescribe who is responsible for what. A campus internship office may be responsible for any number of things, including: serving as a liaison for specific academic departments concerning credit issues and program information; approving internships sites; conducting site visits; collecting required documentation; interfacing with community partners; providing career coaching to students; offering career preparation workshops; and supervising interns. Faculty generally are responsible for determining the learning objectives of an internship or a course, course design, and graded course requirements.

Required documentation. A campus internship office is usually responsible for collecting all the required documentation which can be submitted through an online database with customizable features and be accessed by the faculty of record. The beauty of a campus online database is that it contains student contact information as well as site supervisor information, and in the event of an emergency, this information is readily accessible to faculty as well as the campus internship office team. An online database makes it possible to better track where students are interning and to ensure all students receive a workplace and safety orientation. Faculty should familiarize themselves with the database enough to know what features could ease course management.

Resources and services. The primary work of a designated campus internship office is fostering quality internships. Its directors are likely to attend professional conferences and have a strong network of career services professionals. In addition to the services already described previously, most offer workshops and classroom presentations that can be tailored to assist political science students in finding appropriate internships. Lastly, a designated campus internship office can function as the key point of contact for conducting risk assessments and handling emergencies, and is the liaison to other important campus partners such as Risk Management, Dean of Students, Title IX coordinator, and global education or international studies.

CONCLUSION

With the right kind of help, internships can offer critical experiential learning that leads to greater student success for political science students. As this chapter demonstrates, a dedicated office whose single purpose is fostering quality experiences can steer important administrative aspects of the process, including vetting of worksites and community partners, documentation, and safety orientation. When it is set up to partner with all stakeholders, including students, faculty, and internship providers (what we call community partners), a centralized internship office helps systematize procedures, helps avoid "worst-case scenarios," and deals with thorny issues that arise. When it is staffed by knowledgeable administrators, an internship office is positioned to answer questions such as: does the internship meet the "primary beneficiary test" that courts have used to determine if the student qualifies as an employee and should be paid? Is the site safe for students? Have students been informed what to do in the event of an emergency or if they experience sexual or other types of harassment at their internship site? As our experience shows, a campus internship office can be designed to manage these and other compliance considerations adeptly. As with information technology staff and librarians, a campus internship office can provide invaluable administrative, technical, and informational support so that faculty can focus on the teaching aspects of their internship courses.

REFERENCES

Bialostok, Steven, Robert L. Whitman, and William S. Bradley, eds. 2012. *Education and the Risk Society: Theories, Discourse and Risk Identities in Education Contexts.* Rotterdam, Netherlands: Sense Publishers. doi.org/10.1007/978-94-6091-961-9.

Binder, Jens F., Thom Baguley, Chris Crook, and Felicity Miller. 2015. "The Academic Value of Internships: Benefits across Disciplines and Student Backgrounds." *Contemporary Educational Psychology* 41: 73–82. doi.org/10.1016/j.cedpsych.2014.12.001.

Blau, Gary and Andrea B. Lopez. 2020. "Exploring Correlates for Paid versus Unpaid Internships or Co-Ops for Graduating Business Students." *Journal of Education for Business* 95 (6): 393–401. doi.org/10.1080/08832323.2019.1668744.

Bovill, Catherine. 2020. "Co-Creation in Learning and Teaching: The Case for a Whole-Class Approach in Higher Education." *Higher Education* 79 (6): 1023–37. doi.org/10.1007/s10734-019-00453-w.

Bracic, Ana. 2018. "For Better Science: The Benefits of Community Engagement in Research." *PS: Political Science & Politics* 51 (3): 550–53. doi.org/10.1017/S1049096518000446.

Callanan, Gerard, and Cynthia Benzing. 2004. "Assessing the Role of Internships in the Career-oriented Employment of Graduating College Students." *Education + Training* 46 (2): 82–89. doi.org/10.1108/00400910410525261.

Department of Labor. 2018. *Fact Sheet #71: Internship Programs Under the Fair Labor Standards Act.* https://www.dol.gov/agencies/whd/fact-sheets/71-flsa-internships.

Erdogan, Nivazi, and Carol Stuessy. 2015. "Examining the Role of Inclusive STEM Schools in the College and Career Readiness of Students in the United States: A Multi-Group Analysis on the Outcome of Student Achievement." *Educational Sciences: Theory & Practice* 15 (6): 1517-29. doi.org/10.12738/estp.2016.1.0072.

Fairtlough, Anna, Claudia Bernard, Joan Fletcher, and Akile Ahmet. 2014. "Black Social Work Students' Experiences of Practice Learning: Understanding Differential Progression Rates." *Journal of Social Work* 14 (6): 605–24. doi.org/10.1177/1468017313500416.

Fuller, Rex, and Richard Schoenberger. 1991."The Gender Salary Gap: Do Academic Achievement, Internship Experience, and College Major Make a Difference?" *Social Science Quarterly* 72 (4): 715-726. https://ezproxy.csusm.edu/login?auth=shibboleth&url=https://search-ebscohost-com.ezproxy.csusm.edu/login.aspx?direct=true&db=aph&AN=9201270908&site=ehost-live&scope=site.

Gibson, Suanne, Delia Baskerville, Ann Berry, Alison Black, Kathleen Norris, and Simoni Symeonidou. 2016. "'Diversity' 'Widening Participation' and 'Inclusion' in Higher Education: An International Study." *Widening Participation and Lifelong Learning* 18 (3): 7–33. doi.org/10.5456/WPLL.18.3.7.

Heidelberg, Brea M. 2019. "Evaluating Equity: Assessing Diversity Efforts through a Social Justice Lens." *Cultural Trends* 28 (5): 391–403. doi.org/10.1080/09548963.2019.1680002.

Hernandez, Kristen E., Sandra Bejarano, Francis J. Reyes, Margarita Chavez, and Holly Mata. 2014. "Experience Preferred: Insights from Our Newest Public Health Professionals on How Internships/Practicums Promote Career Development." *Health Promotion Practice* 15 (1): 95–99. doi.org/10.1177/1524839913507578.

Jacob, James W., Stewart E. Sutin, John C. Weidman, and John L. Yeager. 2015. *Community Engagement in Higher Education: Policy Reforms and Practice.* Rotterdam, Netherlands: Sense Publishers.

Johnson Carey, Shelley, ed. 2010. "Internships and Experiential Learning." *Peer Review Journal* Fall (12): 4. https://www.aacu.org/peerreview/2010/fall.

Kappe, Rutger and Henk van der Flier. 2012. "Predicting Academic Success in Higher Education: What's More Important than Being Smart?" *European Journal of Psychology of Education* 27 (4): 605–19. doi.org/10.1007/s10212-011-0099-9.

Knouse, Stephen B., John R. Tanner, and Elizabeth W. Harris. 1999. "The Relation of College Internships, College Performance, and Subsequent Job Opportunity." *Journal of Employment Counseling* 36 (1): 35–43. doi.org/10.1002/j.2161-1920.1999.tb01007.x.

Lei, Simon A., and Dean Yin. 2019. "Evaluating Benefits and Drawbacks of Internships: Perspectives of College Students." *College Student Journal* 53 (2): 181-189. https://csusm-primo.hosted.exlibrisgroup.com/permalink/f/17n5p6l/TN_cdi_gale_incontextcollege_GICCO_A594832701.

Liu, Qin, Doug Reeve, Cindy Rottmann, and Emily Moore. 2020. "Examining Workplace Affordance and Student Engagement in Engineering Co-Op and Internship Literature." *Canadian Journal of Science Mathematics and Technology Education* 20 (1): 116–29. doi.org/10.1007/s42330-019-00074-6.

Lucia, Bill, and Matt Murphy. 2001. "Explosions Force Student Evacuations from Dorms." *Washington Square News*, September 12. https://nyunews.com/2018/09/12/archives-from-9-11/.

McLean, Nicole A., Marilyn Fraser, Nicole A. Primus, and Michael A. Joseph. 2018. "Correction to: Introducing Students of Color to Health Sciences Research: An Evaluation of the Health Disparities Summer Internship Program." *Journal of Community Health* 43 (5): 1011. doi.org/10.1007/s10900-018-0546-5.

Moran, Peter. 2015. "Reacting to Crises: The Risk-Averse Nature of Contemporary American Public Education." *Policy Futures in Education* 13 (5): 621–38. doi.org/10.1177/1478210315579548.

Pew Partnership for Civic Change. *New Directions in Civic Engagement: University Avenue Meets Main Street.* Charlottesville, VA: Pew Partnership for Civic Change. http://www.civicchange.org/resources/newdirections.html.

Public Purpose Institute (PPI). 2021. "Community Engagement Classification (US)." Accessed May 1. https://public-purpose.org/.

Strikwerda, Carl J. 2014. "Risk Managing or Risk Averse? Neither Approach is Fully Suited for Higher Education." *The Chronicle of Higher Education* 61 (11). https://csusm-primo.hosted.exlibrisgroup.com/permalink/f/17n5p6l/TN_cdi_proquest_reports_1625380306.

Student Placement Task Force. 2014. "Student Placement Task Force: Summary Report and Recommendation." California State University, San Marcos.

Taylor, M. Susan. 1988. "Effects of College Internships on Individual Participants." *The Journal of Applied Psychology* 73 (3): 393–401. doi.org/10.1037/0021-9010.73.3.393.

US Equal Employment Opportunity Commission, https://www.eeoc.gov/.

ENDNOTES

1. Disciplinary objectives and requirements count toward the credit-hour commitments and include class meetings, mandatory workshops or lectures, course projects and assignments, and so forth. The credit hour policy at California State University, San Marcos (CSUSM) is 45 hours per one unit, or 135 hours for a three-unit course. This does not mean students have 135 hours of seat time; study hours are factored into the total time commitment. For some departments where the internship is part of a capstone course, students attend weekly seminars that are led by faculty, and internship hours typically total 90 hours.

2. This may be at the college or campus level.

3. Examples include Career Development and Alumni Engagement (California State University, Channel Islands); Career Development Center (California State University, Long Beach); Career Education Community Engagement (California State University, Bakersfield); Center for Community Engagement (Cal Poly Pomona); Center for Experiential Learning; Center for Internships and Community Engagement (California State University, Fullerton); Center for Teaching and Learning (University of California, Berkeley); Office of Civic Engagement (Bucknell University); Office of Integrative Learning and Life Design (Johns Hopkins University); Office of Internships (CSUSM).

4. To date, there is no research that the author is aware of regarding the placement of a campus internship office in the university's institutional structure; therefore, what effects, if any, result from the differences in the institutional structure has not been studied and is beyond the scope of this review.

5. See Johnson Carey 2010; *Journal of Cooperative Education and Internships* published by CEIA; *2020 Internship & Co-op Survey Report Journal of Cooperative Education and Internships* published by NACE

6. I am a full professor at CSUSM. My appointment as the Faculty Director of the Office of Internships is a three-year appointment, renewable upon agreement with the Vice President of Community Engagement and the Provost.

7. The informal survey was posted to a CSU internship listserv in March 2021 and included the following questions: 1) "What unit manages academic (credit-bearing) internships on your campus?"; 2) "Does your campus have a policy/policies establishing standards for any of the following: what documentation should be collected from students; any required training/orientation for students prior to placement; criteria for suitable internship sites; conducting site visits; responsible unit for ensuring compliance?"; 3) "What are the primary functions of a centralized unit for managing academic internships?"

8. The cross-divisional task force included Communication Faculty and Director of the Career Readiness Initiative in the College of Arts, Behavioral, and Social Sciences (Academic Affairs); Associate Vice President of Community Engagement (Community Engagement); Director of Corporate and Foundation Relations (University Advancement); Dean of College of Science and Mathematics (Academic Affairs); Director of Procurement and Contracts (Finance and Administrative Services); and Director of Career Center (Student Affairs).

9. Employer Relations and Event Coordinator, Career Center (Student Affairs); Director of Business Community Relations, College of Business Administration (Academic Affairs); Service Partner Liaison (Civic Engagement); Kinesiology Faculty and Internship Coordinator; Associate Dean, Instructional and Informational Technology Services (Academic Affairs); Biology Faculty and Faculty Director for Service Learning (Academic Affairs); Executive Director, University Auxiliary and Research Services Corporation; Associate Dean of Extended Learning (Academic Affairs).

10. Our student placement information includes a learning plan, emergency contact information, internship site contact information, and a workplace safety and internship orientation. It also allowed for total hours worked to be reported at the end of the internship.

11. Seventeen stakeholders were interviewed, including faculty, deans, and leaders from global education and extended learning.

12. The mission of Community Engagement at CSUSM is to be a "leader in creating positive community impact through meaningful connections and innovative partnerships between the university and communities."

13. Because internships are grounded in both curriculum and community, the Implementation Team recommended the Faculty Director have a dual-reporting relationship to the Provost and the Vice President for Community Engagement.

14. CSUSM uses an integrated web application developed by and for the California State University system called CalState S4 to manage risk concerns and requirements associated with off-campus placements, and those specifically outlined in Executive Orders. There are various career management systems on the market designed to help colleges connect students to internship opportunities, for example: Handshake; Portfolium; Simplicity; Tenlegs.

15. The partnership agreement is a fully executable agreement between the university and the internship site which specifies the terms and conditions of the agreement, including the university's responsibilities and the learning site's responsibilities.

16. This may be a campus database and/or posting from external databases such as Coolworks.com; Glassdoor.com; Global Experiences.com; Idealist.com; Internships.com; Indeed.com; InterMatch.com; LinkedIn.com.

17. The literature on high-impact practices also includes capstone courses and projects, community-based learning, diversity and global learning, undergraduate research, collaborative assignments and projects, writing-intensive courses, learning communities, common intellectual experiences, and first-year seminars.

18. Just making internships available is insufficient for rendering positive benefits. It is important that the internship experience is high-quality, meaning the student is performing purposeful tasks in their chosen career field; explicit learning and career development goals have been identified; and the student has the benefit of supervision and coaching from professionals in the field.

19. Examples include health and safety hazards, property damage, sexual harassment, and discrimination.

20. See: https://www.csusm.edu/careers/internships/forfaculty/faqs.html.

21. For a more in-depth discussion on the mutual benefits of community engaged colleges and universities, see *New Directions in Civic Engagement* by the Pew Partnership for Civic Change (2004).

22. For example, international support services, veteran services, and disability support services.

23. Faculty determine if an internship is appropriate for their discipline. Even if a political science, music, or finance major had the qualifications to be a social media intern, it would not meet disciplinary criteria for these departments; therefore, the experience would not be appropriate for earned academic credit from those departments.

24. In Fall 2015 when CSUSM's campus internship office was established, there were 407 community partners in the database, but only 99 of them hosted at least one of the 295 CSUSM students who were interning that semester. That is, 24.3% of all community partners had at least one intern. There continues to be more numerous internship opportunities than students interested in an internship.

25. Students are encouraged to intern with established community partners to ensure they are covered by the university's liability policy. Students may intern with organizations with whom no community partnership has been established by signing a liability waiver.

CHAPTER 13

Navigating the DC Internship Ecosystem

Michelle L. Chin
Archer Center and The University of Texas at Dallas

Students face an exciting array of internship options in Washington, DC that include public and private sector organizations engaged in domestic and international policymaking and politics. Navigating this ecosystem can be challenging for students and their advisors. This chapter provides faculty advisors with useful, practical information about the internship search, preparing for the DC experience, finding housing, and living in DC. Additional information about starting and managing a campus-, college- or departmental program-affiliated internship program is also provided. Helpful tips for finding a DC internship, descriptions of internship types, a comparison of four existing standalone internship programs, a budget worksheet, and housing, eating, and transportation considerations, are included as Supplemental Internship Resources for easy reference.

Introduction

Internships are filled with many thrilling possibilities. In DC, where local news is often national or international news, an intern can unwittingly change history. In 1972, UCLA student Bruce Givner applied for the Government Internship Program to work in a Washington, DC congressional office. He was sent to intern at the Democratic National Committee instead. On his third day at DNC headquarters at the Watergate Hotel, Bruce worked until 9pm and then remained for several more hours using the telephone service to make free calls to his friends and family. Because Bruce overstayed, a carefully planned break-in by Republican operatives was thrown off schedule and postponed until the intern left after midnight.[1] The burglars were arrested a few hours later, triggering a scandal that resulted in the resignation of President Nixon in 1974. "It is not a huge leap to suggest that without the delay the burglars would have been long gone before anyone noticed [. . .] They might never have been arrested; their ties to Nixon never discovered."[2]

Interns with special language skills can also perform essential duties for their employers. In the summer of 1992, then-US Representative Joe Barton (R-TX) hired an undergraduate intern from Texas A&M University named Jeannie Morrison.[3] At the time, the Congressman was working to build international support for the Superconducting Super Collider (SSC), a large particle accelerator that was being built in his district.[4] After discovering that Jeannie was fluent in Japanese, the Congressman asked her to serve as a translator for a delegation of Japanese dignitaries he had invited to tour the SSC site. She was the only Washington staffer to travel with the Congressman on this important trip and kept in touch with many of the dignitaries. Jeannie credits these connections with helping her subsequently obtain a prestigious scholarship to study at the University of Tokyo.[5] In 2019, Matt Maldonado, an Archer Fellow and senior at The University of Texas at Austin, was an intern at the American Foreign Policy Council (AFPC). Matt, who is fluent in Russian, was asked to greet a visiting delegation from Ukraine and escort them from the airport to DC. He spent four days as the delegation's escort and translator, accompanying them to meetings in the US Senate and a US federal agency, a visit to a Smithsonian museum, and a tour of the US Capitol. Matt could not have predicted that he would sit in the Senate visitors' gallery translating for the Ukrainian delegation as senators discussed the White House memorandum of President Donald Trump's call with Ukraine President Volodymyr Zelensky.[6] After his internship ended, Matt was invited to continue working remotely as a writer for AFPC's Russian news publication, *Russian Reform Monitor*. After graduating in spring 2020, he was hired for a full-time position at AFPC.[7]

Washington, DC internships provide students who are interested in public policy and politics with practical work and learning experiences, opportunities to build their professional networks, and help open doors to new jobs. Students face an array of possibilities: they can participate in programs operated by non-profit organizations, pursue independent internships with public or private organizations, or enroll in their own campus's DC internship, if one exists. Given the enormous variety among opportunities, this chapter serves as a resource guide for faculty who advise students about seeking DC internships or who wish to organize a DC internship program for their department or larger institution. Practical dimensions such as finding an internship, collaborating with established Washington intern programs, locating housing, and working with university stakeholders and the DC government to set up your own internship program are explored.

WHAT KIND OF WORK DO INTERNS DO?

Around town, many organizations depend on interns for similar research and staffing support. For example, interns at think tanks like the Brookings Institution, American Enterprise Institute, Center for American Progress, or Heritage Foundation often work with scholars to conduct research and draft reports. It's not uncommon for these interns to publish blogs with their byline. At lobbying firms or advocacy organizations, interns often work closely with registered lobbyists, collaborating in strategy sessions and attending meetings with members of Congress and their staff. These internships also lead to post-baccalaureate jobs. In fact, the National Association of Colleges and Employers (NACE) reports that "at both the one-year and five-year marks, hires who have interned with the employer (internal interns) are more likely to be retained than hires who interned with other organizations (external interns) and hires with no internship experience."[8]

Interns in media organizations or who are working in communications internships are also given many opportunities to pitch story ideas and/or publish material. For example, one enterprising NPR intern realized the guest speaker in her class would make a good story for the show she was working on. She pitched the story to her producers and was able to book the guest.

Congressional offices often rely on interns to perform direct constituent service such as answering phones, greeting visitors in the front office, staffing constituent coffees, or leading tours of the Capitol. Of course, the interns also perform other essential functions such as opening and sorting mail or attending briefings and conducting research on legislative matters. At the White House, interns help staff a variety of offices. Interns in the Office of the First Lady often are asked to assist with the many social events hosted at the White House, from the annual Easter Egg Roll to holiday parties. At federal agencies, interns can gain experience working with career staff and political appointees, and often the experience is quite substantive. For example, one graduate intern recently worked with the Secretary of Housing and Urban Development on the Opportunity Zone initiative that was a White House priority; as a result, the intern was an active participant in policymaking discussions at HUD and the White House. See the Congressional Research Service's 2020 report on federal government internships for more leads: https://crsreports.congress.gov/product/pdf/RL/98-654.[9]

It is worth noting that Congress tends to operate on an apprentice model of work. For this reason, congressional interns who exercise humility and demonstrate a willingness to perform necessary tasks may experience exciting opportunities and find doors opening to new jobs. Speaking from my own experience, on the first day of my summer Congressional internship, I sat in the front office with another intern awaiting instructions for our work. My new colleague, a student at a large state university, informed me that he would be working on a special project to bring a presidential library to campus. Being from a small town and even smaller private university, I was simply excited to have an internship, but had only a vague idea of what to expect. At the end of the day, we both found ourselves sharing a small cubicle in the back of the office, opening and sorting mail. It was a big letdown for my colleague, who left DC by the end of the week because the work was not sufficiently substantive. At that time, the interns were also tasked with data entry of the annual constituent survey conducted by the representative. We had a daily quota of data entry, which was tedious. One of the graduate interns, who was also responsible for meeting the same daily quota, often got invited to join the legislative assistants in doing policy work (attending hearings and writing memos, for example) and would save his questionnaire entries for the end of the day. Late one morning, the representative's chief of staff informed us that any intern who had completed their daily quota by midday would be invited to join the representative at a White House bill-signing ceremony. The graduate intern was the only intern who could not attend. The following year, after I had graduated from college, I received a call from the representative's chief inviting me to apply for a job. It was a life-changing opportunity that influenced my graduate school research and created professional connections that have sustained my career to date.

UNDERSTANDING THE POLICY ECOSYSTEM

To achieve policy change in Washington, DC, it is often necessary to engage with multiple stakeholders and decision makers. This means that students who are interested in policy change have a variety of internship opportunities to explore (or to create). Each type of stakeholder or policy actor/decision maker in the policy ecosystem represents a different kind of internship opportunity. For example, some policy stakeholders act to influence public opinion by creating messaging campaigns or by issuing scholarly reports to advance their arguments.

Within the policy ecosystem in DC, there are institutions and actors who participate at every stage in the policy process from problem identification to agenda setting, policy formation, implementation, and evaluation. Table 1 provides some questions to help internship directors guide students to find the organizations and internship work that best suits their interests or professional goals.

ACADEMIC CREDIT FOR INTERNSHIP EXPERIENCE

Requiring students to earn academic credit for interning is not a standard rule in DC: intern employers in DC may or may not require it. For example, the House Paid Internship Program requires paid interns to be enrolled in an educational program and to receive credit for the internship.[10] Students can obtain necessary credit by enrolling in an established, academically affiliated program or a program operated through their university. In contrast, the White House Council on Environmental Quality Internship Program does not pay interns and does not require that they earn credit for the internship.[11]

Nevertheless, students on a tight budget may find it difficult to afford the costs associated with a DC internship, especially if it is unpaid. For these students, the best option may be to seek an internship independent of any academic program. For example, a student could obtain a Congressional internship by applying directly to a Congressional office. If they do not seek academic credit for the experience, they would save on tuition expenses and would still gain practical work experience. The costs of these credits will vary depending on the academic institution that provides the internship course. For example, tuition costs for three credits at a state school may be lower compared to a private institution.[12] It is worth noting, however, that students may not be eligible for financial aid from their home institutions if they participate in non-credit programs.

Table 1. Using Policy Stages to Determine What Types of Organizations to Target for Internships

Policy Stages	Problem Identification Defining the policy problem	Agenda Setting Deciding whether the problem is relevant/needs to be solved	Policy Formation Determining a politically-feasible solution (not necessarily the "best" solution)	Implementation Ensuring that the policy is implemented according to Congressional intent	Evaluation Assessment and evaluation of impact and effectiveness
Organized Interests	Who are the organized interests that are actively engaged at the various stages of the policy process? Think Tanks Lobbyists Advocacy coalitions Trade Associations				
Examples of Internship tasks	Research public opinion data. Prepare/proof policy background reports. Create messaging to amplify issue/ create salience.	Research policy priorities of key congressional leaders. Summarize policy reports to create talking points for lobbyists. Develop tracking lists for lobbyists. Attend hearings; monitor Congressional proceedings. Track White House/executive branch actions.		Assist with rulemaking comments and oversight of executive branch actions. Prepare briefing reports for lobbyists with implementation updates.	Develop metrics for evaluating impact and effectiveness. Create messaging to stakeholders about policy success (or need for improvements).
Decisionmakers	Who are the policy actors responsible for making decisions about the policy change? Does the change require amendments to existing law (Congress)? Can the change be accomplished with an executive order (President) or an agency rule or recommendation (federal agency)? Congress President Federal Agency				
Examples of Internship tasks	*Congress*: Prepare materials for Congressional hearings, attend hearings, write briefing memos for legislative staff, attend meetings with constituent groups, draft letters to respond to constituents, assist in planning events to highlight Congressional action or to promote Congressional action on the issue. *President*: Support legislative affairs team in compiling research on Congress members; assist public affairs team meetings with constituent groups; assist with administrative tasks for any member of the President's staff. *Federal Agency*: Prepare relevant responses to Congressional queries; conduct policy research for political appointees or career staff; assist in the implementation of programs and with program oversight.				

HOW DO YOU FIND A DC INTERNSHIP?

There are many options for finding a DC internship, from DIY-internship searches and placements to working with a non-profit organization that provides internship placements, programming, and housing. Students do not need to be affiliated with any program or to pay a program to obtain internship opportunities; however, to obtain credit for the internship, their home institution may require participation in such a program. There are, however, social and cohort benefits from participating in organized internship programs. For example, students are able to build friendships and expand their professional networks in a more coordinated fashion. The following section contains information about various options for internship placements.

ORGANIZATIONS THAT PROVIDE INTERNSHIP PLACEMENT, PROGRAMMING, AND HOUSING

Academically Affiliated Organizations

Students may enroll as visiting students at some of the colleges and universities in DC during their internship term. For example, students can take courses offered through **Georgetown University's Summer Session and Special Programs.** They earn academic credit for these courses but must arrange with their home institutions for approval to transfer the credits. **The Fund for American Studies (George Mason University)** and **Washington Semester (American University)** offer formal internship programs that include academic courses to which visiting students can apply.[13] These programs provide students with internship placements or assistance in finding internships. Once in DC, the students work in part-time or full-time internships and participate in weekly meetings. In addition to the courses, the programs often include a seminar that covers professional development and leadership topics.

Other well-known non-profit organizations that partner with educational institutions to offer DC-based internship programs include **The Washington Center (TWC), Washington Internship Institute, CET Academic Programs,** and **Osgood Center for International Studies.** These programs typically offer some classes for credit. In many cases, the organizations prefer to sign an articulation agreement with an academic institution that sets forth the course credit and billing procedures for the students. These organizations give preference to students recommended by the campus and may offer additional discounts on housing or fees. Partnership opportunities may be available.

A campus or department can customize a DC internship program for their students, or contract with the organization to serve a specific number of their students. The campus or department would be responsible for vetting the students, while the organization is responsible for providing the programming and housing in DC. All of these organizations also accept individual applications directly from students. The program and housing fees are two separate cost items. Programs are offered during the regular academic year and summer term.

A Review of Four Academically Affiliated Programs

This section takes a closer look at four established DC internship programs: American University's Washington Semester Program (WSP), The Fund for American Studies (TFAS) at George Mason University, The Washington Center (TWC), and The Washington Internship Institute (WII).[14] These programs are offered in the fall, spring, and summer terms, and are open to domestic and international students, although some programs will not provide visas. Students work in internships and take classes during the term. They also have access to housing. At a minimum, the organizations prefer to designate campus representatives—a faculty or staff member—who can help promote the internship programs and recruit students. The programs all offer colleges and universities opportunities to establish partnership agreements. These agreements range from simple articulation agreements regarding the transfer of course credits and billing procedures, to agreements to create customized programs for a campus. In some cases, the partnership agreements can result in more favorable fees. See the Supplemental Internship Resources for additional comparison details.

The Washington Semester Program (WSP) at American University (AU) was started in 1947 by AU Dean Harold Davis to "expose students to DC's cultural, educational, and governmental resources and give them 'first-hand acquaintance with possible careers in public service.'"[15] From a class of 24 students from six colleges, the program now serves over 200 students and has partnership relationships with 210 universities.

Admission is on a rolling basis, but application procedures depend on whether the student is from a university that has a partner agreement with WSP. Students who do not attend a partner institution can apply directly to WSP but are encouraged to first check with their faculty advisor about credit transfer, financial aid, and other requirements for off-campus study. Students who are accepted to WSP are enrolled as non-degree students at AU and have the same student privileges as degree-seeking students. They can customize their academic coursework and can take any electives that are listed in the

AU course catalog. At a minimum, students in fall/spring are required to take an internship seminar and one of the listed interdisciplinary WSP seminars, which include topics such as government, international affairs, public diplomacy, business and economics, criminal justice, and law. Summer students are required to take at least one WSP seminar in addition to working at their internship. Depending on the course load they wish to carry, students can add additional WSP seminars or electives from the AU course catalog. The tuition costs will vary depending on the total number of credits a student chooses to take. More detailed information about costs is included in the Supplemental Internship Resources section. All courses are taught by AU faculty.

Housing is available but is listed as a separate fee. Students can opt to find their own housing, live in furnished apartments managed by a third-party housing provider, or seek housing on campus. Students who choose to live on campus must buy a meal plan.[16]

Students receive an AU ID card and have access to all campus resources including libraries, recreation and health facilities, student services, and events. For this reason, students must pay additional mandatory fees for a Metro university pass (U-Pass) that provides access to Metrorail and Metro buses in DC, as well as technology, recreation and health facilities, and student activities.[17]

American University prefers to establish a Memorandum of Agreement (MOA) with its university partners. Typically, the MOA is set for a five-year term and outlines the classes that will transfer, the billing agreement, use of appropriate logos, and the application process. University partners are not charged a service fee and are not required to send a minimum number of students. In fact, there are universities that have no MOA but regularly send students to participate in WSP.

Washington Semester Program maintains a database of internships that students utilize to find internships. A WSP staff member monitors students during their search process and is available to assist in using the database. An AU professor oversees the internship course and meets regularly with the students to discuss their work. During the fall and spring semesters, students work three days and take classes two days each week. In the summer, the students work four days and are in class one day per week.

In summary, the WSP is an established program with a long history. It offers students a rich academic experience in addition to their internship. It is also quite expensive. An undergraduate taking a full load (12–16 credits) would pay tuition and housing costs totaling more than $30,000.

The Fund for American Studies (TFAS) was started in 1967 by Charles Edison, Dr. Walter H. Judd, David R. Jones, Marvin Liebman, and William F. Buckley, Jr. with the goal to provide college students with a "balanced perspective on political and economic institutions," although it has gained a reputation in recent years for being a conservative-leaning program.[18] TFAS programs include academic courses, an internship placement and furnished housing in Washington, DC. Students participate in a variety of exclusive guest lectures, site briefings as well as professional development and networking events. TFAS students leave Washington with 250-plus hours of professional experience.

TFAS originally partnered with Georgetown University but in 2013 established an academic partnership with George Mason University (GMU). TFAS students are enrolled at GMU as non-degree-seeking visiting students and have access to campus resources such as the library and health center and receive a GMU transcript at the end of their TFAS semester.

In DC, TFAS offers academic internship programs each summer, fall, and spring. Summer program students are required to take the 3-credit core class and are encouraged to enroll in an elective class for additional credits. Capital Semester (fall and spring) students will be enrolled in 12 credits. The program is offered in two formats: virtual and in-person. Students select their preferred format when submitting their application. The in-person classes are held at GMU's campus in Arlington, Virgina, which is accessible by Metro.

Capital Semester (fall and spring), students take three classes: Internship Seminar (6 credits), International Economic Policy (3 credits), and a 3-credit government class, either American Presidency (fall) or American Political Thought (spring). In summer, students are required to take one of three core economics courses (3 credits each): Economics for the Citizen, Economic Problems and Public Policies, or Economies in Transition. An optional Economics Boot Camp Seminar is offered during the first week of the program to help students who have never taken any economics classes become acquainted with basic economic principles. Students can also add one of the following 3-credit electives: US Foreign Policy, American Political Thought, Internship Seminar–Public Policy & International Affairs, Internship Seminar–Politics and the Press. All classes are taught by TFAS faculty.

TFAS offers several program tracks: Public Policy and Economics, International Affairs, Journalism and Communications, Business and Government Relations, and Leadership and American Presidency. Guest lectures, Career and Industry Exploration discussions, networking opportunities, and site briefings feature professionals working in fields relevant to the student's program track. Additionally, TFAS offers a mentor program and numerous professional development seminars.

Application deadlines are posted on DCInternships.org and students are notified of decisions within three weeks of completing their application. Scholarships, which are determined based on need, academic excellence, extracurricular achievement, and leadership activities, are awarded at the time of admission.[19] TFAS guarantees that students will find an internship, so each student is assigned a TFAS internship coordinator to work with during the pre-arrival search process.

The program fee includes furnished housing in Washington, DC, enabling students to manage their own meals. During the summer, students live in dormitories on the campus of George Washington University. During Capital Semester (fall and spring), students reside in apartments operated by Washington Intern Student Housing (WISH) in Capitol Hill. Roommates are matched by TFAS with two TFAS students per bedroom. Details are included in the Supplemental Internship Resources section.

Faculty and advisors are invited to nominate students, who then receive priority consideration in the admissions process. TFAS is flexible with university partnerships, which can range from informal partnerships to more formal partnerships that have a memorandum of understanding. TFAS works with each partner on a case-by-case basis. Universities interested in partnering with TFAS may reach out to the TFAS Admissions Department.[20]

In summary, this program has a structured curriculum that focuses on political thought and economics, and emphasizes a cohort experience with the inclusion of housing. This program gives universities the opportunity to collaborate or create a co-branded DC internship program. Program costs, which include housing and tuition, for an undergraduate taking a full load (12 credits) total more than $13,000.

The Washington Center (TWC) was founded in 1975 by the late William M. Burke and his wife Sheila McReavey Burke to provide students with internships and seminars. The program started with 51 students from 35 colleges, and today enrolls between 800–1500 students annually. TWC reports partnerships with over 400 universities in the US and 75 international universities.

In April 2021, TWC announced a School of Record partnership with Elon University, which enables students from institutions that do not have a partnership agreement with TWC to receive an Elon University transcript for up to 15 academic credit hours.[21] Students take one academic course each week in addition to career readiness workshops. TWC offers opportunities for virtually all majors, but particularly those in the social sciences, communications, and business. The course catalogs for each term include courses on various topics depending on interest indicated by the students and university partners. Recent topics include American History, American Politics and Public Policy, Business and Administration, Communication, International Affairs, Law and Criminal Justice, Media and Communications, and Research. The courses are taught in DC by TWC faculty. In addition, each student is assigned a career advisor to provide guidance and support while the students are enrolled in the program.

TWC works with universities to create specific partnership agreements that articulate curriculum expectations, course equivalencies and transfers, program and housing fees, and billing procedures. There is no financial cost to the institution for enacting the agreement, and the duration of the agreement can vary. The agreements typically do not include a minimum number of student enrollments. Students who are applying from non-partner institutions must still obtain university approval for their participation in the TWC program. This ensures that students will receive credit for their internship and classes.

Applications are reviewed on a rolling basis and decisions are made within several weeks of submission. TWC staff review applications to ensure suitability for internship opportunities with TWC partners. Students will not be accepted if TWC determines that there are no internship opportunities that align with the student's stated preferences. TWC has partnership agreements with internship employers and maintains an updated database of internship opportunities. TWC staff work with admitted students to prepare their internship application materials and to facilitate placements.

TWC provides furnished housing in their Residential and Academic Center located in the NoMa section of Washington, DC (see: https://twc.edu/right-home-dc) but does not require students to live there. TWC does not offer any meal plan, since the TWC housing includes furnished kitchens for students to prepare their own meals. TWC offers scholarships and furnishes a list of private and state scholarships available to students (https://twc.edu/programs/private-scholarships).

In summary, the TWC program has a long history of providing experiential learning, a broad network of internship partners, and a diverse list of courses. The diverse and interdisciplinary cohort creates many opportunities for students to build friendships and expand their personal and professional networks. Total program and housing fees for an undergraduate student are close to $16,000 for a semester; however, students who opt out of TWC housing would only pay a program fee of $9,415 (figures current as of 2021).

The Washington Internship Institute (WII) was founded in 1990 by Dr. Mary Ryan, the former vice president for academic programs at The Washington Center. The emphasis was on creating more customized internship programs. The cohorts range from 30–50 students per semester, and classes are small, in line with WII's mission to foster learning through more individualized experiences. WII offers programs for students in fall, spring, and summer. Students intern four days per week and take two classes on the day they are not interning: the internship seminar and one of two core courses (Inside Washington: Politics and Policy, or International and Foreign Policy Studies). Depending on the university partnership agreements, students may add additional online courses to take a full load. There are no evening or weekend classes. WII also offers customizable programs for their university partners, which can take the form of short immersion courses or semester-long courses. The classes normally meet in-person but were virtual during the COVID-19 pandemic. The program fee covers course costs, although students may have to pay to transfer credits if their institution lacks a partnership agreement. These rates can also be negotiated in the partnership agreement.

WII offers furnished housing in the Crystal City section of Arlington, Virginia but does not require students to live there. The housing rates can be negotiated in a university's partnership agreement. Additional information can be found in the Supplemental Internship Resources section.

A notable innovation is the Faculty Fellows program, which WII offers in partnership with the Association of American Colleges and Universities (AAC&U). This program allows faculty to spend a semester or summer in Washington, DC working with a host organization and networking with professionals. Housing is provided. A Faculty Fellow's home institution is required to pay $6,000 which is matched by the Fellow's host organization, but discounts are available to partner institutions. Details about this program can be found at: http://wiidc.org/faculty-fellows.

In summary, WII is a much smaller operation compared to the other three organizations discussed in this section. They offer university partners creative opportunities for customizing a program and for engaging faculty in the DC experience as well. Total program and housing fees for an undergraduate are over $12,000 during the fall/spring term, and close to $10,000 for the summer. Additional details can be found in the Supplemental Internship Resources section.

Minority-Serving Organizations

These civil rights organizations advocate on behalf of constituent groups and seek to increase participation of underrepresented persons in the policy process. Some of the more well-known programs are the **Asian Pacific American Institute for Congressional Studies (APAICS), Congressional Black Caucus Foundation (CBCF), Congressional Hispanic Caucus Institute (CHCI), Congressional Hispanic Leadership Institute (CHLI),** and the **Udall Foundation Native American Congressional Internship Program.** Many of these organizations provide substantial financial support to their interns. For example, the Congressional Hispanic Caucus programs provide housing for their interns. Other minority-serving programs are listed in a document included in the Supplemental Internship Resources.

Paid Internships

Although many organizations still rely heavily on unpaid interns, there has been a move in recent years to change this practice. In 2018, the nonprofit organization, Pay Our Interns, successfully lobbied

Congress to include funding to pay Congressional interns. In 2019, the average total stipend for Senate interns was $1,986 compared to $1,612 for House interns.[22] Their report compared the Congressional internship stipends to stipends offered by external internship programs (see table 2). Paid internships can also be found in other public and private sector organizations.

Table 2. Stipend Amounts of External Internship Programs	
Asian Pacific American Institute for Congressional Studies (APAICS)	$2,500
Congressional Black Caucus Foundation (CBCF)	$3,000
Congressional Hispanic Caucus Institute (CHCI) Summer	$3,125
Congressional Hispanic Caucus Institute (CHCI) Fall and Spring	$3,750
Congressional Hispanic Leadership Institute	$2,000

Source: Table 9 in James R. Jones, Tiffany Win, Carlos Mark Vera. 2021. "Who Congress Pays: An Analysis of Lawmakers' Use of Intern Allowances in the 116th Congress," https://payourinterns.org/wp-content/uploads/2021/03/Pay-Our-Interns-Who-Congress-Pays.pdf.

Extra Work

Most internship programs discourage students from working a second job while completing their internship. The internship should be a priority. In cases where students are also attending classes, there is limited time for a second job. Nevertheless, opportunities exist for students to take on extra work. One student who worked as a barista at a Starbucks in Arizona was able to pick up shifts at a Starbucks in Foggy Bottom to help offset her expenses while working an unpaid Congressional internship. Low-wage Congressional staff also take on extra work; some staffers generated extra income by pet-sitting after signing up with Rover.com.[23] Long before he was elected Speaker of the House, Paul Ryan was just a recent college graduate and Senate staffer who also worked as a server at a Tex-Mex restaurant, Tortilla Coast. According to a *Washington Post* report, this was "a second job that [led] to him meeting his mentor, Jack Kemp... [then] Secretary of Housing and Urban Development."[24]

Living in DC

Having landed a DC internship, the next task is to decide where to live, and how to budget properly to live in DC. In the supplemental internship section, you will find tips for securing suitable, safe and affordable housing, reliable transportation and a worksheet for creating a budget. If you are a faculty member looking to bring a group to DC, general housing options are available.

Student Housing Providers

There are several housing providers used by members of the Washington Program Consortium (dcprograms.org) a forum for institutions that offer experiential education and internship programs in DC. Institutions contract with these companies to provide housing for their students. An institution can reserve space for dedicated use by their own students, an arrangement that helps enhance the cohort experience. Some institutions sign multi-year contracts which can lock in affordable housing rates, while other institutions operate with an annual contract that provides greater flexibility in case of enrollment fluctuations. The contracts may stipulate that the institution pays a lump sum for the housing, or that individual students pay their housing fee separately.

These companies (see table 3) also accept housing applications from individual students working independently. In some cases, a student may be housed with students from other institutions if they do not wish to pay extra for single accommodations. Some companies like **WISH** (https://internsdc.com) and **The WIHN** (https://www.thewihn.com/) also organize social and professional development events for their student residents.

The companies may own or lease the properties that are offered to students. For example, a company may lease several large luxury apartments in addition to owning other townhouses. This means that an institution has options to house their students in a luxury apartment building that is home to other

Table 3. DC Housing Providers Used by Washington Program Consortium Members	
Housing Company	Website
CapStay	capstay.com
Churchill Living	www.ChurchillLiving.com
Elite Intern Housing	https://www.eliteinternhousing.com/
LUXbnb	www.LUXbnb.com
Olympus Housing	https://www.olympushousing.com/
Globe Quarter (Locations in DC & VA)	http://www.globequarters.com/
The Washington Intern Housing Network (The WIHN)	https://thewihn.com
TurnKey Housing	tkhousing.com
ULodging	www.ulodging.com
Washington Intern Student Housing (WISH)	InternsDC.com

working professionals in DC, or in a townhouse that is reserved exclusively for those students.

There are advantages to housing students in a neighborhood of working professionals, including the building amenities—pool, rooftop entertainment area, gym—that increase students' opportunities to network. For example, students housed in one building were surprised to discover a Supreme Court justice shopping at the grocery store. The disadvantage is that when students get rowdy, they may discover that the unhappy neighbor who was disturbed is a senator, White House staffer, or some other interesting person who they might otherwise wish to impress.

Housing students in a townhouse can help foster stronger bonds within the cohort. The house can then be identified as a home for many classes or "generations" of interns. Nevertheless, the maintenance and upkeep on some of these older ("historic") townhomes can be challenging. Students have been known to encounter the famous enormous DC rats scurrying around the alleys behind and between these buildings.

These are not the only options for group housing. For summer programs, local DC-based universities may also offer summer housing on campus. Check with their summer housing department for more information.

A Unique Option for Women

In 1887, Congress chartered "a temporary home for young women coming to [. . .] the District of Columbia."[25] This was known as the Young Woman's Christian Home until 1937 when it was renamed **Thompson-Markward Hall (TMH)**. Today, TMH is located across from the Hart Senate Office Building and offers young women (ages 18–34) an affordable, safe, and temporary residence (minimum of two weeks to maximum of two years). The housing fee includes furnished rooms, daily breakfast and dinner (Sunday through Friday). For details see: https://tmhdc.org/what-we-offer/.

OTHER CONSIDERATIONS FOR SETTING UP YOUR OWN INTERNSHIP PROGRAM

If you wish to establish a DC internship program that carries a university brand, there are some important things to consider. In this section, you will find general guidance for setting up your own internship program. *Please note that this information is not legal advice.* We strongly recommend that you consult with your home institution's general counsel to ensure that you are in compliance with DC law as well as the regulations that govern your home institution.

First, be aware that your home institution must obtain permission from the District of Columbia **Higher Education Licensure Commission** ("HELC", the "Commission") to do business in DC. Institutions that partner with an academically affiliated organization to deliver their programming may not be required to register with HELC; they should consult with their general counsel to be certain. The general counsel for the partner institution should review the HELC regulations and the partner agreement to ensure full compliance. Failure to comply with HELC regulations can result in hefty fines to the institution.

Second, be aware of the requirements and procedures imposed by your home institution, as well as the various stakeholders who have an interest in such a program. For example, the accreditation and program requirements may differ depending on whether a DC internship program is structured as a study-abroad program or set up as a satellite campus. The university president may take a personal interest in the program and its interns if the DC internship program is seen as a way to connect the campus (and students) with alumni and policy influencers (or federal funders).

Finally, peer support is available through the previously-mentioned Washington Program Consortium, a forum for institutions that offer experiential education and internship programs in DC. You can reach out to other program coordinators for ideas and advice about setting up your own program. The group meets monthly and has a Student Life committee that meets regularly to plan collaborative events for their students, such as a field day and a community service day. The meetings usually include a guest/expert presentation about a relevant topic; a recent speaker was the director of the White House Internship Program who explained the process for reviewing and selecting interns. Prior to the pandemic, the consortium would meet in person at member offices, such as the UC Washington Center or the ASU Barrett and O'Connor Washington Center, which allowed people to interact with each other and to also tour the facilities. As of summer 2021, meetings were on Zoom.

DC Higher Education Licensure Commission

The DC Higher Education Licensure Commission is a regulatory consumer protection agency that is authorized to issue educational licenses for postsecondary educational institutions in DC. Any out-of-state institution that establishes an educational program in DC, or which sends students to DC to participate in an educational program, must obtain a license or conditional exemption from the Commission before doing business in DC. The license or conditional exemption must be renewed every 12 months. Information about the application requirements can be found here: (https://helc.osse.dc.gov/topic/helcadmin/institutions/frequently-asked-questions-for-institutions). Please note that failure to comply may result in fines and penalties. The Commission's staff are accessible by email (see: https://helc.osse.dc.gov/topic/helcadmin/about/staff-directory).

University Personnel

In setting up an internship program that carries a university's (or department's) brand, it is important to make sure that you have contacted all the relevant stakeholders at your institution. DC internship programs can be hosted in different units on campus such as a department, a Study Abroad office, or a Career Services office. In some cases, the program may be operated as a multi-campus system program, or as a special program in the president's office. The approval process and chain of command will vary depending on where the internship program is situated.

In alphabetical order, here is a list of key stakeholders to know. Please note that this is not a comprehensive list.

Alumni: Contact your campus's Alumni Office to obtain a list of DC-based alumni. They are often willing and eager to host interns, serve as mentors, participate as guest speakers, and donate. If the institution has not had a strong DC presence previously, then alumni may be excited to establish an official presence and can be relied upon to help coordinate certain aspects of the program. Chance encounters with your institution's alumni can also come into play. In 2002, I was at the Amtrak counter at DC's Union Station when I overheard a conversation between an Amtrak clerk and a man who said he was from "government relations." As then-director of the Arizona State University (ASU) Capital Scholars program, I was always on the hunt for internships, so I introduced myself. Before I could ask about internships at Amtrak, the man smiled and replied, "I used to play football for ASU. Tell me more." To date, Amtrak has hired numerous ASU Capital Scholars as summer interns. When he left Amtrak to join The Madison Group, Marcus Mason also committed to hiring ASU Capital Scholars as summer interns.

Bursar/Billing Services: Knowing the staff in this office will help you sort out the problems that can occur, such as inadvertent overcharges for tuition and fees.

Career Services: Career Services Specialists are excellent allies, for they often have training and expertise in reviewing résumés and cover letters and can work with students to identify skills and knowledge deficits that need attention. They may also have updated information about internship opportunities across disciplines.

Communications/Public Affairs: Work with the institution's external relations/public affairs communications team to share stories of students' successes in DC with the public and with campus recruitment and admissions staff.

Development Office: The campus fundraising team can help you identify sponsors for your program and/or students. Get to know the development director and make sure that any fundraising campaigns you organize are not in conflict with other priorities of the university.

General Counsel/Contracts Officer: Be sure to include your institution's general counsel or contracts officer in your business plan. They should review any contracts for housing or internship articulation agreements or memoranda of agreement that require official signatures.

Government/Federal Relations: When establishing a DC internship program, it is useful to coordinate with the institution's federal relations or government relations team which is responsible for managing the institution's relationships with members of Congress and federal agencies and executives. Often, the federal relations staff can be helpful in identifying internship opportunities and connecting students with policymakers and their staff. They also can act as liaisons to good guest speakers and mentors.

President: The university president may play a significant role in the approval of this program, depending on where the program is situated and how the institution is organized. At a minimum, there are opportunities for publicity and photo ops with the students *before* they travel to DC, while they're in DC, and after they return. At each point, the students have an exciting story to share.

Provost/Dean: Academic officers may play a role in approving the program, depending on where the program is situated and how the institution is organized. These administrators also like to know what their students are doing and can marshal fiscal and human resources to support the program and its students. DC coordinators have a good story to tell, especially when they can demonstrate that the internships help students complete college and obtain gainful employment.

Registrar: Consult with the Registrar to make sure students are properly enrolled for the course or courses during their internship term. The Registrar can also verify that a student's course load is appropriate for maintaining financial aid, and that the program curriculum meets accreditation standards/expectations.

Student Affairs: It is important to communicate with the Dean of Students (or Student Affairs) about the students who will participate in the program, particularly to become aware of any unresolved discipline issues. Student Affairs can help navigate the process if a student experiences an adverse health event that necessitates an ADA accommodation; in that case, the campus ADA coordinator should also be notified.

Study Abroad: In some institutions, the DC internship program is considered a "study abroad" program. If this is the case, you may find it useful to conduct a variety of information sessions about the program to raise awareness outside your department or discipline.

***Title IX Coordinator*:** Interns need to understand their Title IX protections, including how to resist and report inappropriate behavior in the workplace, classroom, and residence. Before students travel to DC, you should contact your institution's Title IX coordinator to provide appropriate training to help students navigate the workplace and residential life experiences. Make sure that your staff are also fully trained about proper reporting protocols.

OTHER PROGRAM MANAGEMENT CONSIDERATIONS

Other important considerations when setting up a DC internship program include planning for emergencies and crises, and responding to incidents of intern misbehavior.

Emergency and Crisis Management

In 2004, Kentucky Governor Ernie Fletcher flew to DC to attend the funeral of former president Ronald Reagan. As the plane approached Reagan National Airport, it veered into restricted air space over the Capitol, triggering fears of a 9/11 style attack and an emergency evacuation of the Capitol.[26] "Sen. Lisa Murkowski, R-Alaska, was on the third floor of the Capitol with her staff when the fire alarms first went off and they started walking out of the building. "We were walking until we were told to run, get out of the building," Murkowski said, as one of her staffers tried to find a lost intern. "I got a little exercise this afternoon."[27]

Help your students plan and be prepared for emergencies while they are in DC by consulting your institution's police department, campus safety officers, emergency management coordinators, risk control and risk management offices. If you are operating a program, your institution's police department or campus security may have access to relevant security alerts that can help protect you and your students. For example, during the days leading up to the 2021 Inauguration, the University of Texas System Office of the Director of Police provided the Archer Center team with intelligence reports about potential security threats in DC. As a result of this information, the Director of Police recommended delaying the students' arrival in DC until after the Inauguration. At the Archer Center, we invite a safety specialist to provide CPR training to all Fellows. We consider having Fellows certified to perform CPR as a life-saving benefit to our program.

Interns Misbehaving

The DC intern experience can be quite stressful, especially if students are required to take classes in addition to working a full-time (or close to full-time) internship. In addition, students may feel greater social pressure to drink, to be extroverted networkers, to perform well at work, to compete against their peers, to prepare to graduate and get a job, or apply for graduate school. Undergraduate juniors and seniors who are thrown together into a new cohort may experience the same type of anxieties they experienced as freshmen when they were transitioning to college life. Students who are unfamiliar with urban life or who prefer wide open spaces with lots of trees and land can become depressed in the concrete jungle of DC. Students from sunny regions may be unprepared for the seasonally affective impact of long, dark, and cold days during the winter season. All of these externalities impact students' mental health and can erode their sense of well-being.

In 2018, a graduate fellow working for a member of the US House of Representatives was arrested and charged with releasing the private cellphone number of Senator Lindsey Graham, chair of the Senate Judiciary Committee, which was holding confirmation hearings for Supreme Court nominee Brett Kavanaugh.[28] The fellow was fired.[29] He later pled guilty to federal offenses and was sentenced to four years in federal prison.[30] He had behaved rashly because "he was angry about his termination in May 2018 from his employment as a computer systems administrator in the office of another US Senator (described in court documents as Senator #1). As a result, from July 2018 to October 2018, he engaged in an extensive computer fraud and data theft scheme."[31]

There are resources to help a student who is experiencing a mental health challenge or struggling to control their anger, or others who are feeling anxious and afraid. Check with the Dean of Students at your institution to see what home campus mental health resources are available to students who are interning in DC. In some cases, telehealth services are available. Students often can use their health insurance to obtain mental health services in DC. There are also providers who will contract with a school to provide services to a group of students. For example, Parkhurst Associates (https://parkhurstassociates.com/university-counseling/) contracts with several universities to provide counseling (in-person and virtual) to students. Parkhurst charges the student a small co-pay for a limited number of individual therapy sessions and then bills the university for the remainder. Clients can schedule additional sessions at the full price.

In crisis situations where a student's behavior has drawn negative public attention, you should also work with your campus public affairs team to coordinate any public communications regarding the incident. Obviously, these situations can draw unwelcome attention to the individual and the institution they represent. For this reason, it is important to ensure that vulnerable students are aware of the supports they can access when interning.

Finally, any student behavior that requires a disciplinary response represents a case that will need to be adjudicated by the Dean of Students on the student's home campus. If you're operating an internship program for your campus or institution, having a good working relationship with the Office of Student Affairs and Dean of Students is essential in these situations. You should also be sure to work closely with the Title IX Coordinator and the director of student accessibility services.

CONCLUSION

After securing necessary approvals from appropriate university stakeholders, faculty members who wish to build an internship program can start by recruiting promising candidates to seek individual internships. While it's natural to look for students in political science departments, students from other disciplines also have interests in DC institutions and the policy process, and they bring a unique perspective to their internships. For example, one engineering student who interned at the House Science Committee was able to use his scientific knowledge to help the committee staffers conduct their research. A pharmaceutical company that was preparing comments for a federal rule was delighted to discover that their graduate intern, a practicing nurse, had clinical experience using their product. As a result, the intern was able to "provide constructive and unique insights... [and to contribute] significantly to formal comments filed...on policy recommendations to improve reimbursements and incentives for novel anti-microbials."[32] So, while internship programs provide students with important professional opportunities and work experience, they can also provide organizations and institutions with vital input and new ideas. As a result, this wonderful, dynamic, exchange of information and experience contributes to a healthy policy ecosystem.

In conclusion, sending your students to live, learn, and intern in DC is an effective way to establish your home institution's reputation for excellence, and to prepare students for professional success. Increasing student enthusiasm for DC internships can generate potential support from key campus stakeholders such as the president, faculty, career center staff, alumni, public relations, and advancement/development leaders. Over time, the internship program can also build new information pathways between university scholars who are creating knowledge and the policymakers in DC who can apply that knowledge to solve policy problems.

ENDNOTES

1. Sharon, Keith. 2019. "The Man Who Stayed Late: The Watergate Story You've Never Heard," *Los Angeles Daily News*, June 14, updated June 18, https://www.dailynews.com/2019/06/14/the-man-who-stayed-late-the-watergate-story-youve-never-heard/.

2. Lewis, Alfred E. 1972. "5 Held in Plot to Bug Democrats' Office Here." *Washington Post*, June 18. https://www.washingtonpost.com/wp-dyn/content/article/2002/05/31/AR2005111001227.html

3. Personal correspondence with Sylvia Jean (Jeannie) Morrison, July 2, 2021.

4. In 1993, Congress cut funding for the SSC and the project was cancelled (see Appell, David. 2013. "The Supercollider That Never Was," *Scientific American*, October 15. https://www.scientificamerican.com/article/the-supercollider-that-never-was/).

5. Personal correspondence with Sylvia Jean (Jeannie) Morrison, July 2, 2021.

6. Personal correspondence with Matt Maldonado, July 2, 2021. For a copy of the memorandum, see "White House memo on Trump call with Ukraine president," accessed July 2, 2021, https://www.documentcloud.org/documents/6429034-White-House-memo-on-Trump-call-with-Ukraine.html.

7. Internships are an important aspect of workforce development, by providing workers with on-the-job training and growing the talent pool for employers. According to Brandon Busteed and Zac Auter with the Gallup Organization, "recent graduates (those who graduated from 2002-2016) who had a relevant job or internship while in school were more than twice as likely to acquire a good job immediately after graduation....Students with these meaningful work experiences are not only finding good jobs quickly, they are also finding them in fields related to their undergraduate studies" (see Busteed, Brandon and Zac Auter. 2017. "Why Colleges Should Make Internships a Requirement," *Gallup Blog*, November 27. https://news.gallup.com/opinion/gallup/222497/why-colleges-internships-requirement.aspx).

8. Gray, Kevin. 2021. "Trends in One-Year, Five-Year Intern Retention Rates." National Association of Colleges and Employers, June 9. https://www.naceweb.org/talent-acquisition/trends-and-predictions/trends-in-one-year-five-year-intern-retention-rates/.

9. Finch, Christina Miracle, Kathleen E. Marchsteiner, and Jennifer E. Manning. 2020. "Internships, Fellowships, and Other Work Experience Opportunities in the Federal Government, Report No. 98-654." Congressional Research Service, updated September 14. https://crsreports.congress.gov/product/pdf/RL/98-654.

10. See "House Paid Internship Program," accessed June 20, 2021, https://cha.house.gov/member-services/house-paid-internship-program.

11. See "White House Council on Environmental Quality Internship Program," accessed June 20, 2021, https://www.whitehouse.gov/ceq/internship-program/.

12. According to Educationdata.org, the average cost per credit hour is $396 at a public, 4-year university (in-state) compared to $1,492 at a nonprofit university (see Hanson, Melanie. 2021. "Cost of a College Class or Credit Hour," June 25, accessed July 2, 2021, https://educationdata.org/cost-of-a-college-class-or-credit-hour). The US Department of Education, National Center for Education Statistics, reports that "For the 2018–19 academic year, annual current dollar prices for undergraduate tuition, fees, room, and board were estimated to be $18,383 at public institutions, $47,419 at private nonprofit institutions, and $27,040 at private for-profit institutions" (National Center for Education Statistics. "Fast Facts: Tuition costs of colleges and universities," accessed July 1, 2021, https://nces.ed.gov/fastfacts/display.asp?id=76).

13. The Semester in Washington Program at George Washington University (https://semesterinwashington.gwu.edu/) operates on a similar model; however, they suspended operations during the pandemic. As of June 19, 2021, they have not announced plans to resume.

14. The Semester in Washington Program at George Washington University suspended operations during the pandemic. Although their website (https://semesterinwashington.gwu.edu/) is still accessible, there is no indication that the program has resumed operations. There was also no response to attempts to phone and email the listed contacts.

15. Frank, Adrienne. 2017. "Eagle Tales: Washington Semester Program," *American University Magazine*, November, accessed June 20, 2021, https://www.american.edu/magazine/article/eagle-tales-washington-semester-program.cfm.

16. As of 2021, the cheapest meal plan is $800 for the semester.

17. As of 2021, these fees are about $400.

18. The Fund for American Studies, "History," accessed June 21, 2021, https://tfas.org/about/history/.

19. TFAS grants more than $1 million in scholarship funding each year; 85% of students attending TFAS programs are on full or partial awards based on merit and/or need. Costs associated with the program cover tuition and furnished housing.

20. More information can be found at: admissions@TFAS.org.

21. Anderson, Dan. 2021. "The Washington Center Sets School of Record Partnership with Elon University." Elon University: Today at Elon [Blog], April 5, accessed June 20, 2021, https://www.elon.edu/u/news/2021/04/05/the-washington-center-sets-school-of-record-partnership-with-elon-university/.

22. Source: Jones, James R., Tiffany Win, and Carlos Mark Vera. 2021. *Who Congress Pays: An Analysis of Lawmakers' Use of Intern Allowances in the 116th Congress.* Washington, DC: PayOurInterns.org. https://payourinterns.org/wp-content/uploads/2021/03/Pay-Our-Interns-Who-Congress-Pays.pdf.

23. According to Millennial Money, a blog on Make It (CNBC), 26-year old Victor Yang, a congressional aide, is living carefully and comfortably on his $45,000 salary (Martin, Emmie. 2019. "How a 26-year-old-Congressional Aide Earning $45,000 Spends his Money in Washington, DC," *CNBC*, December 5. https://www.cnbc.com/2019/12/05/how-a-26-year-old-earning-45000-dollars-in-washington-dc-spends-his-money.html.

24. Kane, Paul. 2015. "From Capitol Hill Tex-Mex Waiter to 54th Speaker of the House." *The Washington Post*, October 29. https://www.washingtonpost.com/politics/from-capitol-hill-tex-mex-waiter-to-54th-speaker-of-the-house/2015/10/29/54b1e8a4-7e61-11e5-afce-2afd1d3eb896_story.html.

25. Conrad, Kent. 2012. "Recognizing Thompson-Markward Hall," *Congressional Record*, Vol. 158, Page 11422, accessed May 12, 2021, https://www.govinfo.gov/content/pkg/CRECB-2012-pt8/html/CRECB-2012-pt8-Pg11422-2.htm.

26. Hsu, Spencer S. 2004. "The Plane That Caused Capitol Evacuation Nearly Shot Down." *Washington Post*, July 8. https://www.washingtonpost.com/archive/politics/2004/07/08/plane-that-caused-capitol-evacuation-nearly-shot-down/2d65e479-88f4-4d17-9642-478366af0ecd/.

27. Associated Press. 2004. "Air Scare Forces Brief Evacuation of U.S. Capitol." *NBC News*, June 9. https://www.nbcnews.com/id/wbna5174887.

28. US Attorney's Office District of Columbia. 2018. "District Man Charged in Investigation of Illegal Posting of Restricted Personal Information of US Senators on Website." Department of Justice, October 4. https://www.justice.gov/usao-dc/pr/restricted-personal-information-us-senators-website.

29. Sullivan, Emily. 2018. "House Intern Arrested, Charged with Doxing Senator During Kavanaugh Hearing." *NPR*, October 4. https://www.npr.org/2018/10/04/654264122/house-intern-arrested-for-reportedly-doxing-senator-during-kavanaugh-hearing.

30. US Attorney's Office District of Columbia. 2019. "District Man Sentenced to Four Years for Stealing Senate Information and Illegally Posting Restricted Information of U.S. Senators on Wikipedia." Department of Justice, June 19. https://www.justice.gov/usao-dc/pr/district-man-sentenced-four-years-stealing-senate-information-and-illegally-posting.

31. U.S. Attorney's Office District of Columbia. 2019. "District Man Sentenced to Four Years for Stealing Senate Information and Illegally Posting Restricted Information of US Senators on Wikipedia." Department of Justice, June 19. https://www.justice.gov/usao-dc/pr/district-man-sentenced-four-years-stealing-senate-information-and-illegally-posting.

32. Personal correspondence with Robert Lively, June 27, 2019.

CHAPTER 14

Internships for Interdisciplinary International Relations and International Studies Programs: Comparing Benefits and Challenges from West to East

Iva Božović, University of Southern California
Alison Rios Millett McCartney, Towson University

This chapter sheds light on processes, challenges, and benefits of International Relations (IR) and International Studies (IS) internships through a comparison of two programs, one on the West Coast and the other on the East Coast of the US. After describing different program structures and resources needed to build IR/IS programs and support international students in the US and abroad, we explore creative ways to expand opportunities for IR/IS students in local communities. We review practical challenges and offer a set of solutions to address them.

INTRODUCTION

Most political science departments have internship programs primarily designed for students to participate "in the political process and [...] gain insight into the nature of political institutions" (Auerbach 2021). These opportunities allow students to participate in work that complements their undergraduate classroom experience and ideally is supervised by an internship advisor or mentor (Ediger 2010, 243). We know from research and practice that these types of opportunities provide an important form of field-based experiential learning that entails applying theoretical knowledge from the political science curriculum to "real-world" and "hands-on" practice, and vice-versa (Bennion 2015). However, due to the interdisciplinary nature of international relations and international studies, which can be standalone interdisciplinary majors based in political science at some institutions, experiential education in these areas must be tailored to apply theoretical knowledge specific to international relations/international studies (IR/IS) problems and analyze actual and potential actions by governments, international organizations, private companies, non-government organizations (NGOs), and citizens. Compared to political science internships that more commonly deal with US political processes or public affairs, IR/IS internships address public service components through the examination of inter-state actions, state-to-non-state actor interaction, or even public organizations that interact with private market participants. As a result, political science internships in local, state, or national levels of government may be of limited interest and utility for IR/IS students. The key challenge, then, is to provide internationally focused internship opportunities for globally-engaged students and do so inclusively.

This chapter seeks to shed light on the processes, benefits, and challenges of serving interns in political science and IR/IS. It begins with a general overview of the parameters of an IR/IS internship and a discussion of initial steps to take in order to offer such internships. After briefly comparing how two programs—one at a private institution on the West Coast of the United States and the other at a public institution on the East Coast—handle these internships, we explore the unique hurdles associated with them and how to overcome them. If political science as a discipline seeks to serve all of its majors equally by offering impactful, experiential learning across subfields, then better understanding of these placements is needed, and sufficient resources must be supplied to support them, potentially in tandem with interdisciplinary programs.

THE IR/IS INTERNSHIP

Compared to political science internships, IR/IS internships encompass a wider range of academic and applied learning options. First, many institutions have interdisciplinary international studies majors, stand-alone international relations majors, or concentrations in IR/IS. Students pursue these majors because they recognize, just as their mentors do, that "international studies offers an integrative, comprehensive, and interdisciplinary approach to issues of global importance" (Anderson et al. 2015, 3). A primary learning goal is that students are able to understand and analyze "global interactions, the tensions that these interactions produce, and the forces and actors that play a role in them" (Straus and Driscoll 2019, 4).

One of the hallmarks of an interdisciplinary major is its flexibility. IR majors are usually housed in or offered in conjunction with a political science major, but IS majors usually integrate knowledge from some or all of the following disciplines: anthropology, economics, geography, history, and political science, in addition to various foreign languages. Other departments' courses may also be used for credit, such as art/art history, music, and sociology. Thus, flexibility creates the need to incorporate learning objectives and offerings from several departments while maintaining an explicitly international or non-native focus. Although the literature clearly defines internships and delineates critical dimensions of an internship, there is nothing that determines disciplinary scope, particularly for IR/IS majors (Maertz 2014). For IR/IS students, the principal internship learning objectives include, among others: professional development through the application of IR/IS-specific content and skills; effective self-reflection; teamwork; career preparation; and networking.[1] The effectiveness of internship placements depends on the extent to which they provide students a chance to study key questions of international security, international political economy, foreign policy analysis, diplomacy, international negotiation, working within and between various cultures and societies, international human rights, and international and environmental justice.

Following Bennion (2015), it is clear that the disciplinary embrace of internships depends on whether the hands-on learning outside of the classroom furthers the discipline-defined learning objectives. Because some IR/IS programs are interdisciplinary, internships must reflect that scope, and thus the parameters of IR/IS internships tend to be wider. Some of these placements, such as embassies, consulates, and NGOs that work with immigrant and migrant groups, often require a working knowledge or fluency in a foreign language. Indeed, global competencies can be important selling points on a prospective intern's résumé even when these are not explicitly required. One of the hallmarks of the IR/IS major is its flexibility, meaning that majors are encouraged to make connections among different silos of disciplinary knowledge to understand and analyze the world around them, and this flexibility helps enlarge their internship options beyond a single discipline.[2]

THE INTERNATIONAL RELATIONS INTERNSHIP AT THE UNIVERSITY OF SOUTHERN CALIFORNIA (USC): AN OVERVIEW

The International Relations Undergraduate Program at the University of Southern California (USC), was formed as an independent School of International Relations (SIR), but is now part of a joint Political Science and International Relations Department.[3]

The undergraduate program in International Relations serves approximately 700 students across four separate majors: International Relations (IR), IR-Global Business (IRGB), IR-Global Economy (IRGE), and the most recently added Intelligence and Cyber Operations (INCO) major. Only the first two participate in the IR internship program, so we will refer only to those in this chapter. The IR major largely appeals to students interested in international affairs and those who wish to understand how global developments affect their lives and work. IRGB is an interdisciplinary major overseen by the IR program and the USC Business School. It attracts students who are interested in relations among states and other international actors in the context of the global economy.

The International Relations internship program was established in 2015 in response to the needs of dual constituencies: students who are eager to find more internship positions and community employers who are looking to hire students in conjunction with school credit.[4] This nationwide move to internships-for-credit is not without critics, particularly as these requirements can be viewed as an excuse for not paying interns (Yagoda 2008). Our IR program recognizes that for some students, the course opens opportunities that are obtainable only during the academic year when they receive financial aid. When enrolled full-time during the school year, students can apply their financial aid to cover living expenses for which they would otherwise be responsible.

The IR internship program is offered as an independent study course that can count as an elective 2-unit upper-division course for any of the majors above. The course can be taken twice for a total of 4 units applied to the major. The instructor of record is in charge of recruiting and assisting with student placement, and there is no formal administrative assistance to run and maintain the program. The course is not a requirement for any of the IR/IS majors, and most students pursue internships, without credit, on their own, or earn non-major credit in other programs such as Political Science.[5] An informal survey of upper-division students revealed that about 60% had completed an internship by fall 2020,[6] yet the formal internship course only serves about 30 students per year.[7] Clearly these numbers indicate that the IR internship program serves only a small subset of students who pursue internships during their time at USC.

Students in the USC International Relations internship program can find help with landing a placement in three main ways. First, because the program is situated in a university with a rich professional network, students have access to a robust job and internship online database.[8] Second, students can get help from a designated social science advisor in the College of Letters and Sciences' own career center who can recommend strategies for a targeted search and offer help to strengthen the student's application materials. The third resource is the department itself: students can approach the internship course faculty instructor when they need assistance with identifying opportunities, even if they ultimately do not sign up for the class. More details about the program and the course (and those at Towson University) are shared in the Supplemental Internship Resources.

THE INTERNATIONAL STUDIES INTERNSHIP AT TOWSON UNIVERSITY (TU): AN OVERVIEW

Towson University (TU) is a public, comprehensive, four-year institution located just outside of Baltimore, Maryland. Enrollment reached close to 20,000 undergraduates for the 2020–2021 academic year.[9] The International Studies (INST) major seeks to develop a global perspective through an interdisciplinary network of courses and learning experiences. The program is based on six "foundation" departments—Anthropology, Economics, Foreign Languages, Geography, History, and Political Science—and draws upon upper-level elective courses from a wide variety of disciplines, spanning Art History, Finance, Philosophy, and Religious Studies. The director is a faculty member from one of the participating departments, and an interdisciplinary committee of faculty members helps to administer the program, which includes approximately 225 students, mostly majors.[10] Because this major was established in the 1970s when the university's enrollment was less than half of what it is today, management of its interdisciplinary aspects, such as enrolling in courses in several different departments and including them as INST electives, was easily achieved. In 2009, a paid, part-time faculty director was added after substantial increases in overall university enrollment had occurred and the number of students majoring or minoring in INST rose to over 150 students, more than double the figure in 1995. The INST internship class counts as the practicum requirement for the major, which can be fulfilled either through an internship, independent study course, or a thesis course in a foundation department with the director's approval or through a 3-credit study abroad course in any department.[11] The number of students enrolled in the designated INST internship course averaged 8.5 students per year from 2004 to 2016 (the 12-year period referenced in this section; including summers), but this total excludes all INST majors who simply did internships for credit without enrolling in the course.[12]

Students are responsible for obtaining their own placements, which can be found through the University's Career Center, the INST website, or INST's physical bulletin board, all of which supply work descriptions and contact information. From 2004 to 2016, about half of TU's 93 international studies internships were in Washington, DC. The remainder were conducted mostly in the Baltimore area, while a handful were in the state capitol, Annapolis, and three were conducted abroad.[13] Gaining local placement—i.e., positions located near the university—was a popular option because most TU students work part-time and lack the time to commute to DC two to three days per week, a general requirement for in-person or hybrid internships. This option also appealed to our non-traditional-age students who often had not only another job but also family responsibilities. Until the COVID-19 pandemic, none were conducted online. When students do their internships abroad, mid-semester check-ins are completed through email communication and assignments are accepted via email rather than in person.

COMMON CHALLENGES WITH INTERNATIONAL INTERNSHIPS AND HOW TO OVERCOME THEM

We identify four key challenges associated with IR/IS internships. The first set of challenges relates to student placements—(those near home, meaning the student's home campus, and those in internships abroad)—and the related issue of how to properly disseminate internship-related information to students. The remaining three challenges are assessment, pre-professional support for students, and those related to costs and financial aid. As we discuss each, we also present actual or possible solutions that faculty, supervisors, and university administrators should undertake or consider. At base, these recommendations also aim to include a wider variety of students in international learning opportunities.

1. Placements

Local Placements (Near the Student's College or University)

Typically, IR/IS students desire opportunities directly related to foreign policy and international security such as the State Department, premier think tanks, and research centers. As the Baltimore area is just over an hour's drive or commuter train ride to Washington, DC, Towson students with adequate time in their weekly schedules are able to fill available positions among the many options in the metro-DC area—in government and at embassies, think tanks, and non-governmental organizations—in addition to those offered through TU's partnership with the Washington Center.[14] A similar option is available to a select few USC students who attend the USC-DC program during the spring semester. Consulates in LA (totaling 99 as of 2021) are attractive to USC students who speak foreign languages. Their work assignments range from media and communications support to policy research, and from business development research to preparatory work for trade negotiations.

Unfortunately, while these opportunities are a natural fit for IR/IS students, they are much more limited elsewhere in the US (outside of major cities), and even East Coast students can be constrained by family, transportation, or economic situations. These limitations complicate academic year placements, particularly for students attending courses in-person. Completely online internships[15] can mitigate some of these concerns, but for students who prefer in-person options, internship programs need to actively expand the scope of what is considered an internationally focused internship. Moreover, not all IR/IS students envision careers in the State Department or internationally recognized policy think tanks; some IR/IS career trajectories lead to the private sector. To prepare our students, internship placements have to complement such career trajectories. We also must consider other options by carving out space for IR/IS projects in domestic internships to accommodate non-traditional age students who have family obligations and thus less flexible schedules. Further, internships that count for IR/IS but are in local, state, or national offices can be the best option for international students who are already studying abroad in the US and need more exposure to American governmental processes.

A successful way of expanding placement opportunities for IR/IS students, we posit, is to connect students with local-global options. For cities such as Baltimore and LA, both multi-ethnic port cities with many businesses engaged in international trade, such options are plentiful. For example, local government internships can be tremendously valuable learning opportunities for students who want to examine how local governance issues are connected to inter-state relations or how the private sector engages with government leaders. For example, USC students have held positions in the Mayor's Office of International Affairs and the Office for Economic Opportunity. Others have worked on expanding educational exchanges, public diplomacy interactions, foreign direct investment opportunities, city transportation contracting, and expanding trade opportunities for domestic firms in foreign markets. LA's successful bid to host the 2028 Olympics created opportunities for students to work in the area of international sports diplomacy, but cities host other major sporting events that require official interaction with international governing bodies or other governments to facilitate contract negotiations, dignitary visits, and cultural exchanges surrounding those events. Increasingly, city governments are procuring goods and services from international suppliers; at the LA County Department of Transportation, students have worked on projects requesting bids from Japanese manufacturers of light-rail train cars. Similarly, government officials may recognize opportunities for student involvement when funders or foreign companies show interest in local investment opportunities. IR/IS students may gain a front-row seat to negotiations that involve questions of regulatory compliance, international trade rules, international financial flows, and international law.

NGOs and non-profit organizations are additional sources of internationally focused internships that examine local-global connections. Locally based organizations such as the International Rescue Committee, the Youth Refugee Project, and the Interfaith Refugee and Immigration Service are dedicated to refugees and immigration-related issues; Catholic Relief Services, Lutheran World Relief, and the Red Cross work on international and humanitarian aid; and others such as Baltimore's Council of Foreign Affairs and the World Trade Center Institute, or LA's World Affairs Council and Pacific Council on International Policy, are devoted to global engagement and international policy. These options are helpful to IR/IS students not just because they offer locally based work related to students' global interests, but also because they often offer programming and events that represent potential learning opportunities for students who intern there.

Additionally, local chambers of commerce and various trade associations, as well as union offices, could accommodate students with interests in international political economy. Students at these sites benefit from studying government-business relations, and they can often capitalize on close access in order to interview or survey business leaders on topics related to their internship class-related research projects. To illustrate IR/IS program flexibility in using a local government experience to satisfy the IR/IS internship requirements, we note the example of local non-profits that join federally-funded efforts to address homelessness; students have pointed out that placements in this area can be valuable for those who want to work in the field of poverty alleviation in international development. They recognize important lessons, such as the fact that provisioning direct assistance and matching services with target recipients are challenges for any aid-based project, and students believe that they have much to learn by comparing local and international initiatives. Fittingly, one USC student interested in international development worked for a non-profit that was serving Syrian refugees in Greece and wanted to adopt a similar model to serve the LA homeless population. Policy issue areas that are also realized on an international scale represent potential places where students can look to apply their IR knowledge, gain skills, and work on projects near the home campus.

One of the more underutilized sources of internationally focused internships is private sector opportunities in local communities, and our experience suggests that they are among the most promising partners in solving the placement problem for IR/IS students. Numerous law firms that work on issues linked to international relations represent a category of such private sector employers. These include firms that work on cases involving human rights abuses, citizenship, migration, domestic abuse, asylum, and workplace labor laws, including unlawful violations exposed by undocumented immigrants. Students with interests in international law and human rights are drawn to them (it is worth noting that they often require students to be proficient in other languages). Other private employers also have opportunities for students to interact with international law, government policy, and government regulations.

Expanding placement options for IR/IS students in the private sector requires dedicated work by the program coordinator to match students' interests and skills to employers' programs and agendas. To do so, rather than focusing solely on the day-to-day activities that the student will perform, the program coordinator should think of the entire sum of the learning experience, including assignments such as research projects that the student will complete as part of their internship program. For example, a student working in the Port of Los Angeles on contract management interviewed the manager and other contacts in Singapore and Norway to complete a project examining how various global ports respond to sustainability initiatives.[16] Similarly, a student interested in journalism was placed with the communications and media team for the Jet Propulsion Laboratory, a NASA space exploration center, typically considered an employer for engineering students in the LA area. The student used her skills to examine more broadly how NASA communications and media campaigns contribute to American public diplomacy and project "soft" power internationally. What these examples purposefully illustrate is how the work for the private employer, when combined with the research project in the internship course, can advance IR/IS learning by enabling students to examine questions, in theory and in practice, that further their education.

Increasingly, large movie studios and entertainment companies like Disney and Sony host interns whose interests lie in open-source intelligence and cybersecurity. These students get a chance to apply political risk analysis learned in the classroom to various projects for private-sector clients who need threat assessments for internationally based asset protection. Students working for real estate and investment firms can also apply theoretical classroom knowledge to day-to-day work. Given that these sectors continue to internationalize in terms of investors and customers, students can engage in work examining compliance with international business law, federal visa policies, intellectual property rights, and international trade trends. Even tech startups can offer relevant opportunities, especially for interns interested in international entrepreneurship and business development; they benefit from broad exposure to business development matters while addressing specific issues such as intellectual property protection, international patent trolling and theft, the influx of international venture capital, or the impact of international trade conflicts. Normally, students interested in public affairs would not be matched to positions in private enterprise, but students who wish to work on private sector development from a public policy perspective could be encouraged to intern for these types of employers in government liaison or government policy capacities. Placing students in these private sector opportunities could have the added bonus of reinforcing business community ties to the university which can be useful for future job placement and potential fund-raising (Alpert 2009).

We maintain that the private sector represents the largest untapped source of creative internationally focused projects, hands-on experiences, and opportunities to build career-enhancing skills. Yet developing these placements significantly increases the workload for faculty instructors who also have to mentor students through the process of self-assessment (to determine interests and goals), and also help find and negotiate placements that strategically match student interests to employer needs. Furthermore, faculty need to invest significant time in seeking out, cultivating, and maintaining ties with the business community in order to expand their base of internship providers. To ensure program stability and sustainability, we recommend that at least one program administrator be hired to assume or share responsibility for dedicated work such as matching students with potential internship employers, identifying and following up with potential providers in local communities, maintaining contact with providers who are already in a database, and offering general administrative support in order to reduce the burdens borne by faculty and strengthen these vital learning opportunities for students.

Placements Abroad

Placements outside the country of the home institution bring additional challenges. First, students must adapt to cultural differences in their social and work lives, and thus it is best to encourage students to investigate these differences before departure. We recommend meeting with the student to discuss how to research, prepare for, and adapt to potentially different workplace norms. If possible, include a faculty or staff member familiar with that country in this meeting, or have them direct the student to credible sources for learning about workplace cultural differences. In many cases, the Study Abroad Office will have resources as well.

Second, any internship conducted in another country, whether in-person or virtually, independently or in conjunction with a course, should include a consultation with the appropriate home campus office about travel, health, resource access, safety, and security issues. For internships conducted abroad, the faculty supervisor should connect with their Study Abroad Office to ensure that the institution's international travel protocols are followed. Simply put, the home institution's Study Abroad Office is the best conduit for legal, security, housing, and health questions because these staff members have the expertise and background experience to navigate these issues. At TU, recent internships conducted abroad were found through the Study Abroad Office and became part of the students' summer away experience.

Students studying abroad almost invariably face employment challenges, given each country's rules and employment regulations regarding the hiring of foreigners, and many international public affairs opportunities remain out of reach for students. Unpaid internships connected with higher education institutions or obtained through personal connections can be an exception. When USC's American students have independently obtained internships in Europe, for example, they have gained these positions through close personal connections, usually working for US companies or contractors operating in Europe. Depending on the country, permissions for private employers may be more lax. This option can be quite valuable for students who desire to learn about different workplace cultures, norms, and policies because they seek careers in international business or in a public or private capacity that requires working in a foreign office.

Completing an internship for credit may also look different when done abroad. Towson's three students who recently interned away from the US were enrolled in a Study Abroad internship course with the INST faculty as the instructor of record, or in a Study Abroad placeholder course. The Study Abroad Office and the faculty member provided advising jointly via common meetings and email exchanges before students' departures; requirements throughout the semester were conducted via email. An obvious distinction lies in the ability of a supervisor to visit the site in-person, so in Towson's case, the INST faculty adviser engages in at least two phone meetings—an activity that occurs with all site supervisors, regardless of location. The first is a preliminary discussion to ensure that course requirements are understood by those working on site; the second is an in-person, mid-semester check-in with the student and a phone meeting with the site supervisor. If phone meetings cannot be arranged, email exchanges are conducted. Required weekly journals are designed to record a snapshot of how the student is doing that week, review major duties, and provide an opportunity for feedback. Students are told not to just list duties undertaken, but instead to focus on one or two key events or activities that week and what was learned or gained from that experience. The event could include what a student learned as a passive observer or as an active participant in the organization; either way, the student is expected to reflect on how that experience influenced them professionally or personally and submit responses via email. The INST faculty adviser replies to each journal entry, sometimes with professional advice and sometimes with needed encouragement. These exchanges with both the site supervisor and the student allow faculty to engage in regular conversations about how the internship is proceeding no matter where the internship is located and provides openings to discuss and bridge any problems, such as those stemming from differing cultural frames of reference.

Many schools, including USC, do not offer international internship placements—that is, experiences based outside the US—because students have to be enrolled in an on-campus course during the regular academic year in order to earn class credit. During the COVID-19 pandemic, USC temporarily allowed remote international internships to count for credit,[17] but USC students typically pursue international internships on their own (i.e., not for credit) during the summer, and limited funding is available for a small number of global programs operated through the Department and the Career Center.[18]

There has been very little demand for a summer internship course at USC because fees and tuition are not typically included in financial aid packages. Even when they cannot earn credit, students who pursue internships abroad outside of school programs often seek assistance with securing placements.[19] Those students should still be encouraged to seek advice from the Study Abroad Office to avoid or address unanticipated issues relating to working abroad as interns.

Information about Placement Opportunities

Related to the challenge of identifying locally available international internships is the issue of how students receive information about opportunities. A general and oft-mentioned problem is that across a campus there can be competing sources of information about internships, a situation that can create frustrations for students who must navigate certain rules about what is (or is not) an appropriate placement. This challenge increases for IR/IS students because typical sources such as the Career Center database, bulletin boards, online job posts, and a variety of university webpages will not necessarily highlight how the work fits into the academic context. Both TU and USC students often express dissatisfaction that there is not a "one-stop-shop" for all of their internship needs which, ideally, should be provided as close to their home department as possible. There is also a sense that students want their departments to give them "VIP access" to select opportunities so that they do not have to compete with other students for the same positions (Chávez Metoyer in this volume offers an additional perspective on this issue). Specifically, because they are enrolled in a course for which they pay tuition, some students expect the department to guarantee access to desirable opportunities. Both USC and TU have opted against this model in order to use the internship search process as a professional development learning experience for students, but having to sort through a wide array of options–including domestic internships that may or may not have international angles–understandably can lead to frustration. To alleviate this problem, two strategies are recommended. First, program websites could maintain an FAQ page that lists recommended steps and sources to consult in the internship search process. USC's page, for example, suggests sources based on how far along students are in the search process and how experienced they are with job searches.[20] To those just starting their search, a visit to the career advisor is recommended, and if going abroad, to the Study Abroad Office; to those knowing what they want, databases are recommended instead (see supplemental resources for a list of international placements).

A second strategy is to advertise the course to students ahead of their potential enrollment in order to create lead time for them to identify desirable placements and also prime them to take action, preferably during the semester prior to enrolling in the internship course. This advertisement at USC is done in person through visits to courses, via postings to learning management systems (Blackboard, Moodle, Canvas) composed by faculty, and in targeted emails sent by departmental staff and academic advisors. Also, particularly if it is incorporated into their syllabus, faculty can promote and showcase students' international internships in public forums—such as symposia, colloquia, posters, or campus conferences, for example—to spread knowledge about the international aspects of their local area. Arranging these presentations requires time and university resources, including faculty and staff commitments, but the benefits to students include teaching others about these contexts, providing examples of such opportunities, allowing prospective interns to ask questions of those who have completed internships, and, for faculty, sharing and learning about the experiences of local-global connections explored by others. Further, this option provides the university with an opportunity to showcase its global-local connections in the public and private sectors.

2. Assessment at Home and Abroad

While our experience shows that students value internships, the tools for assessing learning goals for internship programs are not uniform (Ediger 2010). Two separate types of assessment are worth considering: one, by students enrolled in an internship course, of how they assess the effectiveness of their learning experience; two, by faculty or the institution, as to whether students are meeting the learning objectives through the program (i.e., assessment of student learning). In the former case, we suspect that the challenges associated with internationally focused internships are not much different from those in other internship programs. In the latter case, we have encountered additional challenges, especially with internships conducted abroad. We discuss each in turn.

Student assessment of their learning experience is influenced by the perceived quality of the overall work experience. We know from Alpert (2009) that since internships are conducted off-campus and the work lies outside of the program coordinator's control, a student's experience, if not positive, diminishes their assessment of the overall benefit of the internship program. In practice this means that when students submit course evaluations, a negative internship experience can color their perception of the utility of the internship course that they took. In addition, at both institutions, students tend to complain about the workload associated with these classes, which only earn 2 units/credits at USC and earn a "normal" 3 credits at TU.[21] Some students perceive work and commute hours as part of their coursework, while others begrudge assignments and meetings that require them to put in additional time. Faculty can help to shape students' expectations by addressing these issues from the outset and continuing to emphasize each stage of a course project and other assignments as essential work.

Second, students often fail to grasp the purpose of course assignments and approach requirements as boxes to be checked off, rather than as exercises designed to achieve specific learning outcomes. For example, most students do not implicitly understand the difference between a reflection essay (personal and professional development goals) and a traditional research paper (traditional knowledge and critical thinking goals), and sometimes blend these. This misunderstanding can lead to low quality in the research paper, and as a pass/fail graded class, the faculty member has few incentives for students to invest significant time in this assignment. A partial solution to this problem is to disallow courses taken for the major to be counted as pass/no pass, a strategy which USC, other majors at TU, and other institutions employ; another is to enlarge the audience for their work, such as requiring that students submit their final projects to their supervisors or present them to their peers.[22]

We also know that both the student's assessment and the overall learning experience in the program are enhanced when the advisor takes a close interest in the student's research project in the course. A significant written project is a desirable assessment instrument from the perspective of all involved stakeholders, as documented by Alpert (2009), but our experience confirms that student learning is magnified when their individual research projects receive detailed feedback and support from the mentor. However, the potentially wide range of IR/IS internships poses a challenge for mentors because it requires them to evaluate substantively what students are taking on in their projects. This connection can be further complicated if students take private sector opportunities that have international dimensions.[23] As such, our experience suggests that it is important to identify faculty coordinators in IR who have broad interdisciplinary interests so that they are able to support and assess any one student's project.

Our respective programs emphasize the role of reflective assignments in accordance with the core principle of experiential education which says that "for knowledge to be discovered and internalized the learner must [...] weigh outcomes against past learning and future implications" (Bennion 2015, 356). We can and should insist on this type of assignment in IR/IS internship courses, particularly because of the navigation of cultures, political systems, and/or economic processes that usually occurs. However, we have far less control over the types of related assignments that are asked of students when the internship takes place abroad or outside of the home institution's regular internship course, which can impact the quality of assessments that are performed. Even when they are located in the US, international worksite supervisors may not understand American higher education needs, such as submitting timely evaluations or ensuring that the student does meaningful work, far beyond answering phones and filing paperwork. When the latter has occurred, the faculty member has contacted the worksite supervisor to discuss new assignments and discussed with the student how they might evaluate the cultural differences in workplaces that are leading to this outcome, such as gender-based expectations. When paperwork is late, then the faculty member must send gentle email reminders. In all cases, the faculty member needs to ensure that the student is not placed in the position of "making demands," or being seen as doing so, as in many cultures this positioning could negatively affect the student's situation and further treatment on site. Should problems persist, connecting with the Study Abroad Office may yield some helpful tips relative to that country. Often these kinds of problems can be avoided altogether when relying on the Study Abroad Office from the outset (in fact this is required on many campuses), because their office staff can work closely with the international institution's internship program to ensure that expectations are clear and that those providers who do not fulfill these expectations are excluded from future placements.

3. Pre-professional Support

Required pre-professional development exercises may be of limited utility to some and highly valuable to others, yet all students tend to prefer one-on-one advice, which can be difficult for an individual faculty member to accommodate. In the case of USC, some students perceive very little value in course assignments that involve attending a workshop or a career event on a topic such as business communication, crafting a résumé and writing a cover letter, networking, or salary negotiation because they are too general for their specific needs; these students prefer to use online resources and have someone check their individual résumés and cover letters. Others become dissatisfied when specific events or workshops do not line up with their schedules or are offered too early or too late in the semester. These challenges tend to be more common when programming is created and managed by entities outside the department, such as by a career center that serves an entire campus or college. On some campuses, however, a staff member can be recruited to address a specific class and offer a curated workshop.

We also know that one of the important aspects of internships is to reflect on how the hands-on experience translates into competencies, including abilities, skills, and knowledge (Biswas 2020; NACE 2021). Internship programs can adopt strategies practiced by Study Abroad programs to manage "unpacking sessions" designed to help students articulate and present their marketable skills and competencies in both the job-interview process and on résumés (Malerich 2009, 9). At USC, we have successfully organized a mandatory in-person meeting for the entire semester's cohort to engage in a group exercise with amended résumés as a non-graded deliverable. Naturally, the time burden increases if professionalization workshops must be customized by the instructor or coordinator for the specific cohort each semester. Other ways to help students recognize and highlight international dimensions on their résumés include requiring students to construct and practice a three-minute "elevator speech" about themselves. Given that the international focus may not be clearly identifiable in the title of an internship placement, students often need to be shown how to extract experiences and skills that could be of importance to potential employers who value the IR/IS aspects of the work completed. Malerich (2009) warns that this problem is particularly challenging for IR/IS interns because it often remains unclear to employers which specific competencies were built through the internationally focused experience that could be relevant to a future position (8). Employers can also be quick to dismiss the link between an international working experience and the development of transferable soft skills such as inter-cultural competence, multicultural team building, and language proficiency. Having students reflect on their overall experience and then articulating, for potential employers, specific skills that were obtained through their internships often requires one-on-one attention from faculty or trained career counselors.

4. Costs and Financial Aid

A familiar challenge for all interns are the associated costs. These include direct costs such as tuition, transportation, opportunity costs of foregoing paid employment to do an internship, and indirect costs of room and board. Added costs of internships abroad typically include airfare, communication (cellphone, remote internet connections), additional travel or health insurance, and possibly application and program fees associated with a study abroad program. Often overlooked is the cost of attire, as cultural expectations about proper work dress can differ from what the students expect. Students in large metropolitan areas with competitive rental markets may also have to pay for summer rent in order to "hold" an apartment to which they will return after a summer away. For most students, summer tuition is not covered by financial assistance, and so they avoid taking for-credit internships in the summer. Funding sources available at our respective institutions may cover airfare and a portion of room and board costs, but they are not sufficient to cover all of these additional expenses. As a result, for most students, the total costs are simply the main barrier for taking on an internship abroad. For them, taking a course may be the one way to associate financial aid with an internship opportunity.

Students who are better off socioeconomically are also then better positioned to take advantage of the kinds of international internships that we know advance their employment post-graduation. The costs of unpaid work abroad thus continue to be a barrier to participation and contribute to growing income inequality at home (McDonald 2016), particularly for students who have significant caregiving responsibilities.

The argument for student funding is made elsewhere in this volume, but we wish to emphasize our respective institutional concerns that funds be provided in a way that does not interfere or offset existing tuition support from financial aid, fellowships, and scholarships. In conjunction with a Development Office, other sources of aid might be developed by a program coordinator who maintains close relationships with employers; they could advocate for the creation of employer-based stipends, or consider ways to partner with employers to create new sources of outside funding for students who otherwise would be unable to do an internship. Universities should also make some scholarships available precisely for this purpose. Lastly, universities could investigate ways to reduce tuition costs for summer internships.

LESSONS LEARNED

One lesson learned at both institutions is that we can develop internationally focused internships at home by helping students make local-global connections and relying increasingly on the private sector to do so. For example, students have worked on projects for private firms that lobby foreign governments for tariff reductions in agricultural sectors, for music and entertainment companies that deal with trade-related intellectual property rights, and for startups looking to create new green technologies to alleviate poverty. These opportunities can provide a rich alternative to typical public affairs placements because businesses all over the US increasingly cooperate or compete with foreign partners. We find that our students are uniquely qualified to assist with internationally focused projects of private businesses because of their foreign affairs knowledge and growing research and data skills. These internships also offer an important international learning option for students whose travel status or family obligations may otherwise prohibit this international experience. Faculty can recruit employers by emphasizing students' abilities to assist with analysis of security threats, intellectual property protection, and labor and environmental standards, among others. Students' language and cultural competency skills can be an asset to businesses looking to expand their international connections and enhance their international communication regardless of their location in the US. Uncovering global-local connections is an approach that can be replicated in many university communities, by faculty members who reside far from large metropolitan areas, and in regions where locally based public affairs positions may not be readily available in government offices and policy think tanks. We have found that even employers without internationally focused assignments can help students develop on-the-job skills that can be linked to international relations or international studies with carefully selected, internationally focused research projects. IR/IS students can gain new insight into refugee and resettlement issues, asylum seeking, and immigration issues of concern locally; they can learn about the impacts of international aid, law, and international development and bring that knowledge back to their institutions through presentations and discussions—in their own courses, in recruitment workshops, or in a showcase of student work.

Both institutions covered in this chapter are in metropolitan areas with many options for in-person, internationally focused internships. Some of these internships were initially shut down during the pandemic, but in other cases, the pandemic compelled some organizations and companies to create virtual internships. New technologies and practices will continue to enable more of these positions, especially internationally, opening more opportunities to more students, including those at institutions in rural areas. Virtual IR/IS internships will create new challenges for colleges and universities in terms of vetting, managing, and supervising these opportunities but may also strengthen ties between the Study Abroad Office and an international studies/international relations program.

Another lesson that emerges from the analysis of challenges to internationally focused internships is that many proposed solutions require faculty to devote additional time and resources to ensure student and programmatic success. Whether faculty seek out, develop, and maintain ties to the private sector or work to expand placements abroad, we are suggesting that more responsibility would fall onto the faculty coordinator, as both local and global connections must be created and maintained. Also, by suggesting that faculty customize workshops for the pre-professional development of their interns or advocate for employer-based student stipends, we are asking faculty to step in and provide more administrative work that fills the gap between student learning and student professionalization. Yet faculty loads and fluctuating enrollment numbers do not reflect the level of commitment needed and expected of faculty in many situations.

The editors and other contributors to this volume argue for additional financial support to incentivize and support faculty in these roles.[24] Ultimately, faculty coordinators should be enabled to take on the highly individualized mentoring that a solid internship experience requires, and their work should be accounted for in tenure and promotion decisions. If higher education institutions are serious about an international education mission for all of their students and if political science as a discipline seeks to become more international, then more attention must first be paid to recognizing the efforts of faculty who cultivate and deliver meaningful learning opportunities through IR/IS internships.

CONCLUSION

International studies and international relations (IS/IR) internships provide benefits similar to other internships discussed throughout this book, including improving research, critical thinking, and writing skills, linking classroom knowledge to actual experiences, establishing connections that can lead to more internships and/or jobs postgraduation, and expanding students' abilities to work independently. Their unique benefits center on the international component, whereby students can apply and further their knowledge of current international affairs, including cultural, historical, economic, and political processes, structures, events, and alternative perspectives. As the world of work becomes increasingly globalized, we need to prepare students for the international contexts that await them upon graduation. Political science programs must be ready to extend these global learning opportunities to all International Relations/International Studies students who seek them, whether the positions are based in the US or abroad. When working within an interdisciplinary context, with supportive administrators, and with sufficient financial support, faculty can play essential roles in enriching international internships—efforts that can result in deeper understanding of the global-local connections that exist in every community.

REFERENCES

Alpert, Frank, Joo-Gim Heaney, and Kerri-Ann Kuhn. 2009. "Internships in Marketing: Goals, Structures and Assessment-Student, Company and Academic Perspective." *Australasian Marketing Journal* 17 (1): 36–45.

Anderson, Sheldon, Mark Allen Peterson, Stanley W. Toops, and Jeanne A. K. Hey. 2015. *International Studies: An Interdisciplinary Approach to Global Issues, Third Edition.* Boulder, CO: Westview Press.

Auerbach, Arthur. 2021. "POSC 395: Directed Government and Political Leadership." *Syllabus.* Los Angeles: University of Southern California, Summer.

Bennion, Elizabeth A. 2015. "Experiential Education in Political Science and International Relations." In *Handbook on Teaching and Learning in Political Science and International Relations*, ed. John Ishiyama, William J. Miller, and Eszter Simon, 351–368. Northampton, MA: Edward Elgar Publishing.

Biswas, Bidisha, and Virginia Haufler. 2020. "What Can I Do with This Class? Building Employment-Related Skills in International Relations Courses." *Journal of Political Science Education* 16 (1): 1551–2177.

Ediger, Ruth, and Kathleen Braden. 2010. "International Internships for American Undergraduates: Assessment and Accreditation Challenges." *International Journal of Arts and Sciences* 3 (17): 242–263.

Narayanan, V. K., Paul Olk, and Cynthia V. Fukami. 2010. "Determinants of Internship Effectiveness: An Exploratory Model." *Academy of Management Learning and Education* 9 (1): 61–80.

National Association of Colleges and Employers. 2021. "What is Career Readiness?" NACE. https://www.naceweb.org/career-readiness/competencies/career-readiness-defined/.

Maertz, Carl P., Phillipp A. Stoeberl, and Jill Marks. 2014. "Building Successful Internships: Lessons from the Research for Interns, Schools, and Employees." *Career Development International* 19 (1): 123–142.

Malerich, Jennifer. 2009. "The Value of International Internships in Global Workforce Development." Arizona State University, Working Paper. Accessed June 15, 2021. https://www.aieaworld.org/assets/docs/Issue_Briefs/thevalueofinternationalinternshipsinglobalworkforcedevelopment_malerich.pdf.

McDonald, Paul, Damian Oliver, and Deanna Grant-Smith. 2016. "The Growing Cost of Internships Could Add to Inequality." *The Conversation,* June 20. https://eprints.qut.edu.au/115147/1/The%2Bgrowing%2Bcost%2Bof%2Binternships%2Bcould%2Badd%2Bto%2Binequality.pdf.

Straus, Scott, and Barry Driscoll. 2019. *International Studies: Global Forces, Interactions, and Tensions.* Washington, DC: CQ Press.

Yagoda, Ben. 2008. "Will Work for Academic Credit." *Chronicle of Higher Education* 54 (28): A36.

ENDNOTES

1. See for example USC IR learning objectives posted on their department webpage: https://dornsife.usc.edu/sir/major-requirements/. Towson University INST learning objectives are posted in the catalog online: https://catalog.towson.edu/undergraduate/liberal-arts/international-studies/international-studies-ba/.

2. This situation can help a student by increasing options, but (in some cases and places, such as large cities) it can also add confusion by providing seemingly unlimited options. However, if we return to the key component of IR/IS learning outcomes–an international dimension–this limiting variable can guide decisions about what does and does not count as an IR/IS internship.

3. In 2019, USC Dornsife College of Letters, Arts, and Sciences merged the Political Science Department with SIR to form a joint Political Science and International Relations Department. Hence, the new department consists of two undergraduate programs, one in Political Science and one in International Relations. Each undergraduate program administers a separate internship program.

4. It was clear that students apply for and land internships outside of the school, but we thought that by offering a formal course for credit, we could attract a subset of students who are interested in incorporating internships into their academic learning and training.

5. Dornsife College at USC offers other for-credit internship courses that award university credit but not major credit. For a full list, see: https://dornsife.usc.edu/assets/sites/1078/docs/Do_it_Internship_Search_Guide.pdf.

6. Of those who did not have an internship, 52% said that they have not yet had a chance to do an internship, about 15% reported that they don't have time or resources, 27% don't know how to find one, and only 6% reported that they are not interested. This demonstrates that internships are highly popular among our students but also shows that our program is serving only a small segment of that population. The survey captured responses from 158 students participating in seven major courses during the early Fall 2020 semester.

7. Without detailed information about how many students have an internship per academic year, we cannot estimate the percentage of students served by the program.

8. We should note that while this type of resource may not exist on smaller campuses, software such as Handshake and People Grove that connects alumni to current students can help jumpstart one.

9. Towson University. 2021. "At a Glance." Towson University. Accessed May 4, 2021. https://towson.edu/about/ataglance/.

10. Towson University. 2020. "Major in International Studies." In *Undergraduate Catalog 2020-21*, Towson University. https://catalog.towson.edu/undergraduate/liberal-arts/international-studies/international-studies-ba/.

11. Not all majors at TU require a practicum or capstone experience.

12. Additionally, some INST majors embarked on internships through other departments such as political science and business, and with the INST director's approval, these credits can be used to fulfill the practicum requirement. This option of overlapping credit helps students who are pursuing double majors or minors.

13. The placements in Annapolis, normally reserved for American students focusing on state and local government, were undertaken by international students at TU seeking to learn about another country's political system (in this case, the US). The three study abroad internships were conducted in Ireland, the United Kingdom, and a multi-country program in Asia.

14. The Washington Center partnered with the state of Maryland to offer scholarships for in-state students, now totaling $9,000/semester, which recently has increased enrollment through the Center. See: https://twc.edu/programs/state-scholarships.

15. The State Department, at least, has offered online internships since 2009. See: https://www.state.gov/vsfs-a-great-opportunity-for-students-and-federal-employees-alike/.

16. Specifically, the research project allowed the student to study whether environmental sustainability efforts are more effective when conducted in response to a push from state, sub-state, or non-state actors.

17. The experience with remote teaching and internships has demonstrated that it would be possible for our existing program structure to accommodate internships that our students line up abroad. While the practical experience would be "in person," the academic work would be performed remotely with the faculty instructor "at home." However, we think that few students would pursue this opportunity due to lack of summer tuition funding. Towson students face similar funding challenges, and hence few have pursued this option.

18. The USC Political Science and International Relations Department offers separate internship opportunities in the summer through the Brussels Program for students interested in European security and foreign policy. We offer scholarships to students pursuing internships in Africa and Asia that they have identified on their own. The USC Office for Overseas Studies runs programs in Paris, Australia, Hong Kong, and Mexico City. A popular program offered by the USC Career Center is the USC Global Fellows program, and our IR students are frequent recipients of this fully funded internship opportunity abroad. With political science students, IR students are very competitive for the Rangel International Affairs Summer Enrichment Program. Many also tend to find opportunities while studying abroad. Others turn to federal government opportunities in the CIA, FBI, GAO, OMB such as the Pathways Internship Program and the State Department Student Experience Program, as well as the centralized intern program in the Defense Department. Popular international organizations are major DC think tanks and the Clinton Foundation, Carnegie, OECD, Center for Strategic and International Studies, and the Gates Foundation.

19. Depending on the country, permissions for private employers may be more lax. These issues amplify the need to cultivate more opportunities with private sector actors who may have the resources to navigate employment law regulations and who may enable students to work both at home and abroad. These issues highlight, once again, the importance of working with and going through the Study Abroad Office to overcome these hurdles.

20. See, for example: https://dornsife.usc.edu/sir/internship-program-faqs/.

21. A "normal" IR course at USC carries 4 units/credits.

22. During the COVID-induced switch to remote learning, this rule was relaxed to allow a limited number of courses to be taken pass/no pass in select semesters. This accommodation will be lifted once the campus returns to residential learning.

23. Narayanan, Olk, and Fukami (2010) propose a strategy for screening students to ensure that their interests overlap with the faculty member's research interests and expertise, but this strategy is not feasible in small programs where there is a single faculty coordinator (and a smaller faculty that students can access for additional help).

24. The conclusion to this book contains an extended argument for paying interns and compensating faculty fairly and adequately for their work. We would like to add that there are numerous institutional benefits to providing a clearer workload credit and accounting for expectations for faculty. First, faculty whose expertise focuses only on local or national politics may not be able to help students navigate the international questions and expectations of these internships. A specialized faculty internship coordinator could resolve this problem. Second, clearer expectations and compensation levels could also help institutions to recruit and retain a dedicated faculty coordinator who could create and maintain close relationships with local entities. The benefits for students, faculty, and staff, include creating less burdensome and more helpful major-specific training sessions with institutional career centers, thus making landing these internships a smoother and more successful process for students.

CHAPTER 15

Virtual Public Affairs Internships

Amy Cabrera Rasmussen, California State University, Long Beach
Renée B. Van Vechten, University of Redlands

The expansion of virtual internships following the spread of COVID-19 is likely to persist. This chapter reviews scholarly work on virtual public affairs internships, situating their recent surge within a longer trajectory. The analysis draws on interviews with faculty, site supervisors, and students to improve our understanding of virtual internships' structural features and their effect on the achievement of learning outcomes. Specifically, we focus on students' ability to build competencies related to career and self-development, communication, and professionalism. The chapter also addresses the implications for inclusion, access, and equity, and closes with concrete recommendations for key stakeholders.

INTRODUCTION: TOWARD BEST PRACTICES IN VIRTUAL PUBLIC AFFAIRS INTERNSHIPS

Working and learning remotely are not new, but the COVID-19 pandemic initiated an era of remote internships at an unprecedented scale and speed. In early 2020, untold numbers of student interns were hastily shuffled into virtual environments, and other internships were postponed indefinitely or ended without warning. Within a year, many internship providers had largely adapted to virtual spaces through trial and error. Likewise, many college and university faculty worked to adapt their own pedagogical practices to the challenges and possibilities associated with remote internships. The experiences of student interns helped open a window onto the pitfalls and promises of virtual work-to-learn experiences while also providing lessons that can be applied to any internship modality (in-person, virtual, or hybridized).

Prior to 2020, many multi-national business employers had already recognized the possibilities of attracting a more globalized, diverse intern pool through their efforts to branch into remote settings (Jeske and Axtell 2016). Virtual internships had been developed for educators at least a decade before COVID-19 pushed schooling online (Faucette and Nugent 2015). In the public affairs internship context—where student work is primarily associated with public policy, goods, and governance, and having an impact on political communities, broadly defined—the Virtual Student Federal Service was established in 2009 to harness "the expertise and digital excellence of US citizen students" to advance the federal government's work.[1]

For the relatively few pre-existing virtual internship providers, then, the sudden leap into fully online workspaces required minimal effort. For almost everyone else, the in-person model of undergraduate internships served as a default guide for pivoting to online work, providing a foundation for understanding how to design and deploy experiential learning.[2]

Internships gained greater support on college campuses after they were deemed "high-impact practices" based on their demonstrated contributions to student success and engagement. In particular, they have been shown to have the potential to strengthen intellectual and practical skills through integrative and applied learning (Kuh 2008; 2013). Moreover, as Kuh (2008) and Finley and McNair (2013) have documented, all students have the potential to benefit from experiential learning, but historically underrepresented groups may benefit even more.

Whether remote internships can serve the same educational purposes as in-person ones remains an open question that scholars recently have begun to explore (Adadi 2018; Ruggiero and Boehm 2016). As Pike (2018) points out, "Although online internships are frequently discussed in the popular media, they are still in the exploratory stage in many professional programs throughout the world" (148). Early assessments show that internship outcomes vary with the nature and type of work, specific assignments, institutional organization, and stakeholder goals, among other things. Yet as Hora, Lee, Chen, and Hernandez (2021a) note, this "massive experiment" is largely taking place in the absence of evidence that virtual internships support student success (3).

This study adds to the growing research literature by examining the large-scale natural experiment by which remote experiential learning replaced face-to-face versions. We rely on interviews conducted with faculty, site supervisors, and students, almost all of whom have engaged in both types of internships in the public affairs context, to address three overarching research questions: (1) Conceptually and descriptively, what are the key structural features of online internships? (2) How does the modality of an internship affect student learning or the achievement of learning outcomes? (3) What aspects of online environments impede or facilitate inclusiveness in terms of benefits and access? Finally, to assist those who will supervise and monitor both in-person and virtual internships, which will persist long into the future alongside hybridized versions (Ruggiero & Boehm 2016; Schloetzer 2021), we offer recommendations that move us closer to a set of "best practices" for conducting virtual internships in the public affairs context.

WHAT WE KNOW ABOUT VIRTUAL INTERNSHIPS

Internships in which workplace interaction is mediated through an electronic device (most commonly a computer, phone, or tablet) are variously termed in the literature as *virtual*, *remote*, *online*, *digitally mediated*, *computer-mediated*, and *computer-assisted*. In most cases, students conduct related work in their own physical spaces, which could be a dorm room or local café with a WiFi connection, and they meet with their supervisors, colleagues, or peers only through digital means. The bulk of assignments is conducted independently, either during work hours interns set for themselves or during regular business hours. In hybridized versions, a modest amount of face-to-face interaction with office mates (either offsite or onsite) and in-office work time of varying duration could be included, depending on where the intern is physically located. If we visualize a spectrum of types ranging from strictly online to strictly in-person, internships that mainly take place face-to-face in office settings but involve occasional online meetings generally would not be considered "online" internships per se.[3]

Along with individual faculty, campus career centers have helped facilitate the rapid move to online environments, with demand for their expertise and services spiking as COVID-19 spread in 2020.[4] Virtual internships "arguably became the central modality of work-based learning for students around the world" that year (Hora et al. 2021a, 3; see also Braga 2020; Lumpkin 2020), but public health regulations and widespread economic shut-downs managed to reduce, not eliminate, in-person internships. In their study of mostly STEM majors, Hora et al. (2021a) showed that less than half (45.3%) of all internships in 2020 were conducted online.[5]

Studies about online internships parallel existing research examining work-from-home, telecommuting, and other types of remote employment, which was estimated to be about 15% of the US population prior to COVID-19.[6] Researchers have observed that interns encounter the same practical challenges as employees with respect to technological issues, respecting work-life boundaries, and communicating with others in an organization—all of which affect either productivity or one's ability to learn on the job (Hora et al. 2020b). For example, in Sull, Sull and Bersin's (2020) survey of global human resources managers, keeping remote employees engaged, productive, and connected were frequently mentioned as top concerns; these are the same types of issues that Jeske and Axtell (2017), Hora et al. (2021a), and Criso, Low, and Townsend (2021) have identified in their research on virtual interns. During the COVID-19 pandemic, student interns reported extra stress from the sudden transition to work-from-home arrangements and the tumultuous environment overall, conditions that could influence personal judgments about the overall effectiveness of experiential learning (Bijeau and Peters 2021).

Recent studies of virtual internship experiences have probed the practical issues and challenges that stakeholders such as students, faculty advisors, educational institutions, and internship providers face, and scholars have sought to establish guidelines for success based on comparisons. For example, Bijeau and Peters (2021) studied evaluations of student interns who enrolled in a US university's for-credit internship program and found that the remote work format required students to become more agile and self-disciplined than might have been the case in an office setting, largely because much of their independent work was not monitored closely or could be done at a time of their own choosing.

Much of what is considered to be best practices for in-person internships appears to be equally important for online internships. Ruggiero and Boehm (2016) emphasize the need for solid preparation that includes meeting with students prior to their beginning an internship in order to articulate learning outcomes together. They also suggest establishing academic standards and professional expectations before the internship begins—which is particularly important for students who have had limited exposure to professional settings. Most critically, Ruggiero and Boehm highlight how "explicit, clear communication between clients, mentors, and interns during the virtual internship" helps interns fulfill their duties and meet expectations (2016, 117). Open and frequent communication among stakeholders can reduce "ambiguity and uncertainty about responsibilities and performance thresholds" (Jeske and Axtell 2017, 153) and ultimately avoids wasted efforts by interns who may not fully understand instructions delivered through an electronic screen (see also Werner and Jeske 2021, and Wunch 1985).

Werner and Jeske (2021) emphasize other practical rules for faculty and supervisors who run internship programs: monitor progress regularly, as well as recognize milestones in interns' development; make sure that interns are equipped with the proper technological and research tools to perform assigned tasks; connect students to peers and others in the organization routinely, either through collaborative projects or online meet-ups; encourage independent problem-solving and being proactive; and mentor consistently. While these process-oriented considerations are well-established in the literature on face-to-face internships, Werner and Jeske assert that they are of particular importance in virtual contexts.

These structural aspects of remote internships can provide a strong foundation for learning, and research has demonstrated that internships generally are considered a "high-impact practice" (HIP) enabling students to develop knowledge and skills through direct experience (Kuh 2008). Measurable gains from HIPs include higher persistence to graduation rates (Adadi 2018), higher grade point averages, and deeper learning (Finley and McNair 2013). Finley and McNair (2013) found that for underserved students who engage in HIPs,[7] internships lead to higher self-reported deep learning and self-perceived gains, but overall those gains are relatively lower compared to all other forms of HIPs (with the exception of study abroad). To date, almost all studies that have been done on internships as a high-impact practice are based on aggregate data collected about in-person experiences.

Kilgo, Sheets, and Pascarella (2015) also explored HIPs, finding internships to be a "significant, positive predictor for inclination to inquire and lifelong learning [. . .] and socially responsible leadership" (521). Overall, however, internships had lower levels of impact on a range of outcomes as compared to other HIPs such as service learning or learning communities. Similarly, McClellan, Kopko, and Gruber (2021) observed that regardless of major, students who completed an internship "were more likely to acquire practical competencies, such as crucial interpersonal and career skills" (10), but that internships did not significantly influence other abilities, such as applying and analyzing theories, examining diverse perspectives, or encouraging students to rate their college experience positively (Ibid.). Notably, the authors cautioned that they did not control for the types of internships that were reported in their study or the quality of those internships, remarking that the underperformance of the internship variable "suggests that not all were high-quality learning experiences" (Ibid; see footnote 8, p. 17).

Generally, in high-quality internships, students have the motivation, preparation, tools, space, and external support to attain their goals regardless of format, and they are able to develop transferable skills and qualities that both complement their studies and will enable them to thrive post-graduation.[8] Based on research and in keeping with the overarching objectives of liberal arts education, the National Association of Colleges and Employers (NACE) has articulated eight clusters of core career readiness competencies (knowledge, abilities, and skills) that are strongly associated with professional success. These include: career and self-development; communication; critical thinking; equity and inclusion; leadership; professionalism; teamwork; and technology (NACE 2021).[9] When fortified with these abilities, students are broadly prepared for "success in the workplace and lifelong career management" (NACE 2021). These competencies encompass self-learning (Kuh 2008) or developing perceptions of one's professional preparedness (Berntson and Marklund 2007), as well as practical learning, whereby college graduates entering a profession such as public service learn the norms and values appropriate to professional conduct in that realm—in other words, they are socialized into a profession (Barnett 2012; Dailey 2016).[10] As Carnevale, Fasules, and Campbell (2020) reiterate, in addition to the job skills and knowledge that are demanded by professional employers today, the cognitive competencies of leadership, teaching and learning, problem-solving, and complex thinking "associated with higher education have grown more important over time" (n.p.), a point that underscores the importance of integrative learning through practical application.

As the COVID-19 pandemic lengthened, researchers began to study the extent to which career readiness competencies were being enabled through remote internships. Bijeau and Peters (2021) found that students reported limitations on their ability to network; meanwhile, their supervisors noted declines over the semester in professionalism/work ethic and leadership, but gains in abilities that interns likely demonstrated through projects such as oral/written communications and critical thinking/problem solving. Students acknowledged restrictions on their professional development (compounded by the pandemic lockdowns), but also greater opportunities for self-reflection, growth, and the need to become more disciplined and autonomous. Students also self-reported significant improvements in their digital technology, career management, and oral/written communications competencies. As Bijeau and Peters surmise, it's probable that "digital natives" were able to learn and use software effectively, and that their growth in career management was due to periodic, reflective self-assessments that helped them consider their professional development (2021). Criso, Low, and Townsend (2021) reach similar conclusions in their comparative study of in-person versus remote internships, finding that regardless of type, at least half of all interns noted an increase in their (NACE career competency-related) skills, and that the average difference in skills gain that was perceived by students in remote internships was 3.25% less than for in-person ones, a relatively minor difference.

Apart from the issue of whether a well-designed virtual internship can facilitate goal attainment is the question of whether certain student populations can access these opportunities or are better able to thrive in them—in other words, whether the modality fosters inclusiveness and equity. The idea that students can eliminate a commute, work from home, and create their own schedules has led some to conclude that online internships will increase racial and socio-economic diversity in the intern applicant pool (Jeske 2019; Jeske and Axtell 2016; Knight and Taylor 2021). Likewise, Kraft, Jeske, and Bayerlein (2019) and Hora et al. (2021a) recognize that online internships have been largely perceived "as a potential equalizing force in the internship economy," as low-income and working students, and those students with disabilities or located in rural areas, would theoretically be more able to access virtual opportunities (Hora et al. 2021a, 9). Thus far, studies suggest that rather than easing access, online settings can reinforce existing advantages among those who do not depend on compensation. Hora et al.'s data (2021a) show that online interns predominantly represent upper- and middle-income backgrounds (75.8%) and that there are more unpaid internships in the online format than in-person (42% versus 34.9% unpaid). As internships expand to include previously underserved populations, including racial and ethnic minority and first-generation students, their quality will partly reflect the extent to which they are designed to account for cultural differences and group-specific stressors (Fetter and Thompson 2020; Hora et al. 2021b).

Although research in this area remains under development, it is clear that comparable challenges exist in face-to-face and virtual settings, but the intensity or salience of these challenges may differ depending on context. Jeske and Axtell (2017) report that many of the same aspects of in-person and remote experiences matter, including clarifying goals with interns, communicating, and making them feel valued and rewarded for their efforts. They note that "e-internships provide interns with, not necessarily, any better or worse experience" than they might have experienced in an in-person setting (153–54).

Kuh and Kinzie (2018) also point out that outcomes vary depending on institutional context and the quality of implementation, and a poorly-designed internship—regardless of format—is likely to yield poor outcomes, just as a high-quality internship will do the opposite. This logic also applies to being equity-minded when designing and deploying virtual internships, and more evidence is needed to determine who benefits from online internship placements, who does not, and in what ways. This chapter aims to inform the development of virtual public affairs internships by identifying practices that advance inclusiveness and also equity for student interns.

OUR RESEARCH METHODS

As noted above, our research seeks to understand how online public affairs internships are structured and conducted, how well they allow students to learn and construct knowledge, and how internship practices impact inclusiveness. Our research also aims to provide guidance to faculty and others who seek to ensure that such internships yield educational benefits. Taking a "360-degree view," we focus on all major stakeholders rather than one type alone in our study.[11] During spring 2021 we conducted 19 interviews with three types of respondents who had participated in different aspects of virtual internships: faculty and others who mentored students and worked with a remote internship provider; students who completed online internships; and internship site representatives.[12] We were aware that interviewees' recounting of their experiences could be affected by the condition of living through the COVID-19 public health crisis and kept this in mind as we analyzed the interview material.

Our semi-structured interviews began with a set of designated questions but also responded to the course of each unique interview in order to explore how, from their various vantage points, these stakeholders engaged in and perceived virtual internships (Fujii 2018; Soss 2014). We obtained interviewees through a combination of professional networks and a snowball sampling technique. We continued our recruitment process until we no longer encountered new themes. Interviews were conducted in spring 2021. They lasted approximately 45–60 minutes in length and were conducted virtually via the video-conferencing platforms of Zoom or WebEx and recorded with respondents' informed consent.

More specifically, we asked interviewees about their experience overall with virtual internships and about their specific role and tasks, their perceptions of the strengths and disadvantages of the virtual format, and where appropriate, asked them to compare their virtual internship experiences to those they had done in-person. As it turned out, most participants had experience in both settings and in many cases, more than one experience within each modality. Such multiplicity, it should be noted, made clear that internships are far from homogeneous; as with in-person experiences, variation among virtual experiences is the rule.[13] We queried interviewees about the projects and tasks they considered to be easiest—and most challenging—to accomplish remotely; how supervisors could ensure that their expectations were reasonable; and about lessons learned—things they felt others would benefit from knowing—with attention paid to what they perceived as the (potentially) unique features of the virtual context. Finally, we directly asked interviewees to describe what they considered to be best practices for either hosting, facilitating, or undertaking internships. As researchers, we recognize that our interviewees speak not only from their designated roles (as student, faculty, or supervisor), but also their unique positionalities, and these are reflected in their responses.

Using detailed transcripts and notes of our interviews, we undertook an iterative and recursive content analysis process with these texts, examining responses for commonalities and general lessons.[14] Our goal was to recognize patterns in the responses, continuing until we were confident that we had exhausted the range of emergent themes. From this, we derived a set of insights into what we consider to be best practices for virtual public affairs internships.

THE VIRTUAL PUBLIC AFFAIRS INTERNSHIP: ANALYSIS AND FINDINGS

General Features of Virtual Public Affairs Internships

The general description of virtual public affairs internships that emerged from our interviews largely resonates with the growing understanding of remote work, while also illuminating some features that are specific—but perhaps not unique—to the public affairs field. Our respondents participated in a wide range of settings that included government agencies and departments, nonprofits, labor unions, offices of elected officials, think tanks, political campaigns, non-governmental organizations, political organizations, and consulates, among others. Many of these organizations, especially governmental agencies, feature highly structured internal bureaucracies whose work is substantively specialized and complex. Entry points for students are often narrow; at least in our interviewees' experience, successful placements are often obtained through personal or family contacts or are based on campus connections. Their activities often can have high stakes for the communities or constituents they serve, but ironically, their work often remains obscured from public view. Because organizations' budgets are often tight, interns typically receive little to no compensation.

Our interviews with stakeholders who facilitated, supervised, and undertook virtual public affairs internships demonstrated that these internships include some advantages over in-person varieties. For one, distant organizations, government agencies, and foreign countries—which normally involve prohibitive travel or moving expenses and high costs of living—are accessible. Relatedly, more opportunities are available to international students who were restricted from traveling to the US. Hours are flexible for most students, but some (including those who worked for Congressional DC offices) must adjust to working across different time zones, while others appreciate not commuting and creating a smaller carbon footprint. Workflow could also be inconsistent, and depending on the number of interns and regular check-ins, interns themselves could be neglected ("out of sight; out of mind" as one supervisor admitted). For the most part then, virtual public affairs internships contain many of the overarching features of in-person versions, but a few notable differences emerged.

Some of the starker differences between in-person and virtual contexts arose from the work experience itself. All types of interviewees reported that the online modality constrained their work in some way.[15] In particular, tasks that required quick turnarounds, required input from several or many people, or needed sustained, continual attention became far more difficult, if not impossible, to execute. Examples of these include shadowing a supervisor, obtaining quick answers, and addressing last-minute requests. Said one intern, "I think the amount of time that lapses between 'I've got a problem; I've got to email them; they've got to email me back, then I've got to email them back if it even worked'—it just stretched out longer and longer... you need patience. In person I'd be able to get these problems solved a lot quicker." Even dreaded "busy" or administrative work was a challenge to replicate in virtual form (but this was generally considered a welcome shift): filing, sending mail, photocopying, answering phones, or mundane chores were either eliminated or reduced. Instead, carefully planned tasks, such as research that could be done independently and writing projects such as letters, briefs, reports, and memos, assumed greater importance. On the other hand, without advance strategies or plans, interns could find themselves languishing without much to do or being frustrated that their skills and abilities were not being put to good use.

Some interviewees expressed concerns that the work itself "took up all the space," meaning there was little room for anything except online meetings and work, as opposed to regular workflows driven by personal interactions that normally occur informally, such as through "water cooler talk" (as several interviewees phrased it). Importantly, opportunities to build relationships with coworkers and peer interns through ordinary interactions mostly were reduced to more formal, online meetings, yet peers often found ways to communicate with each other, such as through texting and social media, online meetups, or remote happy hours (organized by supervisors) for socializing and networking.

In a normal workday, there were fewer regular opportunities to express oneself personally, and respondents could not always perceive the impacts of their work in the organization and beyond. A faculty respondent concluded similarly: "I think [virtual internships] are missing a key component, which is that interaction, that engagement. [. . .] Part of why students do internships is to figure out if they want to do this as a starting point. You're not going to know that from a virtual internship for the most part." Without the nearly continuous interaction, improvisation, and serendipity associated with face-to-face internships, our respondents reported less than full immersion in the dynamics of a virtual internship site.

Interns' exposure to their organization tended to be fragmented and/or partial, although less so if they interned for a small agency; it was more difficult to form a holistic understanding of an organizational system, including its professional culture, norms, interpersonal relationships, work cycles and rhythms, and interconnections among different organizational parts—knowledge and understanding that enable personal and professional growth and are common features of a meaningful internship work experience. A federal government intern put it this way: "I think I have an 80 percent grasp of what work at the [government agency] looks like, but I wasn't really able to see what my supervisors were doing beyond just what they told me [. . .] I didn't get the full 'how it really works' at the [government agency]. What's the culture like?..." This fractional view can also hinder student interns' ability to apply classroom-learned political science concepts such as power, hierarchy, and agency to their ground-level internship experiences.

Campus administrators and faculty also encounter differences in the virtual context. It takes additional coordination to ensure that internship providers facilitate work and support interns appropriately. Some students may not be interested in virtual internships, and likewise, site partners may not be willing or able to reframe positions accordingly, which can affect course offerings and program goals. New sites may be drawn to the format or recruited to host virtual interns (relying on alumni networks for instance). For some faculty, their experience in terms of overseeing and reviewing student work does not change a great deal. For others, "going virtual" gives them opportunities to craft new placement processes, build virtual meeting spaces, and design check-in methods that are likely to be utilized again, regardless of format type. In some cases, virtual meeting spaces increase the likelihood that organizational elites and public officials are able to make guest appearances for online community events or campus events, such as those that feature final student intern presentations.

In sum, although certain aspects of face-to-face experiences are difficult to transpose to the online context, our interviewees' experiences demonstrate that virtual internships can be intentionally structured to help internship providers attain their goals and students achieve critical learning outcomes, but they cannot duplicate several aspects of the in-person internship. In the analysis of interview material presented below, we focus on career-related competencies in the virtual space, relying on interview material to isolate how these are developed. The consensus among our interviewees was that the same types of skills could be developed in virtual and in-person contexts at least to some degree, but that a few tend to predominate when internships are fully remote, and some remain especially difficult to develop. Being able to identify which skills are likely to be most valued in an online internship helps inform the judgment of whether a student's unique goals are likely to be accomplished in this context.[16] Virtual internships, even when they are well-executed, generally are not regarded as exact replacements for in-person internships, but are valuable learning experiences nonetheless.

Impact of the Virtual Modality on Student Learning Outcomes

Using the NACE Competencies for a Career-Ready Workforce (2021) as a conceptual framework,[17] we examine the conditions for developing the abilities, skills, and knowledge that college students need for future workplace and career success. Recognizing that internships are a key locus of such learning, we concentrate on three of the eight competencies they describe, namely: career and self-development, communication, and professionalism. All of our interviewees repeatedly addressed these three areas directly or indirectly, indicating their salience in the virtual internship context. Our analysis centers student voices, as interns themselves are best positioned to judge some of the impacts of different actors (such as site supervisors) on their learning experiences. Although overlap among categories is inevitable, we fit themes into the most proximate category. Through this approach we contrast in-person and virtual experiences so that faculty can help students identify appropriate placements, anticipate possible challenges, formulate strategies for overcoming them, and articulate realistic learning goals.

Career and Self-Development

According to NACE (2021), students should continually develop a sense of self and their future career, becoming aware of their strengths and weaknesses and appropriate job opportunities, and networking to build relationships well beyond their campus community.

Isolation from others, as is often the case with remote internships, can reduce a student's potential for professional development. Many virtual interns worked alone, offline, for long stretches—some by design, some not by choice. Online platforms tend to obscure a newcomer's view of how all the parts of an organization and its employees fit together, as well as organizational dynamics and workplace culture and norms. This can make it harder to envision a potential future in that setting. In addition, interns may not be fully immersed in their internship, accessing only parts of the "normal" in-person experience. For instance, one intern said: "At no point for the online DC internship did I interact with constituents. I never once spoke with a constituent." This observation indicates to us that there are some experiences of interest to political scientists that mainly take place "on location." For instance, interns who lack contact with constituents may be less able to solidify their understanding of representation, a concept that is central to the democratic process.

However, some hurdles are surmountable. Many students use internships to lessen the costs of access or to get their "foot in the door," which can be essential for some government or other public affairs sites where internships are a means for identifying talent or expediting more permanent employment. Virtual interns certainly can identify new opportunities and add a line of experience to their résumés.[18] When their work involves independent research and analysis or project-based skills, a supervisor may in fact have a greater ability to assess their potential than if that intern were simply fulfilling more mundane administrative roles. A student interviewee who worked for a Congressional committee was told that if they had been in the office, they primarily would have been "answering phones." Instead, the intern was tasked with researching a concrete policy issue and the data in their report helped inform the committee's budgeting decisions.

Career development also involves networking: "to build relationships within and without one's organization" (NACE 2021), or as one of our student interviewees described it, "figuring out how to do research on people and how to just find points of connection." All interviewees admitted that this aspect of career development was among the most challenging, including one intern who had transitioned from an in-person to a virtual internship during the COVID-19 pandemic:

> I think a lot of the big things that people want out of an in-person internship is making those connections with their colleagues, their peers, but also their supervisors and networking and talking to people [. . . during the in-person internship] I was so excited to go [in] every day [. . .] I felt like I was doing something important. I started learning the names of all the people, [. . .] not just [who] I was working with directly, but the doormen and the women at the desk who check you in and the security guards. And all these little interactions that you have with people, I think is what's really valuable about an in-person internship. And that's what makes it fun. And it makes you feel like, yeah, this is like something that I can do as a job. And it gives you all those skills of how to interact with people if you were in a real job setting. So, you are missing out on that [in a virtual space].

Informal daily interactions, previously described as "water cooler" talk but more broadly construed as the small moments of casual conversation, chats during shared meals, and impromptu discussions of matters both work-related and personal that might occur between meetings, represented missed opportunities to establish relationships. One perceptive intern noted that "with virtual there are no off-camera conversations," and another echoed this message: "At least over a video call, it's a lot harder to have a one-on-one conversation with somebody; it's not like you can pull somebody aside and talk to them for a little bit if you're interested in what they do. Instead, you probably send them your email and try to communicate over that, which is a lot more not awkward, and not as natural."

There did seem to be a silver lining to this situation, however. Some respondents felt that having to try harder to make connections beyond their immediate supervisor or team was actually beneficial because it helped them stretch their abilities. Said one student:

> I was pretty intentional in both my internships, my in-person and my virtual ones, about trying to reach out to almost everyone in both offices for coffee and to get to know people more than in a one-on-one context. And when people ask me for advice about a virtual internship, that's the biggest advice I give them, because [... you're in] a virtual environment where people can forget that you're there and ready to help. And when you sit down with them for coffee, especially early on, and tell them about your interests, it kind of reminds [...] them that I'm here to help you with your projects and probably be interested in what you have to work on. And you can kind of see where my skills might lie.

In sum, especially in public affairs careers, relationships are critical for future success and are often cited as a particularly significant dimension of internships that cannot be replicated from the in-person experience. A student who interned for a Washington, DC policy-oriented nonprofit organization made this point well: "A lot of what you want to do in politics is based on personal connections, and it's much easier to get those in person [...] I got to attend events and meet with people and network with coworkers a little bit. Whereas online, that whole network becomes way harder to get, and requires a lot more work."

Our site supervisors and student respondents also noted the need to find ways to create camaraderie among interns themselves—whether through open office drop-in hours, weekly staff meetings, lunchtime gatherings with guest speakers, or happy hours. They used these meetings to talk about next educational or career steps, check in about a given week, or just get to know one another. In one government agency, the interns asked the supervisor to create an online space where they could "hang together" for an hour at a time or have staff members join them for career-related discussions.

Finally, the increased use of videoconferencing appears to have expanded interns' access to busy public officials, enabling interaction or at least exposure that would not have taken place otherwise (a residual effect of social distancing). One supervisor noted their office's tendency to arrange last-minute meetings, and that online interns on standby could quickly hop into a Zoom call and attend important online gatherings that would normally require staff (but not interns) to travel, thus widening their exposure to certain kinds of office work and leaders in their organization.

Communication

Clearly and effectively communicating in multiple forms is also a key career competency that can be solidified in an internship setting (NACE 2021). Our respondents repeatedly asserted its significance in the virtual context, emphasizing that there was a greater reliance on written communication and less on verbal skills. Many of our respondents reported that their work products were more likely to be formal emails, memos, reports, and other discrete documents that could be edited, rather than delivered via public addresses or even informal conversations. Frequently, interns needed training to produce efficient messages, (in the words of one intern) to "condense intense amounts of information into very digestible, manageable pieces" for memos or briefs, or to craft responses to constituents. Interns were often tasked with research and the drafting of reports that they could do on their own time. Practical outlets and modes for demonstrating knowledge or professionalism, then, were limited.

Online meetings were another important site of communication. Interns occasionally were invited to lead remote meetings, but usually after their supervisors had helped them to prepare well. One supervisor required interns to formulate two questions for every guest who attended their remote lunch hours to facilitate engagement. As described by our interviewees, virtual meetings were not necessarily conducive to developing verbal communication skills: "You get on the meeting, you talk for maybe like one, two minutes, and then [...] everybody does what they need to do so that they can go back to the work that they actually have to do. Whereas like in an office, I feel like I really had to learn how to talk [to others]." The fact that online interaction on campuses and worksites will endure compels students to conquer both writing and speaking in their internships, and to practice different forms of them in class.

Because communication could be delayed and complicated by time zones and technological challenges, students noted that they had to proactively communicate their questions, needs, and progress to be successful. Supervisors echoed that point and expressed concerns that it was often difficult to discern whether interns understood their instructions; facial expressions were generally hard to read online and they lacked the informal cues of tone or clear body language to convey importance or time-sensitivity, as they could do in person. The impersonal, distanced nature of videoconferencing is reflected in a supervisor's comment that, "Even when I speak [...] they're staring, or silent. [I'm wondering:] [...] am I frozen this whole time?" In other words, perhaps with faculty's guidance, students need to develop the confidence to raise questions and ask for clarification when confused, and supervisors should make directions for complicated jobs explicit and not assume that their instructions are always clearly understood. In any case, virtual contexts do permit the development of "soft skills" such as oral communication (through fewer opportunities) and students in almost every case were required to do substantially more writing.

Professionalism

Understanding and demonstrating effective work habits and acting in the interests of the larger community or workplace define "professionalism," dimensions of which include being prepared, punctual, dependable, dedicated, and consistently meeting or exceeding expectations (NACE 2021)—qualities that help distinguish a person's reputation. Our interviewees repeatedly emphasized that although virtual interns had more limited opportunities to interact with colleagues and gain their trust, building a "professional" reputation continued to be essential; after all, site supervisors can play important roles in recommendations for graduate school, other internships, and employment.

In face-to-face internships, students have ongoing opportunities to display their abilities and ethical sensibilities through a broad range of interactions as well as through their work. In contrast, virtual interns are limited to impressing their supervisors almost exclusively through work habits such as punctuality, taking initiative, professional demeanor and appearance, and their work products (usually writing or online communication). Given the fragmented nature of online interactions, the virtual interns we interviewed also had far fewer chances to learn professional habits from supervisors and staff who would naturally model different facets of professionalism. As a supervisor phrased it: "For in-person interns, they'd hear my conversations, see the meetings, see the type of people we're meeting with, or how I handle those types of interactions, and I think that's something they're missing out on by doing it virtually. They [only] get to see it to some extent."

Internship supervisors appreciated and tended to reward those who took initiative and asked for additional work. One who interned at a national nonprofit was noticed because they efficiently met and sometimes surpassed their daily quota of cataloging news articles; the intern was asked to attend weekly staff meetings, given more responsibilities, and eventually was offered a full-time job. Interns who showed initiative also tend to be those who mastered good time management skills, as virtual interns can be given substantial control over their own schedules. For those who entered the internship with fewer organizational skills, completing tasks on time became more difficult. Said one intern: "I'd put things off until last minute, no one physically watching me at that extra level. [If] someone's here in the office, they need it right now, you can talk to them: [it] helps light the fire under you." Successful interns established systems and structure for themselves in a given week and across the scope of the entire internship period, which could include daily or weekly check-ins with supervisors, regular updates about their projects, and designated time to connect with others in the organization who could provide different perspectives.

Many interviewees noted that it was critical to create literal and figurative boundaries when working remotely. Students who worked from home or a dormitory found it especially helpful to separate themselves from their personal spaces when they could. Strategies included partitioning their work areas with physical barriers, finding workspaces outside their home, dressing professionally when working even when no Zoom calls were scheduled, and blocking out regular hours for work to simulate being in an in-person environment.

All in all, students can cultivate professional habits and their reputations through virtual internships, but others' judgments about them are based on a narrower set of observations. Coworkers and supervisors have fewer chances to set an example, while students have fewer opportunities to observe and absorb the lessons of their professional guides.

Virtual Internships and Inclusiveness

A general concern associated with face-to-face internships is that many students cannot afford them: lack of reliable transportation, being unable to move due to family obligations, the need for a regular paycheck, or fitting working hours into overcrowded schedules creates equity-based challenges for many types of students, including those who might benefit from them most.[19] The general consensus among our interviewees (across all stakeholder types) was that virtual internships could advance greater inclusiveness and equity if done well—and on a range of different axes. One faculty respondent remarked: "If we as a university have a mission of equitable access and participation, then we have to think about alternative modes because we have students that have different needs and different availability." How virtual internships could address such needs was repeatedly demonstrated through specific examples that our interviewees supplied.

Among the attributes most closely associated with access to internships was socioeconomic status. Prestigious and well-established public affairs internships are often located in centers of power such as Washington, DC as well as state and international capital cities. Those who attend school in or live adjacent to those areas, and those who have the means to travel and temporarily relocate, are best positioned to seize those opportunities. Conversely, insufficient compensation, loss of income (public internships are "notoriously unpaid," one student quipped), or the need to extend time to graduation (with accompanying tuition and fees) can render in-person internships prohibitively costly. Virtual internships can eliminate or reduce costs and even provide the flexibility to work for pay simultaneously, as one student explained:

> [...] the opportunity cost of not getting a summer job—all of those things are inherently prohibitive to large sections of the population, so in that way, it's fantastic because you can do it at home, you know, it's virtual [...] I know people who did two jobs or maybe if they were like a lifeguard where they were just like sitting at a pool and they could get paid while they were still, like, doing their virtual internships [...] It offers students of different socioeconomic statuses access to the same opportunities, which I think is fantastic.

Virtual internships also help address other kinds of geographic considerations. On the plus side, virtual internships could become more demographically representative than their in-person counterparts by drawing in students from all parts of the US and the world. At least one interviewee noted how their educational choices were conditioned by the work-related opportunities available, and perceived fewer restrictions with virtual internships: "For me, I did a grad program in Washington, DC specifically in part so I could do these kinds of internships; I'm interested in federal government work. But I guess [...] another thing that the virtual environment opens up is you can cast your net way, way wider in terms of location, and it just makes access a lot easier." Not commuting allowed many students to recoup the time and expenses they would have spent on transportation.

Virtual internships also can address some of the issues that derive from identity and positionality. For example, those with certain disabilities or major health concerns can pursue international or distant domestic placements[20]; so can those with home-based caregiving responsibilities, and non-citizens and international students in many cases. Non-traditional age or returning students who have significant family obligations benefit from flexible work hours.[21]

On the other hand, virtual internships can replicate inequities. Remote interns are no more likely to be paid than in-person interns. Students whose equipment is unreliable or who lack fast internet connections experience more interruptions to their communications and workflow. Students of lower socioeconomic status may also lack the ability to sequester themselves in a quiet location without major distractions. One interviewee expressed the concern that a hierarchy among internships may develop, such that in-person opportunities would be valued over virtual internships. Although internship experiences vary considerably, generally speaking, the issues arising from lack of equity, diversity, or inclusion will continue to exist absent additional supports to address their root causes.

IMPLICATIONS OF OUR RESEARCH: TOWARD BEST PRACTICES

Our research makes clear that a range of experiences is possible with virtual public affairs internships, and that some features differentiate those experiences from traditional, in-person versions. Students, internship providers, faculty, and educational institutions can realize a wide range of goals through virtual forms of experiential learning.

As our interviewees conveyed, public affairs interns and their mentoring faculty possess skills, knowledge, and insights that can serve them especially well when navigating online internships. For instance, our disciplinary focus on concepts such as power, institutional structure, and agency are likely to help an intern grasp the context in which they are operating. Students with this understanding are better equipped to build connections between classroom and workplace. In sum, we find that with deliberate effort, virtual internships can be designed to facilitate student success and engagement with the discipline.

With this in mind, we offer a set of recommendations for virtual public affairs internships that is rooted in the existing literature, informed by content analysis of interviews, and complemented by our first-hand experience of managing virtual internships.[22]

We hope to advance the discussion of best practices for virtual internships in political science by addressing questions such as: What do we need to think about to produce better outcomes for all internship stakeholders, but especially student participants? What can help mitigate the aspects that can be lacking or are liable to be less developed in this modality? In short: what needs to be in place to promote the goals of departments, programs, and educational institutions, host sites, and arguably most importantly, interns? We offer suggestions for students, supervisors, and faculty (and their institutions) in turn. As the supervisor takes on an outsized role in the virtual context, several of the most consequential recommendations are intended for them.

Recommendations for Students

As one of our interviewees put it, "I think [virtual internships are] an important experience for a student to have among their portfolio of experiences" in order to test out and prepare themselves for what is likely to be a future in which work contexts may be hybridized or fluid in nature. Ideally, students should be equipped to navigate any modality. One of our student interviewees also suggested that it was important for students to realize that they "can have different objectives for different internships," whether that is building a reputation in an issue area, sharpening their professional research and writing skills, or otherwise. Students are encouraged to perform a clear-eyed self-assessment of their skills, abilities, goals, and priorities both before and after an internship (see supplemental materials for samples).

Students should pursue a virtual internship if there is a good chance it will provide opportunities to develop and improve their skills, especially those that are transferable to non-virtual settings. Those who aim to improve their ability to work independently or gain professional communication skills can thrive in a virtual internship environment. If networking is the primary goal, then interns should be proactive, doing the additional work needed to establish meaningful connections and relationships. The most often repeated advice to potential interns from those who have done virtual internships was to be very intentional about building a network: meticulously cultivate your relationship with your supervisor to help them to see you as an asset, to advocate for you, and frankly to ensure that they do not forget you are there and making contributions in this low-visibility environment. Past virtual interns encouraged reaching out broadly to coworkers, and doing one's research to find points of connection that will produce fruitful conversations.

Some additional practical recommendations for virtual interns include: first, setting boundaries between work and other aspects of one's life through scheduling, professional attire, and physical workspace. We also suggest foregrounding communication via mutually agreed-upon regular check-ins with one's supervisor, prompt and professional responses to email or phone calls, and reminding the supervisor of one's individual contributions to the organization, which could be done through regular progress updates. We recommend systematizing networking efforts by setting and achieving goals for outreach to build relationships (such as setting a certain number of virtual coffee dates). Finally, we encourage students to view and treat their supervisors and faculty as key supporters to their success in this virtual context.

Recommendations for Supervisors and Sites

Interns' range of experiences from positive to negative made clear that a key factor in the success of a virtual internship is the site supervisor. Supervisors are the key point of contact and are responsible for structuring (or not structuring) a student's experience, and in a virtual internship their role assumes greater significance.

Open and regular communication between interns and supervisors is a crucial ingredient of a successful virtual internship. Not only do we recommend immediately establishing communication methods and preferences (when interns should reach out and what channel is preferred, be it email, text, phone call, or Zoom), but also we recommend erring on the side of *overcommunication* throughout the internship (a term that more than one of our interviewees used). Supervisors should clarify deadlines and detail their expectations whenever possible, especially when projects need to be prioritized or are urgent. Without the frequent points of informal contact that make the intangibles of in-person workplaces known, we encourage making "virtual office" norms explicit by re-writing intern and employee guidebooks or manuals to ensure expectations for professional correspondence, formats for written reports, Zoom etiquette, and so forth, are clear.

Another aspect that is especially important in the virtual format is to ensure that interns understand from the beginning (or even prior to their start) the organization's overall structure, including to whom they directly report, what meetings they may attend, and other guidelines that may be specific to a given workplace. This will help them visualize their role in the larger organization and understand how to play an integral role in it. It may also help to avoid misunderstandings that can become more likely in this context where explanations can be inadequate. One supervisor described some of their essential responsibilities this way:

> Setting up expectations beforehand of what are you realistically going to be able to offer to the intern. Setting those goals has really helped in terms of setting objectives, what you want them to get out of the learning experience. Some of it depends on if they are getting academic credit, you need to work with the faculty, or the sponsor—what is it YOU want them to get out of it, and how [the student] wants to utilize their time.

Task development is also an area where we recommend that supervisors engage thoughtfully. Successful interviewees found that a two-track approach was beneficial: by creating both small short-term tasks and larger longer-term tasks or projects, an intern can be more likely to have a consistent workflow. For larger projects, there should still be scaffolding with specific deliverables and deadlines identified and tracked along the way to ensure that an intern is completing the work correctly. Tasks should be meaningful and interns' contributions to the larger team's efforts should be shared whenever possible.

Preparation and advance work help define a successful virtual internship. One student articulated the sentiments of several supervisors when they stated: "Don't build the plane as you're flying it. [. . .] There's so many unexpected [. . .] and logistical things you have to take into consideration in a virtual format." That said, for all stakeholders, flexibility is an inherent part of the virtual internship experience. We encourage supervisors to make contingency plans for the unexpected, to take into consideration the delays that come from mediated communication, and to adjust the work if needed.

Advocating for your interns and helping them network are also ways in which effective supervisors can mitigate some of the constraints of the virtual context. Ideally, supervisors will consider themselves both an advocate and trusted mentor, and in these roles will ask interns about who they might like to meet and facilitate introductions. Good supervisors will be open to having the intern attend extra meetings or create opportunities for learning about the "hidden transcripts" or the underlying context of the workplace, and to help interns recognize where their work fits into the bigger scheme of things. This perception can be especially important in a public affairs internship, as it may affect students' underlying motivation for continuing in the field. More generally, effective supervisors will consider trying to "make space for happenstance" that is all too rare in this context. Being human and creating moments for community-building between the supervisor (you) and the intern, among interns, and between interns and other members of the organization can go far. These efforts can take the form of a virtual happy hour or guest speaker visits over lunch, or "sign-ups" to meet with an intern. If possible, we also recommend finding ways for the interns to present their work publicly to others in the organization. Take an interest in cultivating their learning—their passive and active learning—by assigning readings or making sure that interns gain technical or other sorts of training. A student interviewee described the approach employed by a seasoned virtual internship supervisor:

> He would check in weekly [... and] by the end of the week, I had a set expectation that, okay, I'm going to talk to [him]. So I need to know what I'm doing and what I'm going to show him. [In addition ...] he treated every weekly check-in as kind of like an informal networking situation, too, so sometimes he would bring coworkers [. . .] who I might have mentioned something that I was interested in. And he was like, 'let me bring them in on the call and you can ask them questions.' So I thought that was a great way for me to feel like I was part of the team because somebody was always interested in talking to me and [my supervisor] was the one facilitating those conversations.

As this quote demonstrates, site supervisors' role extends well beyond making sure that a student is doing their work according to the organization's plan. Finding ways to make the intern part of the team—or at least feel a valued part of the organization—is equally important (Jeske and Axtell 2017; Jeske and Axtell 2018).

Recommendations for Faculty and Educational Institutions

Beyond general training to ensure student success in alternative modes of instruction, we encourage faculty, programs, departments, and institutions to acknowledge that virtual internships often demand the creation of additional scaffolding. For instance, placement procedures, onboarding processes, check-in meetings, quick surveys or "temperature checks" may be needed to ensure that students are flourishing in their internships. In addition, students may need supplemental guidance to navigate these professional contexts, and faculty may discover that they need to provide more detail about protocols, processes, and professional norms. Partnering with campus career staff to conduct workshops or bolstering professional development content in an internship course syllabus may be advisable as well.

Course assignments such as a learning agreement and/or contract will help students to communicate with supervisors about their objectives and gain site support for them (see chapter by Simpson, Braam, and Winston; samples can be found in the Supplemental Internship Resources). Even more beneficial than the learning contract itself may be the communication needed among all parties to complete the document successfully. During the semester there may need to be an in-person drop-in time for questions, and the faculty's role may feel more like that of a coach, mentor, or advocate to help students navigate the virtual internship successfully. In particular, students may need assistance building confidence and learning to communicate their needs and goals to their supervisors.

Given the amount of oversight that's needed to operationalize virtual internships successfully, faculty's elevated role may require additional resources in the way of financial support or administrative personnel. As virtual internships become more common (and as public health guidelines allow), departments, programs, colleges and universities may want to systematize technology "checks" as part of on-boarding procedures and create dedicated facilities for student interns working remotely. For example, some campuses have begun to provide physical spaces for students to conduct virtual internships, which they call a "virtual intern hub [... so] they're able to have a community; they're able to have a place to focus, and would not necessarily have any technological challenges."

CONCLUSIONS: THE FUTURE OF VIRTUAL INTERNSHIPS AND THE NEED TO MOVE TOWARD BEST PRACTICES

The COVID-19 public health crisis disrupted many aspects of society, not the least of which were higher education and work. Internships reside at the intersection of these institutions. The relatively slow growth trajectory of virtual internships shifted dramatically in 2020 due to the pandemic, and that extraordinary, exogenous shock likely has transformed internships—and the larger work context—for the long term.

The juxtaposition of virtual internships with the traditional in-person type has thrown some of their differences into sharper relief. Our research demonstrates that those involved in virtual public affairs internships believe that they can produce positive outcomes for students, faculty, programs, and internship partners, given the right inputs. Our investigation shows that a significant amount of concentrated effort by everyone involved is required to make it successful, probably more than is required for face-to-face internships. It appears to take more preparation and intentionality, more strategizing and more advance work, and even with those efforts, some aspects of in-person internships are not replicable. Virtual internships can and do facilitate the development of skills and knowledge that contribute to disciplinary learning; at least this was the clear perception among our interviewees. Remote internships can also address some of the inequities that we seek to mitigate in internships more broadly.

With virtual internships likely to continue expanding, additional research and analysis are required to fully contextualize these changes, and to ensure that virtual internships—all internships, for that matter—contribute to student success before and after graduation. Beyond this, virtual internships have the potential to help us clarify our goals for all modes of public affairs internships.

REFERENCES

Adadi, Elizabeth. 2018. *Supervisory Practices in a Virtual Internship Program: A Multi-Case Study.* FIU Electronic Theses and Dissertations. 3748. https://digitalcommons.fiu.edu/etd/3748.

Allen, Elaine I., and Jeff Seaman. 2014. *Staying the Course: Online Education in the United States.* Newburyport, MA: Sloan Consortium.

Barnett, Kathy. 2012. "Student Interns' Socially Constructed Work Realities: Narrowing the Work Expectation Reality Gap." *Business and Professional Communication Quarterly* 75 (3): 271–290.

Benavides, Abraham, Lisa A. Dicke, and Amy C. Holt. 2013. "Internships Adrift? Anchoring Internship Programs in Collaboration." *Journal of Public Affairs Education* 19 (2): 325–353.

Berntson, Erik, and Staffan Marklund. 2007. "The Relationship Between Perceived Employability and Subsequent Health." *Work and Stress* 21 (3): 279–292. doi: 10.1080/02678370701659215.

Bijeau, Amy Morril, and Beverly Peters. 2021. "Comparing NACE Career Competencies Virtually Through Intern Self-Assessments and Employer Assessments." *NACE Journal*, May 1, https://www.naceweb.org/career-readiness/competencies/comparing-nace-career-competencies-virtually-through-intern-self-assessments-and-employer-assessments/.

Braga, Michael. 2020. "Summer Internship Canceled? Not at These Companies Embracing Virtual Versions." *USA Today*, May 3. https://www.usatoday.com/story/money/2020/05/03/coronavirus-companies-offeringvirtual-internships-humana-goldman/3045256001/.

Brynjolfsson, Erik, John J. Horton, Adam Ozimek, Daniel Rock, Garima Sharma, and Hong-Yi TuYe. 2020. "COVID-19 and Remote Work: An Early Look at US Data." National Bureau of Economic Research, Working Paper 27344. PDF online. https://www.nber.org/papers/w27344.

Carnevale, Anthony, Megan Fasules, and Kathryn P. Campbell. 2020. "The Competencies Students Need for Workforce Success." AAC&U *Liberal Education Blog*, November 20. https://www.aacu.org/blog/competencies-students-need-workforce-success.

Criso, Rachael, Jillian Low, and Kelen Townsend. 2021. "Starting the Debate on Remote Versus In-Person Internship Skills Gain." Unpublished manuscript.

Dailey, Stephanie. 2016. "What Happens Before Full-Time Employment? Internships as a Mechanism of Anticipatory Socialization." *Western Journal of Communication* 80 (4): 453–480.

Faucette, Nell, and Peg Nugent. 2015. "Impacts of a Redesigned Virtual Internship Program on Preservice Teachers' Skills and Attitudes." *International Journal of E-Learning and Distance Education* 30 (2).

Fetter, Anna, and Mindi Thompson. 2020. *Understanding the Impacts of COVID-19 Pandemic for Undergraduate Students attending an HBCU: Insights from Student Voices."* University of Wisconsin–Madison: Center for Research on College-Workforce Transitions, Research Brief 14, November. http://ccwt.wceruw.org/documents/ccwt_report_Understanding%20the%20Impacts%20of%20COVID-19%20Pandemic%20for%20Undergraduate%20Students%20attending%20an%20HBCU.pdf.

Finley, Ashley, and Tia McNair. 2013. *Assessing Underserved Students' Engagement in High Impact Practices.* Washington, DC: Association of American Colleges and Universities.

Fujii, Lee Ann. 2018. *Interviewing in Social Science Research: A Relational Approach.* New York: Routledge.

Hennessy, Bernard C. 1970. *Political Internships: Theory, Practice, Evaluation.* University Park, PA: Penn State Studies.

Hora, Matthew T., Matthew Wolfgram, Rachelle Brown, Jared Colston, Jiahong Zhang, Zhidong Chen, and Zi Chen. 2020a. T*he Internship Scorecard: A New Framework for Evaluating College Internships on the Basis of Purpose, Quality and Equitable Access. Research Brief #11.* Center for Research on College-Workforce Transitions. University of Wisconsin-Madison.

Hora, Matthew T., Brian Vivona, Zi Chen, Jiahong Zhang, Mindi Thompson, and Rachelle Brown. 2020b. *What Do We Know About Online Internships? A Review of the Academic and Practitioner Literatures. Research Brief #10.* University of Wisconsin-Madison: Center for Research on College-Workforce Transitions.

Hora, Matthew T., Changhee Lee, Zi Chen, and Anthony Hernandez. 2021a. *Exploring Online Internships amidst the COVID-19 Pandemic in 2020: Results from a Mixed-Methods Study.* University of Wisconsin-Madison: Center for Research on College-Workforce Transitions. http://ccwt.wceruw.org/documents/CCWT_report_Exploring%20online%20internships%20amidst%20the%20COVID-19%20pandemic%20in%202020.pdf.

Hora, Matthew T., Adrian Huerta, Anita Gopal, and Matthew Wolfgram. 2021b. *A Review of the Literature on Internships for Latinx Students at Hispanic-Serving Institutions: Toward a Latinx-Serving Internship Experience.* University of Wisconsin–Madison: Center for Research on College-Workforce Transitions, Research Brief 16, May. http://ccwt.wceruw.org/documents/ccwt_report_A%20review%20of%20the%20literature%20on%20internships%20for%20Latinx%20students%20at%20Hispanic-Serving%20Institutions.pdf.

Jeske, Debora. 2019. "Virtual internships: Learning Opportunities and Recommendations." In *Total Internship Management: The Employer's Guide to Building and Sustaining the Ultimate Internship Program 3rd Edition,* ed. Robert Shindell, 171–177. Cedar Park, TX: Intern Bridge, Inc.

Jeske, Debora, and Carolyn Axtell. 2016. "Going Global in Small Steps: E-Internships in Small and Medium-Sized Organizations." *Organizational Dynamics* 45 (1): 55–63.

Jeske, Debora, and Carolyn Axtell. 2017. "Effort and Rewards Effects: Appreciation and Self-Rated Performance in e-Internships." *Social Sciences* 6 (4): 154–168. https://doi.org/10.3390/socsci6040154.

Jeske, Debora, and Carolyn Axtell. 2018. "The Nature of Relationships in e-Internships: A Matter of Psychological Contract, Communication and Relational Investment." *The Journal of Work and Organizational Psychology* 34 (2): 113–121. https://doi.org/10.5093/jwop2018a14.

Kebritchi, Mansureh, Angie Lipschuetz, and Lilia Santiague. 2017. "Issues and Challenges for Teaching Successful Online Courses in Higher Education: A Literature Review." *Journal of Educational Technology Systems* 46 (1): 4–29. https://doi.org/10.1177/0047239516661713.

Kilgo, Cindy A., Jessica K. Ezell Sheets, and Ernest T. Pascarella. 2015. "The Link between High-Impact Practices and Student Learning: Some Longitudinal Evidence." *Higher Education* (69) 4: 509–525.

Knight, Leigh, and Anne Taylor. 2021. "Three Reasons Why your Business Should Embrace Virtual Internships." *Harvard Business Review,* March 23. https://hbr.org/sponsored/2021/03/3-reasons-why-your-business-should-embrace-virtualinternships.

Kraft, Carina, Debora Jeske, and Leopold Bayerlein. 2019. "Seeking Diversity? Consider Virtual Internships." *Strategic HR Review* 18 (3): 133–137. https://doi.org/10.1108/SHR-12-2018-0100.

Kuh, George D. 2008. *High-Impact Educational Practices: What They Are, Who Has Access to Them, and Why They*

Matter. Washington, DC: Association of American Colleges and Universities (AAC&U).

Kuh, George D. 2013. "Taking HIP's to the Next Level." In George D. Kuh & Ken O'Donnell, Eds. *Ensuring Quality and Taking High-Impact Practices to Scale.* Washington, DC: AAC&U.

Kuh George D., and Jillian Kinzie. 2018. "What Really Makes a 'High-Impact' Practice High Impact?" *Inside Higher Ed,* May 1. https://www.insidehighered.com/views/2018/05/01/kuh-and-kinzie-respond-essay-questioning-high-impact-practices-opinion.

Lumpkin, Lauren. 2020. "Coronavirus Blew up Summer Internships, Forcing Students and Employers to Get Creative." *The Washington Post,* May 3. https://www.washingtonpost.com/local/education/coronavirus-blew-up-summer-internships-forcing-students-and-employers-to-get-creative/2020/05/03/7f2708ae-83dd-11ea-a3eb-e9fc93160703_story.html.

McClellan, Fletcher, Kyle Casimir Kopko, and Kayla L Gruber. 2021. "High-Impact Practices and Their Effects: Implications for the Undergraduate Political Science Curriculum." *Journal of Political Science Education* 0:0, pages 1–19. doi: 10.1080/15512169.2020.1867562.

Mulki, Jay, Fleura Bardhi, Felicia Lassk, and Jayne Nanavaty-Dahl. 2009. "Set Up Remote Workers to Thrive." *MIT Sloan Management Review,* October 1. https://sloanreview.mit.edu/article/set-up-remote-workers-to-thrive/.

National Association of Colleges and Employers. 2011 (revised 2018). "Position Statement: US Internships." NACE, August. https://www.naceweb.org/about-us/advocacy/position-statements/position-statement-us-internships.

National Association of Colleges and Employers. 2021. "What is Career Readiness?" NACE. https://www.naceweb.org/career-readiness/competencies/career-readiness-defined/.

Pike, Pamela D. 2018. "Internships." In *High-Impact Practices in Online Education: Research and Best Practices,* ed. Kathryn E. Linder and Chrysanthemum Mattison Hayes, 147–163. Sterling, VA: Stylus Publishing.

Ruggiero, Dana, and Jeff Boehm. 2016. "Design and development of a learning design virtual internship program." *International Review of Research in Open and Distributed Learning* 17 (4): 105–120.

Schloetzer, Mattie. 2021. "Virtual internships are Here to Stay—and That's a Good Thing." American Alliance of Museums, February 8. https://www.aam-us.org/2021/02/08/virtual-internships-are-here-to-stay-and-thats-a-good-thing/.

Soss, Joe. 2014. "Talking our Way to Meaningful Explanations: A Practice-Centered View of Interviewing for Interpretive Research." In *Interpretation and Method: Empirical Research Methods and the Interpretive Turn,* ed. Dvora Yanow and Peregrine Schwarz-Shea, 161–182. New York: M.E. Sharpe.

Sull, Donald, Charles Sull, and Josh Bersin. 2020. "Five Ways Leaders Can Support Remote Work." *MIT Sloan Management Review* 61 (4): 1–10.

Werner, Johannes, and Debora Jeske. 2021. "Ten Simple Rules for Running and Managing Virtual Internships." *PLoS Computational Biology* 17 (2): e1008599.

Wunch, James S. 1985. "What Should Undergraduate Internships Do?" *News for Teachers of Political Science* 46: 8–19. doi:10.1017/S019790190000180X.

ENDNOTES

1. See: Office of eDiplomacy. 2021. "Virtual Student Federal Service." US Department of State, Accessed July 1. https://www.state.gov/virtual-student-federal-service/.

2. Almost all extant scholarship on internships can be traced back to graduate positions established in the 1930s and to studies initiated in the 1940s (Hennessy 1970). An offshoot of the apprenticeship model (Benavides, Dicke, and Holt 2013), the traditional internship remains a valued means to apply and test academic knowledge as well as to build skills interactively in a professional setting (National Association of Colleges and Employers (NACE) 2018). Internships provide training through which students become familiar with workday rhythms, professional norms, and organizational workflows that they may not have encountered in other employment. In the case of public affairs internships, for instance, an intern might address constituent needs as a member of a larger team in a Congressperson or City Councilmember's office, help plan an outreach event for a community-based nonprofit, or assist in implementing an anti-hunger program abroad with a nongovernmental organization.

3. This definition might be compared to one offered by Hora et al. (2021a): "An online internship is an experiential, work-based learning program conducted primarily via digital or online technologies, with important variations within the modality with respect to program format and compliance with experiential learning standards. Despite the important differences inherent in an online internship, the same quality and accessibility standards and considerations should apply to all internships regardless of their modality" (6).

4. As the internet and supporting technology have advanced, remote internships have followed suit. Present in some fields for decades, large technology companies such as Google and AT&T were at the forefront of their development (Hora, Lee, Chen, and Hernandez 2021; Mulki et al. 2009). They made a small footprint on the business internship map and by the 2010s had generated enough opportunities that third-party vendors began to establish full-scale services to match employers with potential interns, an industry that continues to expand today. Higher education's increased use of online instructional platforms advanced on a parallel track (Allen and Seaman 2014; Kebritchi, Lipschuetz, and Santiague 2017).

5. In addition, 47.6% were face-to-face, and 7.1% were hybrid. The mixed-methods study that Hora and his colleagues performed with the help of an NSF grant (#2032122) included 9,964 survey responses from 10 four-year universities and one two-year college, with an average response rate of 8.53% (a range of 0.4% to 19.73%). The survey was administered between November 2020 and March 2021 with questions concentrating on students' experiences with internships during the prior 12-month period. Females were also overrepresented (69.3% to 27.9% male and 2.7% non-binary respondents). Most were enrolled full-time (91.1%).

6. Brynjolfsson et al. (2020, published by the National Bureau of Economic Research) report that the results of their representative national survey of the US population (n=25,001) between April and May 2020 revealed 15% of respondents worked from home prior to COVID-19, and that about half of the workforce was working from home during the survey timeframe. They note that their estimates "are broadly consistent with the broader literature, which includes a relatively wide range of estimates" (4).

7. "Underserved" is defined in their study as underrepresented minority, first-generation, transfer, and low-income students.

8. Another approach to evaluating the quality of an internship is explained by Hora et al. (2020a), who develop a scorecard for this purpose: "Our approach differs from NACE (2018) and CAS (2018) because it does not articulate a set of criteria that all internships must meet to be considered 'legitimate' or high quality. Instead, we posit that the specific format and activities of an internship may vary, depending on the goals of each student and/or their academic program, and their level of maturity and preparedness" (10). Among these criteria are: the presence of a plan for learning, nature of tasks, mentoring for job performance, active support of student goals, development of specific skills, growth of professional networks, level of student's satisfaction, the value of the internship for the student's career and academic goals, and other indicators of equitable access.

9. Alternatively, the Georgetown University Center on Education and the Workforce, whose work complements that of the AAC&U's survey of employers and hiring managers, lists five competencies that are consistently in high demand (and are associated with better earnings and higher work satisfaction)—communication, teamwork, sales and customer service (even for public affairs interns), leadership, and problem-solving and complex thinking—the "competencies students need for workforce success" (Carnavale, Fasules, and Cambell 2020). A fuller list of the competencies that employers want can be found in their report.

10. With respect to socialization and workplace norms, the increased participation of historically underserved students in internships is likely to lead to cultural shifts in workplaces. Higher participation by historically underrepresented groups is one element needed to move "institutions to take greater ownership of sustained efforts to change cultural norms and fundamental practices for the benefit of students of color" (Finley and McNair 2013, 36).

11. The projects were submitted for simultaneous review on both principal investigators' home campuses and received approval as Project 2021-08 by the University of Redlands Institutional Review Board and as Project 1737971-1 by the California State University Long Beach Institutional Review Board.

12. Of our 19 participants, eight provided the perspective of (former or current) student interns; five were supervisors at sites that hosted student interns; six were positioned as faculty or other sorts of coordinators of student internship opportunities. Our study participants were affiliated with educational institutions both public and private. In terms of gender, women-identified participants outnumbered male participants by a roughly 2:1 ratio.

13. As shown by our interviews, a range of experiences can exist within the category of a virtual internship (and by extension an in-person or hybrid internship). In cases where students had completed two different virtual internships, they would compare those experiences to each other and also to their in-person experiences. Those perspectives allowed us to gain the understanding that just as the reality of in-person public affairs internships

is mixed, so is the reality of virtual public affairs internships. By understanding the "real experience" of these internships we can recognize their peaks and valleys—and make observations about the virtual context's potential and how to best achieve it in the field of political science.

14. This research is ongoing. Additional research will likely be conducted to assess changes over time and how those changes affect students' outcomes.

15. Where possible, we tried to discern the impact of COVID-19 that would have interacted with or posed separate constraints on an activity. For example, coordinating in-person events became problematic during the pandemic because of social distancing rules and restrictions on large gatherings, but these events were possible to set up and coordinate remotely, and some did take place through videoconferencing.

16. It also followed that there could be conflicts among various stakeholders with respect to their goals. There seemed to be a sense that an internship site more easily would be able to structure things to best accomplish their goals, but it could be more challenging for an intern, for instance, to attain theirs.

17. The current and previous versions of NACE "career competencies" have also been utilized in other research studies to better understand the impact of internship format, including Morrill Bijeau and Peters (2021) and Criso, Low, and Townsend (2021). While other types of assessments might also be applicable, such as the Association of American College and Universities' "essential learning outcomes" (Kuh 2008), we feel these categories are best suited to the goals and scope of our study.

18. Students supplied several examples of how they were unsure of how to obtain government jobs unless they were in the system already. Being a virtual intern allowed them to make necessary connections and get ahead in their job searches, especially if they were looking for federal or other government work.

19. Per Kuh (2008), all students benefit from experiential learning and other high-impact practices, but historically underserved populations benefit even more.

20. Health- and disability-related factors a student considers may include access to known medical facilities, providers, or insurance coverage, among other considerations.

21. Aside from the intersections that race and ethnicity may have with some of these aforementioned identities, these axes were not mentioned specifically by our interviewees. That said, there was repeated attention to how some interns are positioned differently in terms of their identity, and so their experiences within the internship itself may differ. Informal engagement or attempts to advocate for themselves were thought to be perceived differently.

22. Cabrera Rasmussen was involved in the planning and teaching of two cohorts of virtual public affairs interns. One was a small cohort of CSULB students who interned with the City of Long Beach to support local census efforts in spring 2020; while these internships started out in-person, the COVID-19 public health crisis pushed these internships into the virtual context, giving her a rare vantage point on the two formats with the same group of students. In addition, she served as part of a larger team on the CSULB campus that crafted and implemented a new program that paired students with local nonprofit organizations: the Long Beach Community Internship Project. The Project's spring 2021 inaugural cohort interned primarily virtually as state, local, and university public health guidelines required. She also served as the lead instructor on that project and taught the majority of the program's students in her (also virtual) internship course, and so these experiences necessarily informed her analysis of the data. Van Vechten helped facilitate several virtual affairs internships in 2020.

CHAPTER 16

Interning in a State Legislature

Richard A. Clucas, Portland State University

Students have been interning in state legislatures since at least the mid-1950s, yet few studies of state legislative internship programs have been conducted. To help bridge the gap, this chapter provides a brief history of these programs and reviews the limited research on best teaching practices related to them. Analysis of a 2021 survey of 74 state legislative intern coordinators is presented, and the survey data, which include responses to open- and closed-ended questions, provide insight into how these programs are taught as well as informed perspectives about what the coordinators believe are key components of successful state legislative internships.

INTRODUCTION

When the Oregon Legislative Assembly moved to crack down on the predatory practices of the state's payday lending industry, it would have come up short if it had not been for an alert university intern.

The 1990s and early 2000s were boom years for payday lenders in Oregon. A change in state law in the 1980s removed the caps on interest rates for consumer loans, which led to a proliferation of businesses offering loans to customers needing immediate financial assistance. The payday lending industry in Oregon quickly became one of the fastest growing in the nation. The attraction for lenders was understandable: they could charge interest rates of more than 500% a year (Callahan and Mierzwinski 2005; Nelson 2007).

Payday lending had emerged as one of the top issues in Oregon politics by the year in which Galen, the university student, interned in the legislature for a freshman lawmaker from north Portland. Four bills introduced at the start of the session were designed to curtail predatory lending practices and limit annual interest rates to 36%. Among them was one focused specifically on abuses in car title loans.

As the car title bill progressed through the legislature, Galen conducted research on similar laws across the nation as part of her classroom work for her internship. Galen found that car title loan companies in other states were able to circumvent these laws by using an alternative lending practice, one in which customers would use their cars as collateral to receive funds. The customers would then sign a statement saying they had not received a loan and were leasing the automobile, yet the rates these customers paid could be as steep as the worst payday loans, reaching 500% a year. The proposed bill before the Oregon's legislature did not address this type of loan (Oregon Senate Committee on Commerce 2007).

Galen brought what she had learned from other states to the attention of her supervisor in the representative's office. He had never heard of the practice. Galen and her supervisor then met with the representative and the authors of the bill. None of them were familiar with the practice either.

After hearing from Galen, there were two things the representative and these others agreed on: the bill needed to be amended to close this loophole and Galen should be responsible for making it happen. Galen was asked to write an amendment and to testify in committee about why it was needed. The Galen Amendment, as it was called by others in the legislature, was added to the bill and eventually adopted as law.

Galen's experience was unusual for a legislative intern. Most do not play a major role in shaping one of the top bills during a session. Yet the work she did, both in the legislature and in the classroom, fit into what are frequently considered among the best practices for state legislative interns.

College students in every state have the opportunity to intern in the state capitol. There are considerable differences, however, in how these internship programs are structured and what they seek to accomplish. No singular model exists, yet there are some practices that are routinely identified as being essential for creating a successful capitol internship.

In this chapter, I provide an overview of state legislative internship programs, reviewing relevant history and presenting different perspectives on best practices. Few studies have been conducted on state legislative internships or offer empirically-based insights about how they should work. To help fill this vacuum, I present findings from a survey I conducted of legislative internship coordinators, which asked for details about their programs and their insider knowledge about what makes for a successful internship.

A BRIEF HISTORY OF STATE LEGISLATIVE INTERNSHIP PROGRAMS

The creation of the first state legislative internship programs primarily grew out of efforts to replicate at the state level the American Political Science Association's (APSA) Congressional Fellowship Program, with a focus on providing opportunities to recent graduates, graduate students, and new faculty. Over time, however, universities, colleges, and state legislatures began to expand the reach of these programs, opening them to other types of students or creating new ones designed specifically for undergraduates.

The APSA's Congressional Fellowship Program was created in 1953 to provide an opportunity for young college teachers, journalists, and PhD candidates to intern alongside personal and committee staff, giving them an inside perspective on congressional politics. Originally called the APSA Congressional Intern Program, the course of study provided for two months of intensive learning in the Library of Congress, followed by eight months of full-time work in a congressional office. The fellows were paid a stipend to underwrite the costs of living in Washington, DC (Biggs 2003; Lee 1958).

The first state-level program followed just a few years later. California is often cited as having created the first state legislative internship program in the nation in 1957, but the University of Washington's (UW) legislative internship program was launched at least a year earlier. Hugh Bone, a UW political science professor, created the Washington State Legislative Internship Program (WSLIP) for undergraduates in the mid-1950s. Most articles about the Washington program report that it started in 1956, the year Bone received a grant from the Ford Foundation to help underwrite the program, but the National Conference of State Legislatures has found photos of Bone's interns dating to 1955 (Kurtz 2007). Unfortunately, there is little published information available about the early years of the program.

Considerably more has been written about California's program and its ripple effects across the US. Unlike Washington's program, however, the one in California was designed for training graduate students or recent college graduates. The first formal discussion about creating the California program occurred at a conference on Streamlining State Legislatures, which was held at the University of California, Berkeley in 1955. The conference brought together faculty, legislators, lobbyists, and journalists to consider how to improve the functioning of state legislatures. The conference participants agreed to develop an internship program explicitly modeled after the APSA Congressional Intern Program as a way to provide an educational experience for graduate students and greater staff support to legislators (Lee 1958).

Over the next year, representatives from several California universities and the state legislature collaborated to develop the program. A formal proposal was submitted to the Ford Foundation to help underwrite costs. The Foundation agreed to provide $40,000 a year over a five-year period to pay intern stipends and incidental university expenses. The state Assembly agreed to contribute another $30,000 per year. When the program was inaugurated on September 3, 1957, five universities and colleges participated: UC Berkeley, Stanford University, Claremont College, University of Southern California, and University of California, Los Angeles. Similar to APSA's program, the participants worked full-time for 10 months and did not include undergraduates (Lee 1958).

After successful launches in Washington and California, other states began to create their own legislative internship programs. Many of the early ones were modeled after California's program, with a focus on training graduate students. The Ford Foundation played an important role in advancing them across the US, providing funds for programs in Hawaii, Illinois, Indiana, Kansas, Michigan, New York, Ohio, Oklahoma, Puerto Rico, and Texas (Hennessey 1970, 13).

Some states also began to provide internship opportunities for undergraduate students. Although this history has not been studied systematically, Thomas Murphy conducted surveys in both 1971 and 1977 to learn about the growth and features of state legislative internship programs across the county. He found that the number of states with legislative internship programs grew from 14 in 1965 to 34 in 1971. By 1977, legislative interns had worked in all states, although only 44 states had functioning programs that year (Murphy 1979).

One of the most striking aspects of these programs, Murphy emphasized, was their "extreme variability" (1979, 178). Among the ways in which the programs varied were how they were structured (formal or informal), who oversaw them (a university or the legislature), who was allowed to participate (high school, undergraduate, graduate, or law school students), the types of assignments given to interns (with individual legislators or leadership; in research offices, party caucuses, or committees), and whether students were able to receive academic credit for their work.

The National Conference on State Legislatures (NCSL) conducted a similar survey in 2005, which gathered responses from the program coordinators for 69 legislative internship programs across 39 states. As with Murphy's surveys, one of the central findings from the NCSL study was that there was "immense variety" in the structure and workings of these programs. The differences were so great that the authors of the NCSL study characterized the state legislatures as not just providing "laboratories of democracy," but also "laboratories of service and learning" (NCSL 2005, 1).

Structural diversity remains a defining characteristic of state legislative internship programs, reflecting their differing purposes and desired learning outcomes. Yet there is some agreement among the legislative intern coordinators about the pedagogical steps that can be taken to create a better program.

PAST STUDIES ON LEGISLATIVE INTERNSHIP PROGRAMS

Research on state legislative internships has been minimal, especially with respect to best practices. The literature that is available can be grouped into four general categories: histories, surveys of program types, thought pieces, and program assessments. These categories are not mutually exclusive, but they do capture the main topics generally covered by scholars.

Histories

The histories of state legislative internship programs focus primarily on telling the origin stories of these programs, such as Lee's (1958) first-hand essay on of the launching of California's legislative program, Profughi and Thompson's (1972) report on Rhode Island's program, and Hennesey's (1970) overview of political internships generally, including those in state legislatures.

Perhaps the most valuable contribution of these works is that they provide historical perspective on the varied purposes of the programs. California's, for example, was started with two main intentions. One was to provide a training program on legislative politics, public policy, and state government for advanced graduate students and young professionals, and it was designed for individuals on the cusp of their professional careers. The other purpose was to provide additional staff—or labor—for the legislature. To enhance the educational experience, the interns underwent a one-week orientation program similar to the one arranged for new legislative personnel. They also met in a weekly seminar to hold discussions and hear guest lectures about subjects revolving around their work and the legislature's politics (Lee 1958, 462).

Washington state's redesigned program, which commenced in the mid-1990s and continues to this day, differs slightly in its intent; it is meant to improve students' job prospects after graduation by giving them "solid job experience and an educational program that will enhance their work skills" (Best 2001). The competitive program is open to high-achieving college juniors and seniors, most of whom go on to graduate studies. The academic side of the program is multifaceted, including a three-day orientation, regular training sessions, and various educational activities, described in more detail below.

Rhode Island's program was originally proposed in the late 1960s as a way to improve public confidence in state government by involving students in the policymaking process. In an early report, Profughi and Thompson (1972) noted that the program was open to a wider range of students than in many states, including participants from high school through graduate school. The students did not have to be entering the job force or even be upper division undergraduates; neither did they have to be academic standouts, as most tended to have a B average. As in California, the program was created as a way to provide the legislature with much-needed help. The Rhode Island General Assembly lacked personal staff into the 1990s, so the program was of considerable value in providing legislators with research support and other activities. On the educational side, the internship had a much more academic focus than the California program, although it was less rigorous than the one in Washington state. The students met weekly with various faculty members, legislators, bureaucrats, and others to learn about state politics. They were also assigned weekly readings and were required to write an analytical paper on state politics.

Rhode Island's program has evolved since Profughi and Thompson's report was issued. The program has been expanded to provide internship opportunities in state agencies, the courts, and non-profit organizations. The centralized weekly meetings were discontinued, the participating universities took over the academic side, and high school students were dropped from the program. More recently, the program began offering remote internships during the coronavirus pandemic. These internships have proven so successful that the legislative office which runs the internship program intends to offer them after the pandemic subsides. One aspect of the program that has not changed is that it has retained its inclusive character, accepting students with a minimum GPA of 2.5 rather than just top academic achievers (Lynch 2021).

Surveys of Program Types

The second category of studies employs surveys to understand the different types of legislative internship programs across the country, such as the work by Murphy (1979) and the NCSL (2005). The publications based on these surveys are primarily descriptive, providing an overview of how internship programs are structured across the nation.

The NCSL's 2005 national survey is perhaps the most comprehensive study of state legislative internship programs to date. The 47-page report based on the results provides information about who is eligible to participate, who oversees the interns, where interns are placed in the legislature, and the type of duties typically assigned. The report also explains how the educational components of the internship programs are structured.

As mentioned above, the survey recognizes profound diversity among programs. For example, participants could include any number of high school, college, graduate, or law school students. Some programs are overseen by university faculty, some by legislative staff, and some have entirely different oversight structures. Opportunities also differ, as some place students in all types of legislative settings, from individual legislators' offices to staff agencies, whereas others limit interns to specific types of offices. As for assigned duties, undergraduate interns handle constituent services and legislative research in almost all programs, and in some institutions they are given the opportunity to conduct policy analysis, committee support, and media relations. Overall, the report provides a valuable overview of the assorted ways these programs work.

Thought Pieces

A third category of published work consists of thought pieces written by program coordinators or faculty supervisors about what they believe has been most important in ensuring a successful internship. These scholars offer "insiders' perspectives" based on personal experiences and knowledge. Some of these works are targeted to faculty who oversee interns, but others are written for interns or their supervisors.

A good example is the chapter by Christensen and Davis (2002) in Reeher and Mariani's *The Insider's Guide to Political Internships*. They provide advice to students on the best ways to approach interning in state legislatures, covering everything from how to select a legislative position to saying goodbye when the internship ends. The chapter is primarily concerned with explaining how to act professionally in a legislative environment—basic information that all legislative interns need to know. Among their recommendations are that interns need to accept the grunt work that comes along with more glamourous duties, abide by professional ethics, and make an effort to build relationships with the regular staff in the office to which they are assigned.

Pecorella (2007) provides the most well-developed thought piece on best practices in state legislative internship programs. The essay is based on Pecorella's 20 years of experience as the professor-in-residence for the New York State Assembly intern program, but he also brings empirical studies to bear on his perspective. Pecorella makes the case that for an internship "to be truly effective, it must embrace a traditional academic complement that is built around" the intern experience (79). The academic component is essential, he writes, because it provides the "theoretical 'forests' for the empirical 'trees' of the actual experience" (80). Without this theoretical background, he argues persuasively, the educational value of the internship is severely limited. Pecorella then recommends the theoretical material that should be covered. Whether or not one agrees with Pecorella's specific reading recommendations, he makes a strong case for providing a rigorous academic component and for active monitoring by faculty sponsors.

Another short but valuable piece by Rosenthal (2006) draws on a guidebook for state legislative interns that he field tested and developed with three other political scientists in 2000 (Rosenthal et al. 2001). His essay distills 16 recommendations for legislators who are charged with providing student interns an educational experience, chief among them: spend personal time with the interns; introduce interns to relevant staff; give them substantive assignments; and provide some supervision. While legislators and legislative staff are the intended audience, faculty supervisors will also find it valuable.

Program Assessments

Moving beyond the personal observations of individual authors, the final category of published work consists of empirical studies assessing the outcomes of interns' legislative experiences. These studies tend to focus on the overall impact of internship programs, examining how interning for a state legislature influences students' knowledge, attitudes, and behavior. But a few do try to determine what factors lead to more successful internship experiences.

Many of these studies focus on the New York State Assembly. Since at least the mid-1970s, Assembly interns have been given questionnaires at the beginning and ending of the legislative session to determine how they were influenced by their experiences. In the first study drawing on these survey instruments, Balutis (1977) examined "the effects of the internship experience on students' knowledge and perceptions of politics in general and the New York State Legislature in particular" (1977, 321). His findings were not encouraging; he found only minor gains in knowledge about the state's political institutions and the legislative process, but the differences were not statistically significant. He identified no significant changes in students' political opinions, interest in politics, attitudes toward government, or sense of efficacy.

Eyler and Halteman (1981) followed in Balutis's footsteps but employed broader questions and a more sophisticated research design, including using control groups. Like Balutis, Eyler and Halteman noted no gains in political efficacy and knowledge, but they did find increases in political sophistication and skills among legislative interns that were not identified among the control groups. Eyler and Halteman's study provides evidence that legislative internship programs can produce desirable outcomes, but as with Balutis's work, their study does not try to identify the best practices in creating a successful program.

The primary survey work that has attempted to address this deeper concern has been produced by Pecorella and Stonecash, who conducted two studies on New York Assembly interns, one which included Winegar as a coauthor. In both studies, interns were asked to answer a series of questions at the start and conclusion of the internship program. These questions probed the interns' political attitudes, knowledge, and personal backgrounds, along with their experiences in the legislature. The first study analyzed survey responses from 106 undergraduates in the 1988 legislative session (Stonecash, Pecorella, and Winegar 1988). The second examined survey responses from more than 600 undergraduate interns from 1999 and 2005 (Pecorella and Stonecash 2007).

Both studies revealed that three factors were particularly important to a satisfactory experience: the students who reported the greatest satisfaction were ones who said they were treated well in the office, interacted more frequently with their legislator, and were assigned more "interesting work" (2007) or had "broader engagement in legislative activities" (1988). These findings led the authors to conclude that it is particularly important that faculty sponsors closely monitor how student interns are being treated to ensure they are being respected and being given appropriate work. While neither study examines the academic side of the internship, Pecorella and Stonecash argue that the experience should have an academic component.

What We Know From The Literature

The existing literature may be limited but it does provide some valuable perspective on state legislative internships. One precept that can be derived from these works is that the overall experience provided legislative interns should be meaningful, even if interns must execute mundane tasks. Another is that the academic side of the internship should be deliberately planned. As Profughi and Thompson (1972) write, regular class meetings, with appropriate readings, are "key integrating" experiences, allowing the internship to become "an extension of the classroom" (7). A third insight is that interns and legislative office staff, including the legislators themselves, need to develop a good relationship. To accomplish this, Christensen and Davis (2002) write that interns need to communicate regularly to their supervisors about how they are progressing, remaining open to feedback. As for legislators and their staffs, Rosenthal (2006) says they need to spend time getting to know their interns, be generous with praise when work is done well, and recognize their role as teachers. Finally, as Pecorella argues, the only way to ensure that students are given substantive work and that the office environment is conducive to learning is for the faculty supervisor to monitor the student interns (Pecorella 2007; Pecorella and Stonecash 2007).

A SURVEY OF CURRENT PRACTICES

To get a better understanding of best practices for legislative internships, I conducted a survey of legislative internship coordinators to find out about their programs and glean their recommendations. While this approach lacks the rigor of a "high-n" empirical study and takes the spotlight off student learning, it does rely on knowledgeable insiders who have honed their observations through years of experience.[1]

I used two approaches to identify potential survey respondents. First, I sent emails to all the legislative internship coordinators listed on the NCSL's website. Second, because many of these coordinators are legislative staff members, I made a systematic effort also to identify instructional faculty and university staff who work directly supervising legislative interns. I conducted online searches to find at least two universities and colleges in all fifty states that advertise legislative internship programs, and I then reached out to the coordinators of these programs. The discussion that follows includes responses from 74 individuals representing 40 states.[2] The information presented below was supplemented with material from program websites.

Laboratories of Service and Learning

The first lesson from this research is the same as that of Murphy (1979) and NCSL (2005): there is wide variation in the character of state legislative internship programs.

Some programs are centralized statewide operations overseen by the legislature, which provide a structured course of study, full-time work, academic credit, and a stipend. The New York State Assembly, for example, offers opportunities to approximately 150 students each session. Interested students apply through the Assembly's intern committee, which then places them into individual member offices and with research staff. As of the 2021 session, interns are paid a $6,600 stipend, work a minimum of 30 hours a week, and typically earn a full semester of course credit. The program includes an orientation, a structured academic course, and a concluding mock session. The state senate has a similar program that is open to some 30 students a session.

Similarly, Washington state's program provides opportunities for 70 undergraduate students to work with individual legislators or as caucus staff through the entire annual session.[3] Students apply to the house and senate civic education directors, who then oversee placement. Students are paid $1,350 per month and work 40 hours per week. The students are required to attend a three-day orientation, regular training sessions, and educational presentations on topics related to legislative politics, state government, and professional development. As in New York, the students participate in a mock legislature, though they are also given the opportunity to shadow a leading state official and participate in a variety of optional activities, including a field trip to the British Columbia Legislative Assembly. Unlike New York, however, where the students attend a regular academic course taught by the assembly's professors-in-residence, the students' main academic work is determined by their home institutions.

At the other end of the spectrum are programs administered by individual universities, which are part-time and tailored to satisfy the interests of individual students. In these programs, the students seek a placement on their own and then work with a faculty sponsor, who monitors their internship and provides academic direction. Among the many universities that offer such programs are the University of Alaska Southeast, Willamette University (Oregon), Northern Arizona University, University of North Dakota, University of Wisconsin-Milwaukee, and Northeastern.

Broad diversity lies between these two extremes. Some legislatures house a centralized program but are not as highly structured as New York's or Washington's. The Wyoming legislature, for example, accepts around 10 interns per year who work part-time during the session. The students apply through their individual universities but the placement is made by the legislative service office. The academic side is handled by each participating institution, although students must supply their course syllabus to the legislative service office with their application.

Some programs that involve multiple universities are either led by one institution or through a consortium of schools, such as The Harrisburg Internship Semester (THIS), which is overseen by the Pennsylvania State System of Higher Education, or the Maddy Institute's Legislative Intern Scholar Program, a joint program in which four public universities in California's San Joaquin Valley participate.[4] Even among programs run by individual universities, the program structures differ widely. Some are overseen by teaching faculty, others by a staff person. Some require students to intern only a few hours a week and do not have regular class meetings; others set much more demanding requirements.

Goals and Learning Outcomes

More relevant to our purposes are the educational goals and pedagogical approaches of these programs. One of the most notable findings is that the survey respondents identified a wide range of learning outcomes. None of the respondents listed just one or two desired learning outcomes; rather, they identified a variety of potential benefits that they hope students gain from interning in the legislature. Moreover, there is broad agreement among coordinators on these desired outcomes, regardless of program structure.

Respondents were asked in a closed-ended question to identify learning goals and outcomes, and almost all (98.6%) said that they hoped the program would improve students' knowledge about government and politics (see table 1). In a follow-up question, one respondent commented on the importance of legislative internships for giving students a concrete understanding of how the government functions, writing: "Legislative politics and state policies are abstract to students. When they intern in the capitol, it all comes to life. They observe how legislators interact with each other, with their staffs, and with lobbyists. They observe how policy is made and how proceedings are used to shape or kill legislation. Most students have more faith in the system after their internships, and they gain a greater appreciation for state politics and policies."

But the respondents view a legislative internship as valuable for reasons beyond improving student knowledge about government; most also regard it as a path to developing a professional career. The next three most common learning outcomes centered on career development: the experience can help

Table 1: Desired Learning Outcomes								
	Improved Knowledge	Understand Career Options	Build Professional Network	Improve Professional Skills	Compare Academic to Experience	Build Self-Confidence	Job Training	Line on Resume
Faculty Supervisor (49)	100%	93.9%	89.8%	87.8%	89.8%	81.6%	83.7%	61.2%
University Coordinator (17)	94.1%	100%	94.1%	94.1%	82.4%	76.5%	76.5%	47.1%
Legislative Staff (7)	100%	71.4%	85.7%	85.7%	85.7%	100%	85.7%	57.1%
All Respondents (74)	98.6%	93.2%	90.5%	89.2%	87.8%	82.4%	82.4%	58.1%

Note: Number of respondents in parentheses. The All Respondents category in this and other tables includes a director of a large multi-university internship program who does not fit into the three categories.

students better understand potential career options (93.2%), build a professional network (90.5%), and improve their analytical, research, communications, and other professional skills (89.2%).

Many of the respondents strongly emphasized how beneficial legislative internships are for providing students with experience in a professional setting. One respondent wrote succinctly that the interactions with others in the legislature "help model appropriate professional behavior." Another wrote that students "learn a lot about the conventions, mentalities, and habits of professionals in policy-relevant jobs." Others emphasized how valuable students' work can be for advancing their careers. One respondent wrote that the writing and research tasks students are often asked to do "are especially valuable because these are translatable skills."

Finally, the respondents broadly agreed on a variety of other learning outcomes that they hope students gain through a legislative internship, including providing students with an opportunity to compare what is taught in academic studies with first-hand experiences (87.8%), to build their self-confidence (82.4%), and to get the training necessary for a career, specifically in government and public service (82.4%).

In analyzing the survey results, I considered aggregate responses and also broke them down by the type of position respondents held (faculty supervisor, university internship coordinator, or legislative staff member). My particular research aim was to discover whether respondents who directly work with students in a faculty role have distinct perspectives from university and legislative staff with respect to legislative internships.[5]

In general, there is considerable agreement on learning outcomes regardless of the position held by the respondent, but slight variations are worthy of note. University internship coordinators were especially likely to view legislative internships in terms of career development. All 17 university coordinators (100%) identified legislative internships as a particularly good opportunity for students to better understand different career options. Moreover, two other outcomes at the top of their lists are related to general career development: development of a professional network (94.1%) and improved analytical, research, communications, and other professional skills (94.1%). Conversely, legislative staff are more likely than others to view internships as a means to build student confidence (100%).

More notable, however, is respondents' consistent agreement on learning outcomes. The respondents perceive legislative internships as a broadening experience, with multiple potential benefits. Speaking to these, one respondent wrote: "Not all students come out of the internship wishing to stay in the legislature as a career, so I try to show them the value of 'skill stacking' that can extend into whatever path they take.... Hearing about the different backgrounds of our legislative staff helps them to overcome obstacles of imposter syndrome. Finally, the network of professionals and mentors is what can help them turn internships into careers."

Table 2: Most Valuable Duties to Perform										
	Policy or Issue Research	Interact with Elected Officials	Write Policy Briefs, etc.	Observe Committee Meetings	Constituent Service	Bill Tracking	Observe Floor Proceedings	Participate in Staff Meeting	Interact with Lobbyists	General Office Duties
Faculty Supervisor (49)	83.7%	79.6%	77.6%	69.4%	69.4%	63.3%	53.1%	53.1%	38.8%	30.6%
University Coordinator (17)	88.2%	76.5%	70.6%	70.6%	76.5%	47.1%	41.2%	35.3%	29.4%	5.9%
Legislative Staff (7)	85.7%	85.7%	71.4%	100%	57.1%	42.9%	85.7%	42.9%	42.9%	42.9%
All Respondents (74)	85.1%	79.7%	75.7%	71.6%	70.3%	56.8%	52.7%	48.6%	36.5%	25.7%

Note: Number of respondents in parentheses.

Structuring the Internship Experience

Respondents also reviewed a list of 10 activities frequently assigned to legislative interns and were asked to identify ones they think are the most valuable for interns to perform. Table 2 shows that there was a relatively high level of agreement across groups, though less strong than with learning outcomes.

Overall, 85.1% of the respondents identified policy or issue research as among the most valuable tasks. In a follow-up open-ended question, many respondents explained that they value research because it is transferable to other jobs, and a few others noted that research allows interns to develop a deeper understanding of how and why public policy is made. Interacting with legislators and other elected officials was also identified by most of the respondents (79.7%) as among the most valuable activities. One respondent acknowledged its importance simply as something "you cannot do...in class or from the library." Another wrote that personal contact, along with working on constituent matters, are "invaluable for understanding how the legislative process actually works and how citizens interact with elected officials." Finally, three out of four respondents (75.7%) selected "writing policy briefs, bill summaries, memos, or committee testimony" as among the most valuable activities. As one respondent wrote, the writing assignments "are essential in learning how to communicate clearly and concisely," and others noted that, as with conducting research, these tasks help build transferable skills. In general, then, faculty supervisors, university intern coordinators, and legislative staff expressed similar preferences about the importance of these three types of assignments, but beyond these, greater differences in opinion begin to emerge.

Most respondents (71.6%) regarded observing committee meetings as one of the most valuable intern activities, a sentiment that was especially strong among legislative staff members, all of whom identified it as among the most valuable. Committee meetings in which the public and policy experts testify and where the fine details of legislation are worked out are considered the heart of legislative work; observing these proceedings puts students right in the center of legislative politics, so it is not surprising this is valued highly. In making the case for this activity, one respondent wrote bluntly that "committees are the most important stage of the policy making process, where they [student interns] see the interaction among committee members and engagement with the public and organized interests."

A large number of respondents also recognize the importance of having students work on constituent matters (70.3%); university intern coordinators were particularly likely to mention it. Since the groundbreaking work of Richard Fenno (1978) and David Mayhew (1974), legislative scholars have emphasized the importance of constituencies in shaping how legislators behave; assigning interns to work on constituent matters provides them with the opportunity to observe the relationship between legislators and constituents directly, which can help them to understand the arguments of these scholars and how representation works. A few respondents pointed out that it should not be the only duty that students are assigned, however, with one cautioning that if students' "whole experience is policy research or responding to constituents' emails, they miss out on so much of what they might learn and observe by being in the office seeing the capitol and its people interact."

Whereas the remaining five activities are clearly considered less valuable overall, a few respondents emphasized that students should be exposed to the entire gamut of activities, not just to the top two or three. Conversely, a few respondents argued strongly that what constitutes the most valuable activity is not universal, but depends on the students' goals. One wrote, "they all matter, though in different ways to different students."

Providing an Academic Component

Two survey questions probed the academic aspects of internship programs: one about general requirements, asking whether there are regular class meetings, a research assignment, and other required activities; and the other about assigned readings. Most respondents identified an academic component attached to the internship program (although 15.7% reported that they include none of these), and here again there is considerable variation in what is required. The most common academic assignment is some type of research-related paper (see table 3). Nearly three-quarters of the respondents (74.3%) require students to write some type of paper with a research component, including a traditional research paper (45.7%), a policy analysis (27.1%), or a reflection paper evaluating their experience through the lens of scholarly readings (37.1%). Some programs require students to complete more than one of these activities.

Table 3: Academic Requirements

	Research Paper (any type)	Academic Paper	Policy Analysis	Scholarly Reflection	Log of Experiences	Regular Class Meetings	Individual Meetings	Experiential Reflection Essay	Classroom Presentation	Exams or Quizzes
Faculty Supervisor (49)	85.7%	49%	32.7%	46.9%	65.3%	42.9%	18.4%	22.4%	12.2%	8.2%
University Coordinator (17)	47.1%	35.3%	17.6%	11.8%	58.5%	58.5%	35.3%	23.5%	17.6%	11.8%
Legislative Staff (3)	66.7%	66.7%	0%	33.3%	33.3%	66.7%	33.3%	0%	33.3%	0%
All Respondents (70)	74.3%	45.7%	27.1%	37.1%	61.4%	47.1%	22.9%	22.9%	14.3%	8.6%

Note: Number of respondents in parentheses.

The next two prevailing requirements were keeping a regular log of activities and attending some type of meeting with the instructor. In total, 61.4% of the respondents indicated they require students to keep a log, while 60% (not shown) include some type of meeting, consisting of regular class sessions (47.1%), individual meetings with the instructor (22.9%), or both. Other types of work are required infrequently, including: a reflection paper based entirely on experiences without a scholarly component (22.9% of programs); classroom presentations (14.3%); and exams (8.6%).

Breaking down the responses by the respondent's position, the most salient finding is that the faculty supervisors are far more likely than university internship coordinators and legislative staff to include an academic, research-based paper, whereas university internship coordinators are the most likely to require some type of meeting (76.5%; not shown). Legislative staff seem accustomed to leaving the academic side of the internship in the hands of the academics, as more than half of the respondents working in the legislature did not answer this question.[6]

Table 4 shows that almost half of the respondents (47.9%) assign some type of academic reading, with the two most common types relating to the state's political system (35.2%) or those by state legislative politics scholars (31%). Some require material on Congress or comparative state politics (22.5%), or public policy analyses (21.1%). Some programs, however, tailor the reading assignments to individual students (21.1%).

Combined, this means that more than two-thirds of the programs include an academic reading component. In addition, some programs require students to read media coverage of the legislature

Table 4: Assigned Readings									
	Academic Readings (any type)	State's Political System	Legislative Studies	Comparative State Politics or Congress	Public Policy	Varies by Student	Media Coverage	Training Manual	No Readings
Faculty Supervisor (49)	53.1%	40.8%	36.7%	28.6%	24.5%	14.3%	18.4%	14.3%	28.6%
University Coordinator (14)	42.9%	28.6%	21.4%	14.3%	14.3%	42.9%	21.4%	21.4%	14.3%
Legislative Staff (7)	28.6%	14.3%	14.3%	0%	14.3%	28.6%	14.3%	71.4%	0%
All Respondents (71)	47.9%	35.2%	31%	22.5%	21.1%	21.1%	18.3%	21.1%	23.9%
Note: Number of respondents in parentheses.									

(18.3%) or a training manual (21.1%).

In sum, considering learning goals and structure, the great majority of legislative internship programs generally follow Pecorella's (2007) advice, embedding scholarship in the internship experience.

Ensuring a Successful Program

Even if all the components for a successful internship are in place, what steps can be taken to ensure that students meet their learning goals? Respondents were asked to identify all the different factors they believe to be most important to success, and then to explain their selection of those they considered most important.

Respondents (81.1%) wrote that success above all depends on a supportive legislative office staff who work to ensure a successful internship (see table 5). Legislative staff are the ones who oversee the duties assigned, provide opportunities to meet elected officials, and open all the other doors within the legislature; they are positioned to provide the on-site guidance that can ensure interns get the most out of their experience in the statehouse. One respondent wrote that being mentored by legislative staff "is absolutely the most important part of the internship. This means having a staff person in their host site who takes the time to train, support, and include the student(s)." Another said that "if the legislative office staff and the intern's direct supervisor are not invested in the student's growth and learning, and instead simply see them as cheap/free labor, the internship will not be a success." Two activities handled by legislative staff were isolated as particularly important to successful internships: providing the intern

Table 5: Important Factors for Ensuring a Successful Internship									
	Supportive Staff	Meaningful Work	Clear Expectations	Training Program	Student Commitment	Good Match	Coordinator Supervision	Academic Component	Broad Exposure to Process
Faculty Supervisor (49)	85.7%	69.4%	61.2%	38.8%	73.5%	63.3%	28.6%	44.9%	44.9%
University Coordinator (17)	76.5%	88.2%	76.5%	47.1%	70.6%	47.1%	35.3%	23.5%	58.8%
Legislative Staff (7)	57.1%	57.1%	71.4%	57.1%	85.7%	71.4%	14.3%	14.3%	57.1%
All Respondents (74)	81.1%	73%	66.2%	41.9%	74.3%	59.5%	28.4%	36.5%	48.6%
Note: Number of respondents in parentheses.									

with meaningful work (73%) and clear expectations about their responsibilities (66.2%). To a lesser extent, some respondents also believe it is important to have a good training program for incoming interns (41.9%).

Conversely, almost as many respondents (74.3%) pointed to the behavior of interns as being key. These respondents wrote that success depends on such factors as whether the interns are committed, take the initiative, are willing to learn, and work hard. One wrote: "It does not matter (as much) how much effort I put into providing interns with resources. Good interns will take the initiative to get things done and poor interns won't use what they're given."

Ultimately, many respondents recognized that success depends on not just the staff or the student, but on the actions of both (63.5%; not shown). Thus, some internship coordinators consider it essential to find a good match between the student and the legislative office (59.5%). Wrote one respondent: "I think the match is probably most important; the rest of the internships portion sort of goes from there. I try to avoid placing a student in an unsupportive office.... They are also likely to have meaningful work and broad exposure as a consequence." Another wrote simply: "The personalities have to work, and the interests of the students should be engaged in the internship."

Far fewer respondents attributed success to the actions of the internship coordinator,[7] or the academic side of the internship (36.5%), although the faculty supervisors were far more likely (44.9%) to emphasize the importance of the academic component for ensuring a successful internship than were the university coordinators (23.5%) or legislative staff (14.3%).[8] Finally, approximately half the respondents (48.6%) emphasized the need to give students broad exposure to different parts of the legislative process.

What are the takeaways from these responses? Clearly, success depends on the legislative staff and the interns themselves. Legislative staff need to take steps proactively and students need to apply themselves to their positions. Yet there is another takeaway hiding underneath the surface: whereas most legislative internships provide a successful experience, problems do arise, and the results make a case for why internship coordinators need to play an active role in monitoring internships. Coordinators may not be perceived as central to success (only 30% of respondents saw it that way), but as Pecorella (2007) argues, coordinators are there to intervene if necessary, and they can play a critical role in salvaging internships that are not working out.

BEST PRACTICES IN PERSPECTIVE

Survey responses provide an opportunity to learn from those working on the front lines with interns, and the results reveal considerable differences in program structure yet considerable agreement on learning outcomes and pedagogy, which suggests that many coordinators see eye-to-eye on what constitutes best practices in state legislative internship programs. As importantly, much of what these survey respondents had to say is consistent with what has been written in the small body of literature on legislative internship programs.

Drawing from this survey and the existing literature, several best practices can be identified:

Constructive work environment. First, the interns need to be placed in a constructive workplace environment, one in which a good relationship can be created between the intern and the legislative staff, and the interns are able to gain from their experiences. Within that environment, the interns need to be given adequate support, clear directions, appropriate training, and a chance to interact with the legislator.

Meaningful work. Second, interns need to be given meaningful work that improves their understanding of legislative politics and builds professional skills. Assignments should include: policy or issue research; interaction with legislators and other elected officials; writing tasks such as policy briefs and committee testimony; helping with constituency matters; and observation of committee activities. These assignments will foster understanding about legislative politics and skills that are transferable to other professions. While interns may be expected to handle some general office duties, their internships must also involve more satisfying work that has greater educational value.

Academic component. Third, there needs to be an academic component to the program to ensure students do more than just intern in the legislature; they need to gain a broader understanding of what they observe. It is fine to ask students to maintain a log of their experience and write a reflection essay;

both are popular assignments that prompt students to reflect on their internship. But to cement a deeper, more sophisticated understanding of legislative politics through scholarship and practical experience, they should be assigned readings and classroom projects that at least introduce them to related scholarly literature. One way to tie scholarship and experience together is to have the students write traditional term papers on a topic related to what they did or observed within the legislature. Similarly, if a reflection paper is assigned, the students should be asked to compare what they observed with concepts drawn from readings and academic lectures.

Close monitoring. Fourth, internship coordinators (faculty or campus coordinators) need to be engaged in the internships they oversee to make sure the work environment is healthy, that legislative staff are helping interns thrive, and the students are experiencing no serious issues or problems. The coordinators may not need to intervene frequently, but they need to be ready to help.

Galen, the intern in the Oregon legislature, was given a classroom assignment to write a research paper, which had to include scholarly sources. She worked in an office environment in which the legislative assistant was willing to stop and listen to what Galen had found on the payday loan industry. The legislative assistant then opened doors to enable Galen to play a meaningful role in the legislative process. She was given the opportunity to work directly with her legislator, to write an amendment to a major bill, and then to testify in a hearing. The experience also allowed Galen to build a valuable professional network. It also has not hurt her career that the legislator for whom she interned went on to become the Oregon House Speaker. Galen herself went on to work in the majority party office, for the co-chair of the legislature's Ways and Means Committee, and for the governor.

What Galen experienced is the ideal type of outcome that faculty supervisors should try to ensure that each legislative intern enjoys, even if such outcomes are rare. It included a constructive workplace environment, an opportunity to be involved in meaningful work, close monitoring, and a classroom assignment that improved the student's understanding beyond the internship itself.[9]

REFERENCES

Balutis, Alan P. 1977. "Participation Through Politics: An Evaluation of the New York State Assembly Intern Program." *Teaching Political Science* 4 (3): 319–328.

Best, Judi. 2001. "Legislative Internships: A Partnership with Higher Education," *Journal of the American Society of Legislative Clerks and Secretaries* (Fall): https://www.ncsl.org/print/aslcs/Fall01best.pdf.

Biggs, Jeffrey R. 2003. *A Congress of Fellows: Fifty Years of the American Political Science Association Congressional Fellow Program, 1953–2003.* Washington, DC: American Political Science Association.

Callahan, Shannon, and Ed Mierzwinski. 2005. *Preying on Portlanders: Payday Lending in the City of Portland.* Portland: OSPIRG Education Fund.

Chistensen, Joan K., and Sandra L. Davis. 2002. "The State Legislative Internship." In *The Insider's Guide to Political Internships*, ed. Grant Reeher and Mack Mariani, 90–105. Boulder, CO: Westview Press.

Eyler, Janet and Beth Halteman. 1981. "The Impact of a Legislative Internship on Students' Political Skill and Sophistication." *Teaching Political Science* 9 (1): 27–34.

Fenno, Richard F. 1978. *Home Style: House Members in their Districts.* Boston: Little, Brown.

Hennessy, Bernard C. 1970. "Political Internships: Theory, Practice, Evaluation." *Penn State Studies, No. 28.* University Park: Pennsylvania State University.

Kurtz, Karl. 2007. "Oldest Internship Program in the Country?" *The Thicket at State Legislatures, National Conference of State Legislatures*, February 28, https://ncsl.typepad.com/the_thicket/2007/02/oldest_internsh.html.

Lee, Eugene C. 1958. "The California Legislative Intern Program." *American Bar Association Journal* 44 (5): 461–62, 483.

Lynch, Blair I. 2021. Unpublished interview with Rhode Island State Government Internship Program officer by author on May 11.

Mayhew, David R. 1974. *Congress: The Electoral Connection.* New Haven, CT: Yale University Press.

Murphy, Thomas P. 1979. "State Legislative Internships: The Evolving Reality." *Southern Review of Public Administration* 3 (2): 175–188.

National Conference of State Legislatures. 2005. *NCSL 2005 Survey of Legislative Internship Programs*. Denver, CO: National Conference of State Legislatures.

Nelson, Scott. 2007. "Oregon Curbs Payday Lenders." *Consumer Law & Policy Blog, Public Citizen*, June 20, https://pubcit.typepad.com/clpblog/2007/06/oregon_curbs_pa.html.

Oregon Senate Committee on Commerce. 2007. Restrictions on Car Title Loans: Hearings on House Bill 2204. 74th Oregon Legislative Assembly, May 23. Video file available at: https://oregon.granicus.com/MediaPlayer.php?view_id=39&clip_id=16644.

Pecorella, Robert F. 2007. "Forests and Trees: The Role of Academics in Legislative Internships." *Journal of Political Science Education* 3 (1): 79–99.

Pecorella, Robert F., and Jeffrey M. Stonecash. 2007. "Evaluating Successful Political Internships: A View from the Student Seats." *Journal of Cooperative Education and Internships* 41 (1): 4–11.

Profughi, Victor L., and Oliver L. Thompson. 1972. *Annual Report on the State Government Internship Program 1972*. Rhode Island: Commission on State Government Internships.

Rosenthal, Alan. 2006. "How to Guide Legislative Interns." *State Legislatures*, April 1: 36–37.

Rosenthal, Alan, Karl Kurtz, John Hibbing, and Burdett Loomis. 2001. *The Case for Representative Democracy*. Denver, CO: National Conference of State Legislatures.

Stonecash, Jeffrey M., Robert F. Pecorella, and Laurel Winegar. 1988. "Satisfaction with the Intern Experience: Analysis of the New York State Assembly Intern Program." *Journal of Cooperative Education* 25 (1): 25–43.

ENDNOTES

1. This study was approved by the Institutional Review Board at Portland State University, HRPP# 217208-18 and 217209-18 amendment.

2. The survey was conducted in March 2021. A link to the survey was sent to 185 individuals. In a few cases, the recipients forwarded the link to someone they thought was more appropriate to respond. In total, 76 respondents filled out the survey questionnaire. Since my concern is undergraduate education, I excluded the responses from two individuals who oversee programs for graduate students and do not work with undergraduates.

3. Sessions start in early January and run for 60 days in even-numbered years and 105 days in odd-numbered years. Students who attend universities and colleges on the quarter system are allowed to leave the program in odd-numbered years after the end of their winter quarter rather than serve the entire 105 days.

4. Since August 2019 (and as of June 2021), these include the University of California, Merced, and three California State University campuses: Fresno, Bakersfield, and Stanislaus.

5. Some respondents serve both as a faculty supervisor and a university internship coordinator. Two reported serving in all three roles. Since these individuals include the role of faculty supervisor among their multiple responsibilities, I included them with in the faculty category. Along with faculty, the other two categories were respondents who identified themselves as working solely as either a university internship coordinator or a coordinator within the legislature.

6. Most staff members explained that they did not handle the academic requirements. Of the three that did answer, two of them are from the nation's largest and most highly structured programs run by legislatures.

7. However, several wrote that it was important for the faculty supervisor or program coordinator to closely monitor the student interns to ensure the students are being giving meaningful work and are having a worthwhile experience (28.4%).

8. In a quote that echoed Pecorella's (2007) comments, one wrote about the value of class meetings: "In those meetings they hear about the experiences of the other interns, meet guest presenters involved in the legislative process, and learn more about the 'forest' of the legislative process rather than just being familiar with the 'trees' in their individual legislator's office."

9. Author's note: I want to thank the internship coordinators who helped with this study, especially those who wrote notes and called to talk in more detail about their programs. Thank you also goes to Logan Gilles for providing the cover photo of Darren Harold-Golden with Senator James Manning. I would like to dedicate the chapter to Joel Fischer, the legislative aide who helped Galen and many other legislative interns. It is legislative staff like Joel who are central to making legislative internship successful. He will be missed.

CHAPTER 17

Conclusion

Much has changed since the mid-20th century when political scientists began to publish about the few internship programs in existence. The study of internships has developed from personal musings supported by anecdotes into the empirical testing of refutable hypotheses. No longer niche programs that serve a few aspiring public servants, internships have become a standard component of the undergraduate political science major, considered essential by many (Anderson 2014; Jensen and Hunt 2007; Kuh 2008; Mariani and Klinkner 2009; Moore 2013). But much has remained the same: academic internships continue to be a means for students to learn our discipline, with faculty mentors and site supervisors playing crucial roles in facilitating that learning, and interns often using their experiences to jumpstart a career in public service. The preceding chapters have explored these changes and continuities in detail, and they help move the discipline towards identifying a set of best practices in internships that is informed by empirical evidence and expert observation and analysis.

Rather than simply reiterating the contribution of each chapter, in this conclusion we dwell briefly on the overall lessons that they impart and then turn our attention to areas of action for the discipline. We close by suggesting future areas of research that move us beyond the architecture of academic internship programs to the outcomes they produce for stakeholders— faculty, site supervisors, and above all, students.

TOWARDS BEST PRACTICES: WHAT HAVE WE LEARNED?

Each of the chapters in this volume makes a distinctive contribution to our understanding of political science internships. However, some important points emerge at once from several different chapters. First, internships are not simply a means to apply what has been learned in the classroom, nor are they merely a platform for practicing non-academic job skills. Fundamentally, internships involve learning from experience: interns learn some political science, and they learn about themselves. This process takes place in the classroom as well; the difference lies in the medium through which the learning occurs. In the case of internships, learning requires conscious, active experience in an applied setting and then critical reflection on it (Kolb 1984); the process involves reconsidering one's experiences and ideas in light of new information, and then reconciling differences.

Mentoring is crucial for fostering learning. Academic interns should be mentored by a faculty member who will help them stay focused on what they are learning and help them relate their experiences to relevant political science literature. Propositions from that literature can not only be applied to the experience, but tested against it. No doubt some students would do that on their own, just as some might grasp rational choice theory from independent reading; but mentorship helps assure that every intern learns at levels appropriate for academic credit, both in terms of quality and quantity.

At the heart of experiential learning is reflection, meaning that interns think about what they have learned and how that knowledge relates to the discipline. Ideally, it involves a three-way interaction among student intern, faculty mentor, and site supervisor. Reflection should be ongoing throughout the internship, and can be incorporated as assigned journal entries and written self-evaluations, for instance.

Reflection will be aided by evaluative feedback from the mentor from beginning to end of the internship. Without feedback, some interns may drift from a focus on academic learning to the technical details of the workplace; continual interaction, whether through in-person discussion or as comments and questions on interns' journal entries, can keep them on track.

Researchers have found that students learn more effectively when they work toward specific learning goals (Butler and Winne 1995). In classroom-based courses, these goals are commonly set by the instructor and listed in the syllabus. In internships, students set learning goals in accordance with the nature of their worksite. Moreover, since interns tend to know little about the work they will be doing until they begin, it may be more appropriate for the intern and mentor to work them out, with assistance from the intern's supervisor, a week or two into the internship. Learning contracts, examples of which are included in the Supplemental Internship Resources section, can help make these goals specific. Here again, a primary role of the instructor is to assure that the goals pertain to learning political science, not just learning how to do a particular job.

To succeed, students must invest themselves in their internship experience. Normally, such investment flows from the interns' excitement at working at a semi-professional level, with others as members of a team, but above all, as a valued contributor to the operation—as a person who is made to feel what they are doing has genuine worth. This responsibility lies mainly with site supervisors who are entrusted with creating a meaningful work agenda and welcoming interns into their organization to the greatest possible extent. On occasion, faculty may need to help students recognize the educational value of their internship experiences.

In addition to mentoring interns, faculty who direct internship programs need the backing of their own departments in the form of agreement about program standards and objectives, against which progress should be regularly measured, assessed, and furthered through improvements over time. Support is also required administratively and could take the form of a centralized campus internship office, as Chávez Metoyer has described. If no such center exists, faculty should try to form a dependable intra-campus network consisting of those who can assist with specialized tasks or address unforeseen issues: student affairs, career services, admissions, public relations, marketing, financial aid, alumni affairs, legal counsel, and advancement, along with deans, provosts, and presidents. Individuals in these offices will be glad to hear and share interns' stories in order to further the university's goals and mission, which may be served by attracting prospective students, improving retention rates, creating stronger relations with external communities, and contributing to the positive feelings of alumni about their time at the institution.

Beyond campus, intern supervisors are also important stakeholders in an internship program. In addition to hosting interns and playing the role of educators (and sometimes mentors), supervisors may enjoy coming to campus to speak to potential future interns. They should also know that their contributions to the education of student interns are valued. Optimally, supervisors should be offered training by universities so that they are familiar with university protocols, have access to information about best practices, and can establish a foundation for mutual understanding with faculty, administrators, and students.

In theory the sum of these parts should be a high-quality internship, but as COVID-19 reminded us, unanticipated developments can derail even the best-laid plans. Furthermore, the nature of work varies from placement to placement, and some internships are simply more engaging or intriguing than others.[1] Faculty should keep in mind that internships have the *potential* to bring about positive academic outcomes for students, including those from marginalized or historically underrepresented groups, and that *intentionality* and *deliberate effort* on everyone's part are essential to create rigorous, successful experiences. It is not enough to *just do* an internship; *how* it is done matters greatly.

High-quality internships facilitate growth across a range of liberal arts competencies (see NACE 2021)—not just basic employability skills—that are associated with better jobs long-term (Carnevale and Smith 2018; Kuh 2013; Fisher 2019). Quality internships can help pave field-specific occupational pathways that branch into graduate school or an entry-level job; they foster the kinds of connections that are important in public affairs settings where relationships have currency and can be leveraged for career success. Crucially, they help raise the prospects of career success for disadvantaged students—those who are considered low-income, first-generation, with historically marginalized racial or ethnic backgrounds, among others. As Carnevale and Smith (2018) demonstrate empirically, "the true dividing line between higher- and low-income students may be more in the characteristics of their work than the amount of work that they do," and they show that higher-income students are more likely to complete field-relevant internships that give them relative advantages when they seek jobs as graduating seniors (17). Addressing these inequities through more accessible, high-quality academic internships can help level the playing field.

A final takeaway is the need for program sustainability. Many political science internships have been developed by a single individual, often with little support at the beginning. It is often up to them to ensure that the program will continue in their absence. Elements that can help institutionalize a program include the campus-wide and community networks discussed earlier; a database of potential placements that includes contact information and descriptions of the internship; a catalog description and dedicated course number for the internship class; a collection of written forms; and ideally, a manual for future program directors.

ACCESS TO INTERNSHIPS: THE CASE FOR PAYING INTERNS

Equitable access requires that internships be paid. Students who have sufficient resources to pursue their studies full-time and to take time off for an unpaid position constitute only a small portion of the total undergraduate student body. Most find time to do an internship only by reducing the time devoted either to study or work, and, as Yamada argues, they shouldn't have to surrender the protections of labor law when they work as interns.

Ideally, an internship should carry academic credit equivalent to what would be earned for a course requiring a similar amount of work. In this scenario, the student could then take one less classroom course to meet requirements for the political science major. In a different scenario, students might also be given the option of doing an internship for zero units so that it appears on their official records but they are not required to pay extra fees or tuition. Even with these options, the hours-on-task for a classroom course typically include 100 minutes of reading, writing, and study for every 50 minutes in the classroom. Economic pressure can sometimes lead students to scrimp on their study time in order to make ends meet, but they cannot shirk their internship hours. As the chapter by Mallinson demonstrates, the lack of pay for interns' work renders these opportunities less available to students from historically disadvantaged groups. Perlin (2012) makes the same point strongly.

In his book, *Intern Nation*, Perlin (2012) proposes that professional governing bodies demand that interns be paid, as the American Institute of Architects, the Association of Art Museum Directors, and other professional associations have done (Sutton 2019), and argues that the Fair Labor Standards Act (FLSA) be reinterpreted to cover all internships under its minimum wage provisions. Although these changes would go far in making internships more accessible, they would erect new financial barriers for small, underfunded non-profit organizations that typically rely on unpaid labor by interns and volunteers to achieve their ends. Even if nonprofits were able to extract an exemption from FLSA rules, issues relating to equitable and fair access would remain.

The interaction of access and affordability also affects students wishing to intern outside their home city, for example in their state capital, Washington DC, or in another country. Aspiring interns often face prohibitive travel, living, housing, and program fees that may not be covered by financial aid. To avoid reinforcing the same advantages for some who enjoy the freedom to explore in-person options away from home, as well as gain valuable knowledge, skills, and experiences that give them a leg up over their peers, the goal of equity requires that there be financial support for interns who need it; today, such support is largely unavailable. Funding for programs or individuals could be supplied by academic institutions, government, or by charitable funds set up for the purpose, as described by Mallinson, but steady revenue streams are unlikely to flow as long as internships are treated as volunteer positions that lack an educational core or as purely vocational training exercises.

Virtual internships are expanding access in some important respects by enabling far more students to engage with organizations that were once out of their geographic reach—and opportunities continue to improve as internship providers institutionalize their remote programs post-COVID-19. However, as Cabrera Rasmussen and Van Vechten point out, being online carries its own set of challenges, including potential technological barriers such as intermittent connectivity or unreliable equipment, lack of readiness to work in isolation for long stretches of time, and lack of dedicated workspaces that are free of unrelenting distractions. Universities are uniquely positioned to address some of these needs by taking concrete steps that could include offering dedicated internship-work spaces on campus with trusted digital connections and communication devices that are available to those who cannot afford them.

Departments, colleges, and universities could also team up to close other gaps that sometimes prevent students from reaching their potential. A smaller percentage of students will do internships for academic credit than the majority who will find internships on their own, and to maximize the potential educational outcomes for the latter, essential materials (such as the ones located in the Supplemental Internship Resources section of this text or in campus career centers) should be shared with students widely. Campuses could also establish "professional dress closets" where students can obtain professional clothing, or could organize a sponsored shopping excursion for students who are searching for a professional outfit. Disparities, even ones based on self-presentation, can affect how "professional" interns are perceived (Williams et al. 2020).

ADMINISTRATIVE SUPPORT FOR INTERNSHIPS

The chapter by Gentry describes wide variation in institutional support provided for internship programs. In the best case, a faculty member is paid for supervising interns at the same rate as any other course and is assisted by a campus internship center or career services office. In far too many other cases, faculty are expected to supervise interns with no compensation at all. Aside from being exploitative, this practice impairs the educational quality of internships by stretching faculty members well beyond what would be considered reasonable, and as research shows, replicates the same biases that lead to largely invisible, "extra" responsibilities being assumed by more vulnerable faculty (junior, untenured, persons of color, women; see Flaherty 2019; Joseph and Hirschfield 2011; June 2015; Reid 2021; Whitaker 2017).[2]

As several chapters have demonstrated, if an internship is to be more than a part-time job, it must help the intern learn about political science. But such learning is not automatic; it requires mentoring and assistance from the instructor at all stages: placement selection; monitoring through student journaling and reflections, class discussions about readings and experiences, and written reports; and periodic evaluations and prompt feedback. An unpaid instructor simply does not have the time to do all these things, and may have to fall back on sending the intern into the field to report back briefly at the end of the semester. Since students are charged tuition for credited internships, there is no justification for not paying internship instructors. Fairer compensation could include fractional, cumulative credit awarded for internship supervision, and also recognition of internship-related work in the tenure and promotion process.

The discipline has produced limited survey data describing faculty compensation for internships, and as Mallinson and Sciabarra and Gentry explain, we lack a comprehensive picture about the resources that are generally available for internships, in contrast to other characteristics of universities. Such a compilation would contribute significantly to rationalizing the compensation scales and to achieving better alignment of individual effort, pay, and educational mission.

NEW DIRECTIONS IN INTERNSHIPS

Most of the chapters in this book are based on evidence and observations about in-person internships that have involved faculty and/or staff and student interaction, are completed after one (or perhaps two, and on rare occasion, multiple) semesters, and are not compulsory.[3] Several authors have referenced newer forms of internships that might become more prevalent in the future, and it is worth considering whether and how these opportunities might change the way students gain access to or encounter experiential learning. In addition to virtual or remote positions (addressed in Chapter 15), gig internships, mini-internships, and specialized placements for first and second-year students, including those enrolled in community colleges, could expand internship opportunities beyond their current boundaries.

Gig Internships. In the early 20th century, jazz musicians began to use the word "gig" to refer to one-time or temporary performance contracts. Today, the "gig economy" captures the work of free-lancers who lack traditional labor law protections and employee benefits but have more control over their own working conditions or hours (Kondo and Singer 2010; DeRuyter and Brown 2019). "Precarious labor" is sometimes used to describe this class of workers, a group that could include adjunct faculty who, like musicians, tend to "perform" in multiple venues under a limited contract and receive few if any benefits. To navigate the ever-expanding, globalized gig economy, students need to acquire practical knowledge that enables them to perform well across several sectors or in more than one position within an organization or industry. They need to know how to find available jobs; how to move from one position to another; and how to make themselves available for those looking to hire.

Many jobs in politics naturally fit the definition of "gig." For instance, campaign positions fall into this category unless they are filled by permanent, professional consultants who might be campaign managers, field organizers, fundraisers, media relations managers, or pollsters. By design, gig internships enable students to explore multiple sites and employment opportunities in quick succession. They could also be project-based positions whereby students work on parts of a project at one internship location and then work on different parts at another site. Alternatively, following the model developed by the CORO Foundation for public affairs fellows, interns might be assigned a series of projects in a city and be required to work with specific agencies or officials for a specified period of time on separate projects.[4]

Opportunities such as these would allow students to explore several positions within an issue area, or different sites dedicated to the same policy problem, such as working with a homeless shelter, then a local politician, and then a local homeless advocacy group to gain different perspectives about the same policy area through different lenses. Students who are drawn to campaigning would be assigned to work in different divisions of a campaign, gaining skills that are useful across a campaign team, enabling them to make greater connections between theory and practice, and also increasing their odds of gaining employment post-graduation. An internship that exposes students to various aspects of an industry can help uncover areas of interest that they later might pursue in greater depth.

Micro-Internships. Micro-internships are those in which students work intensively on discrete projects for a short duration, such as a solid week, and the emphasis is on exposure rather than development or mastery. According to an organization that promotes them, "Micro-Internships are short-term, paid, professional assignments that are similar to those given to new hires or interns. Unlike traditional internships, micro-Internships can take place year-round, typically range from 5 to 40 hours of work, and projects are due between one week and one month after kick-off." (Parker Dewey 2020). Projects are assigned from a single location and require far fewer hours than a traditional internship. It remains to be seen whether micro-internships can yield the same academic and career-related gains that have been measured in semester-long internships, but we surmise that short but impactful opportunities could be more advantageous to students who are early in their college career, who can spare little time for interning, or want to explore different opportunities (Wingard 2019). For example, a student might be asked to research specific city policies about an issue and compile a report, or create public outreach messaging for a local agency. Although the purpose of these experiences would be to expose the student to a narrow aspect of an organization's operations, if incorporated into a course or a series of courses, then they could be used to advance certain skills, such as policy research and oral presentations, in real-world settings.

Internships for First- and Second-Year Students. Extending for-credit internship opportunities to include first- and second-year undergraduates also represents a path for making them more accessible and inclusive. Some institutions only allow students who have attained junior standing to enroll in an internship course, and articulation agreements do not allow internship credit to transfer from community colleges—a barrier for community college students (see Chapter 9 by Sciabarra and Gentry). This practice seems to stem from concerns about the educational value of internships; after all, experiential learning is not standardized across political science, giving faculty at four-year institutions reasons to remain skeptical of their curricular worth and unwilling to award credit for "just working." In addition, internship credit at four-year institutions is sometimes reserved for junior- and senior-level undergraduates who have acquired foundational knowledge: they are better equipped, the argument goes, with the kinds of time management, writing, research, analytical, and interpersonal skills that will transfer well to a work setting. In this line of argument, advanced students are better prepared to situate their internship in the field, and better able to balance the demands of working both outside and inside the university.

The incorporation of service-learning is a counterfactual to these arguments. Often designed as experiential components of classroom-based courses, but sometimes as freestanding activities, service-learning is often available to first-year students. While service-learning is often considered to be completely different from internships, it may be more productive to think of both as points along an experiential learning spectrum. It is worth remembering that Robert Sigmon, often considered to be the father of service-learning, began his program as what was basically an internship in the North Carolina state legislature (1970).

Given the overall potential benefits of interning for all students, but especially historically underrepresented groups, rules that deny internships to all first- and second-year students appear to be arbitrary. Faculty should be able to assess students individually for their maturity and fitness as interns, and because many students pursue multiple not-for-credit internships both before and after doing one for academic credit (Berg 2014), the reasons for reserving internships for juniors and seniors are potentially more harmful than helpful. Schools should also consider how introductory-level internships might differ from more advanced ones. When restrictions are based on limited faculty resources (i.e., to limit the number of interns to a manageable number), then more creative alternatives—such as elective internship courses—rather than more restrictive rules, should be pursued. At this point in time, the evidence supports removing limitations that lead students to rule out doing multiple internships.

MOVING TOWARDS BEST PRACTICES THROUGH RESEARCH

Qualitative and quantitative evidence overwhelmingly supports the conclusion that internships create educational opportunities unlike those found in a classroom but with measurable academic and personal gains that are similar to what traditional learning settings produce. Experiential learning enables students to operationalize concepts through practice, or apply their know-how to "real-world" settings, and thus build competencies that will advance their academic and career goals.

Because there is so much variation in the types of internships and work that students engage in (arguably, no two internships are exactly alike), it is often easier to focus on the inputs—program design, faculty roles—as this book does, than the outcomes, in order to characterize best practices in internships. Yet even when standard elements such as mentoring, contracts, midterm evaluations, ongoing reflections, or public presentations of interns' work are in place, student outcomes will be influenced by myriad intervening factors, some stemming from the students' personality or life situation, others from the site or site supervisor, and still others from the larger environment. Health status, compatibility among coworkers, reliable equipment—complexities such as these make clear that a qualitative approach to understanding how internships work is sometimes preferable to reducing an experience to quantifiable data. Not surprisingly, much of what has been established about reliable and efficacious internship practices is derived from surveys, interviews, and program assessments.

With the help of large-n, multivariate measures, we will gain greater purchase on many aspects of internships that remain undetermined or not well understood. There is ample room for researchers to test the effects of specific internship practices on students' learning, academic progress, and career paths, and to investigate how newer modes of interning compare to "traditional" in-person forms.[5] Importantly, our discipline would benefit from understanding whether and how internships obtained and conducted independently (or not for credit) yield different outcomes compared to those obtained with assistance from campus staff or faculty, or to those monitored carefully by their site supervisors and faculty mentors, or to those requiring any number and type of assignments (in particular reflections or research projects that are often connected to a class). Assessing the effects of political science internships could include a comparison of post-degree job placement rates for internship participants and nonparticipants, or longitudinal studies.

Given the demonstrated ability of internships as a high-impact practice to enhance the knowledge, abilities, and skills of all students, future research should also examine the conditions under which students from historically disadvantaged groups build competencies in public affairs internships and connect these to academic and career outcomes. Mixed-methods studies are well-suited to this purpose. The evidence these efforts generate could well be used to justify investments in program expansions and adequate pay for those who support internships as a form of experiential learning.

CONCLUSION: REFOCUSING INTERNSHIPS ON LEARNING

Political science credit is awarded for political science learning. This is as true for experiential courses as for those in the classroom. At a minimum, all forms of experiential learning should involve self-reflection by the student, feedback by the supervisor, and mentoring by the instructor. Including these fundamental components can help assure that academic quality is maintained as the tremendous potential of new internship modes develops and spreads. By design, rigorous internships demand significant inputs, and further empirical assessments of outcomes are in order. With the right kinds of evidence, we can set standards for quality internships, meet the demands for them by students and potential internship employers, and justify their inclusion in curricular planning that serves students and graduates well into the future.

REFERENCES

Anderson, Brian. 2014. "High-Impact Political Science Internships in a 'Low-Density Opportunity' Environment." *PS: Political Science & Politics* 47 (4): 862–66.

Berg, John C. 2014. "Two Threats to Political Science Internships: Press Attacks and Incorrect Student Assumptions." Paper presented at the Annual Meeting of the American Political Science Association. Washington, DC.

Butler, Deborah L., and Philip H. Winne. "Feedback and Self-Regulated Learning: A Theoretical Synthesis." *Review of Educational Research* 65 (3): 245–81. https://doi.org/10.3102/00346543065003245.

Carnevale, Anthony P., and Nicole Smith. 2018. *Balancing Work and Learning: Implications for Low-Income Students.* Georgetown University: Center for Education and the Workforce. https://1gyhoq479ufd3yna29x7ubjn-wpengine.netdna-ssl.com/wp-content/uploads/Low-Income-Working-Learners-FR.pdf.

De Ruyter, Alex, and Martyn Brown. 2019. *The Gig Economy*. Newcastle upon Tyne, UK: Agenda Publishing.

Fisher, Julia F. 2019. "Micro-internships: Just a gig or a promising gateway?" Christensen Institute, September 17 [Blog]. https://www.christenseninstitute.org/blog/micro-internships-just-a-gig-or-a-promising-gateway/.

Flaherty, Colleen. 2019. "Undue Burden." *Inside Higher Ed*, June 4. www.insidehighered.com/news/2019/06/04/whos-doing-heavy-lifting-terms-diversity-and-inclusion-work.

Jensen, Jennifer M., and Lauren L. Hunt. 2007. "College in the State Capital: Does It Increase the Civic Engagement of Political Science Undergraduate Majors?" *PS: Political Science & Politics* 40 (3): 563–69.

Joseph, Tiffany D., and Laura E. Hirschfield. 2011. "Why Don't You Get Somebody New to Do It? Race and Cultural Taxation in the Academy." *Ethnic and Racial Studies* 34 (1): 121–141.

June, Audrey Williams. 2015. "The Invisible Labor of Minority Professors." *Chronicle of Higher Education*, November 8. www.chronicle.com/article/The-Invisible-Labor-of/234098.

Klein, Markus, and Felix Weiss. 2011. "Is Forcing Them Worth the Effort? Benefits of Mandatory Internships for Graduates from Diverse Family Backgrounds at Labour Market Entry." *Studies in Higher Education* 36 (8): 969–987.

Kolb, David A. 1985. *Experiential Learning: Experience as the Source of Learning and Development.* Englewood Cliffs, NJ: Prentice-Hall.

Kondo, Alexander, and Abraham Singer. 2020. "Labor Without Employment: Toward a New Legal Framework for the Gig Economy." *ABA Journal of Labor and Employment Law* 34 (3): 331–58.

Kuh, George D. 2008. *High-Impact Educational Practices: What They Are, Who Has Access to Them, and Why They Matter.* Washington, DC: Association of American Colleges and Universities.

Mariani, Mack, and Philip Klinkner. 2009. "The Effect of a Campaign Internship on Political Efficacy and Trust." *Journal of Political Science Education* 5 (4): 275–93. doi: 10.1080/15512160903272160.

Moore, David Thornton. 2013. *Engaged Learning in The Academy: Challenges and Possibilities.* London: Palgrave-Macmillan.

National Association of Colleges and Employers. 2021. "What is Career Readiness?" NACE. Accessed July 1, 2021. https://www.naceweb.org/career-readiness/competencies/career-readiness-defined/.

Parker Dewey. 2020. "Micro-Internships." *Parker Dewey*, Accessed July 10, 2021. https://www.parkerdewey.com.

Perlin, Ross. 2012. *Intern Nation: Earning Nothing and Learning Little in the Brave New Economy.* London: Verso.

Reid, Rebecca A. 2021. "Retaining Women Faculty: The Problem of Invisible Labor." *PS: Political Science & Politics* 54 (3): 504–506. https://doi.org/10.1017/S1049096521000056.

Sigmon, Robert L. 1970. "Service-Learning: An Educational Style." Transcript of speech. ED 086 HE 004 979. Online: ERIC.

Sutton, Benjamin. 2019. "The Association of Art Museum Directors Just Called for Ending Paid Internships." *Artsy.net*, June 21. https://www.artsy.net/news/artsy-editorial-association-art-museum-directors-called-unpaid-internships.

Social Sciences Feminist Network Research Interest Group. 2017. "The Burden of Invisible Work in Academic: Social Inequalities and Time Use in Five University Departments." *Humboldt Journal of Social Relations* Special Issue 39: *Diversity & Social Justice in Higher Education* (2017): 228–245.

Whitaker, Manya. 2017. "The Unseen Labor of Mentoring." *Chronicle Vitae*, June 12. https://chroniclevitae.com/news/1825-the-unseen-labor-of-mentoring.

Williams, Tameka, Daniel K. Pryce, Tyler Clark, and Hydeia Wilfong. 2020. "The Benefits of Criminal Justice Internships at a Historically Black University: An Analysis of Site Supervisors' Evaluations of Interns' Professional Development." *Journal of Criminal Justice Education* 31 (1): 124–140.

Wingard, Jason. 2019. "Why Micro-Internships Will Be the Next Big Thing." *Forbes*, March 6. https://www.forbes.com/sites/jasonwingard/2019/03/06/why-micro-internships-will-be-the-next-big-thing/?sh=1c85bdf9700c.

ENDNOTES

1. Of course, student interests and abilities also help determine the kinds of work they find engaging.

2. Reid (2021) writes that invisible labor involves student-initiated mentorship, in which faculty attend to their students' emotional needs by providing "hands-on attention" to "serve as role models, mentors, and even surrogate parents" (June 2015), especially with respect to diversity and inclusion matters (Flaherty 2019). Reid states: "This time-consuming work often is overlooked and undervalued because it is considered unnecessary and voluntary" (2021, n.p). This type of taxing work can also be associated with mentoring interns, adding many hours to an internship supervisor's week, and ultimately, leading to imbalances in faculty workload.

3. Klein and Weiss (2011) find that mandatory internships do not generate the same positive effects as they do for students who choose to do internships.

4. For more about the CORO Fellowship, see: http://www.corofellowship.org/.

5. For example, examining "mini-internships" could help us understand how number of hours spent on the job influences knowledge and skill development.

Supplemental Internship Resources

3.1 FLSA Rules for Internships

U.S. Department of Labor
Wage and Hour Division

U.S. Wage and Hour Division

(Updated January 2018)

Fact Sheet #71: Internship Programs Under The Fair Labor Standards Act

This fact sheet provides general information to help determine whether interns and students working for "for-profit" employers are entitled to minimum wages and overtime pay under the Fair Labor Standards Act (FLSA).[1]

Background
The FLSA requires "for-profit" employers to pay employees for their work. Interns and students, however, may not be "employees" under the FLSA—in which case the FLSA does not require compensation for their work.

The Test for Unpaid Interns and Students
Courts have used the "primary beneficiary test" to determine whether an intern or student is, in fact, an employee under the FLSA.[2] In short, this test allows courts to examine the "economic reality" of the intern-employer relationship to determine which party is the "primary beneficiary" of the relationship. Courts have identified the following seven factors as part of the test:

1. The extent to which the intern and the employer clearly understand that there is no expectation of compensation. Any promise of compensation, express or implied, suggests that the intern is an employee—and vice versa.

2. The extent to which the internship provides training that would be similar to that which would be given in an educational environment, including the clinical and other hands-on training provided by educational institutions.

3. The extent to which the internship is tied to the intern's formal education program by integrated coursework or the receipt of academic credit.

4. The extent to which the internship accommodates the intern's academic commitments by corresponding to the academic calendar.

5. The extent to which the internship's duration is limited to the period in which the internship provides the intern with beneficial learning.

6. The extent to which the intern's work complements, rather than displaces, the work of paid employees while providing significant educational benefits to the intern.

7. The extent to which the intern and the employer understand that the internship is conducted without entitlement to a paid job at the conclusion of the internship.

---

[1] The FLSA exempts certain people who volunteer to perform services for a state or local government agency or who volunteer for humanitarian purposes for non-profit food banks. WHD also recognizes an exception for individuals who volunteer their time, freely and without anticipation of compensation, for religious, charitable, civic, or humanitarian purposes to non-profit organizations. Unpaid internships for public sector and non-profit charitable organizations, where the intern volunteers without expectation of compensation, are generally permissible.

[2] *E.g.*, *Benjamin v. B & H Educ., Inc.*, --- F.3d ---, 2017 WL 6460087, at *4-5 (9th Cir. Dec. 19, 2017); *Glatt v. Fox Searchlight Pictures, Inc.*, 811 F.3d 528, 536-37 (2d Cir. 2016); *Schumann v. Collier Anesthesia, P.A.*, 803 F.3d 1199, 1211-12 (11th Cir. 2015); *see also Walling v. Portland Terminal Co.*, 330 U.S. 148, 152-53 (1947); *Solis v. Laurelbrook Sanitarium & Sch., Inc.*, 642 F.3d 518, 529 (6th Cir. 2011).

Courts have described the "primary beneficiary test" as a flexible test, and no single factor is determinative. Accordingly, whether an intern or student is an employee under the FLSA necessarily depends on the unique circumstances of each case.

If analysis of these circumstances reveals that an intern or student is actually an employee, then he or she is entitled to both minimum wage and overtime pay under the FLSA. On the other hand, if the analysis confirms that the intern or student is not an employee, then he or she is not entitled to either minimum wage or overtime pay under the FLSA.

Where to Obtain Additional Information
This publication is for general information and is not a regulation. For additional information, visit our Wage and Hour Division Website: http://www.wagehour.dol.gov and/or call our toll-free information and helpline, available 8 a.m. to 5 p.m. in your time zone, 1-866-4USWAGE (1-866-487-9243).

U.S. Department of Labor
Frances Perkins Building
200 Constitution Avenue, NW
Washington, DC 20210

1-866-4-USWAGE
TTY: 1-866-487-9243
Contact Us

How to cite this resource: US Department of Labor. 2018. "Fact Sheet #71: Internship Programs Under the Fair Labor Standards Act." Reprinted with permission in *Political Science Internships: Towards Best Practices* eds. Renée B. Van Vechten, Bobbi Gentry, and John C. Berg. Washington, DC: American Political Science Association.

4.1 Ten Tips for Internships

Shannon McQueen, West Chester University

Clinton M. Jenkins, Birmingham-Southern College

Susan L. Wiley, The George Washington University

Ten Internship TIPS

A key learning experience, an internship can also lead to job and networking opportunities. How do you make the most out of your internship experience? Here are ten tips for doing so, which were condensed from five years' worth of supervisor evaluations of students enrolled in George Washington University's (GWU's) internship program.

#1. Be prepared for Writing and Research Most internships for GWU students involve heavy writing and research components. This includes a wide range of projects that summarize, share, and/or communicate information. Interning students have given presentations, written policy, legal, and research briefs, crafted a new podcast proposal, and developed advocacy documents.

The next most common internship activity is researching: over 33% of all internship supervisors asked interns to complete research tasks. This may involve compiling literature reviews, collecting data, or analyzing data sets. Time to brush up on your writing and research skill set!

#2. Communicate, Communicate, Communicate When asked about how their interns could improve, over 20% of internship supervisors commented on the need for better communication. Strong communication skills include the following;

- Listening closely when your internship supervisor is talking.
- Making eye contact when engaging in discussions.
- Sharing the progress of your work with your internship supervisor and colleagues frequently.
- Asking questions! Internships are a learning experience.
- Responding to emails promptly (within 24 hours).

#3. Show Initiative Taking initiative refers to acting and engaing with the work independently. How do you show initiative at your internship?

- When attending meetings, take notes and look engaged.
- Stay in the present moment while working site.
- Take advantage of opportunities to meet with and learn from staff members.
- Ask for more work when you finish a project.
- Show up on time for your internship.
- Don't be afraid to make suggestions and take ownership of tasks.

#4. Pay Attention to Small Details Before sending that email, memo, or research paper, proofread your work.

#5. Project Calm Confidence You were selected for the internship for a reason and can bring something new to the organization. Try to enter the workplace with some confidence!

- Try a 30-second "power pose" before entering your worksite.
- Create a playlist of music to boost your confidence and listen to it on the way to your internship.
- Visualize what a successful internship experience looks like for you.
- Celebrate your wins! Did you write a great memo? Did your supervisor compliment your data analysis? Pat yourself on the back and accept the praise.

#6. Be on time Plan your commute to show up to your internship on time, every time. This may seem insignificant, but this is a signal that you are interested in the internship process, and ready to engage.

#7. Take advantage of informal networking opportunities Internships are a valuable opportunity to put your most personable step forward. Be kind to those you meet, and use this opportunity to build connections and make relationships.

#8. Stay Organized Interning as a student can be a lot to juggle. Work to keep yourself organized and learn to self-manage your time.

- Find a planner and use it!
- If you find yourself getting distracted online, use website blockers to stay on track
- Put your cell phone away to remain focused on a current task
- Start each day with a "to-do" list of goals
- Plan ahead (i.e. if you know finals are coming up, study a few weeks in advance so you are not overwhelmed during busy weeks)

#9. Remember your boundaries Remember, you are a student first, intern second. It can be difficult to balance an internship and college classes. If you feel overwhelmed with the amount of work you have on your plate, talk with your site internship supervisor or university contact.

#10... and Have Fun! An internship delivers unique opportunities to apply class concepts in a real-world environment. It can be both rewarding and memorable. Enjoy your internship learning experience!

How to cite this resource: McQueen, Shannon, Clinton M. Jenkins, and Susan L. Wiley. 2021. "Supplemental Internship Resource: Ten Tips for Internships," in *Political Science Internships: Towards Best Practices* eds. Renée B. Van Vechten, Bobbi Gentry, and John C. Berg. Washington, DC: American Political Science Association.

4.2 Sample #1, Intern Evaluation Instrument for Site Supervisors

POLITICAL SCIENCE INTERNSHIP
PSC 2987 Internship Supervisor Evaluation

Please note: In order for the student to receive credit for his/her internship, this evaluation must be returned to me by Tuesday 1 May

Please mail, fax, or email the completed form.

Student Name:

Name of Organization:

Supervisor Name: Phone: (

Internship Start Date: Internship End Date:

*Total Number of Hours Worked: ____________

On a scale from 1 (poor) to 5 (excellent), please evaluate the student's performance during the internship with respect to the following criteria:

1. Dependability
(Comments)

2. Work Ethic
(Comments)

3. Attendance / Punctuality
(Comments)

4. Usefulness to the Organization
(Comments)

5. Works Effectively with Others
(Comments)

6. Quantity of Work Produced
(Comments)

7. Quality of Work Produced
(Comments)

8. Level of Initiative
(Comments)

9. Please identify a specific project or situation for which the intern was responsible and comment on his/her performance

10. Please list any overall recommendations for improvement in the student's performance.

11. From your perspective, was the student's internship a good learning experience for him/her?
Yes No____ (Why?)

12. Do you feel that it is appropriate for the student to earn academic credit based on his/her performance? Yes No____ (Why?)

13. Overall, was the student's performance satisfactory? Yes No____ (If no, why not?)

14. Additional Comments or Observations:

15. Have you discussed this evaluation with your student? Yes No____
(Do you want this evaluation to be confidential? Yes___ No)

16. Would you be interested in having another GW intern work for you? (*Yes No___)*

How to cite this resource: Wiley, Susan. 2021. "Sample #1, Intern Evaluation Instrument for Site Supervisors." Department of Political Science, George Washington University.

5.1 Information Needed to Build an Internship Database

Information Needed to Build an Internship Database

By Bobbi Gentry, Bridgewater College

Internship Provider Information
Employer name
Employer address
Internship coordinator or contact (Name, Number, Email)
Internship site supervisor (Name, Number, Email)
Employer mission
Employer website
Paid or unpaid / Pay rate
Number of internships available
Semester availability (e.g., only summer, only fall)
Employer preference for hours at internship per week
Requirements for internship: application, cover letter, academic standing, GPA, interview
Skills and knowledge necessary
Necessary training before internship (e.g., CPR, Excel, statistical programs)
Can this internship be done remotely?
Emergency contact information for student
Alumni contact(s) at internship site
Willingness to come to internship fair?
Big events at internship (for photographs or marketing materials)
Connection to political science/public affairs
Last student intern (Semester and Year of Internship; name and contact information may be protected)*
Information Relevant to Students
Common activities or assigned duties
Previous interns' anonymous feedback about the internship (with or without dates), including what skills are likely to be developed and what learning opportunities are possible
Site supervisor's willingness to write letters of recommendation
Opportunities for future employment at this site
Possible stipends or grants available

How to cite this resource: Gentry, Bobbi. 2021. "Supplemental Internship Resource: Information Needed to Build an Internship Database" in *Political Science Internships: Towards Best Practices* eds. Renée B. Van Vechten, Bobbi Gentry, and John C. Berg. Washington, DC: American Political Science Association.

5.2 Readings for Interns

Readings for Interns

Many, if not most, readings that are covered in an internship course are those selected by students conducting research projects.[1] In some internship classes, professors and instructors assign common readings to promote knowledge, provoke group discussion, inspire individual reflection, or simply provide practical advice. The following compilation includes a few such readings suggested by some of our authors and others,[2] organized alphabetically by general topic and type of internship placement. Excerpts from some of these titles, rather than the entire texts, are often assigned. This list is neither comprehensive nor definitive, and the inclusion or exclusion of titles should be considered neither an endorsement of these or lack thereof. This list contains readings that have been assigned by colleagues who are practiced in the area of political science or public affairs internships, and should be considered a starting point for exploration. It will be periodically updated on the website, APSA Educate.

Bureaucracy and Administration

Fischer, Frank, and Carmen Sirianni, eds. 1984. *Critical Studies in Organization and Bureaucracy.* Philadelphia: Temple University Press. [excerpts recommended]

Campaigns and Elections

Semiatin, Richard, ed. 2020. *Campaigns on the Cutting Edge.* Washington, DC: CQ Press.

Simpson, Dick and Betty O'Shaughnessy. 2016. *Winning Elections in the 21st Century.* Lawrence, KS: Kansas University Press.

Conduct of Internships; Learning by Doing

Brown, John S., Allen Collins, and Paul Duguid. 1989. "Situated Cognition and the Culture of Learning." *Educational Researcher* 18(1): 32-42.

Reeher, Grant and Mack Mariani. 2002. *The Insider's Guide to Political Internships.* Boulder: Westview.

---

[1] At least this was the conclusion that the editors reached after conducting an informal (and unrepresentative) survey of internship coordinators in 2021.

[2] With appreciation for their suggestions, this list was developed with help from the following contributors: John C. Berg, Cynthia Chávez Metoyer, Grant Ferguson, Joshua Franco, Dick Simpson, and two anonymous contributors. Four titles were derived from Ambrose and Poklop (2015): Ambrose, Susan A., and Laurie Poklop. 2015. "Do Students Really Learn from Experience?" *Change* 47 (1): 54–61.

Congress and Congressional Internships

Waxman, Henry, with Joshua Green. *The Waxman Report: How Congress Really Works.* New York: Twelve Publishing.

Grabowski, Sue. 2006 (1986). *Congressional Intern Handbook.* Washington, DC: Congressional Management Foundation. https://www.congressfoundation.org/storage/documents/CMF_Pubs/cmf-congressional-intern-handbook.pdf.

CMF. 2020 (1984). *Setting Course: A Congressional Management Guide.* Washington, DC: Congressional Management Foundation.

State Legislatures

Rosenthal, Alan. *Heavy Lifting: The Job of the American Legislature.* Washington, DC: CQ Press, 2004.

------. *Legislative Life: People, Process, and Performance in the States.* New York: Harper & Row, 1981. (Rosenthal was the long-time director of the study of state legislatures at the Eagelton Institute, Rutgers; both books are comparative studies of what legislators do.)

California

Boyarsky, Bill. 2007. *Big Daddy: Jesse Unruh and the Art of Power Politics.* Oakland: University of California Press.

Micheli, Chris. 2021. *The California Legislature and Its Legislative Process: Cases and Materials.* Durham, NC: Carolina Academic Press.

Starr, Kevin. 2007. *California: A History.* New York: Modern Library Press.

Massachusetts

McDonough, John E. *Experiencing Politics: A Legislator's Stories of Government and Health Care.* California/Milbank Series on Health and the Public. Berkeley: University of California Press ; New York: Milbank Memorial Fund, 2000. (McDonough was in the Massachusetts State House for 10 years; after leaving, he got a PhD in Public Policy. The book matches various theories of public policy with examples from is experience.)

Vermont

Wright, Ralph G. *Inside the Statehouse: Lessons from the Speaker.* Washington, DC: CQ Press, 2005. (Wright was Speaker of the Vermont House).

Wisconsin

Loftus, Tom. *The Art of Legislative Politics.* Washington, DC: Congressional Quarterly Press, 1994. (Loftus was Speaker of the Wisconsin State Assembly)

NOTE: The books by Loftus, McDonough, and Wright let students compare the full-time, highly professional Massachusetts General Court with the very part-time Vermont legislature and the Wisconsin Assembly which is somewhere in between. They are full of anecdotes that illustrate political science propositions.

Judicial or Legal Internships

Breyer, Stephen. 2011. *Making our Democracy Work: A Judge's View*. New York: Vintage.

Gibson, James L. and Michael Nelson. 2017. "Reconsidering Positivity Theory: What Roles Do Politicization, Ideological Disagreement, and Legal Realism Play in Shaping U.S. Supreme Court Legitimacy?" *Journal of Empirical Legal Studies* 14 (3): 592-617. Available at SSRN: https://ssrn.com/abstract=3016684 or http://dx.doi.org/10.1111/jels.12157.

Scalia, Antonin. 1998. *A Matter of Interpretation*. Princeton, NJ: Princeton University Press.

Political Activism

Alinsky, Saul. 1971. *Rules for Radicals*. New York: Vintage.

Graham, Bob, and Chris Hand. 2016. *America, The Owner's Manual: Making Government Work for You*. Washington, DC: CQ Press.

Liu, Eric. 2013. "Why Ordinary People Need to Understand Power." TED Talk, September [video]. https://www.ted.com/talks/eric_liu_why_ordinary_people_need_to_understand_power.

Public Policy

Allison, Graham T. 1971. *The Essence of Decision*. Boston: Little, Brown.

Brown-Dean, Khalilah L. 2019. *Identity Politics in the United States*. New York: Wiley.

Ingram, Helen and Anne L. Schneider. 2005. "Introduction: Public Policy and the Social Construction of Deservedness." In *Deserving and Entitled*, ed. Helen Ingram and Anne L. Schneider. Albany: State University of New York Press. https://www.sunypress.edu/pdf/61060.pdf.

Lindblom, Charles. 1957. "The Science of Muddling Through." *Public Administration Review* 19:79–88.

Meltsner, Arnold J. 1976. *Policy Analysts in the Bureaucracy*. Oakland: University of California Press.

Weiss, Carol H. 1980. *Social Science Research and Decision-making*. New York: Columbia University Press.

Race and Ethnic Politics and Policy

Alexander, Michelle. 2020 (2010). *The New Jim Crow: Mass Incarceration in the Age of Colorblindness.* New York: The New Press.

Kendi, Ibram X. 2019. *How to Be an Antiracist.* New York: One World.

Muhammad, Khalil Gibran. 2019. *The Condemnation of Blackness: Race, Crime, and the Making of Modern Urban America.* Cambridge: Harvard University Press.

Wing Sue, Derald. 2015. *Race Talk and the Conspiracy of Silence: Understanding and Facilitating Difficult Dialogues on Race.* Hoboken, NJ: Wiley.

Non-Academic or Popular Press Readings: Leadership- and Career-Related

Burnett, Bill, and Dave Evans. 2016. *Designing Your Life.* New York: Knopf.

Dweck, Carol. 2012. *Mindset: The New Psychology of Success.* New York: Ballantine Books.

Kahneman, Daniel. 2013. *Thinking, Fast and Slow.* New York: Farrar, Straus and Giroux.

Langer, Ellen. 2016 (1997). *The Power of Mindful Learning.* Boston: Da Capo Lifelong Books.

Maxwell, John C. 2007 (1998). *The 21 Irrefutable Laws of Leadership.* Nashville: Thomas Nelson, Inc.

Pink, Daniel H. 2010. *Drive.* New York: Penguin.

Pollak, Lindsey. 2012. *Getting from College to Career.* New York : Harper Business.

How to cite this resource: No Author. 2021. "Supplemental Internship Resource: Readings for Interns," in *Political Science Internships: Towards Best Practices* eds. Renée B. Van Vechten, Bobbi Gentry, and John C. Berg. Washington, DC: American Political Science Association.

5.3 Career Readiness Self-Assessment Tool

Are You Career Ready?

Career Readiness Self-Assessment Tool

Career readiness is the awareness and development of the skills students need to confidently and successfully meet employer expectations and transition into the workplace.

Take this self-assessment to see what professional competencies you need to develop and practice to be career ready and experience workplace success.

COMMUNICATION:

Articulate thoughts and express ideas effectively using oral, written, visual and non-verbal communication skills, as well as listening to gain understanding. The ability to deliver information in person, in writing, and in a digital world.

need to develop 1 2 3 excelling

Ways to develop this competency:

- Develop and deliver a presentation for a class.
- Check for understanding by asking clarifying questions.
- Proofread on-line and written communication to avoid errors.

Ways I am developing: ______________________________

Next steps for developing: ______________________________

TEAMWORK AND INTERPERSONAL:

Build and maintain collaborative relationships to work effectively with others in a team setting through shared responsibility, empathy and respect. The ability to manage ones emotions and conflict with others while contributing towards a common goal.

need to develop 1 2 3 excelling

Ways to develop this competency:

- Collaborate with others on a class project where responsibility is shared and not divided.
- Handle difficult conversations in person with respect.
- Join a student organization or team on campus where you can help achieve a common goal.

Ways I am developing: ______________________________

Next steps for developing: ______________________________

LEADERSHIP:

Leverage strengths to motivate, collaborate and guide. The ability to use a positive attitude to influence and empower others to reach a shared goal through strategic thinking and effective decision-making.

need to develop 1 2 3 excelling

Ways to develop this competency:

- Take on a leadership role in a group or organization.
- Demonstrate initiative at your job/internship by taking on additional responsibilities.
- Motivate team members with a positive attitude and leverage their strengths when delegating work.

Ways I am developing: ______________________________

Next steps for developing: ______________________________

CREATIVITY AND PROBLEM-SOLVING:
Exercise sound reasoning to analyze issues, synthesize information, make decisions and solve problems. The ability to think critically and strategically to develop original ideas and innovative solutions.

need to develop 1 2 3 excelling

Ways to develop this competency:
- Develop an action plan with specific steps to solve a problem.
- Brainstorm solutions to a problem before bringing it to a supervisor/professor.
- Activate your mind – read, do puzzles, write, etc.

Ways I am developing: ______________________________

Next steps for developing: ______________________________

PROFESSIONALISM AND PRODUCTIVITY:
Demonstrate integrity, resilience, accountability and ethical behavior. The ability to take initiative, maintain effective work habits (prioritize, plan and manage work) to produce high quality results and project a professional presence.

need to develop 1 2 3 excelling

Ways to develop this competency:
- Use a planner or calendar to prioritize work/assignments and meet deadlines.
- Attend the Dining Etiquette program to learn more about professional expectations during a meal.
- Review your social media through the eyes of a future employer and determine appropriateness.

Ways I am developing: ______________________________

Next steps for developing: ______________________________

GLOBAL PERSPECTIVE:
Respect the viewpoints of those from diverse cultures, races, ages, genders, religions and lifestyles to build collaborative relationships and communicate effectively. The ability to appreciate, value, and learn from other cultures and perspectives.

need to develop 1 2 3 excelling

Ways to develop this competency:
- Attend an event on campus that encourages you to step outside your comfort zone.
- Engage in conversation with individuals who have different perspectives than your own.
- Participate in a study abroad or volunteer experience to broaden your horizons.

Ways I am developing: ______________________________

Next steps for developing: ______________________________

DIGITAL FLUENCY
Maximize new and emerging technologies in order to work, learn and live in a digital society.
The ability to apply digital technology to enhance quality, improve productivity and communication, solve problems, and streamline processes.

need to develop 1 2 3 excelling

Ways to develop this competency:
- Create projects and express ideas through digital tools.
- Learn a new technology or design skill through Lynda.com
- Work with a Virginia Tech librarian to find relevant and credible sources through on-line research.

Ways I am developing: ______________________________

Next steps for developing: ______________________________

How to cite this resource: Virginia Tech Career and Professional Development. 2021. "Career Readiness Self-Assessment Tool," in *Political Science Internships: Towards Best Practices* eds. Renée B. Van Vechten, Bobbi Gentry, and John C. Berg. Washington, DC: American Political Science Association.

6.1 Journal Guidelines

SUFFOLK UNIVERSITY
Department of Government
JOURNAL REQUIREMENTS

Keeping a journal will be an important part of your learning experience as an intern. By forcing you to think about what you are doing and what you are learning from it, the writing of a journal can increase the amount you actually learn. It can also make you aware of what you don't know, so that you can direct your efforts toward finding out.

You should write in your journal at least briefly every day that you work at your internship. Keeping current in your writing is important because it lets you keep track of how your perceptions and understanding change from day to day and week to week, thereby documenting your learning.

Your journal should include all of the following elements:

1. A daily log of what you do. This should be as brief as possible, but try to be precise rather than general. E.g., "research at State House library on condominium control bills" is better than "research on bills".

2. Questions. If there's something you want to know, write it down. If you later learn the answer, write that down, too--not necessarily on the same day. Curiosity is the first essential for learning, so the more questions, the better. Try to have at least one question every day that you work.

3. Insights, observations, perceptions, interesting incidents. After you have logged your day's activity, think about what it meant to you, what you got out of it, new things you noticed, et cetera.

4. Essay. Once a week, write a page (or more) in which you discuss some topic of your choice more fully. This should not be a summary of your daily entries, but a real essay in which you discuss a particular incident, explore an issue that interests you, or explain an insight that you have had. Please note – *one* essay per week means *two* essays per journal installment.

5. Likes and dislikes--about the work, the office, the political system, the world, yourself.

6. New words. Once a week, write down any new terms you've learned during the week--or, if you've heard them but not understood what they meant, write that down. Learning specialized vocabulary is a big part of any field.

Please submit your journal through Blackboard every week. Your journal supplies important evidence of what you are learning from your internship, which in turn is used to help determine your grade.

(Adapted from guidelines by Helen Graves)

How to cite this resource: Berg, John C. 2021. "Supplemental Internship Resource: Journal Guidelines," in *Political Science Internships: Towards Best Practices* eds. Renée B. Van Vechten, Bobbi Gentry, and John C. Berg. Washington, DC: American Political Science Association.

6.2 Sample Learning Agreement

SUFFOLK UNIVERSITY GOVERNMENT INTERNSHIP

Internship Learning Agreement

I. Basic Information

Name: ____

Placement agency: ____________________________________

Agency address: _____________________________________

____

Name and title of supervisor: ___________________________

____

Telephone number: ____________ Email: ___________________________

II. Duties

1. What are the basic purposes of the office or agency?

2. What will your job as an intern be? How does it contribute to the purposes described above?

3. Will you be assigned a long-term project? If so, please describe it briefly.

III. Learning goals

1. What special skills do you have which will be useful in doing your job?

2. What skills do you hope to acquire or improve during the course of your internship?

3. What past experiences--work, courses taken, reading, or anything else--have prepared you for this job?

4. What factual knowledge do you expect to gain during your internship?

5. What ethical or moral values are relevant to the work you will be doing as an intern, either positively (values you are expected to observe) or negatively (things which are considered improper)?

6. Are there any ethical issues about which you hope to clarify your own thinking during the course of your internship?

IV. Documentation and evaluation

1. What standards will your supervisor apply in evaluating your work?

2. For purposes of grading, how will you demonstrate to your instructor the degree to which you have achieved the learning goals listed in section III, parts 2, 4, and 6?

3. Will there be any other materials--for example, reports written on the job--which you would like to submit in documentation of what you learn on your internship?

V. Approval

We, the undersigned, have read and agree to the conditions and goals of the internship described in this internship learning agreement.

Intern: ________________________________ Date: ____________

Instructor: ______________________________ Date: ____________

How to cite this resource: Berg, John C. 2021. "Supplemental Internship Resource: Sample Learning Agreement," in *Political Science Internships: Towards Best Practices* eds. Renée B. Van Vechten, Bobbi Gentry, and John C. Berg. Washington, DC: American Political Science Association.

6.3 Sample Placement Agreement

SUFFOLK UNIVERSITY
Department of Government

Government Internship Program

PLACEMENT AGREEMENT

Student's name: ____

Address____

______________________Telephone: __________________________

PLACEMENT:

Name of office or agency: ____

Name and title of immediate supervisor: ___________________________

____

Agency address: ____

Email: ______________________________Telephone: ______________

Intern's duties, including hours and responsibilities:

Approved by:

______________________ ______________________
(intern) (date) (supervisor) (date)

____
(faculty sponsor) (date)

How to cite this resource: Berg, John C. 2021. "Supplemental Internship Resource: Sample Placement Agreement," in *Political Science Internships: Towards Best Practices* eds. Renée B. Van Vechten, Bobbi Gentry, and John C. Berg. Washington, DC: American Political Science Association.

6.4 Sample Self-Evaluation Instructions

Sample instructions for midterm and final self-evaluations

Mid-term self-evaluation (3-5 pp): Midway through your internship, reflect on what you have learned and accomplished so far. Look back at the goals you set for yourself in your learning agreement. Have the goals changed? Are you achieving them? Now that the internship is halfway through, are there any ways in which you need to adjust your expectations? What do you think you will accomplish in the remaining weeks? Be prepared to present your report orally in class.

Final Paper and Presentation (7-10 pp): This is the crux of the course. In your paper, you are to both evaluate your internship and, most importantly, reflect on its importance to your major. In addition to your written report, you should prepare a formal presentation, with A/V, for the final meeting of the class.

How to cite this resource: Berg, John C. 2021. "Supplemental Internship Resource: Sample Self-Evaluation Instructions," in *Political Science Internships: Towards Best Practices* eds. Renée B. Van Vechten, Bobbi Gentry, and John C. Berg. Washington, DC: American Political Science Association.

6.5 Sample #2, Intern Evaluation Instrument for Site Supervisors

SUFFOLK UNIVERSITY
Department of Government
Internship Program

INTERN EVALUATION

Intern's Name:

Please describe briefly the nature of your intern's responsibilities under each of the following headings:

Routine tasks:

Research tasks:

Administrative tasks:

Was the intern assigned a long-term project?

What skills or specialized types of knowledge has your intern demonstrated in doing this work?

What skills or specialized types of knowledge has your intern acquired or developed in doing this work?

What skills or specialized types of knowledge does your intern need to learn in order to do this work better?

How satisfied have you been with your intern's promptness, accuracy, and dependability?

How satisfied have you been with your intern's initiative and creativity?

Additional comments:

Date internship began:

Average hours per week:

Date internship completed:

Signed: ______________________________

Title: ______________________________

Agency: ______________________________

Date: ______________________________

Please assign a tentative grade for student:
(A, A-, B+, B, B-, C+, C, C-, D+, D, D-, F) ______________________________

Please return to:

Professor John C. Berg
Department of Government
Suffolk University
73 Tremont Street
Boston MA 02108
jberg@suffolk.edu

How to cite this resource: Berg, John C. 2021. "Supplemental Internship Resource: Sample #2, Intern Evaluation Instrument for Site Supervisors," in *Political Science Internships: Towards Best Practices* eds. Renée B. Van Vechten, Bobbi Gentry, and John C. Berg. Washington, DC: American Political Science Association.

7.1 Research Internship Sample Syllabus

USC Dornsife
Jesse M. Unruh Institute of Politics

POSC 395
DIRECTED GOVERNMENT & POLITICAL LEADERSHIP
California Policy Research Internship

Art Auerbach, J.D., Ph D.
Associate Professor, Teaching
Internship Director
aauerbac@usc.edu
Office Hours: By appointment only

Meghan Ginley
Manager, Unruh Institute of Politics
ginley@usc.edu
Office Hours:
By appointment only (email Meghan to set up)

IMPORTANT DEADLINES

Due:
Students must register for POSC 395 on WebReg (D-Clearance required prior to registration)

Due:
First political event write-up must be submitted. ***Write-ups are due within one week of event.***

Due:
Final presentations to representatives of partner organization, presentation times are TBD.

Due:
Submit final policy report
Second political event write up

EVENT REQUIREMENTS

All Students *Must Attend*:
- Bi-monthly meetings with Professor Auerbach and Meghan Ginley
- Mid-semester exchange with partnership (TBD)
- 2 Unruh Institute Political Events (2-page write-up is due within one week of each event)
- 2 of the Course Activities (Listed on Page 4)
- (1) One-on-one with Professor Auerbach to discuss final policy report

Please note, Political Events and Course Activities are independent of one another and are not interchangeable

1. Course Description
Students will take part in a team-based research project where they will work to develop potential

USC Dornsife
Jesse M. Unruh
Institute of Politics

solutions in their respective policy areas by conducting original fieldwork, interviewing policy experts, reviewing academic and policy reports, and using other forms of primary and secondary research. At the conclusion of the internship, each group will present their final product to representatives of their partner organization.

2. Internship Hours per Units of Credit

Units/Credits	2	3	4	5	6	7	8
Suggested weekly hours	10	14	18	22	26	30	34
Total hours at internship	100	150	200	250	300	350	400

3. Meetings and Communication with Partnership Organization
An introductory meeting between students and representatives of their partner organization will take place in the beginning of the semester. The Mid-Semester Exchange in which students will share research progress with their partner organization will take place midway through the semester. Each policy group will deliver their final product to representatives of their partner organization. Students should stay in close contact with their partner organization throughout the semester, but are required to include the Internship Director and Community Engagement Director in any communication with them.

4. Meetings and Communication with Unruh Staff
Groups will meet with the Internship Director and Community Engagement Director on-campus twice a month. In these meetings, interns are expected to bring a 2-page summary of their research and share research progress as an individual and as a group. Dr. Auerbach will be in contact with you throughout the semester via the Blackboard system. Check Blackboard on a regular basis for information relevant to POSC 395. During the semester, you should also keep in close contact with Dr. Auerbach and Ms. Ginley to discuss your research progress.

Student groups will present their final product to the Unruh staff before the final presentations. The specific date and time is dependent upon the students' schedules. If a student does not adequately prepare for the run-through presentations, as determined by Professor Auerbach and Ms. Ginley, then he/she may not be permitted to present before their partner(s). Alternative arrangements will be made for students to give their final presentation.

You are encouraged to meet with your policy team at least once a week. The organization of these meetings will be left to group members.

5. Grading
Course grades will be based on satisfactory completion of the required number of hours at the

USC
Dornsife
Jesse M. Unruh
Institute of Politics

internship, the supervisor's evaluation of your performance, and fulfilling other coursework requirements. The final grade for the course will be based on:

Unruh Manager Evaluation	25%
Partner Organization Evaluation	10%
Final Policy Presentation	20%
Final Research Project	35%
Event Write Ups	10%

*NOTE: The Unruh Manager Evaluation will be comprised of attendance at all meetings,, submission of bi-monthly write-ups and participation during all meetings, partner and bi-monthly alike. The Partner Organization Evaluation will include overall performance over the course of the internship.

**NOTE: All late papers will be marked down by 5 points for each day they are late. Also, papers will be marked down 1/3 of a letter grade for every 10 hours of research that the student is short of the required 100 hours).

6. Course Activities

The following list of course activities have been carefully organized with the intention of enhancing each students career development skills. These activities will bring in experts in the corresponding fields to give students an opportunity to gain life-long skills in each category.

- **All students, including students that have previously taken POSC 395 in prior semesters, are required to attend two of the following course activities of their choosing. Students who would like to attend more than two course activities may do so for personal benefit, but will not receive any extra credit or additional course recognition.**

<u>Course Activities:</u>

As each Course Activity approaches, students will receive an email with specific details and RSVP links.

1. **"Politics in the News" with Adam Nagourney (Monday, September 16, from 5:30pm-7pm)**
   Learn from field-expert Adam Nagourney, Los Angeles Bureau Chief for the NYT, about the process and intricacies of political reporting.

2. **"Director's Corner" with Bob Shrum and Mike Murphy at the USC Center for the Political Future (SOS B15)**
   Come learn from our Directors, Bob Shrum and Mike Murphy, how to win friends and influence people in the world of politics.

USC Dornsife
Jesse M. Unruh
Institute of Politics

3. **"How to Win the Presidency in New Hampshire" with Patrick Griffin**
   Learn about the importance of New Hampshire in political campaigns and the inner workings of the New Hampshire caucus - everything you need to know entering the 2020 Presidential campaigns.

4. **Communications with Heather Wilson**
   Learn from a local expert how to handle crises and manage crisis communications for political operations and large-scale organizations.

5. **Jobs Forum**
   Learn about the various political fields by listening to a panel discussion of local professionals, followed by a networking session with the professionals.

6. **Resume Workshop**
   Learn from a professional what a hiring manager is looking for a resume, followed by a hands-on tutorial on how to edit and enhance your resume and cover-letter.

7. Attending Political Events and Write-Ups

You are required to attend at least two (2) politically-focused events during the fall and turn in a short, 2–page write-up for each event. You write-up MUST follow the memorandum format, an example of which is attached to the syllabi. ***Please submit your write-up on Blackboard within one week of the event.*** Your write-up should briefly describe the event, including what was the event, who spoke, at least one page on what was said and at least ½ page on whether you agree or disagree on what was said and why. The first write-up is due no later than _______________.

You are encouraged to find political events that are of interest to you. All events hosted by USC's Center for the Political Future are considered pre-approved events which qualify for the political event requirement for this course. Below is a list of preapproved events hosted by the Center this semester, however, you are more than welcome to attend other political events such as other political events on campus, events through your internship, City Hall meetings, County Board of Supervisor meetings, etc. All events that are not hosted by USC's Center for the Political Future require approval from Professor Auerbach before attending the event.

To find on-campus events hosted by the Center for the Political Future, please check out our event calendar: https://dornsife.usc.edu/unruh/programming/

The Final Written Policy Report & Presentation

You are required to complete a writing assignment in which you analyze your designated area of research and make policy recommendations.

Final written projects should be 8-15 pages (depending on units, see below) and must include substantial *scholarly research*, including consideration of relevant literature. Please discuss your project in detail with the Internship Director and Community Engagement Director throughout the course of the semester.

A) Written Policy Report:

USC Dornsife
Jesse M. Unruh Institute of Politics

The final written component should be in the format of an 8 to 15-page policy report. Papers must be typed and double-spaced in 12-point font with 1" margins. Paper/project length is dependent on the number of credits/units earned:

2 units: 8-10 pages
3 units: 10-12 pages
4 units: 12-15 pages

Students' papers will receive 5 point deductions for failing to meet the minimum page length, failure to include a "references" page and 5 points for every day late. Note: You must use in-text (parenthetical) citations along with your work-cited page. Only include citations in work cited that are used in the paper. **Students are required to submit their final papers on Blackboard through the "Turnitin" system by the deadline.**

B) Policy Presentation:
Presentations will be one hour in length comprised of a 30-minute presentation to representatives of your partner organization followed by a 30-minute Q&A session.

8. Academic Integrity

Because the completion of the internship is a major part of this course, you MUST work all of the hours listed on your internship agreement form. All written assignments for this class must be your original work, completed only to fulfill the requirements of this course. Sources must be cited accurately and completely.

NOTE ON "RECYCLING PAPERS": Your paper/project MUST be original work done for this class and related to your internship. You may not re-use another student's paper, or your own paper from a previous course or a course in which you are currently enrolled.

This is an extremely serious issue, which, according to University policy, can result in failing this course as well as the course from which you "borrowed" your paper.

Please refer to the SCampus chapter on "University Student Conduct Code" (scampus.usc.edu/university-student-conduct-code) or contact the Internship Coordinator if you have any questions.

*Please note that the POSC 395: Directed Government and Political Leadership Syllabus is not a binding contract. Dr. Auerbach has the discretion to make changes as deemed necessary.

How to cite this resource: Auerbach, Art. 2021. "Supplemental Internship Resource: Research Internship Sample Syllabus," in *Political Science Internships: Towards Best Practices* eds. Renée B. Van Vechten, Bobbi Gentry, and John C. Berg. Washington, DC: American Political Science Association.

8.1 Sample #3, Intern Evaluation Instrument for Site Supervisors

American University | Washington Semester Program | Washington, DC

Employer Evaluation of Intern Performance for Career Readiness

Completed by employers at the midterm and end of semester to assess intern performance. Below are 8 NACE career competencies.[i] NOTE: This is a copy of the online evaluation form managed in a content management system. Email prompts provide direction and request evaluation responses.

Student____

Employer name ________________________________

Supervisor ____________________________________

Supervisor phone _______________________________

Supervisor email ________________________________

Approximate hours interned to date:_______________________

1. Critical Thinking & Problem Solving *

Intern exercises sound reasoning to analyze issues, make decisions, and overcome problems. The intern is able to obtain, interpret, and use knowledge, facts, and data in a process, and can demonstrate originality and inventiveness.

1. Failure	2. Poor	3. Average	4. Good	5. Excellent	n/a
O	O	O	O	O	O

Comments

____

2. Oral & Written Communications *

Intern articulates thoughts and ideas clearly and effectively in written and oral forms to persons inside and outside of the organization. The intern has public speaking skills; is able to express ideas to others; and can write/edit memos, letters, and complex technical reports clearly and effectively.

1. Failure	2. Poor	3. Average	4. Good	5. Excellent	n/a
O	O	O	O	O	O

Comments

____

3. Teamwork & Collaboration *

Intern can build collaborative relationships with colleagues and customers representing diverse cultures, races, ages, genders, religions, lifestyles, and viewpoints. The intern is able to work within a team structure, and can negotiate and manage conflict.

1. Failure	2. Poor	3. Average	4. Good	5. Excellent	n/a
O	O	O	O	O	O

Comments

____

4. Digital Technology *

Intern can leverage existing digital technologies ethically and efficiently to solve problems, complete tasks, and accomplish goals. The intern demonstrates effective adaptability to new and emerging technologies.

1. Failure	2. Poor	3. Average	4. Good	5. Excellent	n/a
O	O	O	O	O	O

Comments

____

Employer Assessment | Washington Semester Program | American University | Questions? Contact: morrill@american.edu

[1] National Association of Colleges and Employers (n.d.). Career readiness defined. Retrieved from www.naceweb.org/career-readiness/competencies/career-readiness-defined/.

5. Leadership *

Intern can leverage the strengths of others to achieve common goals, and use interpersonal skills to coach and develop others. The intern is able to assess and manage their emotions and those of others; use empathetic skills to guide and motivate; and organize, prioritize, and delegate work.

1. Failure	2. Poor	3. Average	4. Good	5. Excellent	n/a
O	O	O	O	O	O

Comments

____

6. Professionalism & Work Ethic *

Intern demonstrates personal accountability and effective work habits, e.g., punctuality, working productively with others, and time workload management, and understands the impact of non-verbal communication on professional work image. The intern demonstrates integrity and ethical behavior, acts responsibly with the interests of the larger community in mind, and is able to learn from their mistakes.

1. Failure	2. Poor	3. Average	4. Good	5. Excellent	n/a
O	O	O	O	O	O

Comments

____

7. Career Management *

Intern can identify and articulate one's skills, strengths, knowledge, and experiences relevant to the position desired and career goals, and identify areas necessary for professional growth. The intern is able to navigate and explore job options, understands and can take the steps necessary to pursue opportunities, and understands how to self-advocate for opportunities in the workplace.

1. Failure	2. Poor	3. Average	4. Good	5. Excellent	n/a
O	O	O	O	O	O

Comments

____

8. Global & Intercultural Fluency *

Intern values, respects, and learns from diverse cultures, races, ages, genders, sexual orientations, and religions. The intern demonstrates openness, inclusiveness, sensitivity, and the ability to interact respectfully with all people and understand individuals' differences.

1. Failure	2. Poor	3. Average	4. Good	5. Excellent	n/a
O	O	O	O	O	O

Comments

____

Positive Feedback:* Comments regarding the intern's talents and progress

____

____

____

Constructive Feedback: * Comments regarding areas of improvement for the intern

____

____

____

Optional attachment(s) to provide more details on assignments.

____

Employer Assessment | Washington Semester Program | American University | Questions? Contact: morrill@american.edu

[1] National Association of Colleges and Employers (n.d.). Career readiness defined. Retrieved from www.naceweb.org/career-readiness/competencies/career-readiness-defined/.

How to cite this resource: Lowenthal, Diane and Jeffrey Sosland. 2021. "Supplemental Internship Resource: Sample #3, Intern Evaluation Instrument for Site Supervisors," in *Political Science Internships: Towards Best Practices* eds. Renée B. Van Vechten, Bobbi Gentry, and John C. Berg. Washington, DC: American Political Science Association.

8.2 Student Self-Evaluation

American University | Washington Semester Program | Washington, DC

Student Self-Evaluation of Internship Performance for Career Readiness

Completed by students at the start, midterm, and end of semester for self-reflection about career readiness.

Below are 8 NACE career competencies.[i] Select the choice that best matches your abilities in the given areas. Respond honestly to maximize the accuracy of your career development in the beginning, middle, and end of the semester.

NOTE: This is a copy of the online evaluation form managed in a content management system. Email prompts provide direction and request evaluation responses.

Student ______________________________

Employer name ______________________________

Supervisor ______________________________

Supervisor phone ______________________________

Supervisor email ______________________________

Approximate hours interned to date: ______________________________

1. Critical Thinking & Problem Solving *

I exercise sound reasoning to analyze issues, make decisions, and overcome problems. I am able to obtain, interpret, and use knowledge, facts, and data in a process, and I can demonstrate originality and inventiveness.

1. Failure	2. Poor	3. Average	4. Good	5. Excellent	n/a
o	o	o	o	o	o

Comments

____

2. Oral & Written Communications *

I articulate thoughts and ideas clearly and effectively in written and oral forms to persons inside and outside of the organization. I have public speaking skills; am able to express ideas to others; and can write/edit memos, letters, and complex technical reports clearly and effectively.

1. Failure	2. Poor	3. Average	4. Good	5. Excellent	n/a
o	o	o	o	o	o

Comments

____

3. Teamwork & Collaboration *

I build collaborative relationships with colleagues and customers representing diverse cultures, races, ages, genders, religions, lifestyles, and viewpoints. I am able to work within a team structure, and can negotiate and manage conflict.

1. Failure	2. Poor	3. Average	4. Good	5. Excellent	n/a
o	o	o	o	o	o

Comments

____

4. Digital Technology *

I leverage existing digital technologies ethically and efficiently to solve problems, complete tasks, and accomplish goals. I demonstrate effective adaptability to new and emerging technologies.

1. Failure	2. Poor	3. Average	4. Good	5. Excellent	n/a
o	o	o	o	o	o

Comments

____

Self-Assessment | Washington Semester Program | American University | Questions? Contact: morrill@american.edu

[1] National Association of Colleges and Employers (n.d.). Career readiness defined. Retrieved from www.naceweb.org/career-readiness/competencies/career-readiness-defined/.

5. Leadership *

I leverage the strengths of others to achieve common goals and use interpersonal skills to coach and develop others. I am able to asses and manage my emotions and those of others; use empathetic skills to guide and motivate; and organize, prioritize, and delegate work.

1. Failure	2. Poor	3. Average	4. Good	5. Excellent	n/a
O	O	O	O	O	O

Comments

____

6. Professionalism & Work Ethic *

I demonstrate personal accountability and effective work habits, e.g. punctuality, working productively with others, and time workload management, and understand the impact of non-verbal communication on professional work image. I demonstrate integrity and ethical behavior, act responsibly with the interests of the larger community in mind, and am able to learn from my mistakes.

1. Failure	2. Poor	3. Average	4. Good	5. Excellent	n/a
O	O	O	O	O	O

Comments

____

7. Career Management *

I am able to identify and articulate my skills, strengths, knowledge, and experiences relevant to the position and career goals, and identify areas necessary for professional growth. I am able to navigate and explore jobs options, can take and understand the steps necessary to pursue opportunities, and understand how to self-advocate for opportunities in the workplace.

1. Failure	2. Poor	3. Average	4. Good	5. Excellent	n/a
O	O	O	O	O	O

Comments

____

8. Global & Intercultural Fluency *

I value, respect, and learn from diverse cultures, races, ages, genders, sexual orientations, and religions. I demonstrate openness, inclusiveness, sensitivity, and the ability to interact respectfully with all people and understand individuals' differences.

1. Failure	2. Poor	3. Average	4. Good	5. Excellent	n/a
O	O	O	O	O	O

Comments

____

Positive Feedback:* Out of the eight competencies listed above, describe your strongest ones. How have you put them to use?

____

____

____

Constructive Feedback: * Out of the eight competencies listed above, describe the ones in need of improvement. How are you addressing them?

____

____

____

Optional attachment(s) to provide more details on assignments.

____

Employer Assessment | Washington Semester Program | American University | Questions? Contact: morrill@american.edu

[1] National Association of Colleges and Employers (n.d.). Career readiness defined. Retrieved from www.naceweb.org/career-readiness/competencies/career-readiness-defined/.

How to cite this resource: Lowenthal, Diane and Jeffrey Sosland. 2021. "Supplemental Internship Resource: Student Self-Evaluation," in *Political Science Internships: Towards Best Practices* eds. Renée B. Van Vechten, Bobbi Gentry, and John C. Berg. Washington, DC: American Political Science Association.

8.3 Self-Assessment Questions and Tools

Self-Assessment Questions and Tools

Several chapters, including the one by Lowenthal and Sosland, mention that interns (like all of us) learn more deeply when they consciously ask themselves what they have learned and what they have yet to learn. Below are questions, drawn from various sources, for interns to use in performing self-assessments at different points in the internship process.

Note to the intern: before you begin, how well do you know yourself? Consider taking a personality test that helps you reflect on what you value and what interests you, and understand how your attributes, values, and interests map onto different kinds of work. A campus career center advisor can direct you to these resources and the assessment instruments they have vetted are usually free to students. Links to other online assessments are listed at the end of this document. Although these questionnaires are not likely to reveal your "perfect fit" with a job or type of work, they can help you identify what kinds of work environments you may find more fulfilling and help narrow your job search.[1]

A) Questions to be asked **before searching for** an internship:

- How do I find a job that I like or maybe even love?
- How can I make a difference in the world?
- What do I want to grow into?
- What kinds of work make me feel satisfied, enthusiastic, or inspired to do more?
- Which of my accomplishments or recent successes in college give me the most satisfaction? What do I think made them most successful?
- What are my top five skills? Which of these skills do I want to hone?
- Are there other skills I want to develop in an internship?
- Where do I see myself using my skills in a career?
- What do I see myself doing in the next five years?
- How do I envision balancing my job/internship/career with my academic and family (or other caregiving) obligations?

B) Questions to be asked **every working day** (Burnett and Evans 2020)[2]:

- What did I learn?
- What are the differences between what I observed in the field and what I learned in class?
- What did I initiate?
- What people did I help? How did I contribute to the organization?

[1] Foss, Erica. 2021. "Five Questions You Need to Ask Yourself Before Taking Another Self-Assessment Test." The Muse, n.d. Accessed July 15, 2021. https://www.themuse.com/advice/5-questions-you-need-to-ask-yourself-before-taking-another-selfassessment-test.

[2] Burnett, Bill, and Dave Evans. 2020. *Designing Your Work Life: How to Thrive and Change and Find Happiness at Work.* New York: Alfred A. Knopf.

C) Questions to be asked **periodically**, at least at middle and end of internship, but more often if desired, should help the intern discern how true each of the following is for them.[3]

Development of Political Science Knowledge and Skills:

- I gained a good deal of fact-based knowledge in this internship.
- I learned to identify main points and central issues in the area of my internship.
- I gained a better understanding of concepts and principles that are core to the political science discipline, such as power, authority, governance, self-governance, liberty, fairness, and equality, among others.
- I developed an understanding of ethical issues are common in public affairs.
- I learned how different perspectives on race, class, gender, and culture add to political science.
- I improved my ability to identify and analyze problems.
- I learned to evaluate the quality of work in this field.
- I developed the ability to give appropriate evaluations of others' work.
- I developed the ability to solve real problems by applying what I have learned in college.
- I improved my research skills in my internship.
- I developed the ability to carry out original research in my internship.
- I developed the ability to communicate clearly about the area of my internship.
- I improved my writing skills through my internship.
- I improved my quantitative reasoning skills in my internship.
- I improved my organizational and time management skills in my internship.
- I learned to identify formal characteristics of work in my internship.
- I developed creative ability in my internship.
- I gained a broader understanding of my major by doing this internship.

Self-understanding:

- I gained a better understanding of myself through this experience.
- I increased my awareness of my own interests and skills.
- I developed confidence in myself.
- I increased my awareness of my own interests and talents.
- I gained an understanding of some of my personal concerns.
- I developed a greater sense of personal responsibility.

Development of Interests:

- I deepened my interest in the field of my internship.
- I developed my enthusiasm for the field in which my internship is situated.
- I was stimulated to discuss related topics outside of class.

---

[3] Excerpted from course evaluation questions at American University, online at https://www.american.edu/provost/oira/set/qbank.cfm, and from the Lowenthal and Sosland chapter in this book.

Development of Social Skills and Attitudes:

- I developed leadership skills in this internship.
- I developed greater awareness of societal problems.
- I became interested in community projects related to my internship.
- I learned to value my own viewpoints.
- I learned to consider the viewpoints of my colleagues in this internship.
- I reconsidered some of my former attitudes.

Development of Professional Skills and Attitudes:

- I was introduced to important professional perspectives by guest lecturers or coworkers.
- I developed the specialized skills needed by professionals in this field.
- I learned about career opportunities.
- I developed a clearer sense of professional identity, or a better sense of how I want to make a mark in this field.

Other Self-Assessment Tools

Additional online assessment tools[4] are listed below. Please be aware that not all assessment tools are reliable or valid.

- 16 PERSONALITIES: This questionnaire describes different personality types that are reflected in personal motivation to work and help users understand their strengths and weaknesses. A basic test is free: www.16personalities.com

- CAREER BELIEFS INVENTORY (CBI): This career counseling tool can help students recognize preexisting beliefs and attitudes that could constrain their career choices. It can be self-scored for free. See: https://prezi.com/fx7didwptftm/career-beliefs-inventory/
- The CAREER INTERESTS GAME, developed by the Career Center at the University of Missouri in conjunction with Dr. John Holland: https://career.missouri.edu/career-interest-game/.
- HUMANMETRICS, a series of questions based on Briggs-Myers's and Jung's typological approach to personality assessment: http://www.humanmetrics.com/personality
- O*NET PROFILER , developed through the US Department of Labor and sponsored by the Employment and Training Administration, helps the user identify their interests and how they relate to the working world: https://www.mynextmove.org/explore/ip
- THE VALUES TEST – This assessment tool can help students learn what is important to them in a job or career by helping identify underlying work needs and motivations. Free at: https://www.myplan.com/assess/values.php

[4] The inclusion of these tools does not constitute an explicit endorsement of them. These references and links are included so that faculty can make comparisons and appropriate recommendations for students in need of direction.

- VT CAREER EXPLORATION TOOLS: For more self-assessment for career exploration tools, visit the Career and Professional Development Office on your campus, search for tools through other universities, or explore the collection at Virginia Tech: https://career.vt.edu/exploring/self-assessment.html

How to cite this resource: No Author. 2021. "Supplemental Internship Resource: Self-Assessment Questions and Tools," in *Political Science Internships: Towards Best Practices* eds. Renée B. Van Vechten, Bobbi Gentry, and John C. Berg. Washington, DC: American Political Science Association.

13.1 DC Internship Programs Serving Minority Students

DC Internship Programs Serving Minority Students*

By Michelle L. Chin
Archer Center
The University of Texas at Dallas

A number of advocacy organizations host internship programs designed specifically to increase the participation of underrepresented populations in the policy process. Table 1 alphabetically catalogs some of the more well known programs. Table 2 compares data compiled by the nonprofit organization, Pay Our Interns, about the stipends paid by five of these organizations.

Table 1. Internship Programs for Underrepresented Populations

AAPD (American Association of People with Disabilities) Summer Internship Program
AIPAC - Diamond Summer Internship Program
American Jewish Committee
APIA Vote
Arab-American Business & Professional Association - Internship Placement Program
Asian Americans Advancing Justice (AAJC)
Asian Pacific American Institute for Congressional Studies (APAICS)
CAIR (Council on American-Islamic Relations)
CCAI (Congressional Coalition on Adoption Institute) -Foster Youth Intern Program
CHCI (Congressional Hispanic Caucus Institute)
College to Congress (C2C)
Conference on Asian Pacific American Leadership (CAPAL)
Congressional Black Caucus Foundation
Congressional Hispanic Leadership Institute - Global Leaders Program
HACU (Hispanic Association of Colleges and Universities)
International Leadership Foundation
Islamic Scholarship Fund - Congressional Policy Internship
Japanese American Citizens League (JACL)
Muslim Public Affairs Council (MPAC) - Congressional Leadership Development Program
Organization of Chinese Americans (OCA) - Asian Pacific Advocates
Public Policy and International Affairs Program (PPIA)
Running Start – Congressional Fellowship
SALDEF (Sikh American Legal Defense and Education Fund)
Southeast Asia Resource Action Center (SEARAC)
The Washington Leadership Program
Udall Foundation - Native American Congressional Internship
US-Asia Institute - IMPACT: Filipino-American National Internship Program
US-Asia Institute - Thai American National Internship Program

Table 2. Stipend Amounts of External Internship Programs

Internship Program	Stipend Amount
Asian Pacific American Institute for Congressional Studies (APAICS)	$2,500
Congressional Black Caucus Foundation (CBCF)	$3,000
Congressional Hispanic Caucus Institute (CHCI) Summer	$3,125
Congressional Hispanic Caucus Institute (CHCI) Fall and Spring	$3,750
Congressional Hispanic Leadership Institute	$2,000

Source: Table 9 in James R. Jones, Tiffany Win, Carlos Mark Vera. 2021. "Who Congress Pays: An Analysis of Lawmakers' Use of Intern Allowances in the 116th Congress," accessed April 30, 2021, https://payourinterns.org/wp-content/uploads/2021/03/Pay-Our-Interns-Who-Congress-Pays.pdf.

*Created July 1, 2021

How to cite this resource: Chin, Michelle. 2021. "Supplemental Internship Resource: DC Internship Programs Serving Minority Students," in *Political Science Internships: Towards Best Practices* eds. Renée B. Van Vechten, Bobbi Gentry, and John C. Berg. Washington, DC: American Political Science Association.

13.2 Comparison of Four Academically Affiliated Programs (2021)

Comparison of Four Academically Affiliated Programs (2021)

By Michelle L. Chin
Archer Center
The University of Texas at Dallas

Comparison of Four Academically Affiliated Programs (2021)

	Washington Semester Program (WSP)	The Fund for American Studies (TFAS)	The Washington Center (TWC)	The Washington Internship Institute (WII)
Website	https://www.american.edu/spexs/washingtonsemester/	https://www.dcinternships.org/	https://twc.edu/	http://wiidc.org/
Academic Home	American University	George Mason University	Elon University	Belmont University
Term	Fall/Spring: 15 weeks Summer: 8 weeks	Fall/Spring: 15 weeks Summer: 8 weeks	Fall/Spring: 9 weeks Summer: 9 weeks	Fall/Spring: 15 weeks Summer: 10 weeks
Eligibility	For Fall/Spring programs: 2.5 minimum college GPA At least 36 earned university credits (or home school equivalent). Dual enrollment credits count, but AP/IB credits do not. For Summer programs: All of the above and must be an actively enrolled student in good standing at an accredited 2- or 4-year institution of higher education; or an actively enrolled student in good standing at an accredited graduate-level program; or a graduate of an accredited undergraduate institution in the past academic year. In addition, the candidate must not require visa support from AU to study in the US.[1]	18 years or older High school graduate Must have completed at least one semester of undergraduate study at an accredited college or university. No minimum GPA required, but "applicants with a GPA of 3.0 or higher, relevant professional and volunteer experience, and well-written essays are given the highest scores." "We are seeking well-rounded students who demonstrate ambition, strong academic performance, leadership ability, maturity, time management skills as well as campus and community involvement."[2]	18 years or older Enrolled as an undergraduate student at an accredited college or university. Be a sophomore or above while participating in the program and have completed at least two semesters on campus by the start of our program. Recent college graduates and graduate students considered on case-by-case basis. Minimum 2.75 GPA. Must receive academic credit from home campus for participation in the program. Home campus liaison (or a faculty sponsor if there is no TWC campus liaison) must approve the application. *Home institution may have additional eligibility requirements[3]	Must be a sophomore or above at an accredited college or university when in DC; or have graduated with a bachelor's degree within a year before starting the program. Minimum 2.75 GPA, with special consideration if the GPA is lower. Prior consultation with faculty adviser, Washington Internship Institute campus liaison

[1] American University Washington Semester Program, "Domestic Student Admissions," accessed June 20, 2021, https://www.american.edu/spexs/washingtonsemester/us-student-admissions.cfm.
[2] The Fund for American Studies, "Admissions," accessed June 20, 2021, https://www.dcinternships.org/admissions/.
[3] The Washington Center, "Eligibility," accessed June 21, 2021, https://twc.edu/programs/academic-internship-program.

	Washington Semester Program (WSP)	The Fund for American Studies (TFAS)	The Washington Center (TWC)	The Washington Internship Institute (WII)
Enrollment	Students enrolled as non-degree seeking students at AU, with full student privileges including access to libraries, campus facilities and events, and student services.	Students enrolled as non-degree seeking students at GMU, with full student privileges including access to libraries, campus facilities, and student services.	In general, students retain their home campus enrollment status and their TWC experience is treated as a study away program.	In general, students retain their home campus enrollment status, and their WII experience is treated as a study away program.
Course Credit	Course credit is offered by American University and students receive an AU transcript at the end of the term.	Course credit is offered by George Mason University and students receive a GMU transcript at the end of the term.	Credit for courses is provided by Elon University. Specific university partner agreements will also articulate the course equivalencies and credit transfers.	Students can take a full load (up to 15 credits during fall/spring) through a combination of the WII internship and core courses, and other online classes. The course equivalencies and credit transfers will depend on the university partner agreements. In the summer only, course credit is offered through Belmont University.
Curriculum	Classes are virtual or in-person on campus at AU. Fall/Spring • Internship course (4 credits) • WSP Seminar (4 credits) – pick one of following: *Political Transitions and Policy Implications *Managing the Pandemic in Globalized Societies *Criminal Legal System: Roots of Mass Incarceration and Racial Disparity *National Conversations in Times of Crisis • AU Elective (3 credits) – choose from the catalog Summer • WSP Seminar (3 credits) • May take additional WSP Seminars listed in summer catalog.	Classes held at the GMU Arlington campus (accessible by metro). In the Fall/Spring, students take 3 classes: Internship Seminar (6 credits), International Economic Policy (3 credits), and a 3-credit government class, either The American Presidency (Fall) or American Political Thought (Spring). In the Summer, students are required to take one of three economics courses (3 credits each): Economics for the Citizen, Economic Problems and Public Policies, and Economies in Transition. An optional weeklong Economics Boot Camp is offered during the first week of the program to help students who have not taken any economics classes before. Students can also add one of the following 3-credit electives: US Foreign Policy, American Political Thought, Internship Seminar – Public Policy & International Affairs, Internship Seminar – Politics & the Press.	Classes held at TWC. Students take one academic course each week in addition to career readiness workshops. TWC offers courses on various topics depending on interest indicated by the students and university partners. Recent topics include: American History American Politics & Public Policy Business & Administration Communication International Affairs Law & Criminal Justice Media & Communications Research	Classes are offered in-person at the WII office. These are scheduled during the day; there are no night or weekend classes. The students are expected to intern 4 days a week. WII requires students to take an Internship Seminar and a Core Course. Additional classes may be customized at the request of the university partner.

	Washington Semester Program (WSP)	**The Fund for American Studies (TFAS)**	**The Washington Center (TWC)**	**The Washington Internship Institute (WII)**
Program costs (As of July 1, 2021)	Program Fees (tuition) Total program cost varies depending on the credits, and the length of the term. 2021-22 tuition rates for non-degree students range from $1,684 (for course levels 100-400) to $1,812 (for course levels 500 and above) per credit. Summer program: $3,800 (3 credits) About $400 in additional fees to cover Metro university pass (U-Pass), technology, health and recreation centers, and other student activities. Housing Fees • Off campus furnished apartments (provided by TurnKey): $5500 (Fall/Spring) • On campus (variable rates) - Summer housing ($3080-$3920) - Meal plan required ($800+) Application Fees – none listed	Program Fees (includes housing) Fall/Spring: $13,495 (12 credits) Summer (3 credits): $7,950 Summer (6 credits): $9,150 Application Fees $25 non-refundable	Program Fees Fall/Spring: $9,415 Summer: $7,100 Housing Fees Fall/Spring: $6,570 Summer: $4,990 Application Fees $60 $125 – only for students enrolled in institutions outside the US	Program Fees Fall/Spring: $7,400 Summer: $5,700 Housing Fees Fall/Spring (15 weeks): $5300 Summer (10 weeks): $4200 Application Fees $50 non-refundable $150 for students outside the US
Housing	WSP offers off-campus housing in furnished apartments managed by TurnKey ($5500), or on-campus AU housing (summer only). Students who choose to live on-campus *must* purchase a meal plan. Students are *not* required to live in WSP housing whether on- or off-campus.	Fall/Spring term housing provided by WISH on Capitol Hill. Roommates are matched by TFAS. 2 persons per bedroom. Summer housing is at the George Washington University campus in Foggy Bottom. Students are required to live in TFAS housing.	TWC provides furnished housing in their Residential and Academic Center located in the Noma section of Washington, DC. See https://twc.edu/right-home-dc. Students are *not* required to live in TWC housing.	WII manages metro-accessible, furnished, apartment-style housing in Crystal City, VA. Students are *not* required to live in WII housing.
Internships	WSP maintains a database of internships. Students are responsible for finding their own internship but will have assistance from WSP staff as needed.	TFAS assigns each student their own internship coordinator who works to help place the student. TFAS guarantees an internship placement (see https://www.dcinternships.org/internships/)	TWC has partnership agreements with internship employers and maintains an updated database of internship opportunities. TWC staff work with students to prepare their internship application materials and to facilitate placements.	WII advisors help guide students through the internship search process and remain with their assigned students throughout the student's residency. Staff hold office hours before and after class. A faculty member meets weekly with students in the internship class.

	Washington Semester Program (WSP)	The Fund for American Studies (TFAS)	The Washington Center (TWC)	The Washington Internship Institute (WII)
University Partners	Memorandum of Agreement and Supplemental Materials are negotiated between American University and the university partner. The agreement is typically for 5 years and sets guidelines for credit transfer, billing, and application/admissions protocols. There is no cost to the university partner for entering into the agreement.	TFAS is flexible with university partnerships (informal partnerships, formal partnerships that have a memorandum of understanding), working with each partner on a case-by-case basis. Universities interested in partnering with TFAS may reach out to the TFAS Admissions Department at admissions@TFAS.org. In general, faculty and advisors are invited to nominate students, who then receive priority consideration in the admissions process.	TWC works with universities to create specific partnership agreements that articulate curriculum expectations, course equivalencies and transfers, program and housing fees, and billing procedures. There is no financial cost to the institution for enacting the agreement, and the duration of the agreement can vary. The agreements typically do not require the partner to enroll a minimum number of students.	The agreement designates a campus representative, articulates the application process, course equivalencies and credit transfers, and billing procedures. WII is also willing to customize classes to suit the partner's interests. The partnership agreement is available online (see http://wiidc.org/universities). There is no partnership fee and no requirement for a minimum number of students to be enrolled.

How to cite this resource: Chin, Michelle. 2021. "Supplemental Internship Resource: Comparison of Four Academically Affiliated Programs (2021)," in *Political Science Internships: Towards Best Practices* eds. Renée B. Van Vechten, Bobbi Gentry, and John C. Berg. Washington, DC: American Political Science Association.

13.3 The DC Internship Search: Many Types of Placements

The DC Internship Search: Many Types of Placements

By Michelle L. Chin
Archer Center
The University of Texas at Dallas

In this resource[1] students and faculty will find internship search tips and a review of various types of internship sites in Washington, DC that have established internship programs or tend to hire undergraduate students. Written mainly for students as a practical guide, this list includes programs designed to increase participation of underrepresented populations, nonprofit organizations, lobbying firms and law firms, think tanks, and government organizations. Government options cover state, federal and international organizations.

Internship Search Tips
Although you can Google "internships DC" and find a list of random internship opportunities, there are a couple of reliable search engines that can help target your search. **Chegg Internships** (https://www.internships.com) provides a comprehensive internship search engine and publishes relevant articles, such as "Getting a Summer Internship Guide" (https://www.internships.com/career-advice/basics/how-to-find-internships). **Daybook.com** is another source for DC internships. Although much of their content is hidden behind paywalls, there are often interesting internships to discover. On its site, search "internships" in "Washington, DC".

DC Internship Programs Serving Minority Students
A number of advocacy organizations host internship programs designed to increase the participation of underrepresented populations in the policy process. Table 1 provides a list of some of the more well-known programs.

[1] Document created July 1, 2021

Table 1. Internship Programs for Underrepresented Populations

AAPD (American Association of People with Disabilities) Summer Internship Program
AIPAC - Diamond Summer Internship Program
American Jewish Committee
APIA Vote
Arab-American Business & Professional Association - Internship Placement Program
Asian Americans Advancing Justice (AAJC)
Asian Pacific American Institute for Congressional Studies (APAICS)
CAIR (Council on American-Islamic Relations)
CCAI (Congressional Coalition on Adoption Institute) -Foster Youth Intern Program
CHCI (Congressional Hispanic Caucus Institute)
College to Congress (C2C)
Conference on Asian Pacific American Leadership (CAPAL)
Congressional Black Caucus Foundation
Congressional Hispanic Leadership Institute - Global Leaders Program
HACU (Hispanic Association of Colleges and Universities)
International Leadership Foundation
Islamic Scholarship Fund - Congressional Policy Internship
Japanese American Citizens League (JACL)
Muslim Public Affairs Council (MPAC) - Congressional Leadership Development Program
Organization of Chinese Americans (OCA) - Asian Pacific Advocates
Public Policy and International Affairs Program (PPIA)
Running Start – Congressional Fellowship
SALDEF (Sikh American Legal Defense and Education Fund)
Southeast Asia Resource Action Center (SEARAC)
The Washington Leadership Program
Udall Foundation - Native American Congressional Internship
US-Asia Institute - IMPACT: Filipino-American National Internship Program
US-Asia Institute - Thai American National Internship Program

US Government

Federal Agencies

In 2010, President Obama issued an executive order creating the Pathways Programs, which are three programs designed to improve the recruitment and hiring of students, recent graduates and persons with advanced degrees.[2] The Internship Program provides high school and college students with paid internships in federal agencies. The Recent Graduates Program is for individuals who have completed a degree within the past two years. The Presidential Management Fellows (PMF) Program is for individuals who have completed a graduate or

[2] Office of Personnel Management. "Policy, Data, Oversight," accessed June 19, 2021, https://www.opm.gov/policy-data-oversight/hiring-information/students-recent-graduates/#url=Overview.

professional degree within the past two years. For more information about applying for these programs, see https://www.usajobs.gov/Help/working-in-government/unique-hiring-paths/students/. US government internships typically require a security clearance prior to the internship start date and are limited to US citizens. Some internships may be paid, while other internships are unpaid. Within each agency there are formal internship programs, with details reported on USAJOBS.gov. Agencies may also offer additional student volunteer opportunities, which can be arranged through contacts within the agency. For example, a former Archer Fellow was recently hired by the Consumer Financial Protection Board (CFPB) and recommended that his boss reach out to the Archer Center for interns. Thanks to this connection, the CFPB now routinely hires multiple Archer Fellows as interns each semester.

White House
The White House Intern Program (WHIP) hires undergraduate and graduate interns to work in a variety of offices within the Executive Office of the President. The program is often suspended when there is a transition in power. In addition, because of the sensitive nature of the internship, students should not be surprised if their social media accounts are scrutinized as part of the hiring/vetting process. The Executive Office of the President includes offices such as the Office of Science and Technology Policy (OSTP) or Office National Drug Control Policy (ONDCP) that focus on less polarizing topics, which can make it easier for an individual who disagrees with the incumbent president to feel comfortable interning during the incumbent's term. General information is available here: https://www.whitehouse.gov/get-involved/.

Supreme Court
The Supreme Court Internship Program is over 40 years old and provides undergraduate and graduate interns an opportunity to learn about the role, functions and history of the Court. These internships are unpaid and limited to US citizens. The internships are in four offices: Office of the Counselor to the Chief Justice, Office of the Curator, Public Information Office, and Office of the Clerk. Details are available here: https://www.supremecourt.gov/jobs/internship/internshipprogram.aspx. Note that law students are not eligible to apply for these internships. Presumably this is because the interns do not work with any Justices on cases before the Court.

Congress
There are 535 members of Congress in the US House of Representatives and US Senate. This means there are 535 different internship program coordinators (usually recent college graduates and recent interns!) to contact for jobs. Contact the individual member to inquire about internship options. In addition, the congressional committees also offer internships. The Senate Employment Office publishes a regular list of internship opportunities (see https://www.senate.gov/employment/po/internships.htm). Internship information in the House of Representatives can be found here: https://diversity.house.gov/employment/interns. Members of the House of Representatives have an annual allowance of $25,000 from the House Paid Internship Program to cover compensation for interns, and members of the Senate receive $50,000. These funds can be used to pay interns who work in district offices as well as those who work in DC. However, interns paid with these funds "must be part of a demonstrated education

program and may not be employed by the Member for more than 120 calendar days."[3] Senators are also able to use some funds from their Official Personnel and Office Expense Account to pay intern salaries.[4] Congress members are not obligated to use those funds to pay their interns however.

Library of Congress
The Library of Congress has multiple opportunities for internships and fellowships for undergraduate and graduate students. Most of these are unpaid internships and do not carry a US citizenship requirement. For details, see https://www.loc.gov/internships-and-fellowships/.

State Organizations
Some states have an office of state-federal relations in DC. These are usually connected to the governor's office and may have internship opportunities. The **National Governors Association (NGA)** hosts a variety of interns (see https://www.nga.org/about/careers/). For information about internships with the **Republican Governors Association (RGA)** see https://www.rga.org/internships/. To apply for an internship with the **Democratic Governors Association (DGA),**[5] send a resume and cover letter to internships@dga.net; in the subject line write: "Internship Application, [Your Name]".

International Organizations
DC is also home to many international organizations, such as the **European Parliament Liaison Office in Washington, DC** (https://www.europarl.europa.eu/unitedstates/en/internships) or the **Organization of American States (OAS)** (http://www.oas.org/en/saf/dhr/internships/) that offer internships. At **The World Bank ("Bank"),** internships are mostly for graduate students (see https://www.worldbank.org/en/about/careers/programs-and-internships/internship). However, there are cases where specific programs at the Bank may obtain permission to hire a highly motived and exceptionally talented undergraduate. This information is often generated within personal or professional networks where an intern program director is able to match their talent pool to the needs of the Bank. The **International Monetary Fund (IMF)** internship programs are paid, and open to graduate students and international students (see https://www.imf.org/en/About/Recruitment/working-at-the-imf/fund-internship-program). The **United Nations (UN) Foundation** (https://unfoundation.org/careers/internship-opportunities/) and **United Nations Information Center (UNIC) Washington** (https://unicwash.org/internships/) both have a variety of unpaid internship opportunities for undergraduates and recent graduates. The **Georgetown University School of Foreign Service Graduate Career Center** publishes a helpful list of international organizations with internships in DC: https://sfsgcc.georgetown.edu/services/online-resources/international-organizations/.

---

[3] U.S. House of Representatives Committee on House Administration, "House Paid Internship Program," accessed June 19, 2021, https://cha.house.gov/member-services/house-paid-internship-program. Brudnick, Ida. 2020. "Members' Representational Allowance: History and Usage." Congressional Research Service, updated August 13, accessed June 19, 2021, https://crsreports.congress.gov/product/pdf/R/R40962.

[4] Brudnick, Ida. 2020. "Senators' Official Personnel and Office Expense Account (SOPOEA): History and Usage." Congressional Research Service, updated November 5, accessed June 19, 2021, https://crsreports.congress.gov/product/pdf/R/R44399.

[5] Democratic Governors Association. Accessed June 19, 2021, https://democraticgovernors.org.

Non-Profit Organizations

Within the DC metropolitan region, there are more than 14,000 non-profit organizations, including 900 international development and relief organizations. Many of these organizations offer internships during the summer and/or academic year. CauseIQ.Com provides a comprehensive list of non-profit organizations across the United States, including detailed information about each nonprofit organization such as financial reports and organizational structure. To customize reports and/or research more than five organizations, you will have to set up a free account with CauseIQ. Table 2 lists the top ten most popular nonprofit organizations operating in the DC area.

Table 2. CauseIQ.Com's Top 10 Most Popular Washington DC Area Nonprofit Organizations[6]

The Seed Foundation
Recreation Vehicle Industry Association
National Association of Manufacturers
CTIA – The Wireless Association
Freedom Forum
International Foodservice Distributors Association (IFDA)
National Electrical Manufacturers Association (NEMA)
International Masonry Training and Education Foundation IIMTEF)
American Physical Therapy Association (APTA)
Helicopter Association International (HAI)

Media/communications

While New York may be the capital for television news, it is Washington, DC where daily headline news is often generated and reported. Most major domestic and international news organizations have news bureaus in DC. Check each network's website for internship information. Table 3 provides a partial list of the public, private and non-profit news media and communications organizations that offer DC internships.[7]

Another useful resource is the *Washington Business Journal*, which publishes lists of the largest media and communications organizations in the Greater Washington, DC area (see https://www.bizjournals.com/washington/datacenter/lists/media-and-communications). For example, students interested in marketing/public relations careers might find it useful to see that

[6] "Directory of nonprofits in DC," CauseIQ.com, accessed June 18, 2021, https://www.causeiq.com/directory/washington-arlington-alexandria-dc-va-md-wv-metro/

[7] In 2011, the Federal Communications Commission issued a report, *The Information Needs of Communities: The Changing Media Landscape in a Broadband Age* (https://www.fcc.gov/sites/default/files/the-information-needs-of-communities-report-july-2011.pdf) highlighting the impact of technology on coverage of local and community news. In 2013, the Council on Foundations published a follow-up report, *The IRS and Nonprofit Media: Toward Creating a More Informed Public*, which recommended that the IRS modernize its approach to granting tax-exempt status to "organizations seeking to produce local news and disseminate information in the public interest" (p. 2, https://www.cof.org/sites/default/files/documents/files/Nonprofit-Media-Full-Report-03042013.pdf). These types of reports can yield important clues to internship opportunities by identifying relevant stakeholders and policy debates where interns could perform useful work.

of the top five advertising agencies in the DC area, only one is actually located in Washington, DC.[8]

Table 3. Media & Communications Internships

Broadcasters (tv, streaming/digital, radio) **ABC News** – https://jobs.disneycareers.com **CBS News** –https://viacomcbs.careers (Search for "CBS News Internships") **CNN** – https://warnermediacareers.com/global/en **CSPAN** - https://cspan.applicantpool.com/jobs/ **FOX News** - https://foxcareers.com/students **NBC News** –https://www.nbcunicareers.com/internships (For news, select the Digital Media & Streaming window) **NPR** – https://www.npr.org/about-npr/181881227/internships-at-npr/ **PBS** –https://www.pbs.org/about/careers/internships/
Periodicals (print, digital) **Axios** – News apprentice program (12 months) - https://boards.greenhouse.io/axios/jobs/3068565 **National Geographic** - https://www.nationalgeographic.org/careers/internships/ **Politico** - https://www.politico.com/employment **Roll Call** - https://www.vault.com/internship-program/government/roll-call/internship-opportunities **The Hill** - https://thehill.com/contact/internships **The New York Times** - https://www.nytco.com/careers/entry-level/ **USA Today** - https://usatodaynetworkcareers.com/internships/ **Wall Street Journal** - https://wsj.jobs **Washington Post** – summer internship (https://intern.washpost.com)

[8] Proctor, Carolyn M. 2020. "Largest Advertising Agencies in Greater DC: Ranked by 2019 revenue," *Washington Business Journal*. July 31, revised August 6, accessed May 7, 2021, https://www.bizjournals.com/washington/subscriber-only/2020/07/31/largest-advertising-agencies-in-greater.html.

Media Companies **Atlantic Media** - https://www.atlanticmedia.com/careers/ **Bloomberg** - https://www.bloomberg.com/company/careers/early-career/ **Discovery Communications** - https://corporate.discovery.com/careers/internships/ **Disney** - https://jobs.disneycareers.com **FiscalNote** - https://careers.fiscalnote.com/about/ **Gallup Organization** - https://www.gallup.com/careers/ **NBC Universal** –https://www.nbcunicareers.com/internships **Sinclair Broadcast Group** - https://sbgi.net/careers/ **The Economist Group** - https://economistgroupcareers.com/internships/ **Viacom** - https://viacomcbs.careers **Warner Media** - https://warnermediacareers.com/global/en
Trade Associations **CTIA (The Wireless Association)** - https://careers.ctia.org **Motion Picture Association (MPA)** - https://www.motionpictures.org/who-we-are/#careers **MDDC Press Association** (Maryland, DC Press) - https://mddcpress.com/mddc-reese-cleghorn-summer-internship-program/ **National Association of Broadcasters (NAB)** - https://www.nab.org/careers/default.asp **National Association of Black Journalists (NABJ)** - https://www.nabj.org/page/internships **National Press Club** - https://www.press.org/students **NCTA (The Internet & Television Association)** - https://www.ncta.com/careers **News Media Alliance** - https://www.newsmediaalliance.org/about-us/contact-us/ **RTDNA (Radio Television Digital News Association)** - https://www.rtdna.org/content/about_rtdna
Foundations & Non-Profits **American Press Institute (API)** - https://www.americanpressinstitute.org/publications/api-updates/apply-for-our-summer-internship-in-news-analytics/ **Council on Foundations** - https://www.cof.org/about/work-council **Philanthropy Roundtable** - https://www.philanthropyroundtable.org/home/about/Employment **Pulitzer Center** - https://pulitzercenter.org/about/employment-opportunities **Scripps Howard Foundation** - http://www.shfwire.com/semester-washington-internships-undergraduate-students/

Lobbying Shops (Law firms, lobbying groups)
Lobbying shops come in all sizes. Some are part of a larger law firm or consulting group, while others are smaller firms or one-person operations that focus on specific policy issues or clientele.[9] These groups or practices are closely associated with these terms: government relations, government affairs, regulation, federal relations, public affairs, public policy. These lobbyists assist clients in navigating the legislative process in Congress, regulatory and oversight process at federal agencies, and the political and policy process in the executive branch (White House) and with Congress. The lobbyists may be licensed attorneys or non-lawyers with specific expertise in government service or policymaking. Often these are former members of Congress or their staffers, former members of the executive branch or other former government employees. Lobbyists who are not lawyers but who are employed by a law firm will often be listed with the designation "of counsel" to distinguish them from their colleagues who are licensed attorneys.

Law firms
Law firms that also lobby may offer policy internships that are open to undergraduate or graduate students. These internships are different from the summer legal associate programs which are only available to law students. For example, **Holland & Knight's Public Policy & Regulation Group** hosts an internship program for undergraduates (see https://www.hklaw.com/en/general-pages/public-policy-and-regulations-internship); but this opportunity is not listed on the firm's "Careers" page (https://www.hklaw.com/en/careers). Therefore, be sure to inquire with a law firm's lobbying or government advocacy department about internship opportunities that may not be listed as part of the firm's student programs. This is also where alumni connections can be extremely beneficial in creating internship opportunities and long-lasting relationships between a university and a firm.

The Center for Responsive Politics uses the mandatory quarterly reports filed by registered lobbyists with the House of Representatives and the Senate to compile useful reports of the law firms and lobbyists doing business in DC (see OpenSecrets.org). Between 2016-2020, over $73 million was spent on lobbying by lawyers and law firms according to the Center for Responsive Politics.[10] The top 19 law firms in turn spent over $44 million in campaign contributions to candidates and parties.[11] This list can help you identify firms that are engaged in politics and policymaking, which makes it easier to identify relevant alumni connections to your institution. These individuals are good candidates to donate to student scholarships, to host or help find internship placements, and to mentor your students. These firms also have meeting space that

---

[9] Center for Responsive Politics, "Top Lobbying Firms," accessed June 19, 2021, https://www.opensecrets.org/federal-lobbying/top-lobbying-firms.

[10] The total calculated from the following data: 2016 ($14.98 million, https://www.opensecrets.org/federal-lobbying/industries/summary?cycle=2016&id=K01), 2017 ($16.42 million, https://www.opensecrets.org/federal-lobbying/industries/summary?cycle=2017&id=K01), 2018 ($15.51 million, https://www.opensecrets.org/federal-lobbying/industries/summary?cycle=2018&id=K01), 2019 ($12.91 million, https://www.opensecrets.org/federal-lobbying/industries/summary?cycle=2019&id=K01), 2020 ($13.36 million, https://www.opensecrets.org/federal-lobbying/industries/summary?cycle=2020&id=K01).

[11] Source: "Lawyers & Lobbyists: Top Contributors to Federal Candidates, Parties, and Outside Groups," https://www.opensecrets.org/industries/contrib.php?cycle=2020&ind=K (Accessed 5/11/2021). The list reports the top 20 contributors, but I have omitted the American Association for Justice (#5) since it is not a law firm.

they may be willing to let you use for classes, meetings or social events. For example, the 11-story DC headquarters for the Arnold & Porter Kay Scholer law firm includes some impressive rooftop views of downtown DC, a perfect setting for an alumni reception or meeting with guest speakers.[12]

Table 4. Top DC Law Firms & Total Contributions in 2020

List of Top 19 DC Law Firms[13]	Total Contributions (2020)
1. Kirkland & Ellis	$4,555,042
2. Paul, Weiss et al	$4,019,876
3. Akin, Gump et al	$3,221,795
4. Latham & Watkins	$2,875,184
5. Covington & Burling	$2,640,663
6. Sullivan & Cromwell	$2,633,104
7. Morgan & Morgan	$2,518,604
8. WilmerHale LLP	$2,339,933
9. Sidley Austin LLP	$2,147,205
10. DLA Piper	$1,914,284
11. Brownstein, Hyatt et al	$1,914,137
12. Boyden Gray & Assoc	$1,807,020
13. Greenberg Traurig LLP	$1,752,449
14. Morgan Lewis LLP	$1,685,068
15. Gibson, Dunn & Crutcher	$1,663,654
16. Arnold & Porter Kay Scholer	$1,658,258
17. Skadden, Arps et al	$1,642,797
18. K&L Gates	$1,588,441
19. Holland & Knight	$1,574,504

Lobbying Firms

In Washington, there are many lobbying firms that focus on specific policy issues or industries. Often, these firms are established by former members of Congress, congressional staff, or White House officials. The Center for Responsive Politics includes the following firms in their list of top lobbying firms measured by total income (2020, 2021). Some institutions of higher education hire lobbying firms to represent their interests with federal policymakers, which may generate ready-made internship opportunities. Table 5 provides a list of the top 20 lobbying firms in DC in 2021.

---

[12] HYL Architecture, which designed the office building, provides a description and photos on their website, "Office Snapshots," accessed June 19, 2021, https://officesnapshots.com/2020/08/05/arnold-porter-offices-washington-dc/.

[13] Center for Responsive Politics, "Lawyers & Lobbyists: Top Contributors to Federal Candidates, Parties, and Outside Groups," accessed May 11, 2021, https://www.opensecrets.org/industries/contrib.php?cycle=2020&ind=K.

Table 5. Top 20 Lobbying Firms for 2021[14]

Akin, Gump et al
Brownstein, Hyatt et al
BGR Group
Cornerstone Government Affairs
Holland & Knight
Invariant LLC
Covington & Burling
Squire Patton Boggs
Peck Madigan Jones
Forbes Tate Partners
Mehlman, Castagnetti et al
Capitol Counsel
Crossroads Strategies
K&L Gates
Ballard Partners
Cassidy & Assoc
Thorn Run Partners
Sonoran Policy Group
Van Scoyoc Assoc
Subject Matter

Corporate interests – private sector
Corporate interests, business and industry may be represented by in-house lobbyists and/or by contract lobbyists employed by a law firm or lobbying firm. These companies may have established internship programs or may be open to creating an internship opportunity with the prospect of developing a long-standing internship arrangement with a particular school or program. Reach out to the government relations division or office within the company to inquire about DC internships that focus on policy. Don't be shy about using personal ties (such as alumni connections) to initiate conversations about internship opportunities in these organizations!

Using the Center for Responsive Politics Data to Find an Internship
The Center for Responsive Politics classifies organizations that contribute to federal campaigns according to industry and interest group, making this a great place to start the hunt for a corporate internship in sectors such as health care, finance, communication/electronics, energy & natural resources, defense, agribusiness, construction, transportation/aviation (see https://www.opensecrets.org/federal-lobbying/ranked-sectors). Use this list to guide your search for specific companies and to identify individuals affiliated with that company who might be willing to hire interns.

Table 6 illustrates the way the information is arranged. To find a list of companies doing business in the health sector, select one of the industries listed. In this table, you can see there are five industries listed. In the Pharmaceuticals/Health Products industry there are 371 companies

[14] Center for Responsive Politics, "Top Lobbying Firms," accessed June 19, 2021, https://www.opensecrets.org/federal-lobbying/top-lobbying-firms.

or organizations listed. Since this list provides information about the companies that made campaign contributions in 2021, it is reasonable to assume they may have internship opportunities in DC. These internships could be focused on policy or politics, for example by working with lobbyists on legislative strategy or with the managers of a company's political action committee (PAC) to track and evaluate the PAC contributions.

Table 6. Identifying Companies and Individual Lobbyists Who May Hire Interns

Ranked Sectors[15]	Industries[16]	Clients[17]	Lobbyists[18]
Health	***Pharmaceuticals/ Health Products***	***Pharmaceutical Research & Manufacturers of America*** Pfizer Inc. Roche Holdings Merck & Co AbbVie Inc. Biotechnology Innovation Organization Amgen Inc. Gilead Sciences Johnson & Johnson Pharmaceutical Care Management Association Novartis AG Horizon Therapeutics Eli Lilly & Co. GlaxoSmithKline Teva Pharmaceutical Industries Bayer AG Biogen Sanofi CH Boehringer Sohn Medtronic Inc. Association for Accessible Medicines AstraZeneca PLC Abbott Laboratories Alkermes PLC Siemens AG (+346 other organizations)	*165 individual lobbyists have listed* ***Pharmaceutical Research & Manufacturers of America*** *as a client.*
	Health Services/HMOs	255 organizations	
	Hospitals/Nursing Homes	329 organizations	
	Health Professionals	201 organizations	
	Misc Health	93 organizations	

[15] Center for Responsive Politics, "Ranked Sectors," accessed May 11, 2021, https://www.opensecrets.org/federal-lobbying/ranked-sectors.

[16] Center for Responsive Politics, "Sector Profile: Health," accessed May 11, 2021, https://www.opensecrets.org/federal-lobbying/sectors/summary?cycle=2021&id=H.

[17] Center for Responsive Politics, "Industry Profile: Pharmaceuticals/Health Products," accessed May 11, 2021, https://www.opensecrets.org/federal-lobbying/industries/summary?cycle=2021&id=H04.

[18] Center for Responsive Politics, "Client Profile: Pharmaceutical Research & Manufacturers of America," accessed May 11, 2021, https://www.opensecrets.org/federal-lobbying/clients/lobbyists?cycle=2021&id=D000000504.

Think Tanks (Based in DC or with DC offices)

Information is currency in DC. For this reason, think tanks provide valuable research and analysis to help policymakers make informed decisions. These organizations also depend on interns to assist with research. See the *Global To Go Think Tank Index* for updated rankings on more than 6,000 think tanks (https://repository.upenn.edu/think_tanks/), then go to the organization's website to obtain specific internship information. Most of these organizations host formal internship programs, although many are unpaid internships. Nevertheless, there are perks such as meeting notable scholars or decision-makers, contributing to published research, and building a professional network that can lead to graduate school opportunities or jobs. The **American Enterprise Institute (AEI)** offers its interns "Complimentary breakfast and lunch prepared by AEI's own in-house gourmet chef, served in our dining room."[19]

Table 7. Sample List of Washington, DC-based Think Tanks

AEI (American Enterprise Institute)
Aspen Institute
Atlantic Council
Bipartisan Policy Center
Brookings Institution
CAP (Center for American Progress)
Carnegie Endowment for International Peace
CATO Institute
Center on Budget and Policy Priorities (CBPP)
Center for Immigration Studies
Center for New American Security
Competitive Enterprise Institute
Council on Foreign Relations
CSIS (Center for Strategic and International Studies)
Economic Policy Institute
Freedom House
Heritage Foundation
Human Rights Watch
Inter-American Dialogue
Lexington Institute
Mercatus Center at George Mason University
New America Foundation
Stimson Center
Third Way
Urban Institute
Woodrow Wilson International Center for Scholars
Worldwatch Institute

[19] See https://www.aei.org/internships/program-elements/ (Accessed 5/12/21).

How to cite this resource: Chin, Michelle. 2021. "Supplemental Internship Resource: The DC Internship Search: Many Types of Placements," in *Political Science Internships: Towards Best Practices* eds. Renée B. Van Vechten, Bobbi Gentry, and John C. Berg. Washington, DC: American Political Science Association.

13.4 Dressing for Success: Professional Wardrobe

Dressing for Success: Professional Wardrobe

By Michelle L. Chin
Archer Center
The University of Texas at Dallas

Dressing for success in Washington, DC can be challenging for interns who are used to casual dress on campus. Rebecca Gale (2014) offers this tip: "Learn the office dress code…and err on the conservative side of following it."[1] She also constructed a quick guide for what to wear in DC office settings (see table 1), whether the setting is a Congressional office, a lobbying firm, or a nonprofit organization.

Table 1. Professional Working Attire Tips (Gale 2014)

- "Wear a suit the first day of work. Even if it's recess. Or Friday. Or hot outside. Your first day sets the tone of your internship, and a suit shows you're taking it seriously."
- "Wear a suit (or jacket and tie, or blazer/slacks/skirt for ladies) every day Congress is in session."
- "Dress up every day the boss is in town. Most offices have a relaxed dress code when Congress is out of session, but if the boss is there, take the extra time to dress in business clothing."
- "Follow the office's lead. Don't be the first one to wear jeans or break out into casual Friday polo shirts unless you see your co-workers doing the same thing. And by co-workers, I don't mean other interns. Take the cues from the higher-ups in the office."
- "Cover up. Keep the short skirts and deep V-neck shirts at home. If you aren't sure whether it's office appropriate, it probably isn't."
- "Stay away from jeans, sneakers, T-shirts and yoga pants. No matter how casual Fridays get, you're better off in khakis or dress pants than something more comfortable. Wait for the weekends to wear whatever you want. Or wait until your internship is over."

Source: Gale, Rebecca. 2014. "The Quick Guide to 'Best Intern Ever: How to Ace Your Capitol Hill Internship," *Roll Call*, July 16, accessed April 29, 2021, https://www.rollcall.com/2014/07/16/the-quick-guide-to-best-intern-ever-how-to-ace-your-capitol-hill-internship/.

Comfortable shoes: It is important to find shoes that are comfortable (and look professional) for walking long distances on hard surfaces. One young congressional staffer experienced excruciating pain in her shins after about 6 months on the job. The doctor diagnosed her with shin splints, caused by walking on the marble floors in her stylish, but orthopedically deficient shoes.

Blazer, suit jacket, tie: When Congress is in session, the staff dress code is formal, modest (suits, jacket and tie, blazer or cardigan and slacks/skirts, dresses with sleeves), and tends to be gender-conforming. In the Senate Member's Dining room, there is a closet with a selection of sportscoats and ties that are lent to any man who happens to arrive clad in slacks and a shirt. No jacket and tie; no service!

---

[1] Gale, Rebecca. 2014. "The Quick Guide to 'Best Intern Ever: How to Ace Your Capitol Hill Internship," *Roll Call*, July 16, accessed April 29, 2021, https://www.rollcall.com/2014/07/16/the-quick-guide-to-best-intern-ever-how-to-ace-your-capitol-hill-internship/.

Shopping tips

For students on a budget, finding professional clothing that is affordable and comfortable can be challenging. Some suggestions: check the campus career center to see if they have a "career closet" with donated professional clothing. In DC, Suited for Change collects women's clothing which are available to individuals who need assistance in building a professional wardrobe. A similar organization, Sharp Dressed Man, provides similar services in Baltimore. Across the United States, there are similar organizations that can help students in need.

Programs can also work with consultants to advise students about creating a professional wardrobe. For example, Chanmuny Dy, founder of The Stylery (http://thestylery.co), created a short video for the Archer Center at The University of Texas System that gives students helpful tips about maintaining a professional look.

How to cite this resource: Chin, Michelle. 2021. "Supplemental Internship Resource: Dressing for Success: Professional Wardrobe," in *Political Science Internships: Towards Best Practices* eds. Renée B. Van Vechten, Bobbi Gentry, and John C. Berg. Washington, DC: American Political Science Association.

13.5 Living in Washington, DC: Housing, Food, and Transportation (2021)

Living in Washington, DC: Housing, Food, and Transportation (2021)

By Michelle L. Chin
Archer Center
The University of Texas at Dallas

After having landed an internship in Washington, DC, the next task is to decide where to live, and how to budget properly to survive and thrive in what is arguably one of the most expensive, urban areas of the US. In this resource, students will find tips for securing suitable, safe and affordable housing, reliable transportation; and creating a budget (see also the separate resource, "Sample Budget Worksheet").

Housing

DC rents are typically higher than what most college students are accustomed to paying. Finding safe, affordable and suitable short-term housing can be a challenge for someone who has never traveled to DC. Students can conduct solo searches for housing by looking at long-term hotel or short-term rentals/sublets on sites like **AirBnB** (https://www.airbnb.com/), **Craigslist** (https://washingtondc.craigslist.org/d/housing/search/hhh), or **Intern Housing Hub** (https://www.internhousinghub.com/housing/Washington-D.C.). Just use caution and be aware of scams. For example, the properties may be in unsafe areas or may not be habitable. Virginia Tech provides some helpful tips for avoiding such scams (see https://dc.offcampus.vt.edu/avoid-scams-and-fraud). Students who will be living in DC during the summer should also check with local universities about summer housing. **Local universities (American University, Catholic University, Georgetown University, George Mason University, George Washington University, Howard University, University of Maryland, College Park)** also make dorm space available during the summer term. Go to the university website and look for "summer housing" to find information about availability. Just make sure that the location offers convenient transportation options for safe travel to and from the internship. For example, **Catholic University** (http://pryzbyla.catholic.edu/conferences/housing/summer-intern/non-cua-student/rates.html) offers single-occupancy rooms at $42.00 per night per person on a first-come, first served basis. [1]

Alumni connections are another great way to find affordable housing. Recently one woman posted in her local alumni chapter's Facebook group that her home would be available for free to an alum who could take care of the family cat while they were away for the summer. Living with friends, or **family relatives** is another (obvious) way to save on housing costs. Not many students will be as fortunate as Carlos Molina, a young college student from Healdsburg, CA who spent a week interning in the DC office of Representative Don Clausen (R-CA) and living as a guest of the Congressman and his wife in their home![2] Yet generous people remain. In 1989,

---

[1] The price is current as of June 18, 2021. The stay should be a minimum of 30 consecutive nights, and the rooms are subject to a 14.95% DC occupancy tax. Linens are not included, but a linen pack, which includes a pillow, blanket, two top sheets, pillowcase and towels, is available for rent ($60 for the entire stay).

[2] Untitled. 1968. *Healdsburg Tribute, Enterprise and Scimitar*, August 15, accessed June 19, 2021, https://cdnc.ucr.edu/cgi-bin/cdnc?a=d&d=HTES19680815.2.82&e=-------en--20--1--txt-txIN-%252522congressional+internship%252522-------1.

when I was offered an unpaid congressional internship, I worried about having to decline the offer unless I was able to find affordable housing. Knowing of my predicament, a former supervisor offered her spare bedroom and only charged me $100 for the entire 9 week stay. I had a chance to pay it forward in 2014, when my cousin told me her sister-in-law needed a place to stay during her summer internship in DC. The moral of this story: Make the offer or make the ask!

Eating in DC

Eating In

Food, whether at the grocery store or in restaurants, tends to cost more in DC. It is generally cheaper to cook or meal-prep at home. Many DC residents often depend on grocery delivery services such as **Peapod, Amazon Prime, Instacart**. Major grocery providers that are easily accessible to DC residents include **Whole Foods, Giant, Safeway, Walmart, Harris Teeter, Trader Joe's, Aldi, Target.** Popular meal delivery services include UberEats, Grubhub, Doordash, Caviar.

Eating Out

In a 2019 article, "Washington Is the Most Exciting Food City in America," Kate Krader wrote that "the city has a restaurant scene that mirrors its World Series-winning Nationals—a group of underdogs who are fun to watch as they raise their city to championship levels."[3] There is tremendous diversity in the cuisine available in this region at a variety of price points. The *Washingtonian* magazine publishes a list of best budget restaurants in the DC, Maryland and Virginia area (see https://washington.org/visit-dc/affordable-budget-friendly-cheap-dining-in-washington-dc). Budget-conscious interns can also take advantage of happy hour specials, periodic Restaurant Week deals, request lunch portions (and prices), or make a meal out of an affordable appetizer or several side dishes.

The restaurants in the Dirksen Senate Office Building and Longworth House Office Building offer some affordable meal options in addition to the opportunity to see senators and representatives dining casually. The American Grill in the basement hallway between the Hart and Dirksen Senate office buildings has daily breakfast specials that can be stretched to last for two meals. These and other restaurants in the House and Senate office buildings are also great places to hang out to people-watch or network. There is also a café in the Supreme Court where many of the justices are known to eat meals. One group of visiting students were happily surprised when Chief Justice Roberts sat at the next table and visited with them while he ate his lunch.

Receptions and Meetings with Meals

Under non-COVID conditions, it's common for think tanks, advocacy organizations and other groups to host meetings that include some type of refreshment. Look for breakfast briefings to get coffee and breakfast carbs. Lunch briefings will often yield a box sandwich lunch, occasionally a hot buffet or plated meal. Evening receptions will also offer lots of food and

---

[3] Krader, Kate. 2019. "Washington Is the Most Exciting Food City in America," *Bloomberg*, December 17. https://www.bloomberg.com/news/articles/2019-12-17/washington-d-c-not-nyc-or-l-a-is-the-top-food-city-in-america.

beverage options. If you linger towards the end and come prepared with some zip-top bags or food containers, you can leave with the leftovers that would otherwise be trashed. After one reception that APSA hosted for their congressional fellows, I walked away with a box of cheese, crackers, fruits, and raw vegetables that became ingredients for several dishes (pasta, meatballs, soup). One of my students left a reception with a bag of sliced ham. Unfortunately, by the time he had walked the few blocks to his apartment, he had finished snacking on the meat. ("I should have gotten more!" he laughed when he told me the story.)

Transportation

There are many options for getting around Washington, DC. The District Department of Transportation (DDOT) provides a page (https://ddot.dc.gov/page/getting-around-2) with information about all options for local transportation. Migo (https://www.getmigo.com/coverage/us/district-of-columbia/washington-dc/) provides rankings of the best on-demand transportation apps for DC.

WMATA U-Pass (https://www.wmata.com/fares/Student-Programs.cfm/): The Washington Metropolitan Area Transportation Authority (WMATA) created a program to provide university students with affordable public transportation. Universities contract with WMATA to provide their students with a "U Pass" that allows students to travel on the bus or metrorail for $1 a day. The pass expires at the end of the term.

Scooters: DDOT has a list (https://ddot.dc.gov/page/dockless-vehicle-permits-district) of the companies licensed to provide "dockless vehicles" (scooters) in DC.

Bicycles: DC is a bike-friendly city with dedicated bike lanes throughout the city, and Capital Bikeshare that provides access to 500 bicycle stations in the DC metro area. DDOT provides information about bicycle laws and other resources (maps, parking: https://ddot.dc.gov/page/bicycle-program).

Carsharing: For information about companies licensed to provide on-street carsharing in DC see https://ddot.dc.gov/node/480212. Zipcars are available in convenient locations around town, giving students options for driving out of town. For instance, it's possible to rent a Zipcar to go to the Shenandoah Mountains for a weekend trip.

Bringing a car to DC

It can be costly and perhaps inconvenient to bring a car to DC, unless the housing and/or internship are located outside DC. The primary concerns when bringing a personal vehicle to DC are the cost and availability of parking. According to SpotHero.Com, the monthly cost of garage parking ranges from $150-$411 at commercial garages around DC.[4] Street parking in certain areas of DC is limited to 2 hours without a residential permit, but students may be eligible to obtain a Reciprocity Parking Permit (https://dmv.dc.gov/node/1118916). Some congressional offices may offer free parking for interns, but this varies by office.

---

[4] Based on data accessed April 29, 2021.

Gas stations can be difficult to locate in DC. GasBuddy.com provides a list of top 10 lowest gas prices and best gas stations in DC. AAA reports state average gas prices on their website: https://gasprices.aaa.com/state-gas-price-averages/.

Traffic congestion: DC traffic is subject to many challenges such as sudden street closures to accommodate presidential (or other dignitary/VIP) motorcades, accidents, bike lanes, and one-way streets. According to StreetLight Data, a data analytics company I (https://inrix.pdmdev.co/scorecard-city/?city=Washington%20DC&index=89), Washington, DC is the 12th most congested city in the U.S. with about 29 hours lost in congestion in 2020. Drive times in DC vary depending on the time of day, so an eight-mile drive without traffic might take 20 minutes, but 45 minutes with traffic. In Northern Virginia, the state has instituted congestion pricing on its toll roads to allow drivers to pay a toll to avoid congested roads.[5]

Budgeting & Finances

According to Expatistan (https://www.expatistan.com/cost-of-living/index/north-america), the cost of living in Washington, DC makes it the 4th most expensive city in the United States behind Mountain View, CA, New York City, and San Francisco. Use the sample budget worksheet in section 13.6 to help plan your income and expenses during your DC internship.

Cost of Living

Students can use a cost of living calculator to compare their existing costs with expected costs in Washington, DC. For example, BestPlaces.Net's calculator (https://www.bestplaces.net/cost-of-living/) includes an estimate of cost differences for food and groceries, and miscellaneous expenditures like restaurant meals, prepared food, dry cleaning, cosmetics, and haircuts.

Sales Tax

Sales taxes in DC range from 6% on tickets to theaters and entertainment venues, to 10.25% on baseball tickets at Nationals Park and events at the Capital One Arena. There is also an 8% tax on soft drinks and a 10% tax on restaurant meals.[6]

---

[5] Schaper, David. 2017. "Are $40 Toll Roads The Future?" *NPR*, December 12, accessed April 30, 2021, https://www.npr.org/2017/12/12/570248568/are-40-toll-roads-the-future.

[6] Office of the Chief Financial Officer. "DC sales and use tax", accessed June 19, 2021, https://cfo.dc.gov/page/tax-rates-and-revenues-sales-and-use-taxes-alcoholic-beverage-taxes-and-tobacco-taxes.

How to cite this resource: Chin, Michelle. 2021. "Supplemental Internship Resource: Living in Washington, DC: Housing, Food, and Transportation (2021)," in *Political Science Internships: Towards Best Practices* eds. Renée B. Van Vechten, Bobbi Gentry, and John C. Berg. Washington, DC: American Political Science Association.

13.6 Budget Worksheet for Internship Away from Home

Budget Worksheet for Internship Away from Home

Program Costs	Amount
program free	
housing fee	

Travel Costs (to and from location)	Amount
flight	

Move-In-Related Costs	Amount
bedding	
towels	
toiletries	
extra luggage fee	
other:	
Total	

Move-out-Related Costs	Amount
shipping items home	
extra luggage fee to bring items home	
other:	
Total	

Resources	Amount
estimated monthly income	
financial aid	
other financial award:	
other financial award:	
allowance from parents	
other income/savings	
other campus/program scholarships	
Total	

Monthly Expenses	Amount
cell phone	
insurance	
car payment	
unexpected expenses/emergency	
health care-related	
other:	
other:	
Total	

Weekly Expenses	Amount
local transportation	
groceries	
other meals (lunches/dinners out)	
entertainment	
laundry	
other:	
other:	
other:	
Total	

Other Miscellaneous Expenses	Amount
class items (books, etc.)	
car and insurance payment	
parking (if you bring a car)	
gas (if you bring a car)	
extra medical expenses	
entertainment travel (weekend trips, etc.)	
Total	

Budget Summary

Total resources:

Total travel costs to and from site:

Total move-in related costs:

Total move-out related costs:

Total remaining budget for monthly and weekly expenses:

How to cite this resource: Chin, Michelle. 2021. "Supplemental Internship Resource: Budget Worksheet for Internship Away from Home," in *Political Science Internships: Towards Best Practices* eds. Renée B. Van Vechten, Bobbi Gentry, and John C. Berg. Washington, DC: American Political Science Association.

14.1 Towson University (TU) Program and Internship Course Requirements

Towson University (TU) Program and Internship Course Requirements

The 45 credits required for the major include fifteen 3-credit courses plus evidence of intermediate competency in a foreign language. Depending on a student's level of proficiency, which is determined by a placement test administered by the Foreign Languages Department, this requirement could amount to additional four courses at most. To fulfill the major's core, students must take four courses from three of the five non-language foundation disciplines. Then, students select 10 upper-level courses to focus on a specific world region (Africa, Asia, Europe, Latin America, or Middle East-North Africa) or an international topic (e.g. international development, international security). Students are also required to complete a 3-credit research and practicum course, which can include an internship, study abroad course, discipline-specific research methods course, independent study, or thesis. On occasion, the INST Director can allow an additional course in this area to count as an elective, which is more likely for an internship, independent study, or thesis, whereas discipline-based courses taken in a semester-long study abroad program may be used as electives. The INST internship class, INST 493, falls in this practicum category.

The course learning outcomes were: to develop substantive knowledge of international affairs, including different cultures, histories, economic issues, and political issues; promote critical thinking skills; advance students' abilities to communicate the affective meanings of cultural, historical, economic, or political contexts in written and oral communications; and foster personal and professional skills, including job readiness, networking, and experience connecting classroom knowledge to real-world contexts.

Course requirements for INST 493 (in the period studied) included:

1) Preliminary meeting with the INST internship adviser to ensure internship placement acceptability and review requirements
2) Initial paperwork delineating internship duties on site, signed by internship on-site supervisor
3) Completion of at least 120 on-site hours
4) Weekly journals
5) Ending semester evaluations, which included a student evaluation of the internship and the on-site supervisor's evaluation of the student and confirmation of number of hours completed
6) A 5-page, end-of-semester reflection essay
7) A 10-page research paper

Most of these requirements are self-evident, though it should be added that the INST faculty adviser always conducted at least **two phone meetings** with the site supervisor. The first was a preliminary discussion to ensure that course requirements were understood on site; the second was usually a mid-semester check-in. If phone meetings could not be arranged, email exchanges filled in on the same basic schedule.

The **weekly journals** were designed to get a snapshot of how the student was doing that week, review major duties, and provide an opportunity for feedback. Students were told not to just list duties undertaken, but instead to focus on one or two key events or activities that week and what was learned or gained from that experience. The event could include what a student learned as a passive observer or as an active participant in the organization. Either way, the student was asked to reflect on how that experience impacted them professionally or personally and was submitted via email. The INST faculty adviser replied to each journal entry, sometimes with professional advice and sometimes with needed encouragement.

At the end of the semester, students handed in a **five-page reflection paper** which reviewed overall lessons learned, key experience gained, and the student's self-evaluation of professional and personal gains. The **research paper** addressed a topic agreed upon by the adviser and student around mid-semester and had to be a traditional research product connected in some way to the student's internship placement. For example, a student working with a refugee family from Syria could write a paper on the circumstances which compelled the family to flee or the immigration process.

Although individual requirements composed by the students were given letter grades, the course itself was graded as Satisfactory/Unsatisfactory due to the fact that students conducted much of their work in a wide variety of cultural contexts where common grading norms and performance standards could not be guaranteed. As an S/U graded class, there were also no weighted percentages assigned, and there were few problems in assigning a grade of Satisfactory. While this grading scheme followed accepted practices on campus at the time, updates include readjustments to the percentages counted for different assignments.

How to cite this resource: McCartney, Alison Rios Millett. 2021. "Supplemental Internship Resource: Towson University (TU) Program and Internship Course Requirements," in *Political Science Internships: Towards Best Practices* eds. Renée B. Van Vechten, Bobbi Gentry, and John C. Berg. Washington, DC: American Political Science Association.

14.2 USC International Relations Program and Internship Course Requirements

University of Southern California (USC) International Relations Program and Internship Course Requirements

The International Relations major at USC requires completion of 48 units consisting of four lower-division and eight upper-division courses. Of the eight, one must be from each of the four fields, one must be a regional course, one must be a 400-level course, and the remaining two are electives.[1] In addition, students are required to complete four semesters of a single foreign language. International Relations Global Business students apply for admission into the major with junior standing after they have completed specific courses required for admission with a 3.0 GPA or better. Half of their units include IR coursework and the other half are courses in the Marshall School of Business. In IR, they take one course from the field of International Political Economy, one regional course, one 400-level course and three upper-division electives.[2]

Our internship course is an elective, independent study course centered on the internship experience where students are responsible for their own placements. A central objective is to build a connection between academic training and career possibilities for any IR major. As a result, it does include a significant learning component separate from the work experience itself.

Course requirements include:

1. Orientation meeting with the faculty instructor to discuss internship placement and/or pre-approval of placement.
2. Successful completion of the minimum 120 hours of internship verified with a supervisor evaluation form (35% of the student grade).
3. An 8-10 page original research paper (35% of the grade) on a topic selected by the student and verified by the instructor. Students are encouraged to select a topic that links career interests to their internship work and their research interests. Students meet a minimum of three times with the faculty advisor to review their method selection, outline, and first draft of the paper.
4. Attendance at least one pre-professional session organized by the Career Office in the College of Letters, Arts, and Sciences or another off-campus event that can serve as an appropriate substitute for career exploration and preparation. Students report back by summarizing the key takeaways from the event (15% of the grade).
5. Career-related assignment where students have choice of completing: 1) an informational interview with an individual outside of the University, for those who are unsure of what career path they would like to pursue, 2) an event write-up for those who are pursuing more research-oriented careers or are learning about substantive issues in international affairs, or 3) an exit interview for those who have identified positions post-graduation and need to engage in an assessment of their strengths and weaknesses in a professional setting (15% of the grade).

---

[1] Our fields include 1) Culture, Gender and Global Society, 2) Foreign Policy Analysis, 3) International Political Economy, and 4) International Politics and Security Studies.

[2] IRGE major consists of 48 units distributed across Economics and IR coursework. This is an interdisciplinary major for students who wish to develop strong foundations in economic analysis and to be able to apply these tools in the context of global economy. INCO requires between 51 and 54 units of courses that include a mix of IR and Information Technology courses. This is an interdisciplinary major developed in conjunction with the Viterbi School of Engineering. In the IR Department, students take courses focused on intelligence, technology, security, violence, finance, and regional coverage. It is our impression that the IRGE majors pursue research opportunities during the year and apply for lucrative, paid, data science-oriented opportunities during the summer. The program does not attract students from the INCO major because it is a brand new major for the IR program and their students typically do not take internships for course credit. Opportunities are identified through an established network managed by the student organization Cyborg and their faculty advisor.

How to cite this resource: Božović, Iva. 2021. "Supplemental Internship Resource: USC International Relations Program and Internship Course Requirements," in *Political Science Internships: Towards Best Practices* eds. Renée B. Van Vechten, Bobbi Gentry, and John C. Berg. Washington, DC: American Political Science Association.

14.3 International Internship Listings

International Internship Listings[1]

This document contains listings for internationally-focused internships in the US or abroad. Some are paid (these are marked with an asterisk) but most are unpaid.*

Listings are roughly organized into four separate tables: (A) International Internship Programs, which are full-scale work-and-study programs that tend to offer multiple placements; (B) International Affairs/International Relations Internships; (C) International Policy and Research Internships; and (D) International Studies/International Business Internships.

Note: Search for "internship" on each website if the page does not load immediately.

A. INTERNATIONAL INTERNSHIP PROGRAMS	
Educational Programmes Abroad	https://www.epa-internships.org/
The Fund for American Studies / DC Internships.org**	https://www.dcinternships.org/
Go Overseas	https://www.gooverseas.com/internships-abroad
IES Abroad (Institute for the International Education of Students)	https://www.iesabroad.org/ies-internships/full-time-internship-programs#paragraph-view-5621
IPSL Global Institute (formerly International Partnership for Service-Learning and Leadership	https://www.ipsl.org/
The Washington Center (TWC) Global Competencies Internship Program**	https://twc.edu/programs/global-competencies-internship-program
US Department of State Student Internship Program (in DC or abroad) **OR** US Department of State Pathways Internship Program	https://careers.state.gov/interns-fellows/student-internships/ OR https://careers.state.gov/work/pathways/internship-programs/

Links current as of July 2021
***This program is reviewed in the chapter about DC Internships by Michelle Chin, and more information can also be found in a Supplemental Resource.*

NOTE: Organizations marked with an (*) asterisk offer paid internships.

---

[1] Source: Teaching + Learning Commons. 2021. "Academic Internship Program." UCSD. https://aip.ucsd.edu/programs/ucdc/dc-internships/internship-list/international-affairs.html.
Listings are subject to change. Inclusion in this list is not a guarantee that an internship is available or that a program is being offered. Check with the organization's internship coordinator or visit their website for more information.

B. INTERNATIONAL AFFAIRS / INTERNATIONAL RELATIONS	
Africa-American Institute*	https://www.aaionline.org/
American Foreign Policy Council	https://www.afpc.org/about/internships
American Foreign Service Association*	https://www.afsa.org/internships-afsa
American Israeli Public Affairs Committee	https://www.aipac.org/connect/students/diamond-internship
American Jewish Committee*	https://www.ajc.org/
American Pakistan Foundation	https://shallot-ocelot-bxxc.squarespace.com/apf-fellows-program
AmidEast	https://www.amideast.org/about-amideast
Asia Foundation*	https://asiafoundation.org/
British American Security Information Council*	https://basicint.org/
Commission on Security and Cooperation in Europe	https://www.csce.gov/about-csce/join-our-team/max-kampelman-fellowships
Council on Foreign Relations	https://www.cfr.org/career-opportunities/internships
Council on Hemispheric Affairs	https://www.coha.org/internships/about-internships/
Eurasia Foundation	https://www.eurasia.org/CareerOpportunities
Foreign Embassies of Washington, D.C.	https://www.embassy.org/embassies/
Fund for Peace*	https://fundforpeace.org/internships/
Institute for Science & International Security*	https://isis-online.org/about/internships/
Inter-American Dialogue	https://www.thedialogue.org/careers/
Internships in International Affairs	http://cei-internship.squarespace.com/
Japan-America Student Conference	http://iscdc.org/
Middle East Institute	https://www.mei.edu/get-involved/internships
National Council on US-Arab Relations	https://ncusar.org/internship
National Democratic Institute of International Affairs*	https://www.ndi.org/careers
North Atlantic Treaty Organization	https://www.nato.int/cps/en/natolive/71157.htm
National Endowment for Democracy	https://www.ned.org/about/jobs/
National Security Archive	https://nsarchive2.gwu.edu/nsa/archive/intern.html
Organization of American States	http://www.oas.org/en/saf/dhr/internships/
Search for Common Ground	https://www.sfcg.org/
United Nations	https://www.un.org/development/desa/youth/opportunities-within-the-un/internships.html

U.S. Department of State	https://careers.state.gov/interns-fellows/student-internships/
U.S. Agency for International Development (USAID)	https://www.usaid.gov/work-usaid/careers/fellows-program
World Affairs Councils of America	https://www.worldaffairscouncils.org/

C. INTERNATIONAL POLICY AND RESEARCH	
Alliance for International Educational and Cultural Exchange	https://www.alliance-exchange.org/explore-exchanges/internship-exchange/
American Foreign Service Association*	https://www.afsa.org/internships-afsa
American Jewish Committee*	https://www.ajc.org/careers#internships
Amnesty International – USA	https://www.amnestyusa.org/careers/
The Aspen Institute*	https://www.aspeninstitute.org/careers/career-opportunities/
Atlantic Council	https://www.atlanticcouncil.org/careers/internships/
Center for Immigration Studies	https://cis.org/Center-Immigration-Studies-Internship-Program
Center for International Policy	http://ciponline.org/GFIinternships.html
Center for Security Policy	https://centerforsecuritypolicy.org/about-us/internships/
Center for Strategic & International Studies	https://www.csis.org/programs/about-us/careers-and-internships/internships
Competitive Enterprise Institute	https://cei.org/internships/
Foreign Affairs Information Technology Fellowship	https://twc.edu/programs/foreign-affairs-information-technology-fellowship
Foundation for the Defense of Democracies	https://www.fdd.org/jobs-and-internships/
Fulbright Canada Globalink program	https://www.fulbright.ca/programs/undergraduate-students/fulbright-canada-mitacs-globalink-program
Institute for Policy Studies	https://ips-dc.org/about/jobs-internships/#Internships

Institute for Science & International Security*	https://isis-online.org/about/internships/
Israel Policy Forum	http://www.israelpolicyforum.org/
Latin America Working Group	https://www.lawg.org/internship-application/
National Defense Council Foundation	http://www.ndcf.org/
National Security Archive	https://nsarchive.gwu.edu/jobs-internships
World Jurist Association	https://worldjurist.org/
Washington Institute for Near East Policy	https://www.washingtoninstitute.org/about/employment-opportunities - research-intern
Washington Office on Latin America	https://www.wola.org/get-involved/internships/
Women's Foreign Policy Group	https://www.wfpg.org/internships

D. INTERNATIONAL STUDIES / INTERNATIONAL BUSINESS	
Center on Budget & Policy Priorities*	https://www.cbpp.org/internships
Citizens Network for Foreign Affairs*	https://www.cnfa.org/opportunities/
Corporate Council on Africa	http://www.africacncl.org/careers
Citizens Network for Foreign Affairs*	https://www.cnfa.org/opportunities/
Department of Commerce International Trade Administration	https://www.trade.gov/
Economic Strategy Institute	http://www.econstrat.org/publications/op-eds/56-about-us/about-the-institute/26-esi-internships
European Union in the U.S.	https://eeas.europa.eu/delegations/united-states-america/area/jobs-funds_en
Inter-American Dialogue	https://www.thedialogue.org/careers/
International Law Institute	http://www.ili.org/opportunites/internships.html
Korea Economic Institute	https://keia.org/about/get-involved/internship-opportunity-faq/
Public Citizen*	https://www.citizen.org/internships/
U.S. Chamber of Commerce	https://www.uschamber.com/about/careers#internships
U.S. Russia Business Council*	https://www.usrbc.org/
Washington International Trade Association	http://www.wita.org/internships/

How to cite this resource: Van Vechten, Renée B. 2021. "Supplemental Internship Resource: International Internship Listing," in *Political Science Internships: Towards Best Practices* eds. Renée B. Van Vechten, Bobbi Gentry, and John C. Berg. Washington, DC: American Political Science Association.

15.1 Tips for Facilitating Remote or Virtual Work

CALIFORNIA STATE UNIVERSITY **LONG BEACH**

FACILITATING REMOTE WORK

TIPS FOR INTERNSHIP, SERVICE LEARNING, AND PRACTICA FACULTY AND STAFF

Much has changed on campus and in our local community during the ongoing COVID-19 public health crisis. But what has not changed is that our community partners have needs—in some cases more than ever. As well, our students have important knowledge and skills that they seek to further develop. Faculty and campus staff can play an important role in facilitating this mutually beneficial exchange—even when it will most likely occur remotely.

To help you accomplish this successfully, we start with key steps to make a solid match with a community site. We also offer tips for facilitating remote experiential placements for students. To help you advocate for and coordinate student work, we provide examples of work that can be done well remotely and that can pave the way to productive collaborations. Finally, we offer resources to gather additional assistance and support.

STEPS TO MATCHING WITH A COMMUNITY SITE

- Identify whether the community site complements students' coursework or degree objectives
- Understand the needs of community sites and recognize these needs may have changed since your last contact with them
- Have a conversation with community sites about their new needs. Questions to consider asking:
  - *In the past, I know our students have worked with you on [project]. I am wondering if [project] is still your priority or if your focus has shifted to other projects? Is there an opportunity for students to support this work remotely?*
  - *What type of remote work or projects do you need assistance with now?*
  - *Do you have additional needs that have emerged due to recent events or other emergent social justice issues?*

FACILITATING REMOTE EXPERIENTIAL PLACEMENTS WITH STUDENTS

- Help identify the type of work and community sites related to students' professional goals. Questions to ask students:
  - *What are your professional goals?*
  - *What type of work do you think will help you take the next step towards your career?*
  - *What types of skills and experiences are you wanting to gain in the community?*
- Identify skills students have that could be applied to support their community sites remotely
- Ensure students understand the connection between their coursework and experiential placements
- Recognize students' capacity to complete work remotely. Questions to ask students:
  - *Are there any limitations or challenges you anticipate that might affect you successfully working with a site remotely? (e.g., technology, scheduling). [This might be an appropriate time for instructors to mention to students any special site requirements such as background checks, fingerprinting, etc.]*
  - *Is there any support you will need to be prepared to complete this work assignment?*

How to cite this resource: Cabrera Rasmussen, Amy, and Sarah Taylor. 2020. Facilitating Remote Work: Tips for Internship, Service Learning, and Practica Faculty and Staff. California State University Long Beach: Division of Academic Affairs, Interim Dean for Student Success, and Center for Community Engagement. https://csulb-my.sharepoint.com/:b:/g/personal/amy_rasmussen_csulb_edu/ERYGuT9eOqtFrBdrwhHoGa4Bbux7_LGJEk_NpX1faGKyLg?e=bgn3cS

About our Contributors

Art Auerbach received BA degrees in political science and environmental studies from the University of California, Santa Barbara. He went on to attain a JD from Pepperdine University School of Law and practiced as a state prosecutor for 10 years with the California Attorney General's office in Los Angeles. In 2000, he left the practice of law to pursue a PhD, and earned his degree from the University of Southern California (USC). Auerbach is a teaching professor within the Department of Political Science and International Relations at USC and teaches a variety of courses within Public Law. He is also the internship director of the Jesse M. Unruh Institute of Politics where he works with undergraduates at all stages of their academic careers to help them gain real-world experience prior to graduation.

John C. Berg recently retired after 42 years at Suffolk University. He is the founding chair of the Section on Political Science Education, a former chair of the New Political Science Section, and former Reviews Editor of *New Political Science*. His latest book, *Leave It in the Ground: The Politics of Coal and Climate*, was published by ABC-CLIO in 2019.

Iva Božović is an Associate Professor of Teaching in the Department of Political Science and International Relations at the University of Southern California. Her research explores the interaction of formal and informal institutions with implications for private sector development, governance, and corruption. Her published works have examined the role of social capital and social networks in the growth of small- and medium-sized businesses in post-communist economies. Bozovic also consults with international development organizations and their partners about issues related to private sector development. She teaches courses in international political economy, development, economic institutions and trade, and is also the head of the International Relations Undergraduate Internship Program. She received her PhD in Political Economy and MA in Economics at USC.

Scott Braam is a doctoral candidate at the University of Illinois at Chicago (UIC) and is currently a political science and urban politics adjunct professor at Elmhurst University. He worked closely with university student interns and instructed the Political Science Internships course at UIC, 2016–2019. Braam studies urban neighborhood transformation via gentrification and the role of urban aesthetics including public art murals. Currently he is working on his dissertation, titled, "Reflections of Power: Three Eras of Muralism in Chicago's Pilsen Neighborhood."

Amy Cabrera Rasmussen is Professor of Political Science at California State University Long Beach. She has been an active participant in a variety of spaces, both on-campus and off, regarding matters of equity-driven student success, life design, and community engagement. She has for years taught an internship course for CSULB's College of Liberal Arts, was part of the team that launched an innovative and equity-minded nonprofit internship project, and is the director of Design Your Long Beach—a program to help students design careers to positively impact the local community. Cabrera Rasmussen is also one of the founding directors of APSA's Institute for Civically Engaged Research (ICER) and is a long-time participant in a local environmental justice collaborative. She teaches and researches US politics and public policy with a focus on health and the environment. She earned her PhD at Yale University and has received fellowships from the Ford Foundation and the American Association of University Women, among others.

Cynthia Chávez Metoyer is Professor of Political Science at California State University San Marcos. She joined the faculty in 1994 to develop the Latin American politics curriculum and has served as Political Science Department Internship Coordinator since 1999. Her teaching and research interests include Latin American politics, gender and development, and comparative politics. Since June 2015, Chávez Metoyer has served as the founding Faculty Director of the University Office of Internships and has developed a university-wide internship course to serve students whose majors do not offer an internship course. As a first-generation college graduate, she believes experiential learning is essential to students' success.

Michelle L. Chin (PhD, MA, Texas A&M University) is the academic director for the Archer Center, the Washington, DC campus of the University of Texas system. Prior to joining the Archer Center, Michelle was senior researcher and policy analyst at the Learning Policy Institute. She is a former APSA Congressional Fellow (2006–07) and congressional staffer, working for more than eight years as an education policy advisor for US Senator John Cornyn of Texas. Chin's college internship with Rep. Joe Barton (Texas) led to a full-time job in his office the following year; she left after four years to attend graduate school. From 2001–2006, Michelle was an assistant professor of political science at Arizona State University where she also served as program director of the ASU Capital Scholars Program (2002–04).

Richard A. Clucas is Professor of Political Science in the Political Science Department at Portland State University and the Executive Director of the Western Political Science Association (WPSA). Clucas has written extensively on legislative politics, state government, and Oregon politics. Among other works, he is co-author of *The Character of Democracy* (Oxford University Press), co-editor of *Governing Oregon* (Oregon State University Press), and the set editor for the encyclopedia series, *About State Government* (ABC-CLIO). He has directed the Political Science Internship Program at PSU for 26 years.

Bobbi Gentry is Associate Professor of Political Science at Bridgewater College as a scholar of teaching and learning who focuses on improving student engagement in the classroom through simulations, policy problem/solution proposals, and research projects. She is also a youth voting scholar and does extensive research in political identity development. Gentry has recently published her book, *Why Youth Vote: Identity, Inspirational Leaders, and Independence* (Springer, 2018). Her current work on the scholarship of teaching and learning includes best practices in internships, curriculum review in higher education, and identity development in the political science classroom.

Clinton M. Jenkins is an Assistant Professor of Political Science at Birmingham-Southern College. He studies political behavior and political communication. His current research focuses on political socialization and the political development of adolescents. In addition, he is engaged in scholarship on teaching and learning in political science. He is a frequent participant at APSA's Teaching and Learning conferences, where he has presented multiple papers on internships and teaching writing to political science majors. He holds an MA and PhD in American Politics and Quantitative Methodology from The George Washington University. In addition, he holds a BA in Political Science from York College of Pennsylvania.

Diane J. Lowenthal is an Assistant Professor at American University (AU). She spent seven years as Associate Dean and Senior Associate Dean in the School of Professional and Extended Studies after 12 years teaching in the Washington Semester Program. She earned her PhD in Social and Decision Sciences from Carnegie Mellon University and her AB from the University of Michigan. She has authored several articles studying decision making in different political contexts and co-authored "Making the Grade: How a Semester in Washington May Influence Future Academic Performance" (*Journal of Political Science Education*, 2007) and "The Forgotten Educator: Experiential Learning's Internship Supervisor" (*JPSE*, 2016). This research received awards from the APSA (2014) and National Society for Experiential Education (2019).

Daniel J. Mallinson is an Assistant Professor of Public Policy and Administration at Penn State Harrisburg. His research and teaching interests include policy diffusion, federalism, health policies, and pedagogy. He serves as a member of the APSA Committee on the Status of First Generation Scholars in the Profession (2021–2023). In 2020, he received the Theodore J. Lowi Award for the best paper in the *Policy Studies Journal* from the APSA Public Policy Section.

Alison Rios Millett McCartney (PhD, University of Virginia) is Professor of Political Science and Faculty Director of the Honors College at Towson University. She is co-editor of *Teaching Civic Engagement Across the Disciplines* (2017) and *Teaching Civic Engagement: From Student to Active Citizen* (2013; both APSA publications), and also publications and webinars on European politics, civic engagement education, and pedagogy. She has received numerous awards for service and teaching, including the University of Maryland Board of Regents Faculty Award for Mentoring, and the Distinguished Service award from the Political Science Education section of APSA, of which she is a past president. Currently she sits on the Steering Committee of the American Democracy Project of the AAC&U and the Executive Board of the Maryland Collegiate Honors Council. She co-created and co-chairs the Towson University-Baltimore County Model United Nations conference, a free civic engagement program for local youth. She teaches diplomacy, civic engagement, and European politics.

Shannon McQueen is an Assistant Professor of Political Science at West Chester University. Her research focuses on the importance and influence of women's involvement in politics, the mobilization of women's groups, and the institutional, cultural, and policy obstacles women face when running for office. Additionally, she is engaged in scholarship concerning internships, civic engagement, and metacognition in the classroom. She earned an MA and PhD in American Politics and Public Policy from The George Washington University.

Christina Sciabarra is a faculty member in Political Science and in the Neurodiversity Navigators program at Bellevue College. She previously served as the Director of the Center for Career Connections and the Women's Center and facilitated the creation, implementation and teaching of Bellevue College's First-Year Seminar program. Sciabarra holds a PhD in Political Science from the University of Arizona and her research focuses on post-civil war peacebuilding.

Dick Simpson has taught for 55 years. At the University of Illinois at Chicago (UIC) he received the highest awards given for teaching, including the UIC Silver Circle Award, CETL Teaching Recognition Award, the UIC award for Excellence in Teaching, and the APSA and Pi Sigma Alpha National Award for Outstanding Teaching in Political Science. He also received a Lifetime Achievement Award from the Political Science Education Section of APSA. He was UIC Political Science Department Head from 2006–2012. He has published over 25 books and over 100 journal and magazine articles, and newspaper op-eds.

Jeffrey K. Sosland is an Assistant Professor at American University. He teaches Global Economics and Business for the Washington Semester Program. He is author of *Cooperating Rivals: The Riparian Politics of the Jordan River Basin* (SUNY Press, 2007) and co-authored "Making the Grade: How a Semester in Washington May Influence Future Academic Performance" (*JPSE,* 2007) and "The Forgotten Educator: Experiential Learning's Internship Supervisor" (*JPSE,* 2016). This research received awards from the APSA Political Science Education Section (2014) and National Society for Experiential Education (2019). He earned his PhD from Georgetown University and AB at Harvard University.

Renée Bukovchik Van Vechten (PhD, University of California, Irvine), Professor of Political Science, holds the Fletcher Jones Endowed Chair in American Politics and Policy at the University of Redlands. She is the author of *California Politics: A Primer,* now in its 6th edition (CQ Press/SAGE), and is the recipient of several grants and awards for teaching, including the Rowman and Littlefield Award for Innovative Teaching in Political Science (2008). She is actively engaged in the scholarship of teaching and learning, and received the best APSA conference paper award presented through the Political Science Education section in 2020 (with Maureen Feeley, co-author). She is a former APSA Council member, having chaired the Teaching and Learning Policy Committee (2017–19); she is also a past president of the PSE member section of APSA. Van Vechten also advises UofR's Pi Sigma Alpha honor society chapter and is an executive board and executive committee member of the national organization.

Susan L. Wiley is an Associate Professor of Political Science at The George Washington University. Along with her teaching duties in Political Science she serves as the department's Director of Undergraduate Studies, leads the undergraduate internship program, and teaches quantitative methods in the Graduate School of Political Management. She received her PhD from the University of Maryland in Political Behavior and Public Policy, and holds a BS in Applied Mathematics from The Georgia Institute of Technology.

Myron D. Winston is a graduate student and Research Assistant at the University of Illinois at Chicago. He is a research assistant with the Race and Trust in Government Study, a joint University of California, University of Illinois, and Northwestern University research project, and is a research assistant in the Institute for Research on Race and Public Policy at UIC. Winston serves as a Teaching Assistant in the Department of Political Science and was an instructor for the Political Science Internships course at the University of Illinois, 2019–2020.

David C. Yamada is a Professor of Law and Director of the New Workplace Institute at Suffolk University Law School in Boston. He is a nationally recognized authority on legal matters relating to internships, having published leading law review articles on the topic and co-filed amicus curiae briefs in support of unpaid interns seeking back pay and protections against discrimination in cases before the US Court of Appeals. He served as a subject matter expert for Pro Publica's investigative project on unpaid interns and has been interviewed by national media on the legal rights of interns, including the *New York Times, Wall Street Journal, Washington Post,* and *Boston Globe.* Yamada is also an internationally recognized authority on the legal and organizational implications of workplace bullying and abuse. His blog, Minding the Workplace, is a popular source of commentary on workers' rights and employment relations. Yamada's educational background includes degrees from New York University School of Law (JD, 1985) and Valparaiso University (BA, 1981).

www.ingramcontent.com/pod-product-compliance
Lightning Source LLC
Chambersburg PA
CBHW080326270326
41927CB00014B/3116
9781878147660